Essays in Modern History

Companion Volume

Essays in Medieval History

EDITED BY R. W. SOUTHERN

Essays in Modern History

SELECTED FROM
THE TRANSACTIONS OF
THE ROYAL HISTORICAL SOCIETY
ON THE OCCASION OF
ITS CENTENARY

Edited by Ian R. Christie

MACMILLAN
London · Melbourne · Toronto
ST MARTIN'S PRESS
New York
1968

© The Royal Historical Society 1968

Published by MACMILLAN & COMPANY LTD
Little Essex Street London WC2
and also at Bombay Calcutta and Madras
Macmillan South Africa (Publishers) Pty Ltd Johannesburg
The Macmillan Company of Australia Pty Ltd Melbourne
The Macmillan Company of Canada Ltd Toronto
St Martin's Press Inc New York

Library of Congress catalog card no. 68–14234

Printed in Great Britain by RICHARD CLAY (THE CHAUCER PRESS) LTD
Bungay, Suffolk

Contents

Contents

Preface

The essays printed in this volume have been selected from the first four series of the *Transactions* of the Royal Historical Society, beginning in 1871 and ending in 1950. For their ready consent to their republication here the Council of the Society gratefully acknowledges the kindness of the Community of the Resurrection, Mirfield; Professor Sir John Neale; Professor Gordon Donaldson; Professor F. J. Fisher; Sir Henry Phillips; the Trust Officer, Barclays Bank Ltd., St. Aldate's, Oxford; Mrs. T. W. Morgan and Miss Katherine Morgan; Professor H. N. V. Temperley; Mrs. Dorothy George; Mr. Nicholas Burn; Miss B. Sumner; and Professor Edna Purdie. No changes have been made in the text of the essays. But the notes have been standardised, and on occasion amplified.

I. R. C.

1 Respublica Christiana

I think it was Lord Halsbury, in the Scotch Church case, who stopped one of the advocates in his use of the word Church,[1] saying that they as a Court had nothing to do with that, and that they could only consider the question as one concerning a trust. In other words, with a religious society as such they could not deal, but only with a trust or a registered company. This is only one instance of a fact exhibited in the whole of that case: namely, the refusal of the legal mind of our day to consider even the possibility of societies possessing an inherent, self-developing life apart from such definite powers as the State, or the individuals founding the body under State authority, have conferred upon them explicitly. In this view, apart from the State, the real society — and from individuals the living members of the State — there are no active social unities; all other apparent communal unities are directly or indirectly delegations, either of State powers or of individuals. To such a view the notion is abhorrent of a vast hierarchy of interrelated societies, each alive, each personal, owing to the State loyalty, and by it checked or assisted in their action no less than are private individuals, but no more deriving their existence from government concession than does the individual or the family. In other words, these phrases of Lord Halsbury are but the natural expression of the concession theory of corporate life which sees it as a fictitious personality, the creation by the State for its own purposes, and consequently without any natural or inherent powers of its own. This theory is not so universally accepted as was once the case, but Professor Geldart's inaugural lecture on 'Legal Personality' shows how great are the obstacles still to be encountered by that theory of realism which is for most of us associated with the name of Gierke,[2] and was popularised by Maitland. The latter, moreover,

[1] Cf. R. L. Orr, *Free Church of Scotland Appeals 1903–4* (Edinburgh, 1904). All the speeches and judgements are there set forth in full. It is to be noted that Lord Macnaughten did take the more liberal view, advocated by modern writers.

[2] O. F. von Gierke, *Das Deutsche Genossenschaftsrecht* (4 vols., Berlin, 1868, 1913), especially vols. ii, and iii, is the prime authority for the discussion of this

has shown how this very English institution of the *trust* has preserved us from the worse perils of the rigid doctrinaire conception of the civilian.[1] For under the name of a trust many of the qualities of true personality have been able to develop unmolested. But this has not been all to the good. It has probably delayed the victory of the true conception, by enabling us to 'muddle through' with the false one. Moreover, the trust is and assimilates itself always rather to the *Anstalt* or the *Stiftung* than to the living communal society, the true corporation, with its basis in the *Genossenschaft*; and consequently, as was proved in this Scotch case, the necessary independence of a self-developing personality is denied to it, and its acts are treated as invalid on this very ground — that it is only a trust tied rigidly to its establishing terms, and not a true society with a living will and power of change.

However, it is not the truth or falsehood of the concession theory, or its realist adversary, that I am to discuss here, but rather its origin. I want to try for a little to see what lies behind it. The doctrine of which we speak could hardly be of modern origin. In the infinitely complex life of modern civilisation and its religious heterogeneity we observe, as a matter of actual fact, the phenomenon of vast numbers of societies all acting as though they were persons. They do manage to do all or most

---

topic in reference alike to historical development in the ancient medieval world and in the post-Renaissance state, and to theoretical truth. In another work, *Die Genossenschafts Theorie und die deutsche Rechtsprechung* (Berlin, 1887), Dr. Gierke shows, by an elaborate analysis of recent decisions both in state and federal courts in Germany, how entirely impossible it is to work with the rigid civilian theory; and how the courts and judges, while often paying lip-service to 'Romanist' notions, are driven in spite of themselves to make use of the more vital early Teutonic notions. The whole matter is intimately connected with that conflict described by G. Beseler in *Das Volksrecht und das Juristenrecht* (Leipzig, 1843). There is a short lecture of Gierke, *Das Wesen des Menschlichen Verbandes*, which is also very illuminative. Professor Jethro Brown in an Appendix to the *Austinian Theory of Law and Government* is worthy of study. There is a somewhat meagre account of the various theories in C. T. Carr, *The General Principles of the Law of Corporations* (Cambridge, 1905).

[1] Cf. Maitland, *Collected Papers*, ed. H. A. L. Fisher (3 vols., Cambridge, 1911), vol. iii. Other papers in this volume are also important on this topic. But valuable above all is Maitland's long introduction to his translation of Gierke's *Political Theory of the Middle Ages*.

of the things which they would do even if the concession theory were not dominant. Indeed, it is only by a series of very transparent fictions that their activities are brought under this rubric. To all intents and purposes they act, not as fictitious but as real legal personalities. Of course the metaphysical question, what this personality really means, lies outside our limits, just as the question whether the will is free or determined has nothing to do with the State in its treatment of the individual. No one is debarred from believing determinism because the State treats its citizens as free agents. Further than this the *Taff Vale* decision is significant, for it tended to show that corporate life was a thing natural and arising of itself in bodies of men associated for permanent objects, and that it could not be destroyed by the process of ignoring it; in other words, that Trades Unions were personalities, in spite of their own wishes, and in spite of the Act of Parliament which had allowed to them much of the liberty of corporate personality while preserving them from its liabilities. That the House of Lords upheld Mr. Justice Farwell in this case, and at the cost of much odium, is also evidence that the concession theory is not really congruous with the facts of life, and that it is not of modern origin, but is in some way an inheritance from the past. We see, in fact, the horizons of the legal mind changing, and we gather that this mentality must relate to some time when, to speak of the two great bodies whose clash has been unending, State and Church were so bound together in unity that they could not be conceived, either of them, as a separate society with a separate life, but each appeared as different aspects or functionings of one and the same body. Such a time is, of course, remote from the world we live in.

Let us now take an instance from a continental country, France. In France the concession theory has long reigned practically unchecked, alike as a legal theory and even as a political maxim. It burst into renewed activity only the other day in the Associations 'Loi'. Rousseau and his followers have always been opposed to allowing any inherent rights to bodies other than the sovereign people. There were, at least in earlier theory, rights of man and there were rights of the State. There were no rights of any other society. But for their obsession with this doctrine, the statesmen of the Revolution could never even have dreamt of such a project as the *Constitution Civile* of the clergy. Now, however, men have gone even farther, and deny all rights at all except those of the Republic one and indivisible. M. Emile Combes put it, writing in an English review, 'There are no rights but the rights of the State; there is no authority but the authority of the Republic.' As I said, it is the origin, not the validity, of this conception with which I am concerned this evening. On this very controversy there was published a volume of collected speeches by M. Combes, with a preface by M. Anatole France. It is called 'Une Campagne laïque'.[1] That title contains, in my view, the key to the mystery. Consider for a moment that M. Combes is not a layman, but an unbeliever; he is a fanatical anti-Christian, and would repudiate with scorn any notion that he was a lay member of the Catholic Church. He is a Secularist, pure and simple, and the whole campaign for the laicisation of the schools, whether in France, or Spain, or Portugal, is a campaign for their entire secularisation, as we well know and is never denied. The ludicrous difficulties into which the need of removing all Christian and Theistic reference sometimes leads the compilers of textbooks have been frequently observed. Laicisation might very well describe the Kenyon–Slaney clause in England and is a not unfair description of some parts of the undenominationalist movement, for that is, at least in name, a Christian movement, and is directed to removing education from clerical control, direct or indirect, and substituting a purely lay authority — still Christian. In France, of course, no such aim was ever suggested, and the Extremists have never made any difficulty about declaring that their object was to *de-Christianise* the nation. Why, then, should M. Combes use a term so essentially ecclesiastical as *lay* to describe his campaign? I answer that it was because he could not help it; the distinction that has ruled Europe for so many centuries has been a distinction, not between Christian and non-Christian societies, but between cleric and layman, between the spiritual and the temporal power, each of them exercised within the Church; between the ecclesiastical and the secular governments, each of them functioning within the body politic. M. Combes used the word *laïque* as an unconscious survival of the day when an attitude similar to his own could have been rightly described by that term. He slipped into

[1] *Une Campagne laïque, 1902–1903* (Paris, [1904]).

4

it, because the categories of our thought are still ruled by influences that breathe of a different world. He was unconsciously, and in spite of himself, recalling a time when troubles between Church and State were not troubles between two societies, but between two departments of one society; not between Church and State conceived as separate social entities facing one another, like the College and the University, but rather as between Churchmen, i.e. ecclesiastics and statesmen, between the King's Court and the Papal Curia, between lawyers and bishops, between kings or emperors and popes. Only some sort of odd historical survival affords any explanation of the use of such a term as *laïque* (which has no meaning except in relation to the Church and the clergy) by so violent an anti-Christian as M. Emile Combes. But this is not all. It seems to point to a narrower use of the term Church than that in vogue today. In common parlance the Church in the Middle Ages meant not the *congregatio fidelium* — though, of course, no one would have denied this to be the right meaning — not the whole body of baptised Christians as distinct from those who were not, but rather the active governing section of the Church — the hierarchy and, I suppose, the religious orders. The common use of any term, especially a collective name, is to be found, not by what it sometimes means nor by what it ought to mean by that for which the society stands, but by what other set of people it is used to distinguish from — and this is the case with the word Church. In the Middle Ages the Church is used to distinguish the spirituality from the laity, and in nine cases out of ten it means the ecclesiastical body; in modern times the word Church is used to distinguish Churchmen from Dissenters of one kind or another; so that, whereas in the Middle Ages 'I am a Churchman' would mean I am *not* a layman, nowadays the phrase means I am not a Dissenter.

When we talk of the Church we commonly mean the body of Churchmen as against those who are not Churchmen. The reason is that we live in a society which is religiously heterogeneous; so that no one nowadays thinks of everybody as *ipso facto* in one Church, but as a member of this or that Christian community, all equally tolerated; or, indeed, of many other bodies semi-religious or secular, like the Theistic Church, the Positivist body, the Labour Church, the Theosophists, the Christian Scientists and so forth.

But even here we are not consistent. In common speech men are always dropping quite unconsciously into the older habit of talk, which treats the Church as primarily the clergy. Let me give an instance common in nearly all our experience. How many a youth has been rebuked by some stiff Churchman, probably an uncle, an archdeacon home from Barbadoes, for saying that he 'is going into the Church', when he means taking Holy Orders? He is bidden to remember that he is in the Church as a baptised and confirmed member; that the Church does not mean the clergy; that if that is the sort of doctrine he is going to preach he had better adopt some other calling, etc., etc.

Now I cannot help feeling that the unfortunate schoolboy has a far better defence than he commonly imagines. He might reply in something of this sort: 'True, my dear uncle, I made a slip, and I regret it. It is less important than you think. For since you left England for the Barbadoes, thirty years ago, things have greatly changed. We live in days of religious chaos, when no one is likely to think Churchmanship a matter of course. But I should like to point out to you that if the phrase I have used is theologically heretical, which I do not deny, it is *historically orthodox*, and by my use of it (a pure slip, due to the uprush of the subliminal consciousness) I am witnessing to the unity of history in a way which, with all your correct Tractarianism, you fail to comprehend. In the Middle Ages, and indeed a very long time since the Middle Ages, as you may see if you will study novels, the Church did mean in ordinary speech the Church as an effectively organised body, a hierarchy (there were no Houses of Laymen in those days), and nonconformity to the established religion was either non-existent or a crime. If you and I had been living in the thirteenth, fourteenth or even the sixteenth century, and I had ventured to say to a person of your dignity [for your dignity was as great as your chances of salvation were said to be small in those days], "I belong to the Church," meaning by it I belong to that branch of the Church established in this realm, what would have happened? You would have been surprised, nay shocked. You would have charged me with incipient heresy because to say I am a Churchman in that sense implies that I have my choice, and that, if I chose, I might be something else. Even to contemplate such a possibility borders upon heresy. If not treason, it is very near akin to *misprision of treason* to Holy Church. And as your nephew I should have been fortunate to have escaped with a sound avuncular whipping. If, however, I had said I belong to the Church, meaning by it what you have just rebuked me for — meaning, namely, I am a clerk in Holy Orders or in minor orders going on to greater things — then you would have quite understood me. You would have strongly approved, and you would doubtless have given me, though only sixteen and a half years old, a couple of livings and one prebend to be held in plurality, and *in commendam* with a *non-obstante* dispensation from the Holy Father permitting absence, in view of the other livings and offices which a person so important as an archdeacon's nephew would certainly have held. So I'll trouble you, after all, for that five-pound note you threatened to withdraw.'

That is the point. The word Churchman means today one who belongs to the Church as against others. In the Middle Ages there were no others, or, if there were, they were occupied in being burnt. A Churchman meant one who belonged to the Church in the narrower sense of its governing body — an ecclesiastic, as the word implies; just as statesman today means not a member but an officer, actual or potential, of the State. In medieval Europe folk would be more doubtful whether you were an Englishman or Bavarian than whether you were or were not a Churchman in our sense, but they might be greatly concerned to know whether you were clerk or layman. Churchmanship was co-extensive with citizenship, and, indeed, with more than citizenship, but the Church as a hierarchy was not; it was not the realm but an estate of the realm.

When the Church came in conflict, as it often did, with the State, it meant the clash of the ecclesiastical with the civil hierarchy of officials. Both these bodies were composed of Churchmen, in our sense, and both existed in the one society — the commonwealth.

All this leads to the main thesis of this paper — that in the Middle Ages Church and State in the sense of two competing societies did not exist; you have instead the two official hierarchies, the two departments if you will: the Court and the *Curia*, the kings' officials and the popes'. But in these controversies you have practically no conception of the Church, as consisting of the whole body of the baptised set over against the State, consisting of the same people, only viewed from a different standpoint and organised for a different end. It is a quarrel between two different sets of people — the lay officials and the clerical, the bishops and the justices, the pope and the kings; it is not thought of under that highly complex difficult form of a quarrel between two societies, each of which was composed of precisely the same persons, only one is called the State, for it deals with temporal ends, and the other Church, as the Christian community. Such a notion would only be possible if the sense of corporate personality in Church and State had been fully developed. This was not the case. The conception of the State was indeed very inchoate, and there was very little power of distinguishing it from its officials; and even in the Church this weakness led to the increasing power of the popes, for the Church took over its conceptions of government from the ancient world, and the Republic had latterly been entirely identified with the emperors.[1] There was no

[1] Cf. the notion of the Church when 'von der Kirche als Rechtssubjekt die Rede sei. Dies sei die Bedeutung von Ecclesia im Sinne des lokalen Verbandes. *Einen solchen aber konnte man bei der damaligen Verfassung naturgemäss nicht in der Gemeinde, sondern lediglich in der klerikalen Genossenschaft finden.* Und so kam man zu einer Definition, wie sie Placentinus aufstellt: *ecclesia dicitur collectio vel coadunatio virorum vel mulierum in aliquo sacro loco constitutorum vel constitutarum ad serviendum Deo.* So war in der That die Kirche als Rechtssubjekt in das korporative Schema gebracht und man konnte onne Weiteres die *Ecclesia* zu den *Universitates* und *Collegia* rechnen und den für diese geltenden Rechtssätzen unterstellen. Ja es sollte ihr, weil sie die privilegiirteste unter den Korporationen sei, kein bei irgend einer Korporation vorkommendes Recht fehlen können, weshalb sie namentlich der *respublics* und *civitas* gleichgestellt wurde.' — Gierke, iii. 195.

Again, 'Si enim aliqua universitas privilegiata est, hodie, potius privilegiata est ecclesia.' 'Ecclesia aequiparatur reipublicae.' But this is of individual churches. 'Weniger als je wurde den Gemeinden irgend ein aktives kirchliches Recht verstattet, immer entschiedener trat die Kirche, als ein fremder und äusserer Körper dem Volk gegenüber. Erschien sie dem Deutschen dieser Zeit vorzugsweise als eine grosse Innung oder Zunft, so war sie ihm doch keineswegs eine Innung aller Gläubigen, eine Gemeinschaft, die jeder Laie mit einem Teil seiner Persönlichkeit bilden half, sondern sie war ihm die Zunft des geistlichen Standes. . . . Freilich war es dem Laien unerlässlich für sein Seelenheil, an dem von der Kirche besessenen und verwalteten Heilsschatz Anteil zu erlangen; aber zu diesem Behuf verhandelte und verkehrte er mit ihr *wie mit einer dritten Person,*

personal substratum behind of which he was the mere representative. To make my meaning clear let me quote two passages from Maitland's *Lectures on Constitutional History*. On pp. 101-2 we read:

While we are speaking of this matter of sovereignty, it will be well to remember that our modern theories run counter to the deepest convictions of the Middle Ages — to their whole manner of regarding the relation between Church and State. *Though they may consist of the same units, though every man may have his place in both organisms, these two bodies are distinct. The State has its king or emperor, its laws, its legislative assemblies, its courts, its judges; the Church has its pope, its prelates, its councils, its laws, its courts.* That the Church is in any sense below the State no one will maintain, that the State is below the Church is a more plausible doctrine; but the general conviction is that the two are independent, that neither derives its authority from the other. Obviously, when men think thus, while

---

kaum anders wie mit der Kaufmannsoder Gewerbezunft, wenn er ihrer Waaren bedurfte. *Die Kirche war in Allem ein geistlicher Staat für sich,* in welchem der Laie keines Bürgerrechts genoss.' — Gierke, i. 427 (cf. also 287). 'Bei dieser Auffassung der staatlichen Rechtssubjectivität konnten es die Römer zu Wort und Begriff der Staatspersönlichkeit nicht bringen. Sie blieben bei der Subjectivität des *populus,* und spätre des Kaisers stehen. Diese Subjectivität aber unterstellten sie, weil einzig in ihrer Art, keinem höheren Gattungsbegriff.' — Gierke iii. 50 ('Das Deutsche Genossenschaftsrecht'). Cf. also the following passage in regard to the Church. After describing the Church as God-planted, 'Wenn einer so konstruirten Gesammtkirche Rechtspersönlichkeit beigelegt wird, so kann Quelle derselben nicht *die den Körper bildende Gesammtheit, sondern lediglich Gott und mittelbar dessen irdischer Stellvertreter sein.* In der That hat daher nach der Lehre der Kanonisten der göttliche Stifter selbst seiner Kirche zugleich mit der Heilsvollmacht die für deren Durchführung erforderliche Rechtssubjektivität verliehen. Und allein von Gott und seinem Vikar sind fort und fort alle einzelnen Privilegien und Rechte abzuleiten, welche der Gesammtkirche um ihres geistlichen Berufes willen zustehen, während auch die höchste weltliche Macht diese Rechte nicht zu mindern, sondern ur rein weltliche Privileginen hinzuzufügen vermag. Ebenso aber findet die einheitliche Kirchenpersönlichkeit ihren obersten Träger und Repraesentanten nicht in der Gesammtheit, sondern in Gott selbst und mittelbar in dessem irdischem Statthalter, so dass sogar als Subjekt der Rechte, welche für die *ecclesia universalis* in Anspruch genommen werden, Gott oder Christus selbst und vertretungsweise dann auch der Papst bezeichnet werden kann.' — Gierke, iii. 250.

they more or less consistently act upon this theory, they have no sovereign in Austin's sense; before the Reformation Austin's doctrine was impossible.

In regard to the theory of sovereignty, this statement is doubtless true of the smaller States. It is not true of the papacy; the *plenitudo potestatis* being simply sovereignty in the Austinian sense, developed by the canonists from Roman law and applied to the pope. It is not true of the more extreme Imperialist doctrine; the lawyers who told Frederic Barbarossa that the property of all his subjects was really his, and the normal civilian were, in theory at least, strong Austinians. Indeed, it is from Rome, first imperial and then papal: i.e. from civil and canon law, that the modern doctrine of sovereignty derives. In its modern form it goes through the medieval canonists to Renaissance thinkers like Bodin, thence through Hobbes and the supporters of Divine Right to Austin. Even in the fourteenth century it is applied to the minor States. Baldus, I believe, was the first to say that *rex est imperator in regno suo*, and we find one of our own kings claiming to be *entier empereur dans son royaume*, and this, the claim to sovereignty, is the true meaning of the preamble to the great statute of appeals 'this realm of England is an Empire'. Moreover, it is not quite true to assert that no one said that the Church ought to be below the State. For that is the exact argument of the twelfth-century Erastian treatise by Gerard of York, printed by Böhmer in the *Libelli de Lite*. He declares, indeed, not that the Church is below the State, but that, in the one commonwealth, which you can call either kingdom or church at your pleasure, the secular power is above the ecclesiastical. Still, of course, it is true that in the main Austinian doctrine is not applicable to the feudal commonwealth of the Middle Ages.

It is not of this matter that I want to speak at length, but of the sentences in italic. Later on in the book there is an even more emphatic expression of the same view:

> The medieval theory of the relation between Church and State seems this, that they are independent organisms consisting nevertheless of the same units. — p. 506.

To that statement I say *quod non*. I make this criticism with much diffidence, for every word that Maitland wrote is worth its weight in gold. Yet we must remember that these lectures were not written to be published, and that they were delivered in 1887, before he entered upon those studies which resulted in his work on 'The Canon Law'[1] and his translation of Gierke. To say the very least, it is not certain that he would have written thus fifteen years later. Nor, again, do I desire to assert an 'absolute not'. I do not deny that such a view of Church and State was possible to acute minds in the Middle Ages, any more than I assert that because men normally meant by the Church the hierarchy they did not quite frequently mean the *congregatio fidelium*. I think that in the later Middle Ages men were moving in that direction. Judging by his letters and manifestoes, I think it not impossible that Frederic II held this view or something like it. What I do think is that this view in no way represented the ruling thought of the Middle Ages, that it was not the necessary background of their minds, that all, or nearly all, the evidence points the other way, and that, if we accepted Maitland's view, we should be left with no intelligible explanation of certain phenomena in the sixteenth century, to say nothing of existing controversies and modes of thought.

When we do find one pope speaking of God's vicar as master both of the terrene and the spiritual empire, he shows by his words that he cannot think them apart. The notion of a single society is so universal that, even where in words the popes admit two, it is in order to deny it in fact and to claim for themselves the lordship of both.

Moreover, when the Inquisition handed a heretic over to the secular arm, what was intended by the figure? Surely, that the two arms, the secular and spiritual powers, were arms of the same body — or else the metaphor makes nonsense. Yet the view we combat would make two different bodies.

Let me put before you the following considerations: Is it not rather improbable that this difficult position of two corporate bodies, each of the same individual persons though totally distinct as corporate personalities, should have been thought of in a world whose ideals were symbolised in the Holy Roman Empire, whose true respublica is the

[1] *Roman Canon Law in the Church of England: six essays* (London, 1898).

civitas Dei? Even in our own day, when there is so much to favour it, views of this sort, at least in regard to established Churches, are not accepted readily or without argument. How would it have been in a world where the unbaptised and the excommunicate were outlaws, and citizenship and Christianity were inextricably bound up? Nobody in the Middle Ages denied that the king was God's minister, or that the bishops were great lords in the commonwealth. Pope and emperor, when they quarrelled, quarrelled like brothers, as members of the same society; the *civitas Dei*.

The fact is, *ecclesia* and *respublica* are more often than not convertible terms in medieval literature. One writer, who is well known, describes much in Maitland's way, viz. 'a system of two sets of law and courts'; but it is of two sets of people that he is thinking — the clergy and the laity, and it is within the whole — the one society, the *civitas*, which he says is the *ecclesia* — that these two bodies are to be found. I do not say but that later on, after the crystallisation of national states and the development through S. Thomas of the habit of arguing about the Church as one among a class of political societies, some such view as Maitland suggests may not have been now and then discernible. But I think it was very rare.

And what we want to know is not how some theorist formulated the matter, but what were the 'common thoughts of our forefathers'. Supposing that I had graduated, not at Cambridge but at Bologna in the thirteenth century, that I was a *doctor in utroque jure*, a protonotary apostolic and an auditor of the rota, should I have declared the kingdom or the empire to be a society quite distinct from the Church, though containing the same units? I trow not. I am much more likely to have said that the limits of the kingly power were determined by the Church, meaning the hierarchy, and that the king must do his duty because he was the minister of God and must therefore be subject to His vicar. So far from denying the king *qua* king to be a member of the same society as my own, I should have made his membership the ground of a due reverence for *protonotaries apostolic*. Supposing again, I had been a clerk of the king's Court or a royal justice or one of the barons at Merton, who were not going to have the laws of England changed to suit the bishops, should I have asserted that they were members of a different

State; should I not rather have claimed that, though specially and even reprehensibly privileged, though forming a distinct order in the commonwealth, they were yet English lieges and should be made, willy-nilly, to do and forbear those things lawful to English lieges, and none others? Even if — pardon the impertinence — I had been either a pope on the one hand or an emperor on the other, should I have thought of my rival as the head of another society with which my own relations were strictly international? Hardly. I should rather have deemed him a 'dear colleague' and felt it as a God-imposed duty to prevent him injuring his character by attempting a dictation over me, which for God's cause and solely as a matter of duty, I was determined to resist. Nor was there warrant in antiquity for this notion of the two societies. The conception of a religious society as distinct from the State had not dawned upon the unified civilisation of Greece and Rome. It was alien alike from the City-State and the Pagan Empire. When it did dawn upon some men's minds, what was the universal response? *Christiani ad leones.* Sir William Ramsay has made it clear that the persecution of the early Church was a matter of policy, and that it was directed against this very notion, the claim to be a separate society, while still remaining Roman citizens. It was the Church as upholding 'a new non-Roman unity' that men feared. That primitive Church was without question a society distinct from the Roman State.[1] As she grew to

[1] 'Dagegen lag allerdings von vornherein eine gewaltige negative Umwälzung der antiken Anschauungen von Staat und Recht in *den vom Wesen des Christenthums untrennbaren Principien* welche dem staatlichen Verbande einen grossen Theil seines bisherigen Inhalts zu Gunsten der religiösen Gemeinschaft und des Individuums entzogen. Einmüthig bekannte man sich zu dem Glauben, dass das innere Leben der Einzelnen und ihrer religiös-sittlichen Verbände keiner weltlichen Macht unterworfen und über die Sphäre der staatlichen Daseinsordnung erhaben sei. *Damit entschwand die allumfassende Bedeutung des Staats.* Der Mensch gieng nicht mehr im Bürger, die Gesellschaft nicht mehr im Staat auf. Das grosse Wort, dass man Gott mehr gehorchen soll als den Menschen, begann sienen Siegeslauf. Vor ihm versank die Omnipotenz des heidnischen Staats. Die Idee der immanenten Schranken aller Staatsgewalt und aller Unterthanenpflicht leuchtete auf. Das Recht und die Pflicht des Ungehorsams gegen staatlichen Gewissenszwang wurden verkündigt und mit dem Blute der Märtyrer besiegelt.' — Gierke, *op. cit.*, iii. 123. Cf. also the author's remarks on the effect of S. Augustine's *De Civitate Dei. Ibid.*, 124-7.

strength and threatened to absorb the whole population there was every likelihood of the view arising, outlined by Maitland.

But it did not arise. The old conception, that of Pagan and Jew, was too strong for it. After Constantine granted the peace of the Church, it was not long, at most three-quarters of a century, before the old conception ruled again of a great unity in which civil and ecclesiastical powers were merely separate departments. Had the world been ripe for toleration of rival bodies things might have been very different. But it was not ripe. The emperors, as you know, were treated almost as ecclesiastical powers; coercion was employed on both sides in the Arian controversy; finally the Catholics conquered under Theodosius the Great. Arianism was made a crime; Paganism was suppressed; and the world was ripe for that confusion of baptism and citizenship which ruled the Middle Ages. True, there were many struggles between the different authorities, and their issues varied with time and place. But neither emperors nor prelates were treated as rulers of rival societies. The code of 'Justinian' was compiled subsequently to the 'De Civitate Dei' of S. Augustine. The whole spirit of both is to identify Church and State. The Pagan State was also a Church, and the medieval Church was also a State; *the* Church and *the* State in theory. Each governs the whole of life and the problem is not whether you take power from one society and give it to the other, but where you tilt the balance of authority — on to the side of the lay officials or to that of the clerics. Shall power belong to him who wields the sword or to him who instructs the wielder? Roman law, as it entered the medieval world, is the law of a medievalised empire, and the code begins with the rubric, *De Summa Trinitate et Fide Catholica.* Much of the liberty afterwards claimed by canonists could be supported by adroit quotations from the imperial law.

All this was crystallised in the ideal of the *Holy Roman Empire*, the governing conception of a great world, Church-State, of which it is hard to say whether it is a religious or a temporal institution. Half the trouble came from the fact that popes and emperors were heads, in theory co-equal, of the same society. The argument so constantly repeated, that the unity of the society needs a single person as the centre, and that, therefore the secular power must be subject to the spiritual, owes its force to the very fact that men were incapable of seeing two societies, and that the theory of two co-equal heads under Christ as King did not work in practice. The pope, we must remember, is the emperor's archbishop; foreign he might be to England and France as nationality crystallised, but no emperor could afford to treat him as foreign. That would have been to give up all claims to Italy.

The lesser conflicts were all conducted under the shadow of this conception. Although in countries like England or France it may have been easier to see the distinctions of the two powers, its meaning was not grasped till later, and men did not talk of two societies separate, though composed of the same individuals.

But it will be said, what of the Canon Law? Here is a separate body of legal rules modelled in its form on the civil law and claiming sometimes to override it, possessed of a higher sanction, so that towards the close of the Middle Ages a French writer can say that *omnia jura civilia sunt canonica*.[1]

Now it is true that in so far as the Canon Law governed the laity, and existed by the side of national laws, its existence points towards a belief in two distinct social organisms; yet I do not think that this inference was drawn at the time. The passage I alluded to above treats it as mainly *law for the clergy*, and so far as that was usual, this view would tally with all I have been saying. The popes, however, doubtless thought they were legislating for all Christians, but these popes were claiming a

---

[1] The following passages are a fair indication of the common view: 'Si auctoritas sacra pontificum et potestas imperialis vere glutino caritatis adinvicem complerentur; nihil est enim in præsenti seculo pontifice clarius, nihil rege sublimius.' Cf. also Henry IV to Greg. VII, Jaffé Bib. Rer. Ger. ii. 46: 'Cum enim regnum et sacerdotium, ut in Christo rite administrata subsistant, vicaria sua ope semper indigeant.' From the following sentence from the Deposition of Frederic II, it can readily be seen how intimately connected are canon and civil law: 'Nonne igitur hec non levia, sed efficacia sunt argumenta de suspicione heresis contra eum, cum tamen hereticorum vocabulo *illos jus civile contineri asserat*, et latis adversus eos sentenciis debere subcumbere qui vel levi argumento a judicio catholice religionis et tramite detecti fuerint deviare?' (Deposition of Frederick II. J. L. A. Huillard-Bréholles, *Historia Diplomatica F. II*, vi. 326.) Elsewhere he is accused of treason towards the pope. 'Non sine proditionis nota, et lese crimine majestatis.' *Ibid.*, 322.

plenitudo potestatis over kings and princes, which implied that all secular law was merely allowed by them. Moreover, in those days of feudal courts, men were in the habit of seeing every kind of competing jurisdiction without definitely claiming that it destroyed such unity in the State as they were accustomed to see. The very looseness of structure of the medieval State, if we are to use the term, enabled the canonists to do their work alongside of the secular courts without drawing all the conclusions we should do. Unification was the work of the Renaissance and the Reform, and it was not till then that men would come to argue that it must either exist by the allowance, express or tacit, of the prince, or else that the prince must be in reality a subject.

Moreover, I do not think people sufficiently realise how systems, apparently competing, went on together in practice. Legal writers, like Bartolus on the one hand or Innocent IV on the other, quote the canon law and the civil law indiscriminately, and never seem conscious of them as being the laws of two separate societies. I cannot find this conception in Innocent's great commentary on the 'Decretale of Gregory IX'. Bartolus wrote a treatise on the differences between the two systems, but there is no hint that he regarded them as the laws of two different States.[1] The fact is that it was the two together, treated as an ideal rather than coercive law, which ruled men's minds; and out of this amalgam arose modern politics and international law.

Again, if you take the 'Unam Sanctam' of Boniface VIII, that does not assert the power of the Church over the State. Rather it asserts the power of the Pope over every human being.[2] In fact the personalisation of authority in popes, kings and feudal lords and prelates was one of the causes that retarded the growth of such theory as that of the two kinds of *societas perfecta*. The conflicts between the two powers are habitually spoken of as struggles between the *sacerdotium* and the *regnum*; although the wider terms *respublica* and *ecclesia* are not un-

[1] It is not certain that this attribution is correct. But it makes no difference to this point, whether the book was by Bartolus or another lawyer.

[2] Cf. Henry of Cremona's interesting treatise on behalf of Boniface VIII printed in R. Scholz, *Die Publizistik zur Zeit Philipps des Schönen*, App. 475: 'Sunt diversi ordines,' etc. Is it possible that a passage like this would have been written in a day when Church and State were conceived as two societies, each consisting of the same units?

known, it is surely reasonable to interpret them by the former. I give one or two stanzas of a doggerel poem by Gualterus de Insula from the *Libelli de Lite*.[1] They represent the natural categories into which men's thoughts fell when they discussed the topic.

> Per Noe colliginius summum patriarcham
> Totius ecclesiae caput et monarcham.
>
> Ergo vel ecclesiae membrum non dicatur
> Caesar, vel pontifici summo supponatur.
>
> Major et antiquior est imperialis
> Dignitas quam cleri sit vel pontificalis,
> 'Major' dico tempore, semper enim malis
> Regibus subiacuit terra laycalis.
>
> Imperator Esau major quidem natu,
> Papa quidem Jacob est, minor enim statu:
> Ille sceptro rutilat, iste potentatu,
> Ille major viribus, iste dominatu.
>
> Caesar habet gladium sed materialem,
> Hunc eundem pontifex sed spiritualem.
> Caesar ergo suscipit usum temporalem
> Ab eo, qui possidet curam pastoralem.
>
> Igitur si vera sunt ista quae promisi
> Nichil habet penitus imperator, nisi
> Ab eo, qui possidet claves paradisi,
> At Petri vicarius; *non est sua phisi.*

The famous passage of Pope Gelasius about the two powers, so often quoted, is no evidence the other way; it refers to the two governing authorities of the *mundus*, which one writer declares to mean the State, not two separate societies. Its date alone is sufficient proof that it had reference to the Christianised ancient empire, when such a decision was not to be thought of.

John of Salisbury, in his *Policraticus*, holds very high views of the function of the priest in the State, but it is a power within, not outside, the State that is to rule it, like the soul in the body.

[1] iii. 559–60.

One writer, Jordan of Osnabruck, equates the three powers, the *sacerdotium*, the *imperium*, and the *studium*, as all equally needful for the health of the Church. The *sacerdotium* he assigns to the Romans as the senior, the *imperium* to the Germans and the *studium* to the French as being more perspicacious. That such a view could even be thought of is evidence how far asunder were the medieval notions on the subject from those natural to us.[1]

Wyclif, in his *Speculum Militantis Ecclesiae*, declares that the ecclesia or commonwealth consists of three sections — lords, clergy and commons. The argument of the book is that if the Church were disendowed the nobles would be richer and have less motive to oppress the poor. Whether that result followed the dissolution of the monasteries we need not here determine. What is certain is that it never occurred to him to conceive of Church and State as two distinct societies composed of the same units. The same is the case with Marsilius; but his Erastianism is so marked that it may be thought that his evidence is not to the point. It is notable, however, that he states (while disapproving the fact) that in ordinary use the Church meant the clergy and not the whole Christian people, at least, he says, that is the most common usage.

Lastly, let us note the surprise of Archbishop Whitgift at the doctrine of two societies. Cartwright, the Presbyterian protagonist, was strongly imbued with the notion of two kingdoms, Whitgift seems hardly able to believe his eyes as he reads it. This comes out *passim* in Whitgift's answer to Cartwright.

I need hardly point out that this is also the view of Hooker. And that is the point; how did that view arise? The very general Erastianism of most of the Reformers is well known. It came from this very fact. Society being conceived as fundamentally one, and the clergy in their eyes not having done their part in removing abuses, recourse must be had to the other power in the Church, the secular government. When Luther appealed to the German princes to take up the work of Reform he did not mean that he was appealing from the Christian Church to a secular State, but merely from the clerical to the civil authority. Any other view is preposterous.

[1] Cf. Jordanus von Osnabruck, *Buch über das Römische Reich* (ed. G. Waitz, p. 71).

My point is that this distinction of the two societies is either very primitive, dating from the days of persecution, or else very modern, dating from the religious divisions of Europe. I think that it came about in some such way as this:

(1) The analysis of political forms, begun by S. Thomas on the Aristotelian basis, set on foot the habit of reasoning about political societies. The facts of the great schism and the conciliar movement drove men to discuss the character and constitution of the Church, considered as a community, and comparable to states and king-doms.

(2) This tendency was furthered by the growth of compact national states, by the decay of feudalism, and by the practical abeyance of the Holy Roman Empire; although, even after Constance, the concordats are not between Church and State, but between pope and king, bishops and nobles, etc., of France or other countries.

(3) Then came the Reformation. So far as this was political and princely it made no difference, save that it tilted the balance of power from the clerical to the lay officials. On the other hand in the Empire, as a whole, religious unity was destroyed and after the Religious Peace of Augsburg the Church could no longer be identified with the Empire. But where either prince or people were not able to make their own religion supreme or universal within the territorial state, the conception of two distinct societies tends to grow up. It is not really in the thought of Calvin, but the organisation of the Huguenots was very important in influencing men's minds. It was so local, so compact, so distinct, that it helped to forward the idea among all persons placed as they were. I do not think that Knox, any more than the other reformers, had any real notion of this distinction. But towards the end of Elizabeth's reign it is certainly to be found in Cartwright and the whole English Presbyterian movement. Andrew Melville developed it in Scotland; and Robert Browne, the originator of the Independents, was inspired by this notion in the pamphlet 'Reformation without tarrying for any'.

In England both the Laudian and the Puritan party were medievalist; they believed in a State which was also a Church and were essentially theocratic. What developed the contrary notion was the non-juring schism. This compelled its adherents, and many High Churchmen who were not its adherents, to think of the Church as the body of all the faithful with rights and powers inherent and unconnected with the State. Union with Scotland increased this tendency, for there was thus before men's eyes the spectacle of two different established Churches. Thus Hoadly gives no hint of any other notion than the old, and his idea of toleration was merely a comprehensive Erastianism, very similar to certain schemes we hear of now. Warburton, on the other hand, develops explicitly and in set terms, in his *Alliance between Church and State*, the doctrine that the two are independent organisms consisting of the same individuals, but existing for different ends, each to be treated as a *corporate personality*. His theory comes at the end, not at the beginning of the development I have been describing, and I cannot help feeling it would have been incomprehensible to men such as Gerard of York or S. Thomas of Canterbury. I should also add that the Jesuits, who had to consider the question of the relations of Church and State in reference to the changed conditions of a divided Europe, were forward in developing the notion of the two societies. In Gierke's view they were the first to develop a frankly secular theory of the State. On the other hand, royalists like Barclay in France, who were yet strong Catholics, in order to combat Bellarmine's doctrine of the indirect temporal sovereignty of the Pope were driven to be equally explicit as to the State being a *societas perfecta* no less than the Church, and to claim that the two societies were in a sense distinct.

But it may be asked, What difference does all this make? Nobody denies that Henry IV went to Canossa,[1] or that Boniface VIII issued the 'Unam Sanctam,' or that Frederic Barbarossa held the papal stirrup, or that his grandson was deposed by a Church council. What difference can it possibly make whether we assert that these incidents were the result of conflicts between two separate societies, each of them a State, or between two sets of officials in one and the same society? If what has been said is well founded, we must view these conflicts as of the nature of civil war. Does that get us any 'forrarder'? If I were a scientific historian I should use great and desolate words about truth, and say that the less it mattered the better was it worth studying. However, instead

[1] At least I do not. I understand that doubt has been thrown even on this event.

of this I shall make the modest claim that such view helps us to understand better both history and ourselves.

(1) It explains the quick drop into Erastianism all over Europe in the sixteenth century. The campaign of the Reformers was just *une campagne laïque*. They were not attempting to take power out of the Christian society, but merely out of its clerical officials. All coercive power was to be rested in the prince, but in theory it was always the godly prince, 'most religious'. So long as they had him on their side, men so different as Laud and Luther felt that they were safe. The sixteenth century witnessed an undoubted victory of the secular over the ecclesiastical power; but it was not for the secular power as a society distinct from the Church, it was a victory for the temporal authority within the one society which can be called either Church or State according to the aspect prominent at the moment. Erastus himself declared that he was only discussing the case of a State which tolerated but a single religion *eamque veram*, a statement which shows how far he is removed from the modern form of the system which derives its name from him.

(2) Many problems and controversies of modern times are rendered more intelligible to us, if we adopt the view which I suggest. Slowly, but only very slowly, has the notion of separate societies with inherent rights developed, just as it is only now that the doctrine of true corporate personality is being realised. The *Kulturkampf* was simply due to the incapacity of Bismarck to realise that there could be any corporate life with inherent powers of its own, unwilling to accept the *sic volo, sic jubeo* of the State. As we saw, the same notion was at bottom of the difficulties in the 'Free Church of Scotland Appeals'. Nor does it take much ingenuity to discover it lurking in recent judicial pronouncements about the *Deceased Wife's Sister Act*, or about the controversy between Churches and undenominationalism in regard to education.[1]

---

[1] 'Hinsichtlich der Enstehung der Korporation geht das Corpus Juris durchweg von der Auffassung aus, dass aus der natürlichen oder gewollten Vereinigung von Individuen zwar das thatsächliche Substrat, niemals jedoch die rechtliche Existenz einer Verbandseinheit hervorzugehen vermag. Vielmehr stammt zunächst die publicistische Verbandswesenheit während der Staat selbst als die mit und über den Individuen gegebene Allgemeinheit keiner Zurück-

(3) The unity of history is a cant phrase and is often made to bear a burden too heavy. But it may be pointed out how strong a testimony to this doctrine is afforded by the persistent notion of the republic, one and indivisible, which has come down to the modern world by descent through the medieval papacy, the Christianised ancient empire, the pagan empire, whither it migrated from the compact all-absorbing city-state. Mr. Carlyle, in the first chapter of his history of political theory in the West, was able to show us how the doctrines of Rousseau anent the fundamental equality of man and modern democracy can be found implicit in the Roman jurists, in Cicero, and to witness to a change in feeling between the aristocratic doctrine of Aristotle and the universalist theories of the great republic. This view has been encountered in our own day by the revival of aristocracy proclaimed by Nietzsche, and the doctrines of the fundamental inequality of men based partly on the subjugation of the tropics, partly on Darwinian theories of natural selection and the struggle for existence. The doctrine, however, which I have been considering is even more venerable than that of human equality. For it goes back, with hardly a break, to the omni-competent and universally penetrating supervision of Sparta and Athens. It is only when we have traced it right back to its origin that we see its inapplicability to the complex life of a modern world-empire.

---

führung auf einen besonderen rechtlichen Begründungsakt bedarf, auf allen übrigen Stufen vom Staat. *Staatliche Verleihung gilt als die Quelle der publicistischen Existenz auch solcher Gemeinwesen,* welche vor ihrem Eintritt in das römische *jus publicum* als selbständige Staaten bestanden haben; aus staatlicher Verleihung fliesst die Korporationsqualität auch derjenigen Verbände, deren thatsächliches Dasein freier Vereinigung verdankt wird; auf staatliche Verleihung gründet sich die publicistische Verbandseinheit auch der christlichen Kirche, welche selbst ihren Bestand aus göttlicher Stiftung herleitet. Überall aber verfährt hierbei der Staat hinsichtlich des rechtlichen Elementes der engeren Verbandswesenheiten wahrhaft constitutiv. *Alle körperschaftliche Existenz erscheint als das Werk frei schaffender Gesetzgebung,* durch welche der Staat, sei es in der Form der *lex specialis* für sad einzelne Gebilde, oder sei es in der Form genereller Regeln für einen Komplex gleichartiger Verbände, seine eigne Gliederung setzt und ordnet. Darum bedarf es in keiner Weise einer Normirung bestimmter Voraussetzungen für die Errichtung einer Korporation.' — Gierke, *op. cit.*, iii. 142–3.

The theory of sovereignty, whether proclaimed by John Austin or Justinian, or shouted in conflict by Pope Innocent or Thomas Hobbes, is in reality no more than a venerable superstition. It is only true to the facts in a cosy, small and compact State, although by a certain amount of strained language and the use of the maxim, 'whatever the sovereign permits he commands', it can be made not logically untenable for any conditions of stable civilisation. As a fact it is as a series of groups that our social life presents itself, all having some of the qualities of public law and most of them showing clear signs of a life of their own, inherent and not derived from the concession of the State.

The State may recognise and guarantee (and demand marks for so doing) the life of these societies — the family, the club, the union, the college, the Church; but it neither creates that life any more than it creates the individual, though it orders his birth to be registered. It is the problem of the future, as Mr. A. L. Smith showed at the close of his lecture on Maitland, to secure from legal theory the adequate recognition of these facts, and in regard to religion the problem is raised in an acute form, and it will be the service of multiplied sectarianism to a true, that is a realistic political, philosophy if it forces the recognition of the truth that smaller societies live by their own life, and exercise real authority over their members. The struggle for liberty nowadays is the struggle to secure that recognition. What I have tried to indicate is the causes of that struggle being arduous. The atmosphere in which law has lived for more than one millennium (apart from the Teutonic and feudal influences) has been all in favour of the doctrine which recognises two and only two social entities, the individual on the one hand and the State on the other. In that atmosphere law not only gets out of relation to living facts and precipitates struggles like the *Kulturkampf* and absurdities like those involved in the case of the *Free Church of Scotland*, but political philosophy, which is always largely dependent on law, oscillates between an unreal individualism and a wildly impossible socialistic ideal. The facts of life are hostile to both, but injury, both practical and theoretical, is always done by trying to ignore facts, especially facts so tremendous as the complex group-life which is to most of us more than the State. What I have tried to show is that this error is not of modern origin, that it did not come into our world at the Renaissance, though it may have been accentuated then, but that it is part of the *damnosa hereditas* from the Civil Law of the Roman Empire, of which Stubbs once said that, whenever it had been dominant, it destroyed any real idea of civil and religious freedom.[1]

J. NEVILLE FIGGIS

[1] I do not claim to have proved the view here set forth; still less to have set out the whole evidence. I am not certain of any hard and fast categories in the topic. But I would ask the student to study the ecclesiastico-political controversies throughout this course, from the *Libelli de Lite* down to the modern newspaper and platform speaker, and to ask himself whether the view here put forward does not fit more readily into the words and modes of thought of thinkers on all sides than that which I have combated. Even if it be only a difference of emphasis, it seems to me one of those matters when the emphasis makes as much difference as the distinction between a stroke of the cat and a stroke of the cane.

2 The Commons' Journals of the Tudor Period

In 1914 Professor Pollard read a paper before the Royal Historical Society on 'The Authenticity of the Lords' Journals in the Sixteenth Century',[1] in the course of which, by revealing how inadequate a presentation of the manuscript originals was contained in the printed journals, he showed that the original journals might be a valuable field for historical gleanings. In addition to Professor Pollard, Professor Maitland and Mr. L. O. Pike also examined the manuscript of an Elizabethan Lords' journal;[2] but in 1916 two American scholars, Professors Notestein and Usher, turned to the Commons' journals of the early seventeenth century, and in advocating a critical survey of the manuscript originals, challenged the conventional view of their authenticity which an uncritical edition of them has easily created.[3] The fact is, of course, that even an accurate edition of a document — and *a fortiori* an inaccurate one — may destroy valuable historical evidence if it convey no clear idea of the appearance of the original manuscript. It is one thing to visualise a large folio sheet of print: a materially different impression may be obtained from the manuscript original. In common with the work of these English and American scholars, the present survey, dealing with the manuscripts of the Tudor Commons' journals, has been prompted by this canon of historical research. Its result will not be to impair the reliability of the printed journals in the way that Professor Pollard's paper did, if only because the manuscripts presented less opportunity for their editors to err. But cognate, as well as new, problems will be raised, and the research

[1] *Trans[actions of the] Roy[al] Hist[orical] Soc[iety]* 3rd series, viii. 17.

[2] *Eng[lish] Hist[orical] Rev[iew]*, xviii. 531. *Constitutional History of the House of Lords*, Pref. vii.

[3] 'The Stuart Period: Unsolved Problems', by Professor W. Notestein, and 'Unsolved Legal and Institutional Problems in the Stuart Period', by Professor R. G. Usher, in *Annual Rep. Amer. Hist. Assoc.* (1916), i. 395, 403.

embodied in it will be found to be complementary to the work of Professors Pollard and Notestein in their different spheres.[1]

The original journals of the Tudor House of Commons that are extant are bound in two volumes, the first covering the years 1547–66, and the second the years 1571–80/1; while for the later Elizabethan Parliaments, from 1584–1601, the manuscripts are missing. The grouping of the surviving journals is necessitated by their size, but the division at 1571 coincides with a change in the clerkship of the lower house, and the volumes are quite distinct from subsequent journals in bearing the names of the two clerks as their titles. The earlier is known as 'Seimour', a name by which it is referred to in the precedent books of the early seventeenth century;[2] and the later, 'Onslowe', a title seemingly unknown to the compilers of those books, and probably given it by analogy with the 'Seimour' volume, after the complete disappearance of Onslow's later Elizabethan journals. 'Seimour' is only 6 in. by 8 in. in size, and is as surprising in internal, as in external, appearance. From 1547–52 its journals are fair copies made from the notes taken in the House, but from 1552/3–66 they are the notes themselves; a distinction which is made quite clear by a close examination of the manuscripts. Thus the earlier journals, which cover the first Parliament of Edward VI, are written in a fair hand with regular spacing between entries and days, contrasting markedly with the irregularity and distention of the entries after 1552. Their margins are ruled, so differing from the double fold of the quire which served later. The journals from 1552/3–66 are, however, in a hurried, uneven hand that varied with the speed of writing. Different quills and ink have resulted in a patchwork appearance, the variations coinciding with fresh sittings of the House;[3] and where additions were made to the entries of a day

---

[1] Professor Notestein's researches deal with the early Stuart Commons' journals, but have not yet been published. I am indebted to him for knowledge of his work and for the light which it has thrown upon my studies.

[2] Cf. B.M. Harl. MS. 6283.

[3] From October 1553 on, Seymour entered the word 'assent' in the margin against Bills that received the royal assent. Being written at the close of a session, the word often seems foreign to a day's entries which were written in a different shade of ink. Probably for this reason the editors of the printed journals confused it with marginalia of the early seventeenth (?) century, added to

at the next sitting, they can frequently be distinguished by the different shade of ink used on the second day, or by being cramped into an inadequate space.[1] Erasures and interlineations are numerous, and they, too, yield instructive evidence. Thus an entry recording the dispatch of certain Bills to the Lords is cancelled, and their transference noted again on a later day, no doubt because the messenger found the Lords risen on the first occasion, and so redelivered the Bills to the clerk.[2] As a rule each of the journals in this first volume is headed only by the year in figures, but in 1558/9 and 1652/3 Seymour added his Christian name 'Johannes'. Bound in at the beginning and end of the volume are a number of leaves, some evidently the unused folios, and others, which are soiled, the outer sheets, of the journals while they were still un-bound. They contain several notes. A quotation from the Vulgate is on the same page with a Parliamentary jotting,[3] and on the next folio appears an entry of a Member's licence of departure.[4] Two soiled sheets at the end of the volume contain, the one, 'Amen per me Johannem', and the other, statistics on the decay of the navy probably taken down during a debate in 1562/3.[5] The second volume of journals, 'Onslowe', which covers the years 1571–1580/1, requires but a brief description.

---

facilitate the use of the journals for precedent purposes. Yet 'assent' is an integral part of the manuscript journals.

[1] Cf. Seimour, fol. 133b, where the Bill, 'that the Subjectes of this Realme shall not bring in foreign wares', clearly had the words, 'of dyverse sortes' added, in accordance with the extended title given it on the following day (fol. 134a).

[2] Seimour, fol. 226a (Feb. 11), 227a (Feb. 15); *Lords Journals*, i. 590, 591.

[3] Ecclesiasticus, cap. x. verse 17. 'Leonard baryngton a wytnes for Mr. Mynne' (cf. *Commons Journals*, i. 44).

[4] Humphrey Bradbourne, knight for Derby County in 1552/3 and 1555 (*Official Return of Members of Parliament*, pt. i. 378, 393).

[5] 'the decayes of the navy/in shippes and maryners/within xxty yeres in the cinque portes 258 now 69 shippes bot[toms?]/Lyme xiiii now 2 for. [*sic*]/ maryners 3c.c. [600]/grete shippes in englend for marchantes/London and Thamys xxvii maryners xxvm. [25,000]/2c [200] houses of religion besides celles fryers colleges femelyes of/bishops dyd eate fishe on wensdayes kept advent xviiim. iic. xlii [?] [18,242 ?]/fed xxxm. [30,000] people in those tymes.' (Cf. *Commons Journals*, i. 68; S.P. Dom. Eliz., xxvii. No. 71.) The bars in the trans-cription denote the end of each line of writing.

It is 8 in. by 13 in. in size, and is in striking contrast with 'Seimour'. Its journals are all carefully finished manuscripts, the four margins of which are ruled, and they are free from the irregularities which distinguish and disfigure the earlier volume.

From the seventeenth century until the present day, conflicting views have been held regarding the origin of the Commons' journals. The one accepts the evidence of survival, and regards the 1547 journal as the first of its class. The record is so meagre, it urges, that anything more rudimentary is hard to conceive.[1] On the other hand, Coke[2] and Petyt[3] in the seventeenth century, and Harding[4] and May,[5] Parliamentary clerks of the eighteenth and nineteenth centuries, have maintained that a journal was kept in the reign of Henry VIII, basing their assertions upon an Act passed in 1515 to regulate the departure of knights and burgesses from Parliament, wherein it was stipulated that licences granted to departing Members should 'be enteryd of record in the booke of the Clerke of the parliament appoynted ... for the Common house'.[6] 'The Clerk's Book and the Journals,' said May, 'were unquestionably the same.'[7] The occasion serves to point an excellent moral, for this passage from the Act of 6 Henry VIII depends for its significance upon the connotation of the term Clerk's Book, and consequently the insertion of a title, 'Journals', which is absent from the Tudor manuscripts, must be regarded as not least among the editorial errors of the printed Commons' journals. The journals were first referred to within their own pages as the clerk's 'Book of Notes', and this in 1580/1;[8] while even in 1641 Hakewill was able to write of 'the Clerkes booke or journal'.[9] The first use of the modern term that I have found occurs late in Elizabeth's reign and then refers to the Lords' journals.[10] Of its being

---

[1] Cf. *Trans. Roy. Hist. Soc.*, 3rd series, viii. 27.

[2] *4th Institute* (1671), 23.   [3] *Jus Parliamentarium* (1680), 223–4.

[4] *Commons Journals*, xxiv. 263.

[5] *Parliamentary Practice* (9th edn.), 258. Sir R. F. D. Palgrave abandoned this view in editing the 10th edn. Also cf. Sir C. P. Ilbert, *Parliament* (Home University Library), p. 179, where an accurate statement based on the Act of 1515 conveys the impression of there having been earlier journals.

[6] *Statutes of the Realm*, iii. 134 (6 Hen. VIII, c. xvi).

[7] *Op. cit.* 258.   [8] *Commons Journals*, i. 116.

[9] *The Manner how Statutes are enacted* ... 32.   [10] *Lords Journals*, ii. 195.

applied to the Commons' journals, I have discovered no instance in the Tudor period. Apparently the practice began under James I; and one of the two journals extant for 1604 is headed 'Diarium', a title which does occur in the original manuscript.[1]

Yet I hope to show that the argument from the Act of 1515 to a contemporary journal, though it may be more valid than has perhaps been thought, is neither necessary nor accurate. A casual examination of even the printed journals will disclose the fact that the journal of 1547 is quite distinct in its character. In the manuscript it is headed, 'In Anno primo Regni Regis Edwardi Sexti, &c. A note of the Bylles when they were redde in the Commen House in the first Session'; and its title is descriptive of its contents. In only five instances is this limitation exceeded, when the names are added of Members to whom the clerk had temporarily committed certain Bills. It would surely be a distortion of terms to call this a 'Journal of the House of Commons', which had no concern with a day whereon no Bill was read, and which quite consistently omits all mention of the opening days of the Parliament.[2] The change, then, is a fundamental one when the journal of the second session includes orders, privilege cases and licences of departure, in addition to the readings of Bills. We have now a real journal of the proceedings of the House, and its scale, adopted for the succeeding journals, gives us entries of the dissolution of Edward's first Parliament at the close of its fourth session, and of the opening of his second Parliament in 1552/3.

There can be little doubt that this transition between 1547 and 1548 was due to the entry upon office of John Seymour, who on 10 May 1548 succeeded Richard Ormeston as clerk of the House of Commons.[3] Hence the 'notes of the Bylles . . . redde . . .' may be regarded as the closest approximation of Ormeston to a Seymour journal. But if at the end of thirty-two years of service[4] he kept such a memorandum, it is practically certain that it was not unique, and that earlier manuscripts once existed. Indeed, memoranda showing the progress of Bills through the House became indispensable as the legislative activities of

---

[1] *Commons Journals*, i. 933. Also cf. i. 385, vi. 117.
[2] 4 and 7 November, cf. *Lords Journals*, i. 293–4.   [3] Pat. 2, Edw. VI, pt. v.
[4] Pat. 7, Hen. VIII, pt. ii. No. 12. *L. and P. Henry VIII*, ii. pt. i. No. 185.

the Commons developed, and the three readings were stereotyped in procedure.[1] But Ormeston must also have kept other types of memoranda. By the Act of 1515 he was compelled to make entries of licences granted to departing Members; while the exigencies of procedure must have led to notes, however rough, of any orders the execution of which devolved upon himself.[2] In all probability the sum of these separate memoranda differed only slightly from the total entries in Seymour's first journal. Nevertheless that journal was novel, its novelty consisting in a synthesis of the isolated and possibly unvalued notes that Ormeston kept, into a single memorandum in diary form. When once begun, a diary invites both expansion and preservation, and so the impetus was supplied which originated a new class of Parliamentary records.

Ormeston's memoranda do not survive, and it is improbable that any of them were deliberately preserved by him. His note of the readings of Bills in 1547 came into Seymour's hands, but was rewritten to introduce Seymour's own journals with some record of the first session of Edward VI's reign; and it survives as a transcript in the same hand as the three subsequent journals. Had a regular series of memoranda been inherited by Seymour, he would scarcely have duplicated the record of 1547, merely to serve as a preface to an enlarged continuation of this series.[3] The accession of Seymour, therefore, marks the taking of so definite a step to record the proceedings of the House of Commons, and his 1548 journal is so different from any memoranda that preceded it, that we may say that the Commons' journals originated, not with the journal of 1547, but with that of 1548. So far as one can tell, not only was Seymour the instrument by which Ormeston's random notes were

---

[1] Under Burghley the clerk had periodically to furnish statements of the positions of Bills in the House on a given day. Cf. S.P. Dom. Eliz., cvii. Nos. 59, 63, 86; cxlviii. No. 1.

[2] A stray, soiled sheet of paper, containing desultory jottings, is inserted in the MS. Lords Journals (ii. 130) before the journal of 3 Edw. VI. It illustrates the need of odd notes, of which the following may serve as examples. 'Re To searche owt the acte for thuse of hand gonnes.' 'ii. bookes of regrating committed to Mr. Sollycitor.'

[3] Hobart knew of no earlier 'journal' than that of 1547 (*Reports* (1678), p. 109).

transformed into a journal, but the initiative was his. He certainly has preserved no order of the House instituting a record, and while it would be a dangerous expedient to argue from the silence of the early journals, one may turn to the appearance of the manuscripts for corroboration: for records so jejune, with the blemishes and peculiarities that have been described, cannot easily be considered official memoranda. They undoubtedly suggest a casual origin.

The thesis upheld by Coke, Petyt and the Parliamentary clerks cannot, therefore, be maintained, for even Ormeston's sessional notes cannot be the Clerk's Book referred to in the Act of 1515, since their contents were the readings of Bills only. The argument, indeed, ignores the fact of evolution in a journal, and an Act of Parliament would probably not have taken cognisance even of Seymour's earlier journals. But the reference must be to some book, and the determination of the document is a matter of historical interest.

From Tudor, if not from earlier, times to the present, it has been the duty of the Clerk of the Crown in Chancery to prepare a list of the elected Members of Parliament from the writs and returns, and to certify a copy into the House of Commons, where it serves as evidence of a Member's return.[1] The lists are long, narrow quires, which, when originals, appear to have been of parchment and to have been indorsed, 'Liber Parliamenti'. At the Crown Office they are extant from Mary's reign onwards; but there is no reason to suppose that they did not once exist for earlier Parliaments, the more so as the records of this office seem to have been in jeopardy both in Tudor and in modern times.[2] In fact, a Hatfield manuscript is almost certainly such a list, dating from Edward VI's reign.[3] The copies certified into the House of Commons were used there for calling the Members at the opening and in the

---

[1] Cf. *Commons Journals*, i. 51, 140; D'Ewes' *Journals*, 570a.

[2] Townshend, *Historical Collections*, 214–15; *Roy. Com. on Pub. Rec.* (1910), *2nd Rep.*, ii. pt. iii. 71–2.

[3] *Hist. MSS. Com., Hatfield MSS.*, pt. i. 51. Mr. W. S. Dann transcribed this for a thesis, 'Parliamentary Representation in the 16th Century', submitted for the University of London M.A. degree in 1911. The formulas of the manuscript are those of the Crown Office lists. Mr. Dann considers the list to be for the last session of Edward VI's first Parliament.

course of a session, and were spoken of as the 'Clerk's Book'. 'After this,' wrote a Member in 1592/3, 'the house was called by the clarkes booke. . . .'[1] They were official in character, and the conclusion seems irresistible that licences issued to Members on departure before the close of the session were entered against their names in the 'Liber Parliamenti'[2]: incidentally, subsequent callings of the roll would have been facilitated by such a procedure. It is unfortunate that the Commons' copies of the lists have not survived. Those earlier than 1625 were lost before the fire at Westminster Palace in 1834,[3] disappearing, perhaps, early in the seventeenth century.[4]

From the seventeenth century until the present day the Tudor Commons' journals have presented two historical problems. With the one, the origin of the records, I have just dealt. The other is concerned with the loss of the manuscripts for the years 1584–1601. Sir Simonds D'Ewes' collection of Parliamentary journals for Elizabeth's reign was compiled in the years 1629–30,[5] and as there was then no gap from 1584–1601 in the official Commons' journals, it includes a text of manuscripts that are now missing. D'Ewes' work is known in the version published by Paul Bowes in 1682. But the original is extant in the Harleian collection of manuscripts at the British Museum,[6] and it includes a prefatory table giving references to the folios of the official Commons' journals for each day's entries. This Bowes omitted in the published work, and he also abridged the preface, both of which contain much information concerning the official manuscripts extant in 1630. By checking the folio references with the two volumes, 'Seimour' and 'Onslowe', at Westminster, it is clear that they are the same volumes that D'Ewes used: although they have since been rebound. The missing journals, D'Ewes shows in his preface, were bound in a bulky, folio volume, along with a fragment of the 1580/1 journal, of which, however, a complete manuscript still exists in 'Onslowe'. They were, he adds,

[1] Cotton MS. Titus F., ii. fol. 70b.

[2] Marginal comments were common: e.g. 'mort' was entered against a deceased Member's name and the new Member's name added.

[3] *Roy. Com. on Pub. Rec.* (1910), 2nd Rep., ii. pt. ii. 106.

[4] Cf. *infra*, p. 45.   [5] D'Ewes' *Autobiography*, i. 409, 436.

[6] Harl. MSS. 73, 74, 75.

exceeding difficult to be read, and were certainly the very notes taken and entered into the said Volume by Fulk Onslowe ... during the Continuance of the Parliament. ... In all which the said Notes being written in a fast running hand, and in every Page almost much inter-lined, and sometimes enlarged by several Additions, disposed into such vacant places as the page afforded, often distant each from other, it required ... much time to discover, ... not only what was written, but also how each particular was to be disposed into its due place.[1]

The passage is clear in its meaning, and it is well that it is so, for its implications are important. There was a very real distinction between the clerk's rough *notes* and the *journal*.[2] The latter was the record: the former but the minutes taken in the House, out of which the record was compiled. And the journal might not, and did not, faithfully reproduce the notes. In his description of the manuscripts D'Ewes is explicit enough to prove the general truth of his statement; but its particular application to each of the documents is not so certain, and we must seek for corroborative evidence in his edition of them.

Fulk Onslow is in D'Ewes' work the chief victim of the editor's uncritical avidity for strictures. Charges against him of negligence are repeated *ad nauseam*. But these assume an entirely new significance when they are now found to be crowded into the later journals, for they are indicative of remarkable omissions and defects, which alone characterise the clerk's rough notes. The numerous omissions that D'Ewes points out, were, according to his comments, almost all denoted in the manuscript originals by blank spaces, often extending into pages. Speeches were frequently left out, or only partially repor-ted, as when, for example, the opening only is given of a speech by Sir Walter Mildmay in moving for a committee of supply, and three blank pages left to mark the deficiency.[3] Reports to the House, embody-ing the deliberations of Committees or the substance of conferences, were often left incomplete, an instance of which is the following trun-cated entry: 'Mr. Comptroller and the residue returning from the

[1] D'Ewes' *Journals*, Pref.

[2] Cf. *Eng. Hist. Rev.*, xxviii. 533, and *infra*, p. 36. note.

[3] D'Ewes' *Journals*, 431a. Also cf. in 1584/5, *ibid.*, 334a, 351–2; in 1586/7, *ibid.*, 392a, 418b; in 1588/9, *ibid.*, 429a, 454b, 455a; in 1592/3, *ibid.*, 470a.

33

Lords, Mr. Secretary shewed that in the debate of the . . .'[1] Then, on one occasion, the names of a committee and the place and time of its meeting are omitted.[2]

We are perfectly familiar with the reporter's habit of relying upon written speeches where these are procurable. There is nothing essentially modern in the practice, and in all probability Onslow's irregularities are to be explained by his reliance upon manuscripts of speeches and orders, and other miscellaneous papers, which he acquired either on loan or as part of the routine memoranda of a session. A fact of wider interest is really involved here, for we should be helped in reconstructing the working of the House of Commons in an important century, if only we knew what its routine memoranda were; and the anxiety of the 1910 Record Commission to extract information concerning a class of Commons' Manuscripts parallel with the Lords' Manuscripts, is witness to the interest of the question.[3] Unfortunately the sixteenth-century papers, with the exception of the journals, did not survive even until the Westminster fire of 1834.[4] However, the journal of 1604, the first compiled by Onslow's successor, Ralph Ewens, is plentifully interleaved with miscellaneous papers, both originals and transcripts. Among the original papers are a warrant, a writ of habeas corpus, various letters and petitions; while among other papers similarly inserted in the journal, are precedents, decisions by Committees, a speech by the Speaker, and a list of the names of a Committee giving the time and place of its meeting. Probably the interleaving is in part strictly contemporaneous with the compilation of the journal; but certain of the papers, judging from their creases and

---

[1] D'Ewes' *Journals*, 584b (1597/8). Also cf. in 1584/5, *ibid.*, 352a; in 1586/7, *ibid.*, 402a; in 1588/9, *ibid.*, 452b, 454b; in 1592/3, *ibid.*, 478a.

[2] *Ibid.*, 337b. Also see *ibid.*, 451a (in 1588/9); *ibid.*, 508a (in 1592/3).

[3] Cf. *Roy. Com. on Pub. Rec.* (1910), *2nd Rep.*, ii. pt. iii. 73. It is probably worth calling attention to a Lansdowne Manuscript (No. 553) in the British Museum, which is a calendar of the House of Commons' books and papers from 1547–1732. It is a substantial folio of 502 folios, and while all the Commons' books and papers referred to in the catalogue reprinted by the 1910 Record Commission (*2nd Rep.*, ii. pt. ii. 106) are not included, its detailed character makes it a useful supplement to that catalogue.

[4] *Ibid.*, *2nd Rep.*, ii. pt. ii. 106.

soiled dorses, were pigeon-holed for a considerable time before being incorporated in the journal, and were, perhaps, inserted after a review of the journal by a Committee in 1607.[1]

The value of Ewens' manuscript is not to show that Onslow initiated the practice of interleaving; probably he did not. It is to suggest that the omissions in Onslow's rough notes generally represent the existence of separate papers in his possession; and in point of fact, most, if not all, of the defects which D'Ewes has instanced, could have been made good by papers similar to those in Ewens' journal. Nor is it unlikely that such papers existed in the latter half of Onslow's clerkship. The same spirit which during Elizabeth's reign caused an increasing definition and formalisation of Parliamentary procedure, must have developed the practice of setting down reports, orders, speeches and memoranda, in writing, for more accurate presentation to the House. Occasional references in the journals bear out this conclusion;[2] while the Mildmay and Sadler Papers which have survived,[3] along with other miscellaneous Parliamentary papers, show that it was customary for the more formal speeches, at least, to be written out in full.

Their omissions and deficiencies stamp the later Onslow journals which D'Ewes used, with the character of minutes. But one would expect such manuscripts, written in long-hand, to contain disjointed notes serving as reports of lengthy speeches. A speech of Sir Christopher Hatton's does, in fact, furnish an example.[4] Yet the result of a general search would be disconcerting were one not familiar with D'Ewes' standards of editorial accuracy and criticism. The text of his documentary sources was not sacrosanct to him, and he did not hesitate to make sense where he thought it lacking, or to frame fragmentary notes into a readable narrative. A detailed study of his journals reveals this very clearly, but for our immediate purpose we are not without confessions of his to revisionary work on disjointed reports. A long relation of the

[1] *Commons Journals*, i. 390.

[2] Cf. D'Ewes' *Journals*, 296b, 417b, 479a. See *ibid.*, 559a, for a reference to a Committee list, and cf. an actual list from the House of Lords in S.P. Dom. cclxv, No. 18.

[3] B.M. MSS.: Sloane 326; Add. 33591.

[4] D'Ewes' *Journals*, 408. But even this has probably been retouched.

results of a conference, made to the House by the Treasurer, 'is set down in the Original Journal-Book . . .', wrote D'Ewes, 'in this (or rather a more imperfect) manner . . .':[1] and so, no doubt, many ill-reported speeches have been disguised in his edition of them.

From 1601, however, the only omission in the official manuscripts noted by D'Ewes is of the closing ceremonies of the Parliament,[2] and against this deficiency must be set his comment upon the unusual full-ness with which the opening ceremonies were recorded.[3] The truth is, he was so well served in this instance by an elaborate journal of Hey-wood Townshend's, that the occasions did not arise, if the defects existed, for editorial strictures upon the official manuscript; and con-sequently we must find other data for its classification. Now a clerk's rough notes, written daily, and into several distinct quires of paper, may be expected to have begun the entries of many more days with fresh pages in the manuscript, than did the journal which was a fair copy written as a single and continuous memorandum. An analysis of the table of folio references in the original manuscript of D'Ewes' work, fully establishes this distinction, as between the earlier Onslow journals from 1571–80/1, and the rough notes of 1584–97/8:[4] and as its evidence is conclusive also for the 1601 manuscript, we may safely classify this as the rough notes of the clerk. Indeed, Onslow's fair journals from 1571–80/1 offer so marked a contrast with the manu-scripts of D'Ewes' description, that an exception of the 1601 manuscript would undoubtedly have been made, had it been a finished journal.

Thus D'Ewes' characterisation of the third volume of official manu-scripts is confirmed. But the volume possessed two peculiarities which

---

[1] D'Ewes' *Journals*, 359b. Also 356a.

[2] Harl. MS., No. 75, fol. 293b. This note (like many others) was omitted by Bowes in publishing D'Ewes' work. The date, and an entry of the Act of Pardon, we learn, were the only entries for 19 December, in the official manu-script. A blank space denoted the omissions.

[3] D'Ewes' *Journals*, 622a.

[4] The following list gives the proportion of days which begin a fresh page, to days which do not.

Journals: For 1571, 24: 20; 1575/6, 11: 19; 1580/1, 21: 31.

Rough Notes: For 1584/5, 18:6; Feb.-Mch. 1586/7, 15: 10; 1588/9, 42:4; 1592/3, 28: 11; 1597/8, 56:2; 1601, 38: 6.

need to be mentioned, for they have a bearing upon the unfolding of our problem. The first concerns the manuscript of October–December 1586. In a prefatory note to his table of folio references for this, D'Ewes remarks that 'diuers daies are entred into two seuerall places out of boath which somtimes (when one place supplied anie matter defectiue in the other) the ensuing Journall was framed and therefore all the said Number-folios where the said double entrances were found though farr distant each from other are for the most parte extracted . . .'.[1] The table itself shows a strange confusion of pages before 18 November, but as the data given do not allow of a reconstruction of the manuscript, it is possible only to conjecture that the superfluous entries were stray sheets from the actual *journal* for 1586, salvaged from a dispersal of the Commons' papers, and bound carelessly with the surviving rough notes.[2] The partial salvage is quite explicable if we assume that the journal was unbound at the time of its loss. Support for such a conjecture as this may be found in the second peculiarity of the volume. For the fragment of the 1580/1 journal which it contained, and

---

[1] Harl. MS. 73, fol. 17. I give the part of the table affected, adopting a columnar rearrangement which both simplifies and helps to explain the confusion.

31 Oct.			197a.
3 Nov.		176a	197a, 198a, b.
4 Nov.	171a.	176b.	199a.
5 Nov.	171b, 172a.		
7 Nov.	172b, 173a, b, 174a.	177a.	
8 Nov.	174b, 175a.		
9 Nov.	175b.	177b, 178a, b, 182.	
		183a, b, 184a.	
10 Nov.		178b.	
11 Nov.		178b, 179a, b, 185, 186a, b.	
12 Nov.		179b.	
14 Nov.		179b, 180a, 188a, b.	
18 Nov.		189a, b.	
19 Nov. etc., regular.			
2 Dec.			196a, b.
15 Feb.			200a, b.

And thereafter regular.

[2] This hypothesis would explain the two versions of the Norfolk election dispute, given by D'Ewes under different dates (*Journals*, 396, 398).

which seems misplaced in a volume covering the years 1584–1601, was part of the rough notes of the session.[1] It, too, was evidently salvaged, and on account of its character was bound in with the rough notes of the later Parliaments.

I have now postulated a finished journal, as well as the clerk's rough notes, for the Parliament of 1586, and in so doing have predetermined an important question. We have already seen that the official manuscripts from which D'Ewes compiled his Commons' journals for 1584–1601, were not, as is supposed, the journals themselves, but merely the rough notes of the clerk. If, then, we assume that Onslow did write up journals from his notes of these later Parliaments, we rediscover the existence of a set of Parliamentary manuscripts, hitherto unknown to modern scholars. They have left us no text, and had disappeared before the beginning of D'Ewes' labours in 1629. Much therefore depends upon whether we can be sure that Onslow completed his clerical duties in these years. It is incredible, however, that he did not. He wrote up journals from his rough notes consistently from 1571–80/1, and as the surveillance of the House over their clerk was increasing, and not decreasing, a sustained lapse from 1584–1601 is highly improbable: while, as we have seen, there is reason for supposing that a finished journal existed for 1586. Apart from D'Ewes' uncritical disparagements, I know of no cause for thinking that Onslow was indifferent or negligent. The length of many of his draft entries in the later years, bespeaks a personal interest in Parliamentary affairs, and so, one imagines, does the word 'better' which crept into his rough notes for 1580/1, and has been preserved by D'Ewes:[2] 'the *better* side had the greater number', he wrote in recording the carrying of Paul Wentworth's motion for a public fast; and one must remember that Elizabeth wrathfully dis-

[1] Cf. D'Ewes' *Journals*, 278a. D'Ewes embodied its additional information in his Commons Journal, and one can detect it by comparison with the official printed journal. It is inconsiderable, and ceases with January 28: but one cannot be sure that D'Ewes made exhaustive use of the fragment. An interesting feature is the insertion of Members' names several times in the rough notes, when they are omitted in the journal. Thus Paul Wentworth's name as that of the proposer of the motion for a public fast is given in the rough notes only. (D'Ewes' *Journals*, 282b; *Commons Journals*, i. 118.)

[2] D'Ewes' *Journals*, 283a.

approved of the motion. However, direct evidence upon the question probably exists in one of the State Papers, which is a transcript, in a hand of the late sixteenth or early seventeenth century, of the Treasurer's report to the Commons, made after conference with the Lords on 29 March 1589.[1] In D'Ewes' journals, which are in this case the clerk's notes, the report breaks abruptly off after a few lines: yet in the State Paper the complete transactions are given. Nor is this manuscript a transcript of the mere report that was probably written out by the Treasurer for delivery in the House: it is couched in the form of a journal entry, and includes the subsequent decision of the Commons. In fact, the conclusion can hardly be avoided that the manuscript is a

[1] S.P. Dom. Eliz., ccxxiii. No. 34.

A° 31° Eliz.   Die Sat: xxix. Martis, 1589.

Mr. Threasurer in the name of the rest of the committees appointed for conference with the Lords this present forenoone sheweth that their Lordshipps haue ymparted (by the mouth of the lord Threasurer) unto the committees of this House the effect of a conference, which their Lordships haue had amongst them-selfes, and of their resolucion therin, which is, That (considering the great practizes, treasons, invasions, and attemptes (lately intended and pursued by the Pope the King of Spaine, and their adherentes for the subverting of true religion, her majestie, and the whole state of the Realme) as their said Lordships together with this House haue yealded, and granted unto her majesty an extra-ordynary and most liberall supply of theire treasure for the necessary defence of her said majesty's state, and kingdome against the like daungerous attemptes of such mighty enemyes. So likewise (for the causes aforesaid) haue their said Lordships not only upon the said conference resolued to offer unto her Highnes the expence, and ymploying of their landes and handes, But also of their bodyes, and lyues. And likewise for the more honorable performance of the same defence to become humble sutors unto her most excellent majestic (yf yt so shall seeme good unto her said highnes) for denouncing of warre, and for preuenting of like attemptes to use all honorable meanes aswell offensiue as defensyue against the said King of Spaine, and his adherentes, at such tyme and occasion, as to her highnesses wisedome and princely good pleasure shalbe thought conuenient. And that if ty stand with the good likeing of this house, to ioyne with their said Lordships in peticion unto her majestic for the same, And also that Mr. Speaker doe delyuer the same peticion in the name of the Lords and of this house in his oracion to her majestie in the upper house this afternoone ymmedyately after the offering and deliuerie of the graunt of the fifteenes, and subsedyes. And this upon the question was resolued to be accom-plished accordingly.' Cf. D'Ewes' *Journals*, 454b.

copy of an entry in the actual *journal* for 1588/9, made before its loss. The formal date heading seems to suggest an official transcript made for precedent purposes.

Two sets of manuscripts covering the years 1584–1601 have therefore disappeared, and as an initial step in determining the date and circumstances of the losses, it is necessary to trace the vicissitudes in the custody of the Commons' journals. The House of Commons was for a long period at a disadvantage, compared with the House of Lords, in storing its papers. In some measure this can be ascribed to the character of the medieval Parliament, which had determined that the one Clerk of the Parliaments officiated in the Parliament chamber, which became later the House of Lords. When Parliament, in Henry VII's reign, able now to conceive of a more immediate repository for its records than the Chancery, retained the original parchment rolls of Acts in its own keeping, the custodian of those documents was the Clerk of the Parliaments. Accordingly, the allocation of the Stone Tower in Old Palace Yard as a Parliamentary repository was its allocation to this official, who, as clerk in the House of Lords, thus ensured the safe custody of the Lords' papers. On the other hand, the clerk in the House of Commons was simply 'Subclericus Parliamentorum'. His papers, probably inappreciable in bulk before Elizabeth's reign, were not comparable with the Parliamentary Acts for authority and importance; and his private residence had consequently to serve as the Commons' repository.

During the Tudor period the House of Commons apparently did not concern itself with the custody of its papers. But the first Parliament of James I began an agitation that was to continue intermittently throughout the century before it attained its object. The Commons agreed in that Parliament to a motion for securing a room, which should serve as the clerk's office, and as a repository for 'the Register, and Records, and Papers' of the House.[1] A warrant was signed by the Speaker, and the Earl of Dorset, then Lord Treasurer, was approached. Dorset issued a warrant to the Surveyor of Works ordering the preparation of a room, which warrant is now one of the interleaved papers of the 1604 journal: but what hitch prevented its fulfilment is not recorded. We only know that the motion for a repository was repeated in 1614, and in 1620/1.[2]

[1] *Commons Journals*, i. 215.   [2] *Ibid.*, 465, 513.

The next entry of the raising of the question is in 1640 when a Committee was authorised to consider, not merely the matter of securing 'some certain Place, for the constant keeping of the Records', but also the duty of the clerk towards their safe custody.[1] What eventuated we are not told. But in the following year a complaint that the clerk allowed journals and papers to be taken by Members from the table in the House, resulted in a ruling that he 'ought not to suffer any Journal or Record to be taken . . . out of his Custody'.[2] This, however, did not touch the real problem of their safe keeping. In 1645 and 1646 an effort was made to turn out the records of the Court of Requests from certain rooms near the House of Lords, and to house there the Commons' papers: but it appears to have foundered in the House of Lords.[3] The agitation was next renewed in January, 1648/9,[4] on the occasion of the transference of the House's papers to Henry Scobell, from Henry Elsyng who had resigned the clerkship. A committee was ordered to fit up a room, but it seems very doubtful whether the order was executed.[5] Perhaps the question lost its urgency on account of the abolition of the House of Lords in the following month, for the clerk in the upper house, John Browne, was thereupon dispossessed of office and of the Stone Tower in Old Palace Yard, with his adjoining official residence, and these, with their documentary contents, were transferred to Scobell, now Clerk of the Parliament.[6] A temporary solution of the problem of housing the Commons' manuscripts was thus offered, which Scobell ultimately, if not immediately, grasped by moving his papers to his new and official residence.[7]

[1] *Commons Journals*, ii. 22.   [2] *Ibid.*, ii. 337.

[3] *Ibid.*, iv. 273, 522; *Lords Journals*, viii. 283.   [4] *Commons Journals*, vi. 108.

[5] *Ibid.*, 111. In 1650/1 the House was again taking order for a repository. *Vide infra*, note 7.

[6] *Commons Journals*, vi. 168, 209.

[7] Cf. *ibid.*, vii. 588 (26 January 1657/8). In 1650/1 the House ordered that the clerk should have the rooms 'over the Parliament House' as a repository. It is difficult to say whether anything came of the order. When a room over the Parliament House was repaired in 1656, the records mentioned as there were those of the Common Bench. (*Commons Journals*, vi. 542, vii. 448; *Cal. S.P. Dom.*, 1656–7, pp. 147, 159, 199.) Certainly the House of Commons' records were in the Stone Tower in January 1657/8.

In January 1657/8 Scobell ceased to officiate in the House of Commons, presumably because his services had to be given to the newly constituted second chamber;[1] and although, under the Rump, a return was made to a single chamber, it left him still in possession of the Stone Tower and dwelling-house, which he held by virtue of an Act of Parliament that was not abrogated before the Restoration.[2] Therefore, in January 1657/8, the manuscripts belonging to the House of Commons resumed their peripatetic character. The Commons first thought of storing them in the room over their own House, and then in the 'boarded House' within the Court of Requests;[3] but it is clear that they were in the clerk's private custody in May 1659,[4] and in July 1661 the Commons were once more attempting to secure a repository and an office.[5] It is remarkable how often they had been baulked; yet again they failed. For in 1671 Joseph Williamson was endeavouring to discover where the journals were, in the absence of the clerk from London;[6] and in January 1673/4 the House of Commons was renewing its efforts and approaching the Lord Great Chamberlain for the use of the inner room of the Court of Wards.[7] No more is heard of this, the last recorded act in the agitation for a repository. If it failed, success could not long have been delayed, since in June 1712 the House moved for improved accommodation, the old being 'very strait and inconvenient' in consequence of the recent increase in the number of its records.[8]

In centring attention upon the custody of the Commons' manuscripts, we have undoubtedly discovered the main cause of the loss of the Elizabethan journals and rough notes. Their storage in the clerk's private residence, unguarded by close supervision and regulations, involved grave risks. It facilitated their loan, and so made it possible for documents to be missing at the death of a clerk, and to be irrecoverable

[1] *Acts and Ordinances of the Interregnum* (Firth and Rait), iii. p. [xxxvii].

[2] The Rump prepared an Act to effect this abrogation. It was engrossed, but not passed (*Commons Journals*, vii. 659, 752, 814). Cf. *Lords Journals*, xi. 3.

[3] *Commons Journals*, vii. 581, 587, 590.

[4] *Ibid.*, vii. 650. The presses mentioned in the Journals, for which Smythe was paid, were private ones, whereas the Surveyor of Works would have furnished any for rooms within the palace.

[5] *Commons Journals*, viii. 310.   [6] S.P. Dom. Chas. II, ccxcii. No. 216.

[7] *Commons Journals*, ix. 295.   [8] *Ibid.*, xvii. 250, 266.

for lack of a memorandum of the loan. When D'Ewes compiled his collection of Elizabethan journals, he found no difficulty in borrowing the official manuscripts from John Wright, his friend and Clerk of the House of Commons. More significant still, he thought it well to note in his *Autobiography* that on each occasion he had most faithfully restored them:[1] and Sir Robert Cotton's reputation is perhaps sufficient extenuation of this extreme caution of his contemporary. Again, it is quite likely that a clerk drew no sharp distinction between his private and his public papers, and the risk may thus have been increased of the two sets being confused at his death, and some of his public papers falling into the hands of executors. Even the growing concern of the House of Commons could not protect the manuscripts during the intervals when Parliament was not sitting. And if at first the journals were unbound, the danger of their loss must in this way also have been enhanced. Hakewill has an illuminating comment upon these risks in his treatise, *The Manner How Statutes are enacted . . .*, which was published in 1641.[2]

> If [he wrote] there were some provision made . . . for the safe preserving of them [the journals] answerable to that which the Lords have, whose Clarke hath a house belonging to him, and his successors, where all their Records are kept to posterity; the Journalls and Records of the Commons house, would not (as now they may) come to the hands of Executors or Administrators, and bee removed to and fro in hazard of being lost, or corrupted and defaced, as is well knowne that some of them have beene, and that in passages of the greatest moment.

Turning now to the actual problem of the lost documents, it would seem that we shall best locate any dispersals of the Commons' manuscripts in the seventeenth century, by reviewing the changes in the clerkship of the lower house, at which times the occurrence of irregularities may have jeopardised the documents, and when, also, any losses that had taken place were likely to have been revealed. Employing this method, it is a simple matter to delimit the period within which the finished journals probably disappeared. The manuscripts which John Wright lent to D'Ewes were assuredly the ones which he received from

[1] *Autobiography*, ii. 53.   [2] Pref.

his predecessor's papers, at his assumption of office on 19 November 1613.[1] This gives one extreme date, and the other is furnished by the death of Onslow on 8 August 1602,[2] when we may conclude that all his own journals were extant. After his death, an interval occurred before Ralph Ewens was appointed clerk on 31 January 1603.[3] But it is unlikely that the journals disappeared then, if only because it is most probable that they vanished at, or after, the death of Ewens in 1611. On 30 August in that year the Lord Chancellor, Ellesmere, wrote to the Earl of Salisbury as follows concerning Ewens' papers: 'For the bokes and papers concernyng the lower howse, I gaue direccion this mornyng to william pynches, to whome the reuercion was graunted that he shulde calle for thym, and tak the care and charg of thym, for being now the officer in possession, to whome yt deth properlye perteyne, he ys to undertak yt. . . .'[4] But William Pynches apparently did not officiate as clerk. I have failed to discover any grant to him of the office or its reversion, and his name does not occur in the list of defunct clerks recited in later patents. No session of Parliament was held until April 1614, and by then John Wright had succeeded to the office. Therefore the interval between Ewens' death and the accession of Wright, when no Parliament was in session, presented an opportunity for the dispersal of manuscripts that was unparalleled in this period. That some loss was suffered, may be inferred from the proceedings in the House of Commons when next it met. On 15 April Sir Edwyn Sandys renewed the motion for a repository for the journals and papers of the House, in order, as he said, that they might not 'come into the Hands of Executors'. On 20 May the subject was again before the House, and Sir Thomas Rowe declared 'that Mr. Wilson is thought to have many of the Books and Papers belonging to this House, which came to my Lord Treasurer's Hands by Mr. Ewens' Will'. Therefore he moved that Wilson might 'be ordered, by the Committee for Privileges, to bring to them what he hath, and to discover what he knoweth about them'; but, unfortunately, the journals remain silent upon any further proceedings.[5]

[1] Pat. 10, Jac. I, pt. viii.   [2] *D.N.B.*, *sub* 'Onslow, Richard'.
[3] Pat. 45, Eliz., pt. viii.   [4] S.P. Dom. Jac. I, lxv. No. 90.
[5] *Commons Journals*, i. 465, 491.

However, these entries must reflect the disappearance of a number of manuscripts, and so we may conjecture that between August 1611 and November 1613 the finished journals for 1584–1601 were lost, probably along with many miscellaneous papers belonging to the House. The clerk's rough notes for those years were, however, saved, as also were a fragment of the notes for 1580/1 and perhaps a few leaves from the journal proper for 1586. Echoes of the catastrophe may probably be detected in the passage already quoted from Hakewill[1] and in the reference of the House of Commons in 1645 to 'the Prejudice' its records had formerly suffered 'by coming into the Hands of Executors upon the Death of former Clerks';[2] for, late as are both these statements, they do not refer to the event which has now to be traced, the loss of the volume of Onslow's rough notes.

John Wright, who lent D'Ewes this volume, was succeeded by Henry Elsyng in December 1640,[3] while Parliament was in session; and as an alert House would not have remained inactive if its papers had fallen into strange hands, we may interpret the silence of the journals as implying the safety of the Commons' records. When Elsyng resigned his office on 1 January 1648/9, a Committee was appointed 'to take an Account, Where the Books and Records of this House are', and to prepare an inventory;[4] and the absence of further proceedings from the journals is presumption that the Committee was satisfied. Our advance is therefore secured to the next clerk, Scobell, whose clerkship in the House of Commons came to an end in January 1657/8. At this date, the volume of rough notes was probably safe in his possession, and was transferred to the new clerk from its lodging in Old Palace Yard, where Scobell had kept both Lords' and Commons' manuscripts.[5] It is, indeed, very probable that some of the Commons'

---

[1] *Supra*, p. 43.   [2] *Commons Journals*, iv. 273.
[3] Pat. 15, Car. I, pt. xxii.   [4] *Commons Journals*, vi. 108.
[5] *Supra*, p. 41. In 1656 Scobell published a treatise entitled 'Memorials of the Method and Manner of Proceedings in Parliament in passing Bills . . . Gathered by Observation and out of the Journal Books from the time of Edward 6. By H.S.E.C.P.' (H. Scobell, Esq., Cler., Parl.). A collection of precedents, some of its illustrations are drawn from the period 1584–1601. But precedent books were as old as the century; by using previous collections he may have got his precedents only at second-hand 'out of the Journal Books' —

manuscripts were overlooked in this transfer; and a Charles I journal, discovered by the Historical Manuscripts Commission[1] among the Lords' manuscripts, is probably a derelict of the occasion. But the House of Commons appointed a Committee to supervise the restoration of their papers, a vigilant body, as Burton's Diary shows.[2] Miscellaneous papers, or even a single journal, might have escaped the inventory; but a gap of six Elizabethan Parliaments, covering some twenty years, could surely not have been ignored.

From Scobell's custody the Commons' papers passed back to the old routine of private storage, with its normal risks greatly enhanced during two years of political confusion. Each Parliamentary assembly during these years appointed its own clerk. John Smythe served the Parliament of 1658 and was appointed again in 1659; Thomas St. Nicholas officiated for the restored Rump; and William Jessop for the Convention.[3] When it is added that no inventory of the papers was apparently taken at the dispossession of Smythe and St. Nicholas, and that for a few days pending the attendance of St. Nicholas, the assistant clerk also was responsible for them,[4] it will be clear that many possible factors of a loss were operative during these years. At no other period, so far as one knows, between 1630, when D'Ewes used the volume of Onslow's rough notes, and 1682, when Bowes referred to their loss[5] in publishing D'Ewes' *Journals*, were conditions so favourable for the dispersal of bulky and important manuscripts.[6] There is needed, only, some such

---

although I doubt whether this was altogether so, even for 1584–1601: and one therefore hesitates to stress the implications of this treatise.

[1] *Rep.*, vi. pt. i., p. viii. The journal covers 21 June–5 July 1625.

[2] *Commons Journals*, vii. 588, 590; Burton's *Diary*, ii. 403–4.

[3] *Commons Journals*, vii. 578, 594, 650; viii. 1.   [4] *Ibid.*, vii. 652.

[5] In his dedication. The reference can only be to this loss. The only other gaps that *may* have occurred in the official manuscripts since 1630 are a few odd days in the Lords' journals of 1558/9 and 1597/8 (*Trans. Roy. Hist. Soc.*, 3rd series, viii. 21; *Eng. Hist. Rev.*, xxxiv. 587).

[6] An entry in the Journals of 1694/5 might seem to refer to an appreciable leakage of manuscripts after 1669, the probable date of some loose papers found in private custody (*Commons Journals*, xi. 255). Between April 1661, however, and the date when we have evidence that the Onslow notes were missing, two clerks officiated, father and son, both named William Goldsborough (Pat. 13.

evidence that documents were actually missing, as that obtained for the earlier loss from the Parliamentary proceedings of 1614.[1] On this occasion it is probably implicit in the following order of 11 May 1660, which rehearsed a similar order issued three days earlier:

> that all Acts Ordinances, Journals, Records, Books, Papers, or Proceedings, belonging to this House, or concerning the same, or the Proceedings thereof as well as the Time it acted as a single House, as before, which are now in the Custody of Henry Scobell Esquire, Thomas St. Nicholas Esquire, or any others, or that hath come into their hands as Clerks of this House, be forthwith delivered to William Jessop Esquire, now Clerk of this House.[2]

However, it would be foolish to claim that in either case final results have been obtained in dating the two losses of manuscripts. In the absence of any direct evidence, the method adopted here has enabled one to select from the evidence available the two most probable occasions; and perhaps in the earlier instance a higher degree of certainty has been achieved than in the later. The ultimate fate of the manuscripts is a mystery. They may be safe, but unrecognised, in some private collection.[3] Possessing no obviously official character by which the casual searcher might recognise them, their survival is quite probable: but for the very same reason destruction may have befallen them. If my hypothesis be sound, that a few stray sheets of the *journal*

Car. II, pt. xliv. No. 7; *Cal. S.P. Dom.*, *1673*, 590; S.P. Dom. Car. II, cdv. No. 112). The risks attendant upon changes in the clerkship were thus eliminated. The son must have known of the gap in the Elizabethan Journals, and it is incredible that either he or his father was responsible for the loss. The researches of Professor Notestein, when published, will show that several Stuart Journals have also been lost, and while these may not have disappeared at the same time as the Onslow notes, it is quite feasible that they did. In either case the period of loss must have been one of lax supervision and unusual risks.

[1] *Supra*, p. 44.   [2] *Commons Journals*, viii. 23–4.

[3] I have examined the Petyt MS. Collection at the Inner Temple, and certain journals in the possession of the Earl of Winchilsea (cf. *Hist. MSS. Com. Rep.* xi, App. vii, 227 *sq.*; *Rep.* i, App. 31). Neither collection includes any of the missing official manuscripts. A Petyt MS., which Professor Firth thought to be one, is a copy of the anonymous Members' journal for 1592/3 used by D'Ewes (cf. *Roy. Com. on Pub. Rec.* (1910), 2nd *Rep.*, pt. ii, 107a; D'Ewes' *Journals*, 468).

for 1586 were rescued from the earlier loss,[1] then that manuscript was probably destroyed, and its fate may have been shared by the other manuscripts which disappeared at the same time. The rough notes, however, were bound in a volume, and destruction, in their case, would not have been easy.

Records bear the impress of the life of the individual or body whose offspring they are, not merely in their verbal contents, but also in their own evolutionary history. In consequence, we are dealing in a documentary study of the Commons' journals with a subject that has a wider application in constitutional history; and in tracing the development of the journal, in this final section of the paper, we cannot ignore its relation to the evolution of the House of Commons, a subject still wrapt in a great deal of obscurity.

The scale on which Seymour began his Commons' journal was most exiguous, and its development painfully slow. One must contrast the privilege entries of 1548 with those of the first session in 1554, to be reassured that the seeds of expansion had in the meantime been active. But they were responding to two forces: the one was the need of evolving an adequate scale and form for the journal, the outgrowing, that is, of the diarist's immaturity in his art; the other, the pressure of an increasing interest which the proceedings of the House of Commons possessed. In the session of November 1554 an innovation was the recording of the Speaker's petitions;[2] and Cardinal Pole's mission of reconciliation so far influenced the journal in the same session, that messages to the House were now noted for the first time.[3] The accession of Elizabeth was the beginning of a new epoch, even in the Lilliputian world of 'Seymour': the opening proceedings of her first Parliament were more fully described than before, and the reply to the Speaker's petitions noticed as well as the petitions themselves;[4] the privilege case of John Smith was entered at greater length than any previous case;[5] and even the saying of the Litany was recorded.[6] In the journal of 1566 the relatively long account of Speaker Onslow's election would almost seem promise of a new scale:[7] but the fact is that Seymour's conventions and technique had allowed no very appreciable expansion upon

---

[1] *Supra*, p. 37.   [2] *Commons Journals*, i. 37.   [3] *Ibid.*, i. 38.
[4] *Ibid.*, i. 53.   [5] *Ibid.*, i. 55.   [6] *Ibid.*, i. 54.   [7] *Ibid.*, i. 73.

the journal of 1558/9. His modest notes were easily written down in a readable form, and did not necessitate transcription. Consequently he failed to initiate the practice of taking rough notes from which to compile the fair journal:[1] and adopting a primitive procedure, he produced a primitive record. When a debate interested him, he abstained from a report of it in his journal, not on the principle which excludes debates today, but because he could not adapt his technique to so elaborate an entry; and accordingly he jotted it down, in more or less unintelligible notes, on the outside sheet of the journal.[2]

It is possible now to understand the importance, in the evolution of the Commons' journal, of the accession of Fulk Onslow to the clerkship on 22 December 1570.[3] His extant journals are fair copies, and it was he who introduced the double process in the compilation of the journal, which has been followed until the present day. Probably he took such copious notes in 1571 that he found himself compelled to rewrite them: so personal a matter was the development of the Commons' record. The new procedure gave the journal great plasticity, so that it was now able to respond adequately to the activities of the House. Compared with Seymour's last manuscript, the first Onslow entries were amplified, and the journal noticeably extended by the new practice of giving complete lists of the names for a committee. The scale of the two following manuscripts remained that of 1571, but in 1580/1 there took place a notable expansion, which is accentuated in the

[1] This statement might seem at variance with the manuscripts of 1548–52, which, along with Ormeston's memorandum of 1547, are fair copies (*supra*, p. 26). But they were not written separately at the close of each session, but were most probably all transcribed after the close of the fourth session of this first Parliament, in 1552. The proof of this is to be found in the fact that the sessions are keyed into one another in the manuscripts by the occurrence medially, and not terminally, of all such variations as denote the breaks in the labour of transcription. The transcription falls into the following sections: Nov. 1547 — 2nd entry, Feb. 23, 1548/9; 3rd entry on same day — 3rd entry, Nov. 5, 1549; 4th entry on same day — date heading, Feb. 16, 1551/2; the single entry of same day — end of session. Conceivably the transcription marks the determination of Seymour in 1552 to preserve his memoranda as of more than ephemeral interest.

[2] *Supra*, p. 27.   [3] Pat. 13 Eliz., pt. vi.

manuscript by the use of larger folio sheets. Reports and motions were entered at considerable length; and a single day's proceedings in Hall's case has filled four columns of the printed journals.[1] But its most noteworthy feature was the reporting of speeches. The modern journal is a record of the acts, and not of the speeches, of the House; but from 1580/1 until 1628, when the practice was declared unwarranted,[2] members' speeches were noted by the clerks. Further development may have been effected by Onslow in his later journals, but what they were it is impossible now to say, for, as I have already shown, the text preserved by D'Ewes is not that of the journals themselves.[3]

The 'Seimour' volume provides an excellent corrective to exaggerated conceptions of the constitutional rôle played by the House of Commons, so late as the middle of the sixteenth century. It accords with its meagre proportions that the journal should have been, as I have suggested it was, a creation of the clerk's: but the regular entry of memoranda into orderly quires, must at last have led members who had sat in several sessions, to regard it as part of the customary procedure of the House; and its acceptance as such by the individual was the prelude to its acceptance by the body of the Commons. One can be certain that this later stage had been reached by 1571, for John Hooker wrote a treatise from his experience in the Parliament of that year, wherein he made the following statement:

> There is onely one Clark belonging to this house, his office is to sit next before the Speaker, at a Table upon which he writeth and layeth his books. He must make true entrie of the recordes and Billes of the House, as also of all the orders therof.[4]

The growth of control out of recognition of the journal was a question of time: but control was assured, if only because its extension, and the development of the competency of the House, were interdependent. The journal, in fact, served to consolidate new or disputed powers by registering decisions and proceedings, thus converting them into precedents, the citation of which was an excellent defensive and offen-

---

[1] *Commons Journals*, i. 125–7.   [2] *Ibid.*, i. 885.   [3] *Supra*, p. 36.
[4] *The Order and Usage of the Keeping of a Parlement* . . . by John Vowel *alias* Hooker (? 1575), *sub. tit.*, 'Of the Clark of the lower house'.

sive weapon. Ostensibly a conservative habit, the Elizabethan Parliamentarians proved, what their Stuart successors were to reveal more strikingly, that the appeal to precedents might enforce, rather than stultify, progress: a selective activity and false interpretation sufficed. Obviously, however, precedents lacked such potentiality when, in prejournal days, they reposed only in the memories of experienced Parliament men. They were then but matter of opinion while the experienced and authoritative memories, no doubt, were chiefly official ones.[1]

The first recorded use of the journal for precedent purposes was in 1580/1. In the interval between two sessions the Speaker had died, and Sir Francis Knolles, the Treasurer, in discussing the procedure for securing a new Speaker, cited a similar occurrence in 1562/3, and offered the House a copy of the precedent. However, runs the entry, 'because ... the Clerk ... had there his Original Book of Notes, out of the which the said Copy was taken, he was commanded to read' it out of 'his Book ....'.[2] References have survived to the use of precedents in deciding various questions.[3] Doubtless the most fertile were those concerning privileges and disputed elections, and the practice of appointing a standing committee for such cases, which originated in 1588/9, must have regularised their solution.[4] That committees occasionally failed in their search for precedents, one may be certain, and it is possible that they then ensured the entry of their own decisions, by securing an order to that effect from the House. Whether this surmise, however, be correct or not, the fact remains that the ordering of specific entries was the first stage in the establishment by the Commons of direct control over the compilation of the journal.[5] Beyond it they had not got by the close of Elizabeth's reign; and it was the work of James' first Parliament to convert the partial control of the Tudor period into

[1] Cf. the following entry in the Colchester journal of 1485: 'Than it pleased the Recorder of London for to shew the custume of the place. This was his seyeng: Maister Speker, and all my maisters, there hath ben an order in this place in tymes passed ...' etc. (W. G. Benham, *The Red Paper Book of Colchester*, 62a.) Or cf. the example of 1580/1 cited on this page.

[2] *Commons Journals*, i. 116.

[3] Cf. D'Ewes' *Journals*, 343a, 354a, 404a, 412b, 431b, 440b, 553b, 572a, 638a.

[4] *Ibid.*, 429b, 471a, 552a, 622.

[5] Cf. *Commons Journals*, i. 96, 126; D'Ewes' *Journals*, 399a, 417b.

complete control. One can detect its approach in the first session, when an order of the House contained a ruling regarding the preparation of a journal: '... all Acts, Resolutions, and Judgments of the House', it stated, 'which are there entered and registered by their common Servant, the Clerk, should be written and ingrossed in One fair Register Book....'[1] But the machinery was lacking for supervision of the journal. This was evolved in 1607, when the general committee for privileges was ordered to review the entries of privilege cases during the first three sessions of that Parliament, and, as a result, the clerk was instructed to perfect his journal before the next session: 'no matter', the House decided, 'concerning Privilege, Order, or Matter of Message, or Conference, or Resolution of the House, proceeding thereupon, shall be of Record, or in Force, till such Time as the same be perused, and perfected, by a Committee to be chosen the next Session of Parliament...; and that from henceforth the Committee for Privileges do, every Saturday in the Afternoon, peruse and perfect the Book of Entries, in all such Matters as aforesaid ...'.[2] Thus was initiated the procedure, which afterwards became customary, of appointing a standing committee each session to supervise the compilation of the journal:[3] and here at the consummation of the movement for control by the House we may leave the question of the evolution of the Commons' journal. It remains only to relate our survey more directly to the constitutional development of the House of Commons.

It may seem strange that a review of the evolution of the Commons' journal suggests a House of Commons in 1548 with a very immature corporate sense. But before the appearance of a journal, the domestic history of the Commons is unreported and obscure, while to appreciate the expansion of their power in Tudor times, we must rid ourselves of modern constitutional conceptions in thinking of medieval parliaments. The High Court of Parliament of the middle ages was not an assembly

[1] *Commons Journals*, i. 215.

[2] *Ibid.*, i. 390, 392. The journals do not make it clear whether the committee was appointed in the next session; but probably it was, and the original journal of 1604 bears evidence of such an overhauling as was suggested (*supra*, p. 35).

[3] Cf. *Ibid.*, i. 520, 575, 669, 673, 761, 818, 885, 924; ii. 4, 22; vi. 297; vii. 588; viii. 7; ix. 263.

consisting of two more or less co-ordinate chambers; but its essence was the meeting in the parliament chamber, the core of which was the King in council.[1] The Commons withdrew from this meeting, usually to the Chapter House, for their own deliberations, and in the exercise of their rôle as petitioners. But their discussions were not *in* parliament, and were not recorded on the parliament roll. Moreover, since the Commons possessed no corporate identity as a distinct 'House', they naturally produced no domestic record: their petitions, which were presented to the King in parliament, were no doubt regarded as adequate records of their deliberations.[2] In modern times, however, the original judicial character of Parliament has been quite overshadowed by its legislative work. An outgrowth of Parliament's jurisdiction as a court, this work involved a gradual extension of the role of the Commons, so that all Acts came eventually to be read by both Lords and Commons, and the familiar procedure of three readings was slowly defined.[3] In correspondence with the facts of this change, there must have arisen a consciousness that the Commons constituted a chamber, parallel, if not co-ordinate with the assembly of Lords in the parliament chamber: and so the personification of the term 'House' was made possible.[4]

As a rule, the chief interest in the development of a corporate body, as in that of an individual, is the growth of self-consciousness: and in the case of the House of Commons the increase in its competency was closely dependent upon the quickening of its corporate sense. It is pre-eminently to the sixteenth century that one must attribute this process; although in the very nature of things it is difficult to trace, especially in

[1] Cf. F. W. Maitland, *Memoranda de Parliamento*, Intro. For this and succeeding statements, see also, C. H. McIlwain, *The High Court of Parliament*, and Pollard, *The Reign of Henry VII from Contemp. Sources*, Intro., xxviii *sqq.*

[2] *Trans. Roy. Hist. Soc.*, 3rd series, viii. 27.

[3] In both cases procedure was fluid in the early Tudor period. For the assent of the Commons in legislation, cf. A. F. Pollard, *The Reign of Henry VII* . . . xxxi–ii; for an unusual number of readings, see the *Lords Journals* of Henry VIII's reign, *passim*, and the *Commons Journal* of 1547.

[4] The earliest reference which has been traced to a 'House' of Lords, is in 1544. C. H. Parry, *Parliaments and Councils of England*, xlii, referred to in Pollard, *op. cit.*, xxxiii.

its initial stages before the appearance of a journal. The effect of the long Reformation Parliament on its development can be imagined rather than measured: but anyone who has paid close attention to the procedure of the House of Commons from 1547–1601, must be conscious of the important expansion which a study of Parliamentary procedure for this period will reveal. Or if we turn to the unofficial Parliamentary sources of the period, the journals, speeches, and memoranda, of individual Members, which are no less tokens of the new interest in itself that the House of Commons was developing; it is no accident that the stream of manuscript material trickles only at the opening of Elizabeth's reign, and gathers breadth and volume as the reign progresses. If we except a remarkable but very jejune example in 1485,[1] private journals commence in 1571,[2] and through several intermediate manuscripts, finally reach the fullness of Townshend's 1601 journal on the eve of the Stuart period.[3] Local researches, it is true, may bring other Parliamentary manuscripts to light, but the present chronological balance will not be materially redressed, for it depends upon the growth of self-consciousness in the House of Commons and not upon the ravages of time.

Now, in the stages by which the House entrenched upon the freedom of the clerk in making and preserving his journal, one may see a reflection, vague, no doubt, but suggestive, of the stages by which it became fully aware of its corporate identity and interests. With the inception of the journal, the Commons had probably nothing to do; but it argues a certain measure of self-concern that they came to regard its compilation as part of the customary procedure of the House, so that in 1571, Hooker, as a Member of the House, was able to consider it a duty of the clerk. So far as one can tell, it was a later step, as it was undoubtedly a maturer policy, to order specific entries to be made, so limiting the discretion left to the clerk by a mere assumption that they were made. The final stage was reached, when in 1604 the Commons began to concern themselves with the safe custody of the journal, and

[1] W. G. Benham, *The Red Paper Book of Colchester*, pp. 60–4.

[2] Cf. D'Ewes' *Journals*, 155; and Hooker's Journal in *Transactions of the Devonshire Association*, xi (1879), 442–92.

[3] *Historical Collections*, 173 *sqq*.

when in 1607 its compilation was completely subordinated to the wishes of the House, and machinery evolved to ensure that important proceedings should be properly recorded. That these two events, both so indicative of a highly developed self-regard, were practically coincident in date, is some assurance that the shadowy lines which I have assembled, and perhaps too exactly defined, are the reflection of a real growth. But they are too few and uncertain to be anything more than suggestive of the picture, which a careful study of sixteenth-century Parliamentary procedure would no doubt reconstruct. When that study is completed, we shall, perhaps, have a more rational background to Stuart constitutional history.

J. E. NEALE

3 The Attitude of Whitgift and Bancroft to the Scottish Church

The friendship and understanding which had joined the reformed Churches of England and Scotland in the early years of Elizabeth's reign were not menaced until shortly after Whitgift's accession to the see of Canterbury in 1583. The new primate had to deal with problems which had been quite unknown to his predecessors — problems arising from the success of the Scottish presbyterians and the efforts of their English imitators. The constitution of the Scottish reformed Church, after developing in the direction of 'conformity with England', had not attained stability before being undermined by the emergence of intransigent Presbyterianism. In 1581 the general assembly had approved the full Presbyterian programme, and in August 1582 a *coup d'état*, the 'Ruthven raid', by the ultra-Protestant party among the Scottish nobles had produced a government favourable to the first brief Presbyterian experiment. In England also the struggle between Presbyterianism and Episcopacy had begun, and Whitgift himself had been the protagonist of the Episcopalian cause. The English Crown was immune from such *coups d'état* as made possible three changes in the constitution of the Scottish Church within five years; but the English Presbyterians had powerful friends among the radical politicians and diplomats. Already there were signs of co-operation between the ecclesiastical rebels in the two British kingdoms, and the incipient alliance soon had political repercussions, for the conduct of Anglo-Scottish relations was during several years in the hands of Francis Walsingham and William Davison, two diplomats who, as secretary and ambassador, consistently used their influence on behalf of the Scottish Presbyterians, whom they alleged to be the only sincere supporters in Scotland of the cause of 'amity with England'.

King James of Scotland escaped from the 'Ruthven raiders' at the end of June 1583. Whitgift was nominated to Canterbury in August, and the initiation by him of a policy of severe repression of Presbyterianism in England coincided with the opportunity presented to Archbishop Adamson of St. Andrews by a new Scottish government — the 'anti-Presbyterian dictatorship' of Captain James Stewart, earl of Arran. The character of Archbishop Patrick Adamson suffered severely at the hands of his Presbyterian opponents in his own day, and few attempts have been made in subsequent generations to ascertain the truth about him; but even his enemies paid tribute to his ability, particularly in letters and oratory, and rated him as a highly dangerous, although treacherous and dishonest, adversary.[1] His portrait seems to show an intelligent, strong and capable nature which might have fitted a lawyer, or even a man of action, better than a cleric. A search for weapons against the Presbyterians, who claimed a divine right for their system, led Adamson to assert the scriptural and apostolic origin of Episcopacy; and, from the moment of his appointment as archbishop (1576), he had made it clear that he would not be subordinate to the general assembly.[2] With these convictions there apparently went the idea — present in the minds of some other moderate men among his contemporaries — that Episcopal government in the Scottish Church would contribute to Anglo-Scottish friendship and smooth the way for the Scottish king's accession to the English throne.[3] It was not only in government, but in worship also, that Adamson sought conformity with England. A commission given to him when he was at the height of his power referred to 'a uniform order in form of common prayer'. The phrase meant more than insistence on the use of the Knoxian *Book of common order*, for it is known that Adamson used 'the English ceremonies' in celebrating a marriage, and that his enemies accused him of

---

[1] James Melville, *Autobiography and diary* (Wodrow Soc., 1842), pp. 53, 293; John Row, *History of the kirk of Scotland* (Wodrow Soc., 1842), p. 115; *Historie and life of King James the sext* (Bannatyne Club, 1825), p. 205; B[ritish] M[useum], Cotton MSS., Calig. C. ix. fo. 161.

[2] Calderwood, *History of the kirk of Scotland* (Wodrow Soc., 1843), iii. 371–2; iv. 500.

[3] Cf. Cal[endar of] S[tate] P[apers] Scot[land], ii. no. 439; vi. no. 705; viii. no. 56.

'filthily adulterating the state of public prayer with the simplicity of rites in ministration of the sacraments'.[1]

On the initiative of Adamson, there was co-operation between the English and Scottish primates. The narrative of the Scottish archbishop's mission to England in the winter of 1583-4, described briefly by sixteenth- and seventeenth-century historians, can be reconstructed more fully from the original sources, including the correspondence which passed between the two archbishops.[2] Adamson had numerous motives for making a journey to England. There seems no reason to doubt that he wished to leave Scotland and visit the continent for the sake of his health. At any rate, the English ambassador in Edinburgh accepted this without question, King James's letter of credit and his licence to leave the kingdom are explicit about it, and even after the excuse, if excuse it had been, was no longer necessary, Adamson persisted in it.[3] It was alleged that he was glad to escape from impending excommunication by the general assembly; and it is possible that the Scottish Government considered that the pursuit of its ecclesiastical policy through a critical stage would be easier in the absence of one against whom the full fury of the Presbyterians was directed. There was, in any case, important diplomatic business which necessitated that Adamson should have audience of the queen of England, but it was realised from the first that the journey had significance for ecclesiastical affairs, and the rumour was current that the archbishop would go to Geneva and other places over-

---

[1] Calderwood, *op. cit.*, iv. 145, 163; Wodrow Soc., *Miscellany* i (1844), p. 417.

[2] There are accounts of Adamson's mission in James Melville's *Diary* (p. 141), Calderwood's *History* (iii. 763; iv. 49, 55, 431-2), Calderwood's *Vindiciae contra calumnias Johannis Spotsuodi* (edn. 1623. p. 54) and B.M., Add. MSS. 32092, fos. 42-5. The Whitgift–Adamson correspondence, which is used throughout this and the succeeding paragraphs, is as follows; (*a*) Adamson to Whitgift (copy, undated, but either late December 1583 or early January 1583/4), B.M., Add. MSS. 32092, fo. 75*v*; (*b*) Whitgift to Adamson (copy, dated 4 January 1583/4), *ibid.*, fo. 76*r*; (*c*) Adamson to Whitgift (copy, undated, probably late April 1584), *ibid.*, fo. 76*v*; (*d*) Adamson to Whitgift, 16 June 1584, B.M., Harl[eian] MSS. 7004, fo. 3 (copy in B.M., Add. MSS. 32092, fo. 79*v*), printed (except the endorsement) in Thomas McCrie, *Life of Andrew Melville*, (2 vols., Edinburgh, 1819), appendix iv.

[3] S.P. Scot. Eliz., xxxiii. nos. 71, 74, 94 (*Cal.*, vi. nos. 681, 684, 707); Registrum secreti sigilli (H.M. Gen. Reg. House, Edinburgh), xlix, fos. 175*v*-176.

seas to obtain from the continental reformed Churches condemnation of the Scottish ministers and their opinions.[1]

The mission was arranged by 29 October 1583; but three weeks elapsed before Adamson left Scotland, travelling south on the *equi gradarii* ('ambling nags') suitable for a sick man. His arrival in London on 30 November was immediately noted by one of Walsingham's agents, who reported to his master that the archbishop 'keeps himself quiet as yet'.[2] Adamson proceeded with diplomatic work, but also communicated with Whitgift, sending him 'articles' which contained a statement of the views of the Scottish Presbyterians — *propositiones ministrorum Scotiae serenissimo regi oblatae* — with a refutation of them, and asking for an interview.[3] Whitgift, although personally willing to accede to this request, decided not to act without reference to the government, and he therefore sent a copy of Adamson's 'articles' to Burghley, whose advice he asked. Perhaps acting on Burghley's recommendation, he sent his chaplain to Adamson to explain to him that the queen's permission must be obtained before the two archbishops could meet. Meanwhile, Adamson had learned, to his great distress, that a copy of the 'articles' had fallen into the hands of Walsingham, of whose enmity he was well aware, and he foresaw their use by the English secretary and his friends in Scotland to discredit the Scottish Government and Adamson himself. Whitgift, when he wrote to Adamson on 4 January 1583/4, declared that the leakage was unaccountable, as he had retained the original of the 'articles', and Burghley, he believed, had retained the copy sent to him. The inference must be that a copy had been abstracted from Burghley's office by an agent of Walsingham. The English primate reiterated that Adamson must take the initiative in asking for the royal consent before Whitgift could hold any discussion with him, but promised to give him his opinion of the 'articles'. It was, of course, through Mr. Secretary Walsingham that Adamson had to apply for the queen's permission to live for a time at Oxford or

---

[1] *Cal. S.P. Scot.*, vi. nos. 691, 696, 703, 706; *Border papers*, i. no. 188.

[2] *Ibid.*; *Cal. S.P. Scot.*, vi. no. 702; Registrum secreti sigilli, *loc. cit.*

[3] *Cal. S.P. Scot.*, vi. nos. 705, 706; Adamson's 'articles', of which there is a copy in Latin in B.M., Add. MSS. 32092, fos. 73–5, are printed (in translation) in J. Melville's *Diary*, pp. 148–53, and Calderwood's *History*, iv. 50–5.

Cambridge and to confer with Whitgift or any other learned men whom Elizabeth might think it fit that he should consult. The necessity for sending such an application was, he felt, hardly consistent with his dignity; but he wrote a courteous letter to the secretary and offered to make him a present of a 'Galloway nag'.[1]

Adamson succeeded in part of his mission. He visited Lambeth Palace and had a conversation with Whitgift, receiving a copy of one of the English primate's books against the Presbyterian Cartwright and promising that in return he would give Whitgift copies of some of his own writings. Moreover, he was entertained by the archbishop of York at his house, and met the bishop of London, who lent him money which Adamson 'dishonoured his country'[2] by failing to repay. He also despatched copies of his 'articles' to the French Church in London and to Geneva and Zürich, and spent part of his time in preparing some books for the press. The difficulties which he encountered were, however, more notable than his successes. Copies of his 'articles' found their way not only to Scotland but also into the hands of the English Presbyterians who thought that they contained matter suitable for discussion at their conferences.[3] The enemies of the archbishops put obstacles in the way of further conversations between them and spread a rumour that they were conspiring for the restoration of Romanism, with the result that Adamson had to expound his Protestant faith in four or five public sermons. His son-in-law and biographer, Florence Wilson, tells us that in these sermons Adamson gave such high praise to King

---

[1] Adamson's application to Walsingham, which is undated (like most of his letters), has been attributed to December 1583, but was probably written after Whitgift's letter of 4 January 1583/4. S.P. Scot. Eliz., xxxiii. no. 94 (*Cal.*, vi. no. 707).

[2] Sir James Melville, *Memoirs* (Bannatyne Club, 1827), p. 315.

[3] Hist[orical] MSS. Comm[ission], *Report*, xii, pt. ix, 149–50. The MS. collection which includes the minute book of the Dedham *classis* contains a copy of *Propositiones ministrorum Scotiae serenissimo regi oblatae* among writings which were 'inserted . . . because they were conferred of in our meetings'. The leakage of Adamson's 'articles' into the hands of the English and Scottish Presbyterians may have taken place through Jean Castel, minister of the French Church in London (cf. Cotton MSS., Calig. C. ix. fo. 161), or through Walsingham and William Davison.

James that Elizabeth commanded him to desist, and that he continued in private to advocate the right of the Scottish king to the English Crown.[1] A number of influential Englishmen — *nobiles quidam* is Adamson's phrase — who desired the overthrow of Episcopacy approached the Scottish archbishop with a suggestion that he should engineer the abolition of bishops in Scotland in order to set an example to England. But it was more to the archbishop's mind to defend Episcopacy and to warn England against Presbytery; and this he did.[2]

The English Presbyterians showed their interest in Adamson's mission and their appreciation of the danger from it, not only by accusing the archbishops of Romish tendencies and by urging Adamson to change his policy, but also by criticising Whitgift for negotiating with the Scottish primate. Their spokesman was Robert Beale, who was a member of Walsingham's group of left-wing and pro-Puritan politicians and whose interest in Scottish ecclesiastical affairs is proved by the existence of his collection of manuscripts relating to the Scottish Church.[3] On 7 May 1584, shortly after Adamson had left England, Beale wrote to Whitgift, alleging that it was 'vehemently suspected that the archbishop of St. Andrews is lately departed hence with such an approbation of our rites here as carryeth with it a condemnation of the form used there; whereon it is not unlike but at the first some hold will be taken to the great disadvantage of the Church'. Whitgift sent the letter to Burghley, and with it a refutation of the charges against him: 'It may be that I have spoken in the mislike of the churches in Scotland, but not of late nor upon any conference with the bishop of St. Andrews, for whatsoever my opinion is of that platform, yet I have learned not to be curious *in aliena republica*. All the conference that ever I had with the bishop of St. Andrews I made known to your lordship, since which time I have not seen him; neither hath he my hand to anything.'[4] Whitgift, although clear in his own mind as to the character

---

[1] P. Adamson, *Poemata sacra* (1619), sig. A. 3 *verso*.

[2] P. Adamson, *Opera* (1619), sig. T. 2 *verso*.

[3] Hist. MSS. Comm., *Report*, ii. 45. For Beale's character and views see T. Fuller, *Church history*, ix. v. 9.

[4] Strype, *Whitgift* (1822), i. 295, iii. 97; Hist. MSS. Comm., *Bath MSS. at Longleat*, ii. 23.

of Scottish Presbyterianism, had been discreet. His discretion saved him from censure by the civil authorities, and it was of service to the English Government, which avoided serious friction with the English Puritan party or with the Scottish Presbyterians, who might at any time regain power. But it did not guard him from the suspicion of the Scottish ministers, among whom distrust of the English bishops was now for the first time sown, and it impeded Adamson's efforts to secure a united front against Presbyterianism. The letter written to Whitgift by the Scottish primate shortly before he left England is in a tone of disappointment. Adamson's sense of failure at the rather meagre results of his mission was aggravated by other difficulties. On his arrival in England he had given away as presents the horses which had brought him south (his enemies called him a spendthrift), and he now found himself without mounts for the return journey. His health had not recovered sufficiently for him to use a swift horse, and he asked Whitgift to give him a sturdy beast to carry him home, promising to let the English primate have a better one in return before Whitsunday.

It was at the end of April or the beginning of May 1584 that Adamson went back to Scotland, boasting of his intention to abolish presbyteries and restrict the power of the ministers,[1] and shortly after his return the Scottish Parliament passed the 'Black acts' which overthrew the Presbyterian system and established the most effective Episcopacy which Scotland had known since before the Reformation. The Scottish Presbyterians were in despair, and the irreconcilables among them crossed the border into England, where they were befriended by Walsingham and welcomed by the English Puritans. The English Government's attitude towards the refugees remained one of indifference, in spite of pressure on one side from Walsingham and other Puritan politicians, who wanted support for the Scottish malcontents in order to bring about the fall of the pro-episcopal Arran Government, and on the other from the Scottish Government itself, which, after an attempt at conciliation, urged the English Government to banish the exiled ministers or at least to restrict their activities.[2] Adamson, flushed

---

[1] *Cal. S.P. Scot.*, vii. no. 138.

[2] *Ibid.*, nos. 138, 146, 149, 161, 165, 167, 175, 195, 208, 241, 267, 349, 479, 508, 542; Calderwood, *History*, iv. 352, viii. 267–8; Wodrow Soc., *Miscellany*,

with his success at home, had an exaggerated idea of his influence on the English notables whom he had met,[1] and attempted to persuade Whitgift to advise hostility towards the exiles. On 16 June 1584 he wrote to the English archbishop explaining the Scottish Government's policy. Presbyterianism had been overthrown, he said, not only because it was repugnant to the scriptures and to the practice of antiquity, but because the democratic assemblies had shown themselves to be instruments of sedition. The ministers who had gone to England had not been banished, but had fled before violence had even been threatened, and they ought not to be allowed to remain in England, or, if they did remain, to preach. He had not yet had an opportunity to send 'your grace's Galloway nag'. Whitgift, with his usual consideration for the civil power, notified to the queen the receipt of this letter, and presumably informed her of its contents.[2] The primate's scrupulous subservience to the Government made it impossible for him to do more, although his antagonists, the radical politicians, had no such scruples and allowed their ecclesiastical preferences to influence their politics. There is no evidence that Whitgift continued to correspond with Adamson; but in January 1584/5 he received from Scotland a letter from an unnamed Scotsman which indicates that he continued to be interested in developments north of the border.[3]

On the downfall of the Arran Government in November 1585 the Episcopacy which the 'Black acts' had established was not at once overthrown; and both the Episcopalians and the Presbyterians of England were keenly interested in the fate of the Scottish Church. At the critical general assembly of May 1586, when the full Presbyterian

---

i. 413–14. These references give evidence of the friendly attitude of Walsingham, Davison and other English politicians to the Scottish Presbyterians, of Walsingham's dealings with the exiled ministers in London, and of the policy of the Scottish Government.

[1] *Cal. S.P. Scot.*, vii, nos. 233, 236.

[2] The letter (Harl. MSS., 7004, fo. 3) is endorsed 'The receat of his letter I signifiet to her majestie at Nonesuch in Sommer anno 1584'.

[3] [*Blank*] to Whitgift, 10 Jan. 1584/5, B.M., Add. MSS. 32092, fo. 78*v* (copy). This letter, written in Scots and dated from Holyroodhouse, contains only invective against the Scottish Presbyterian ministers.

programme was once more accepted, Dr. Giles Fletcher was an obser-
ver, and he sent an account of the proceedings to his brother Richard,
dean of Peterborough, who retailed them to Whitgift, adding some
unfavourable, if obscure, comments: 'I have sent your grace these
first proceedings of the ecclesiastical general assembly in Scotland lately
begun there: but not likely to end in haste for their manifold matters so
saltly according to their fyrie humour controverted.'[1] Whitgift, still
interested and critical, was not the man to begin open war against the
Scottish Presbyterian Church. The task had to be undertaken by a
cleric who felt less obligation to the civil power and to political considerations and occupied a less responsible position. It was soon alleged
by a Presbyterian writer that the English and Scottish bishops were
conscious of identity of interest and were co-operating,[2] but this propaganda had as yet, so far as the evidence shows, very little foundation
in fact. It was, however, prophetic of the course of events in the next
few years.

The intense activity of the English Presbyterians between 1584 and
1587 had resulted in vigorous repression. In taking the initiative and
forcing the Puritans to the defensive, the Anglicans had to strike at the
Scottish Church, whence the rebels derived some of their strength; and
for their first overt attack on Scottish Presbyterianism they selected no
obscure occasion but a sermon preached from the open-air pulpit beside
St. Paul's Cathedral, the scene of many great public sermons. The day
chosen was the first Sunday of Elizabeth's seventh Parliament (9 February 1588/9) and the preacher was Richard Bancroft, a London
rector and canon already noted for his opposition to Puritanism. In
making a spirited defence of Episcopal government Bancroft used conditions in Scotland as a warning against the 'busy and turbulent
humourists' who endeavoured to infect England with the 'corrupt
opinions' which had triumphed among the Scots. He was resolved to
show that the establishment of the 'presbyterial government' did not,
as the 'consistorians' maintained, result in the disappearance of all vice

[1] Nat[ional] Lib[rary of] Scot[land] MSS., 6.1.13, fos. 33–4; copy in B.M.,
Add. MSS. 32092, fo. 88*v*. Giles Fletcher described the assembly's proceedings
to Walsingham also (*Cal. S.P. Scot.*, viii. no. 407).
[2] John Udall, *Diotrephes* (ed. Arber, 1880), p. 7.

and crime and the establishment of 'a very paradise upon this earth'; and, in order to illustrate the 'fruits of this new government where it was erected', Bancroft drew on two unfavourable accounts of Scottish Presbyterianism. The first was *A declaration of the king's majesty's intention and meaning concerning the late acts of parliament* (a manifesto drawn up by Archbishop Adamson in defence of the 'Black acts') which had been published in London in 1585 and subsequently appeared in the 1587 edition of Holinshed's *Chronicles*. This work gave Bancroft material on the association of Scottish Presbyterians with the rebellious proceedings of the 'Ruthven raiders' in 1582 and 1584. Bancroft's second source was a letter of Robert Browne, the English separatist, who had seen Presbyterianism in action when he visited Scotland in 1584 and had criticised it severely, commenting that the régime of pastors, doctors and presbyters produced 'instead of one pope a thousand, and instead of some lord bishops in name a thousand lordly tyrants in deed'. Bancroft welcomed Browne's remark that he had 'seen all manner of wickedness to abound much more in their best places in Scotland than in our worse places here in England'. Had the English preacher confined himself to repeating the allegations of the *Declaration* and of Browne's letter, criticism of his sermon could have come only from Scottish ministers and their English friends. But he took it on himself to say that King James had not altered his views since his suppression of Presbyterianism in 1584, and implied that he was merely waiting for an opportunity to re-establish Episcopacy. This suggestion, it will appear, had serious consequences. By referring to George Buchanan's *De jure regni apud Scotos*, a work composed to justify the Scottish revolution of 1567, Bancroft showed that he was already disposed to lay emphasis on the politics of Presbyterianism as the most discreditable and dangerous part of that programme.[1]

Bancroft desired to obtain fuller information about conditions in

---

[1] Bancroft, *A sermon preached at Paules crosse* (1588), pp. 72–6; Robert Browne, *A new year's guift* (ed. C. Burrage, 1904), pp. 8, 25–6 (the MS. of this work [B.M., Add. MSS. 29546, fos. 67–72] was used by Bancroft, who underlined the passages which he quoted). Bancroft afterwards explained in a letter to Burghley the line of thought which he had followed in his sermon (Nat. Lib. Scot. MSS., 6.1.13, fos. 46–55).

Scotland in order to justify his views. The necessary instruments were ready to his hand. John Copcot, master of Corpus Christi College, Cambridge, had been engaged in combating the Puritans' insistence on the necessity and value of the eldership, and in one of his writings he had used *A declaration of the king's majesty's intention and meaning* to show 'what stay to civil government' the eldership had been in Scotland, and how it had been 'injurious to their sovereign's estate and the cause of great troubles'. The Scottish king, he said, had wisely foreseen 'that some went about to establish an ecclesiastical tyranny . . . under pretext of new invented presbyteries'.[1] Copcot, clearly, would be willing to assist Bancroft, and it happened that he was friendly with Robert Naunton, who was at this time attached to the English embassy in Edinburgh. Naunton was not sympathetic to the Presbyterians, and in a letter to Copcot, dated 12 November 1589, he described 'the old inveterate grudge conceived by this clergy against Mr. Doctor Bancroft for intermeddling with their anarchy here established'.[2] Copcot showed this letter to Bancroft, who realised that he could make use of Naunton to equip himself for the controversy which, as the letter clearly showed, must ensue. When Copcot wrote again to his friend Naunton, on 1 January 1589/90, he enclosed a letter in which Bancroft asked Naunton to endeavour to obtain copies of correspondence between the Scottish ministers and Beza or other continental divines and to send him answers to questions aimed at discovering the details of the Presbyterian organisation in Scotland, particulars of the ministers' attitude towards the king, and the political ideas of the Kirk. From the way in which the questions are framed, it appears that Bancroft wished to compare the Scottish organisation with the English Presbyterian platform, to condemn it as inefficient, to denounce the Scots as rebellious and seditious, and so, by implication, to discredit the English Puritans. He was not fastidious about the means by which his purpose was to be achieved, for he suggested that Naunton should 'insinuate' himself into the ranks of the Scottish Presbyterian party 'as one desirous to embrace their devices', in order to have access to papers which the ministers might

[1] Lambeth Palace MSS., vol. 374, fos. 135, 228, 229; Dudley Fenner, *Defence of the counterpoyson* (1586), preface and Sig. A. 3.
[2] B.M., Add. MSS. 32092, fo. 106.

regard as confidential.[1] Naunton was urged by Bancroft to take pre-
cautions to ensure the secrecy of their correspondence, but evidently
there was some kind of exposure. Naunton had to leave Scotland
shortly after receiving Bancroft's letter,[2] and it seems probable that he
therefore deputed John Norton, an English bookseller resident in
Edinburgh to obtain the information required by the Anglican churchman. A letter from Norton to Bancroft was intercepted, and when the
bookseller was examined (on 12 February 1589/90) he loyally accepted
all responsibility — presumably he had agreed to shield his employer —
and declared that he had received from 'his uncle, old Norton' the
questions which had in fact been directed to Robert Naunton.[3] A paper
containing a series of answers to these questions is extant. It may have
been written by Norton and intercepted before reaching Bancroft;
but there is reason to believe that either this or another copy of the
answers may have come into Bancroft's hands.[4] Bancroft had another
instrument in his quest for information — John Gibson, a young
Scotsman who had gone from Glasgow university to Cambridge in
1583 and, after graduating in 1585/6, been ordained in England. To him
Bancroft signified his 'earnest desire thoroughly to know the order and
accustomed fashions concerning the elderships as they are now erected
in Scotland', and Gibson sent him a long account, based partly on his
own observation and partly on what he had heard from others, of the
proceedings of the Scottish Church courts. He was able to satisfy

[1] B.M., Egerton MSS., 2598, fos. 240–5 (*Cal. S.P. Scot.*, x. no. 337); cf. R. G.
Usher, *The reconstruction of the English church* (2 vol. London, 1910), i. 56–7.

[2] *Cal. S.P. Scot.*, x. nos. 349, 353.

[3] Calderwood, *History*, v. 77. It is possible that there was no connection
between Naunton and Norton and that Bancroft had employed the Nortons
independently. On the other hand, Calderwood's account may be inaccurate,
and Norton's confession may in fact have implicated Naunton.

[4] Nat. Lib. Scot. MSS., 6.1.13, fos. 37–8. Dr. H. W. Meikle identified this
paper as being a series of answers to Bancroft's questions. The same volume
includes (at fos. 33–4) a letter to Whitgift of which there is a copy in the British
Museum (Add. MSS. 32092, fo. 88*v*) and (at fo. 42) a letter from a Scotsman
which undoubtedly reached England; it is therefore likely that the papers
directed to Bancroft which it contains came into his hands safely. It is noteworthy that Calderwood, who had access to a copy of the questions, did not
apparently see any answers to them.

Bancroft that 'the success of that government generally in all men concerning reformation in godliness and manners is very small'. This letter from Gibson exists today in the volume of manuscripts which contains the answers to the questions sent by Bancroft to Naunton.[1]

Scottish indignation at Bancroft's 'slanderous and infamous' sermon had been growing throughout the year 1589, and on 9 December the presbytery of Edinburgh decided to direct a petition to Queen Elizabeth 'desiring her majesty to take order with Mr. D. Bancroft'.[2] Two versions of a letter to Elizabeth were written,[3] and in them the ministers boldly pointed out that they had rendered service to England by supporting the English interest in Scotland, alleging that danger to the 'amity' came from English clerics who were inspired by 'Satan that old serpent' to calumniate the Scottish Kirk. This hostility had first been shown when *A declaration of the king's majesty's intention and meaning* was 'received, diligently read, and that in the ears of divers chief personages of the realm [of England] . . . printed again at London, and with an odious new preface prefixed thereunto reprinted again . . . also insert . . . in the Chronicles of . . . Holinshed for the perpetual memory thereof'. The petitioners proceeded with their chief complaint: 'Secondly, one Bancroft . . . with most impudent mouth took upon him to traduce us, our ministry and whole church openly at Paul's Cross on Sunday the 9 of February last in time of parliament . . . where . . . he entered upon us, not sparing our very dead, but railing against that famous father Mr. Knox'. Thirdly, they complained that 'we, our discipline and whole ministry are most ridiculously flouted, as we hear, in their stage plays, pamphlets and pasquils imprinted day by day' and they concluded this part of the letter with a hint to the queen that she was 'highly provoking our patience' and with a threat of 'a fearful curse within your own bowels'. They went on to request that the *Declaration*, being a forgery by Patrick Adamson, should be deleted

---

[1] Nat. Lib. Scot. MSS., 6.1.13, fos. 39–41. The identification of Bancroft's informant is conjectural; see Register of presentations to benefices (H.M. Gen. Reg. House), i. 144; ii. 113, 115*v*; Venn, *Alumni Cantab.*, ii. 211; Hew Scott, *Fasti Eccl. Scot.*, i. 353.

[2] Wodrow Soc., *Miscellany*, i. 470.

[3] *Ibid.*, 489–96; Calderwood, *op. cit.*, v. 72–7.

from Holinshed; that Bancroft should apologise publicly; that some action should be taken against the authors of the plays and pamphlets; and finally — most astonishing request — that 'it may please you after the example of good Josaphat to proclaim a public fast out-through your realm with preaching and supplication'. The Scottish king had gone overseas to fetch home his bride, and in his absence the audacity of the ministers was unrestrained.

There is no evidence that these immoderate demands ever reached Elizabeth; but the course actually taken by the Scots was sufficiently distasteful to the English Government. John Davidson, a minister who had been associated in the preparation of the presbytery's petition, composed a little book, *Bancroft's rashnes in rayling against the Church of Scotland*, which brought out the strength of feeling against the English preacher for his attack on the Scottish Kirk and king. In the general assembly of August 1590 James Melville preached a sermon on discipline, making the most extravagant claims for the necessity of the Presbyterian courts and for their powers over kings and nobles as well as common men, and he said that his subject was specially apt because 'the belly-god bishops of England by all moyen and money were seeking conformity' between the two churches. This declaration of war was made in the presence of Robert Bowes, the English ambassador. King James, who had returned to Scotland in May, had expressed displeasure with Davidson for writing *Bancroft's rashnes*; but he was unwilling to condemn the book's argument, since his own annoyance at Bancroft's aspersions on his sincerity was genuine enough; and it was in the same general assembly that he made his well-known outburst against the Church of England — 'As for our neighbour kirk in England, it is an evil mass said in English, wanting nothing but the liftings.'[1] On 24 October 1590 Robert Bowes wrote to lord treasurer Burghley, enclosing a copy of Davidson's book and explaining that although the king had endeavoured to confiscate the entire edition some copies had in fact escaped. The matter, he went on,'hath had sundry consultations and been diversely tossed' for it was 'stomached' in Scotland that Bancroft had charged King James with manifest dissimulation and had

[1] Wodrow Soc., *Miscellany*, i. 503–20; J. Melville, *Diary*, pp. 280–1; Calderwood, *op. cit.*, v. 100–1, 106, 112.

used the *Declaration*, which was officially pronounced to be an un-authorised publication by Archbishop Adamson. James and his chancellor were unwilling to make a protest directly to the English Government, and on the ambassador, therefore, fell the stigma of taking action, involving as it did a loss of credit with at least the more extreme section of the Scottish ministers.[1]

On receiving this report from Bowes, Burghley sent for Bancroft. The cleric, who had read Davidson's newly published attack on his sermon, guessed why he had been sent for, but, although he was thus prepared, the interview was unpleasant. Burghley pointed to the passages in Davidson's work dealing with Bancroft's remarks about James, told him that the pulpit was 'not a place to deal in much with princes', and appeared to be 'greatly moved'. Bancroft was 'in sort dismayed', and, as time was short and the lord treasurer had many other people to interview, he thought it best to frame an explanation or defence — it is that rather than a recantation — in writing. In a long letter to Burghley, he first explained his motive in making a reference to Scotland, and went on to examine the character of the *Declaration*. He gave illustrations of the violence of the Presbyterians and of their seditious attitude towards the king, and praised the 'Black acts' for the check which they had imposed on the ministers. He then explained how calumnies about James had been circulated and how the *Declaration* was set forth to refute them, and he reminded Burghley that neither had the *Declaration* (originally published *cum privilegio regali*) been disavowed nor Adamson censured for publishing it. Bancroft next dealt with the central point, his remarks about King James, protesting that there was a difference between the words which he had spoken in the pulpit and the printed copies of his sermon and urging that no man in his senses would wittingly have offended the Scottish king, since he was Elizabeth's ally. But at the worst, he continued, his words could not bear the construction put on them. He proceeded to carry the war into the enemy's country by referring to the violent language used by Knox and, more recently, other Scottish ministers, about the English Crown and the English Church. 'The consistorian humour is of a strange mixture. They will censure and gall every man, but they must

[1] S.P. Scot. Eliz., xlvi. nos. 48, 58 (*Cal.*, x. 482, 492).

not be touched'. Before leaving this part of his subject, Bancroft returned to his favourite point about Presbyterian politics, describing the writings of Knox and Buchanan as 'trumpets of rebellion'. He went on to justify his use of Robert Browne's letter, and concluded by asserting that 'advertisements' which he had received from Scotland since he preached his sermon had tended to confirm him in his critical attitude towards the Scottish ministers.[1]

A copy of Bancroft's letter of explanation was sent to King James, to whom it gave only partial satisfaction. The king regretted that Bancroft had not abandoned Browne as a source of information, and would have preferred that the English preacher should either at Paul's Cross or some other public place, admit his errors and explain his true meaning. A letter from Burghley to the lord chancellor of Scotland helped to mollify James, who reflected that the differences between Bancroft and the ministers might be debated without involving his honour and that to press his own wishes further might bring contention rather than profit.[2]

Bancroft had laid himself open to attack by the English Puritans, who were ever watchful for aspersions on the Scottish Church. They now had a surer basis for their attack than they had when Beale criticised Whitgift for negotiating with Adamson. John Penry in his *A briefe discovery of the untruthes and slanders contained in a sermon preached the 8 of Februarie 1588 by D. Bancroft* (1590) mentioned Bancroft's insinuation that the Scottish king 'is a deadly enemy unto the present government established in his kingdom, and watcheth but his time to overthrow it' and his allegation that the Scottish ministers were seditious; these charges, he said, would be answered by the Scots themselves, but he argued that rebellious conduct on the part of the ministers did not prove their form of Church government to be false. He also censured Bancroft for giving credit to a letter of Robert Browne, whom he described as 'a known schismatic' and a 'proud ungodly man'.[3] Bancroft had read Penry's book before he wrote his *apologia* to Burghley. After John Davidson had stated the case for the Scottish king and Church, a more

---

[1] Nat. Lib. Scot., MSS., 6.1.13, fos. 46–55.
[2] S.P. Scot. Eliz., xlvi. nos. 69, 71; xlvii. no. 4 (*Cal.*, x. nos. 505, 517).
[3] Penry, *A briefe discovery*, pp. 42–4.

studied criticism of Bancroft appeared in a Puritan petition to the queen, possibly written by Henry Barrowe. The author of this work suggested that Bancroft had turned to Scotland for illustrations of the rebellious tendencies of Presbyterianism because he could not find evidence in England, and asserted that he had implied that King James was a 'flat hypocrite'. This writer dismissed the *Declaration*, on which Bancroft had based much of his argument, as 'counterfait by the graceless archbishop of St. Andrews', and expressed his belief that the king was a sincere supporter of the Presbyterian polity. He emphasised the most vulnerable point in Bancroft's sermon — the attack on James — by quoting from Davidson's *Bancroft's Rashnes*.[1]

Bancroft apparently attempted to make contact with Archbishop Adamson. It is alleged by the Presbyterian historian Calderwood that in 1590 or 1591 Bancroft sent letters secretly to the Scottish prelate, telling him that he had read some of his writings, assuring him of support in any attempt to restore Episcopacy, and promising him a welcome if he visited England. It is true that Adamson, although no longer exercising any episcopal functions, was still regarded as dangerous by the Presbyterians and was charged in 1591 with having assisted the English anti-Puritan controversialist Matthew Sutcliffe in the compilation of one of his works. Calderwood's story, although it may be an unfounded accusation which had formed part of a propaganda campaign against Adamson, is not inherently improbable.[2] But the Scottish archbishop was a dying man, and Presbyterianism was in the ascendant, when Scottish episcopacy was offered the English countenance which had been sought in vain from Whitgift seven years earlier. Bancroft, but not Adamson, lived to see the time when the restoration of episcopacy in Scotland would again be practicable.

Bancroft was little affected by the censure which he received for his sermon and by the opposition which he encountered, and he continued the castigation of the Scots in two books, *Daungerous positions*

---

[1] 'A petition directed to her most excellent majestie', B.M., Harl. MSS. 7581, published probably in 1591 (*Short title catalogue*, 1521). The section dealing with Scotland is on fo. 28 (p. 51) of the MS. and p. 46 of the printed version.

[2] Calderwood, *op. cit.*, v. 118–23; J. Melville, *Diary*, pp. 281–2; *Cal. S.P. Scot.*, x. no. 548.

and proceedings and *A survey of the pretended holy discipline*, both published in 1593. His line of argument, indicated in the famous phrase 'English Scottizing for discipline', was that a great deal of English Puritan thought could be traced to Scottish sources, and he paid particular attention to the subversive politics of the Scottish Reformation (as illustrated in Knox's *History of the Reformation* and as reasoned in Buchanan's *De jure regni*) and to the association of the Presbyterian party with the successive *coups d'état* of 1582–5. He was now equipped with a more adequate knowledge of Scottish affairs than he had displayed in 1589, when, in compiling his sermon, he had drawn on Adamson's *Declaration* and Robert Browne's *A new year's guift*. Of printed books, he had now read the first *Book of discipline*, the 1584 London edition of the Anglo-Genevan service book (*The book of common order*), John Davidson's reply to his sermon (*Bancroft's rashnes*), Penry's *A briefe discovery*, the volume of Robert Bruce's *Sermons* published in 1591 and the 1587 edition of Holinshed's *Chronicles*, which was a useful source for recent Scottish history.[1] Most important among printed books, however, was Vautrollier's edition of Knox's *History*, which Bancroft studied carefully and from which he drew illustrations of his conception of the politics of the Scottish reformers.[2] In manuscript he had, presumably, the answers to the questions which he had sent to Robert Naunton and the information which he had received from John Gibson, besides other 'advertisements'. He quoted from one of Archbishop Adamson's letters to Whitgift — an indication that the primate may have taken an interest in Bancroft's work and given him some assistance. He referred also to 'James Gibson's conference with the king, penned by himself and delivered abroad in many copies', an account of an interview in the course of which the most audacious of the Scottish ministers had called the king a persecutor who maintained 'the tyranny of bishops, and absolute power'.[3]

---

[1] Bancroft, *Survay*, pp. 48–9, 75, 78, 147, 174, 186, 458–60; *Daungerous positions*, p. 6.

[2] *Survay*, pp. 48–9, 228; *Daungerous positions*, pp. 10 ff.

[3] *Daungerous positions*, pp. 5, 27. For James Gibson, see Calderwood, *op. cit.*, iv. 484–8. One cannot fail to comment on the fact that B.M., Add. MSS. 32092 (which contains a transcript of the Adamson–Whitgift correspondence,

The only immediate result of Bancroft's work was to foster an atmosphere of tension in which there flourished the belief of the Scottish Presbyterians that the English bishops were conspiring with King James — a belief which had not, so far as we know, much foundation in fact.[1] Bancroft's principal aim had been to discredit the English Puritans by stressing the taint of sedition which was attached to their Scottish allies. Whatever his wishes, he could exert no influence in Scotland in the 1590s, for the episcopal cause there was dead and its resurrection not yet possible. But if there was little ground for the Scottish ministers' suspicions, there was ample justification for apprehension about the future, as the first seven years of James's English reign — roughly the period of Bancroft's tenure of the primacy — were to see the complete restoration of Scottish episcopacy as part of Bancroft's scheme for Anglican reconstruction.[2]

GORDON DONALDSON

---

letters which passed between Beza and Scottish divines, various papers relating to Scottish ecclesiastical affairs, and a letter from Robert Naunton to John Copcot) is such a volume as might have been compiled for Bancroft's use. With Nat. Lib. Scot. MSS., 6.1.13, it provides the principal material for this subject.

[1] J. Melville, *Diary*, p. 679; S.P. Scot. Eliz., lxiii. no. 85; Peter Heylin, *Aerius redivivus* (1672), p. 355.

[2] R. G. Usher, *op. cit.*, ii. 154–74.

4 The Development of London as a Centre of Conspicuous Consumption in the Sixteenth and Seventeenth Centuries

Of all forms of historical writing, that which deals with particular places is perhaps the most pregnant with the possibilities of boredom, for the general reader can seldom hope to share the parochial enthusiasms by which the study of local history is so often inspired. But local history, and particularly urban history, can be approached from two different points of view. It can seek to portray the changing pattern of life within the few square miles which it takes for its field of study. Or it can endeavour to interpret that changing pattern as a symptom of greater changes in the nation as a whole. For, as the sociologists are never weary of reminding us, a town is essentially a social product. It is brought into being by forces external to it. It continues to exist because, and only so long as, it serves a social purpose. During the sixteenth and early seventeenth centuries the population of London and its immediate suburbs grew much more rapidly than the population of the country as a whole. Confronted by that fact, one of the obvious tasks of the historian is to make clear the purposes which that metropolitan expansion served; to indicate the wider developments of which it was a symptom; and to explain why, to contemporaries, it appeared as a symptom of disease rather than of health in the body politic. For that the growth of London was widely considered to be a morbid growth is incontestable. Topographers and chroniclers might write with admiration and affection of the city whose contours they described and whose history they told. But the pride of the city fathers was tinged with dismay at the problems of housing, public health and poor relief which they saw mounting before them. And outsiders were openly abusive. 'Soon,' wrote King James, whose dislike of the city was notorious, 'London will be all England,' and for once he echoed the sentiments of a large proportion of his subjects.

The major reason for the growth of the metropolis is obvious enough, and needs to be mentioned merely in order to give the rest of the story some degree of perspective. Giovanni Botero, the translation of whose work on the magnificence and greatness of cities is itself indicative of the rising interest in urban problems, confidently laid it down that the largest towns were always based on trade and usually built on the banks of navigable rivers.[1] To that generalisation, London was clearly no exception. All contemporary descriptions emphasised its commercial importance. Most of them pointed out the degree to which that importance was due to the river on which the city stood. In that respect, the growth of London was a symptom both of the expansion of English trade as a whole and of the concentration of that trade upon the Thames. It was widely held to be a morbid symptom, for many contended that London waxed fat at the expense of the outports, and grew rich only by sucking the wealth of the country to itself. To explain that expansion and concentration and to examine that contention would, no doubt, be fruitful tasks, but would lead into more purely economic fields than that with which this paper is concerned.

For the city and its suburbs had a second function. Not only did they constitute a centre of production where substantial incomes were earned from industry and trade; they were also a centre of consumption where men expended the revenues which they had acquired elsewhere. During the sixteenth and early seventeenth centuries a number of factors combined to swell the volume of that expenditure. Irrigated by the fertilising tide of provincial money, the metropolitan economy not only expanded but began to bear new fruit. And to that extent the development of the capital became a symptom of something more than the nation's commercial progress. The factors which combined to produce that result are not far to seek. Botero postulated three condi-

[1] G. Botero, *A Treatise Concerning the Causes of the Magnificencie and Greatness of Cities* (trans. R. Pearson, 1606), ch. x.

tions under which cities tend to develop as centres of consumption. Each of those conditions can be shown, not only to have existed in Tudor and Stuart London, but to have considerably increased in influence. In the first place,

> It doth infinitely availe to the magnifyinge and making Cities greate and populous [to have] the Residency of the Prince therein, . . . for wheare the Prince is resident there also the Parliaments are held and the supreame place of justice is kept. All matters of importance have recourse to that place, all Princes and all persons of account, Embassadores of Princes and of Common weales . . . make theire repaire thither . . . All such as aspire and thirst after offices and honors run thither overcome with emulation and disdaine at others. Thither are the revenues brought that appertain unto the state, and there are they disbursed out againe.[1]

Many years ago Professor Tout pointed out the importance in London history of the fact that the seat of government was established at Westminster.[2] As the policy of centralisation increased the work of that government, and as the mounting extravagance of court life increased its social expenditure, so the significance of that fact grew.

In the second place, Botero insisted upon the economic implications of the law courts.

> Cities, that have Courts of Justice must needs be much frequented as well for concourse of people that have cause of Suite unto it as also for the execution of Justice. For it cannot be ministered without the help of . . . advocates, proctors, sollicitors, notaries and such like. Nay more than that (which it greeves me to think on) Expedition of justice cannot be made these our daies without ready money.[3]

Judicial history is a field in which a mere economic historian must obviously hesitate to tread, but at least there seems to be a prima facie case for arguing that the sixteenth and early seventeenth centuries saw a

[1] Botero, *op. cit.*, p. 65.
[2] T. F. Tout, *The Beginnings of a Modern Capital; London and Westminster in the Fourteenth Century* (British Academy, Raleigh Lecture, 1923).
[3] Botero, *op. cit.*, p. 45.

significant increase in the amount of judicial business conducted in the capital. Looking back from the later seventeenth century, Hales noted a long-term tendency for common law cases to be heard at Westminster rather than in the provinces. If the volume of extant records is any criterion, there was a substantial growth in the work of Chancery. Clearly, the age of the Tudors and early Stuarts was the heyday of the prerogative courts. And on two points, at least, contemporary comment leaves no room for doubt. The first was the growth in the number and wealth of London lawyers — a growth which it is difficult to explain except as the result of a similar growth in the volume of the business which they handled. The second was the vital importance to the economy of Westminster of the tide of men and money that flowed in with every term.

But it is Botero's third postulate that throws most light upon the factors which were operating to mould the pattern of London life.

> Experience teacheth that the residence of noblemen in cities makes them to be more glorious and more populous, not onely by cause they bring their people and their families unto it, but also more by cause a nobleman dispendeth much more largely through the accesse of friends unto him and through the emulation of others in a Citie where he is abiding and visited continually by honourable personages then he spendeth in the country where he liveth amongst the brute beasts of the field and converseth with plaine country people and goes apparelled among them in plain and simple garments.[1]

A significant feature of the sixteenth and early seventeenth centuries was the increasing extent to which the revenues spent in London were the revenues of that junior branch of the nobility, the country gentry. If the rise of the squire-archy to social and political pre-eminence was a major theme of the history of those times, their growing urbanisation was a minor theme upon which contemporary comment was abundant and which the historian cannot afford to ignore.

It was a curious development, for it sprang from two immediate causes that were contradictory, although in a sense they shared a common origin. By the early seventeenth century two streams of gentry

[1] Botero, *op. cit.*, p. 63.

can be seen converging upon the capital, the one carried along by its growing wealth, the other driven by its growing poverty. It was, no doubt, the former who inspired Hume's comment that 'could humanity ever attain happiness, the condition of the English gentry at this period might merit that appellation'. And Professor Tawney has recently shown how, faced by a secular rise in prices, a substantial section of that class not only held their own but raised themselves to new levels of affluence, partly at the expense of the Crown, the Church and the peerage whose estates they acquired, partly at the expense of the tenants whose rents they raised and whose faces they ground.[1] But as they acquired the estates of their betters, so they took on some of their social habits. As their revenues rose, so their eyes turned citywards and they established ever closer social contacts with the capital.

In many cases, those contacts began early in life for, by the early seventeenth century, London had become an important educational centre and more than one country squire obtained his first taste of London life as a schoolboy. Some may have gone to St. Paul's; some certainly went to the Merchant Taylors' School; more probably went to Westminster, although the imperfections of the records make generalisation dangerous. But, in addition to those foundations, there were private schools which catered for the sons of the nobility and gentry. Of these by far the best known is that of Thomas Farnaby, who, after an adventurous youth spent voyaging with Drake and Hawkins and soldiering in the Low Countries, became a leading classical scholar of his day and established a school in Goldsmith's Alley where he is said to have had upwards of three hundred noblemen and others under his care.[2] Farnaby was no doubt exceptional both in the reputation which he acquired and in the colourful life which he led, but he was not unique in his occupation. Nor was a London education a masculine monopoly. For Sir Simonds D'Ewes tells us that his sisters were sent to school in Walbrook,[3] and the niece of Andrew Overton,

[1] R. H. Tawney, 'The Rise of the Gentry, 1558–1640', *Economic History Review*, xi (1941), pp. 1–38.

[2] See the article on 'Farnaby' in the *Dictionary of National Biography*.

[3] *The Autobiography and Correspondence of Sir Simonds D'Ewes* (ed. J. O. Halliwell), i. 157.

among others, was sent to London to learn 'her needle, dauncing, and such qualities becoming a gentlewoman'.[1]

For most of the gentry, however, the significant introduction to the capital must have come when they enrolled at one of the Inns of Court, partly to obtain that minimum knowledge of the law essential to a landowner and justice of the peace, but principally to acquire that modicum of the social graces without which no gentleman's education could be considered complete. The rôle of the Inns of Court as schools of law and manners was not, of course, new. But in the sixteenth and early seventeenth centuries the number of their students rose. Admissions to Gray's Inn, for example, which had amounted to only two hundred in the third decade of the sixteenth century, had risen to seven hundred and ninety-nine in the last and to twelve hundred and sixty-five in the ten years between 1611 and 1620.[2] Already by the middle of Elizabeth's reign three of the four great Inns were faced by that too familiar symptom of educational expansion, an accommodation problem that could not be solved by the obvious device of doubling up in chambers.[3] By the reign of Charles, that champion of right thinking, Archbishop Laud, was insisting upon the necessity of appointing proper officials in the Inns because 'almost all young gentlemen spent part of their time in one or other of the Inns of Court and afterwards, when they return to live in their several counties, steer themselves according to such principles as in those places are preached to them'.[4] Under Elizabeth, Sir Humphrey Gilbert had complained that 'the estate of gentlemen cannot well traine upp their children within this Realme but eyther in Oxford or Cambridge', where 'they utterly lose their tymes if they doe not follow learning merely, for there is no other gentleman-like qualitie to be attained'.[5] In 1615 Sir George Buck could write with some justification of a third University, the University of London,

---

[1] P[ublic] R[ecord] O[ffice], Chancery Proceedings, Chas. I, bdle. 6, no. 3. Cf. Star Chamber Proceedings, Jas. I, bdle. 116, no. 1, and Cal[endar] of S[tate] P[apers] D[omestic], *1637*, p. 422.

[2] J. Foster, *Register of Admission to Gray's Inn, 1521–1889* (1889).

[3] S.P.D. Eliz., xcv, no. 91.

[4] *Cal. S.P.D. 1633–4*, p. 340.

[5] B[ritish] M[useum], Lansdowne MSS., xcviii, no. 1.

which offered a range of studies as extensive as it was peculiar.[1] Although they might still waste part of their youth on the banks of the Isis and the Cam, by the reign of Charles I the majority of the country gentry were spending the most impressionable years of their lives on the banks of the Fleet and the Thames, in an area admirably situated for tasting the pleasures of both the City and the Court, and in institutions which, far from following learning only, were sufficiently of the polite world to cultivate a taste for music and the drama and sufficiently broad-minded to finance that taste by turning their libraries into gambling saloons.[2]

Once settled on his family estate, there was a multitude of reasons why the thoughts of the country squire should constantly return to the capital. In one of the greatest ages of land speculation in English history, London was the very centre of the land market; for the estates that were being sold were above all those of the Crown, and the normal method of sale was through the agency of London financiers. In an age of universal borrowing, London was the great money market and London merchants the great lenders. In an age when a judicious marriage was often the easiest way to fortune, London was not unimportant as a marriage market, and the widows and daughters of citizens were not the least attractive stepping-stones to affluence. In an age of furious litigation, a substantial number of the gentry sooner or later found themselves involved before one or other of the courts at Westminster. Above all, in an age which was characterised by the successful assertion of the claims of the gentry to a share in political power, Westminster was the very centre of the political map. To say that the thoughts of the gentry constantly turned to the metropolis is not, of course, to argue that their bodies always followed. Lands could be bought, money could be borrowed, marriages could be arranged and lawsuits could be fought without the physical presence of the landowner concerned. But three generalisations may be made with confidence. The squire who stayed in the country when such questions were at issue had of necessity to be represented by an agent in town; an agent who was likely to be a member of his own family. Whoever the agent might be, his employ-

[1] J. Stow, *Annales* (ed. E. Howes, 1631), pp. 1063–87.
[2] *Cal. S.P.D. 1631–3*, p. 215; *1639–40*, pp. 304–5.

ment entailed the expenditure of money which helped to develop the capital as a centre of consumption. Above all, far from being reluctant to visit London on business, a substantial number of the gentry were anxious to do so even when business offered no pretext. 'I am resolved to spend the greatest part of the rest of my lyf for the wynter and springe quarter abowt london,' wrote John Wynn of Gwydir in 1605, and in so resolving he was no more than conforming to a fashion already well established.[1] Whatever else they may have learned from their sojourn at the Inns of Court, it had revealed to the landowners of England that rural delights did not span the whole gamut of human pleasures. By the early seventeenth century, in fact, there had developed a clearly defined London season which began in the autumn, reached its climax at Christmas, and was over by June. The Duchess of Newcastle, for example, has left it on record that her sisters spent nearly every winter in London.[2] Two sisters, no doubt, do not make a season. But from her account of their normal activities when in town it is clear that, in paying their annual visit, they were following less some personal idiosyncrasy of their own than the social habits of their class. Not every squire went to London every winter, or necessarily stayed for the whole season when he did go. But, by the early seventeenth century, from October to June London always contained a substantial population of rural landowners. And the more regular that system became the more it grew, for the more men could rely upon finding company to their taste.

The townward migration of the gentry, however, was not a purely seasonal phenomenon, and by the reign of Charles I a significant number had become permanent residents of the city and its immediate neighbourhood. And it is at this stage that the story becomes more complicated, for it is here that the second stream of the gentry begins to appear — the stream of those who were driven citywards by their poverty. It is reasonable to suppose that the bulk of the seasonal visitors were comparatively affluent and came because their revenues provided

[1] Wynn MSS., no. 348. The Wynn MSS., in the National Library of Wales, are an invaluable source for illustrating the relations of a county family with the capital.

[2] H. B. Wheatley and P. Cunningham, *London Past and Present*, iii. 295.

a surplus which could be spent on the pleasures of the town. Some, no doubt, who came to take up permanent residence did so from deliberate and unfettered choice. But many were driven by compulsion. For though the gentry as a class emerged victorious from the difficulties into which they had been plunged by the rise in prices, the struggle had not been bloodless and the victims had not been confined to the ranks of the peasantry and the peerage. More than one county family found its expenses rising above its income, and the author of *The Commonweal of this Realm of England* explains how many of them sought a way out of their dilemma. 'Seeinge,' he says, 'the charges of howsehold so much as by no provision they can make can be holpen, they give over their howseholds and get them chambers in London or abowte the courte, and there spend there time, some with a servaunte or 2, wheare he was wounte to kepe 30 or 40 persons daily in his house.'[1] By the early seventeenth century it had become a commonplace that landowners were moving to London in order to save the charges of housekeeping in the country, although not all who did so were reduced to living in a single room. Moreover, even those families that successfully weathered the storm often did so only by means of a rigorous system of primogeniture. It was a system which often bore heavily on widows, and more than one moved Londonwards to ease the strain upon her scanty means. In particular, it was a system which bore heavily upon the younger sons who, to use Thomas Wilson's inelegant but expressive phrase, had only 'thatt which the catt left on the malt heape, perhaps some smale annuytie during his life or what please an elder brother's worship to bestowe upon us if wee please him and my mistress his wife'.[2] To such, London had obvious attractions. Thus the permanent residents which London recruited from the landowning classes were by no means a homogeneous group. Some were wealthy and able to support themselves with style if not with ostentation. Others were merely concerned to eke out a modest income. Others sought to supplement an income that was woefully inadequate to their needs. The efforts of this last group constitute a not unimportant factor in

[1] *A Discourse of the Commonweal of this Realm of England* (ed. E. Lamond), p. 81.
[2] *Camden Miscellany*, xvi (1936), p. 24.

English history. On the one hand, they fertilised both commerce and the professions. On the other, they were largely responsible for the rash of patents and monopolies which from time to time disfigured the political and economic complexion of England. Those who succeeded in making or mending their fortunes must, by that very fact, pass largely beyond the scope of this paper. For to them London became the milieu in which they earned an income rather than spent revenues acquired elsewhere. But to ignore them completely would be an error. For many continued to draw some income from the provinces and, in so far as they retained the tastes and habits of the class from which they came, they served to reinforce the influence which their more fortunate kinsmen had upon the pattern of London life.

Neither the chronology nor the volume of that townward drift is easy to determine. It had existed in some measure during the Middle Ages. A few attempts were made to check it in the first three-quarters of the sixteenth century. But if the volume of contemporary comment may be taken as a criterion, it reached significant proportions in the last two decades of that century, two generations after the rise in prices had burst upon the landowning classes and at a period when the processes of eviction, enclosure and rack-renting and the sale of royal and monastic lands had all progressed sufficiently for the factors outlined above to have had some effect. By the early seventeenth century it had become great enough to inspire James to an ungallant outburst against 'those swarms of gentry who, through the instigation of their wives and to new-model and fashion their daughters (who, if they were unmarried, marred their reputations, and if married, lost them) did neglect their country hospitality, and cumber the city, a general nuisance to the kingdom'.[1] More important, it led to a series of prohibitory proclamations which not only stirred to fury the gentry with whose social activities they interfered, but also stirred to remonstrance the city in whose economic life that influx had come to play a part of some moment. According to Salvetti it had become, by the early years of Charles's reign, the custom for the greater part of the gentry to winter in town.[2] Since both Wilson at the beginning of the century and King

[1] I. Disraeli, *The Curiosities of Literature* (1849 edn.), iii. 402.
[2] *Cal. S.P. Venetian 1632–6*, p. 38, note.

at the end estimated the total number of gentle families at between sixteen and seventeen thousand, that statement, if true, would imply a seasonal influx of thousands of individuals. To take it literally would, no doubt, be naïve; diplomatists are notoriously bad statisticians, and the Italians were worse than most. But at least it suggests that the numbers concerned were of some magnitude, and the same conclusion is borne out by the fact that, in 1632, some two hundred and fifty peers, baronets, knights and gentlemen were prosecuted in the Star Chamber for having been found in London after a proclamation had ordered them home.[1] For it would surely be to underestimate both the law-abidingness and the ingenuity of their class to suppose that a much larger number had not either obeyed that proclamation or else escaped detection when it became clear that the Government intended to act.

By the early seventeenth century, therefore, the economy of London and its suburbs was called upon to adapt itself to a substantial seasonal immigration of rural landowners, many of them accompanied by their families. It had to accommodate itself to an ever-changing and steadily growing student body which had already, under Elizabeth, exceeded a thousand. It had to absorb an uncertain but not inconsiderable number who, from either poverty or choice, from either boredom or ambition, had abandoned their country seats for permanent residence in the town. The incomes of those immigrants no doubt varied, but their total revenues must have been substantial. The result of their expenditure was to create a series of demands which it became an important function of the metropolis to fulfil and which significantly increased the influence that the Court had for long exerted on the pattern of London life. As Botero had pointed out, an invariable characteristic of the gentleman come to town was his ostentatious display. Or, in the more homely words of Ben Jonson, 'First, to be an accomplished gentleman — that is, a gentleman of the time — you must give over housekeeping in the country and live together in the city amongst gallants where, at your first appearance, 'twere good you turned four or five acres of your best land into two or three trunks of apparell'.[2] From that tendency towards

[1] J. Rushworth, *Historical Collections*, ii. 288–92.
[2] C. Knight, *London*, i (1841), p. 378.

conspicuous consumption the luxury trades of the city inevitably waxed fat. As in all ages, the gentleman come to town required transport, and it was during the early seventeenth century that the coach became a familiar part of the London scene. By the reign of Charles I, not only were hackney coaches to be found in their hundreds, but the cab rank had become an institution and the sedan chair was ceasing to be a curiosity.

What was of greater moment than either luxuries or transport, the gentleman come to town needed entertainment. Some, no doubt, he found at Court. But the facilities of the Court were limited, and by the Civil War the visiting and resident gentry had begun to build, or to help build, the leisure institutions that were to be characteristic of polite society in London at least until the end of the eighteenth century. The origin of English club life, it has been argued, is to be found in the associations of gentlemen, usually organised upon a county basis, who regularly met in their favourite taverns to drink, talk and criticise the Government in the manner common to all club men at all times. By the reign of James, the gentry were already manifesting that taste for parks and pleasure gardens that one normally associates with a later age. By the reign of Charles, Hyde Park, which had still been used for hunting under James, had become a parade ground for the coaches of the fashionable, and, although Ranelagh and Vauxhall still lay in the future, the Spring and Mulberry Gardens were indicating the form which they were to take. That the Spring and Mulberry Gardens were both, strictly speaking, part and parcel of the royal parks is no doubt true. But that they were becoming commercialised is obvious from the contemporary descriptions which survive. As Garrard wrote to Wentworth in 1634:

> The Bowling in the Spring Garden was by the King's Command put down for one day . . . there was kept in it an ordinary of six shillings a meal (when the King's proclamation allows but two elsewhere) continual bibbing and drinking of wine all day long under the trees, two or three quarrels every week. It was grown scandalous and insufferable; besides, my Lord Digby being reprehended for striking in the King's Garden, he answered that he took it for a common bowling place where all paid money for their coming in.

When, in the next year, the Spring Garden was closed to the public, the immediate result was the opening of a new one as a private business venture.[1] Above all, there was the theatre. Lord Keynes is reported once to have said that England obtained Shakespeare when she could afford him. Presumably his meaning was that Shakespeare could flourish only in a commercial theatre, and that a commercial theatre could flourish only when there was sufficient surplus wealth to pay for it. If that argument is valid, then perhaps the urbanised and semi-urbanised gentry of Elizabeth and the early Stuarts may claim at least some share of reflected glory, for it was their demand for entertainment that helped to bring the commercial theatre into being. Describing how, in the days of Charles I, her sisters spent their London seasons the Duchess of Newcastle wrote: 'Their customs were in the winter time to go sometimes to plays or to ride in their coaches about the streets to see the concourse and recourse of people, and in the springtime to visit the Spring Garden, Hyde Park and the like places, and sometimes they would have music and cup in barges upon the water.'[2] It was a routine which would have seemed familiar to the eighteenth century. It would have been incomprehensible to the fifteenth.

Moreover, not only did the demands of the newly urbanised country gentry for entertainment lead to a pattern of leisure activities that was to persist for generations, but their demand for accommodation eventually opened a new chapter in the history of architecture. To a large extent, of course, that demand was for purely temporary accommodation and was met by the expansion of what would now be called the hotel and catering trades, and references abound to the great inns that were going up in and around Holborn and to the taverns and cookshops to which the gentry proved such good customers. But of more interest to the historian was their demand for permanent accommodation, for by the time of Charles I that demand was being met in ways which were to leave a lasting imprint upon London topography. On the one hand, those who were content to live near rather than in the metropolis began to build up the old villages of Clerkenwell and Islington, Hampstead and Chelsea as residential suburbs. On the other, those who wished to be in the centre of things settled in the area which

[1] Wheatley and Cunningham, *op. cit.*, iii. 294–5. [2] *Loc. cit.*

was being developed in the parish of St. Giles-in-the-Fields. As Mr. Summerson has recently pointed out, in developing that area Inigo Jones, the Earl of Bedford and William Newton laid the foundation-stones of two centuries of London taste. Lincoln's Inn Fields, Covent Garden and Great Queen Street inspired the work of the great builders of the eighteenth century. The character of the Georgian town house was fixed under Charles I, and it was fixed to meet the needs of the country gentry who were becoming townsmen.[1]

To discuss at length the process by which the spending of these rural revenues gradually modified the pattern of London life in one detail after another would, however, be to lapse into that parochial enthusiasm which the local historian should never parade in public. But two general remarks may perhaps be permitted. The new urban society that was growing up in the city and its suburbs, a society that still had its financial roots and many of its interests in the countryside, created an environment which helped to foster two of the most interesting phenomena of Tudor and Stuart England. The first was the development of the lay professions. Of all the unexplored fields of English economic history, none is less known than the story of the English professional classes, and where the historian knows little it behoves him to say less. But clearly, when that story comes to be written, an important chapter in it will of necessity be devoted to the sixteenth and early seventeenth centuries, for those years saw, not only the spectacular rise of the lawyers but also a significant development of the doctors and architects, the scriveners and journalists. Nearly the whole of that development took place in London and Westminster, for it was only in the capital that the demand for professional services was sufficiently great to make their provision on any scale a source of profit. And a not unsubstantial part of that demand came from the gentry. In the second place, it was this period that saw firmly established the connection between the capital and scholarship, both professional and amateur; the Academy which met weekly from 1572 to 1604 stands on record as the first of the learned societies of London.

By comparison with the rural tide which flowed towards the capital after the Restoration, this earlier movement may seem modest. To an

[1] J. N. Summerson, *Georgian London* (1945), ch. ii.

age which takes urban life for granted, it may reasonably appear as a sign of economic progress. But to contemporaries it was a phenomenon of ill-omen. Some of the opposition which it encountered was, no doubt, inspired by motives which do not appear on the surface. For, as the Venetian ambassadors pointed out, an order that the gentry should disperse to their country homes could on occasion serve as a means for breaking up a Parliamentary opposition or as an instrument of taxation. But the major roots of official disapproval lay deeper, for the migration of the gentry towards London offended against some of the major social principles of the time. In an age when both economic and re-ligious theory demanded a régime of some austerity, the gentleman come to town indulged in luxuries which not only threatened him with personal ruin but which endangered that favourable balance of trade to which so great importance was attached. In an age when the problems of city government were becoming ever more acute, the responsibility for those problems was in large measure laid at his door. For, it was argued, where the gentry went there the idle and dissolute among the lower orders were bound to follow. And in following the gentry to the capital they created problems of housing and poor relief, disease and high prices, which were intolerable in a well-ordered commonwealth. Above all, in an age when every social class was deemed to have its obligations as well as its rights, the gentry threatened to become para-sites upon the body politic. As the Attorney-General argued in the Star Chamber:

> For where by their residency and abiding in several Counties where their Means ariseth, they served Your Majesty in several places according to their Degrees and Ranks in aid of Government, whereby, and by their Housekeeping in those Parts, the Realm was defended and the meaner sort of Your People were guided, directed and relieved; but by their residency in the said cities, and parts ad-joining, they have no employment, but live without doing any service to Your Majesty or Your People.[1]

By so neglecting their traditional functions, the gentry threatened to undermine the whole structure of local government. Consequently it is not surprising that sporadic efforts were made to discourage the new

[1] Rushworth, *op. cit.*, ii. 289.

fashion, efforts that became more vigorous and more frequent as the fashion grew. Sometimes, those efforts were indirect. 'We have very plausible Things done of late,' wrote Garrard to Wentworth in 1634. 'To encourage Gentlemen to live more willingly in the Country, all Game Fowl, as Pheasant, Partridges, Ducks, as also Hares are by Proclamation forbidden to be dressed or eaten in any Inns, and Butchers are forbidden to be Graziers.'[1] More often, however, the method used was that of ordering the gentry back to their country residences. That in the long run those methods failed is obvious. But the efforts of the Crown were not entirely devoid of results. For the resentment which those orders aroused must be counted among the minor causes of the growing rift between the landowning classes and the monarchy.

F. J. FISHER

---

[1] W. Knowler, *The Earl of Strafforde's Letters and Dispatches*, i (1739), p. 176.

5 The Last Years of the Court of Star Chamber 1630–41[1]

On 31 May 1641 in the House of Commons, Edmund Prideaux, the member for Lyme Regis, reported the findings of the Committee on the Star Chamber in a Bill for the abolition of that Court.[2]

There was at once a commotion. Before the Speaker had an opportunity to put the question for the engrossment of the Bill, Mr. Coventry, member for Evesham, rose to his feet to complain that the Committee had exceeded the bounds of its prescribed duty in bringing in such a Bill. Sir Robert Hatton thereupon desired that the original instruction for committal might be read, and, on this being done, it was found that Coventry was correct.[3] On the previous 1 April, a Bill for the 'Reforming of the unlawful Proceedings' of the Court had been given its second reading. It was consigned to the Standing Committee on the Star Chamber. But, on the day following, the Committee was ordered to take into its consideration another Bill, which had not yet received a second reading and which had been introduced to the House on 26 March.[4] This was a Bill for 'Declaring and Regulating the Power' of the Star Chamber. The Committee was moreover instructed to make one good bill out of the two.[5]

Mr. Coventry was supported in his complaint by a certain Mr. Vahun, who is most probably Mr. Vaughan, the member for Car-

---

[1] I desire to express my grateful thanks, in the first place to Professor J. E. Neale, of the University of London, for the invaluable assistance and advice with which he has always been ready to guide my researches, and secondly to Mr. J. F. Mathias, B.A., of Yale University, with whom I have had many valuable conferences, and whose help in the preparation of this Essay for the press I have greatly appreciated.

[2] *Commons Journals*, ii. 162.

[3] This account is taken from the manuscript diary of the Long Parliament by Sir Simonds D'Ewes in the British Museum. Harleian MS. 163, f. 635.

[4] *Commons Journals*, ii. 113.   [5] *Ibid., idem*, p. 115.

marthen,[1] and he too emphasised the fact that the House had originally intended the regulation, not the abolition of the Court. It was now the turn of Sir Simonds D'Ewes, who had been a member of the Committee.[2]

> If the order were generall [he said] to make one good bill out of two and the irregularities of the Court had been soe extreame as that could mee [*sic*] noe moderatinge of them, then the Committee must either have extinguisht and abolisht the Court or they could never have performed the order by making a good bill.

This artless excuse seems to have satisfied the House. D'Ewes records no further speeches on the subject; and the Commons proceeded to vote the engrossment of the Bill as it stood. It was read the third time on 8 June.[3]

Thus it was in these two months in Committee that the fate of the Court was finally decided. Is it possible to assign a reason for the taking of this extreme step? D'Ewes does not appear to have kept minutes of the proceedings of the Committee; we cannot, therefore, venture even a guess in this matter. Yet a possible clue is provided by Clarendon.

The account as set down in D'Ewes's Diary differs from that given by Clarendon in one important respect. According to the latter, the Bill, as originally committed, was reported to the House with certain amendments. Upon which,

> it was suddenly suggested (by a person not at all inclined to confusion, or to the violent party that intended that confusion), 'that the remedies provided by that bill were not proportionable to the diseases; that the usurpations of that court were not less in the forms of their proceedings, than in the matter upon which they proceeded; insomuch that the course of the court (which is the rule of their judging) was so much corrupted, that the grievance was as much thereby, in those cases of which they had proper connusance, as it was by their excess in holding pleas of that, in which, in truth, they had no jurisdiction . . . .'.

[1] The constituencies represented by the Members of Parliament concerned in this scene are to be found in *Return of Members of Parliament*, I, pp. 488, 496, 498.

[2] The Committee had been appointed on 3 December 1640. *Commons Journals*, ii. 44.   [3] *Ibid.*, *idem*, p. 171.

Clarendon then goes on to say that the Bill was recommitted by the House, with an order that it should be so amended as to take the Court away entirely. Thus the Bill as eventually passed received only one reading.[1]

D'Ewes was a day-by-day reporter of Commons proceedings, whereas Clarendon was writing after the event, and the word of the former is thus the more credible. Yet the student is loath to condemn the interesting speech which Clarendon quotes.

Can the two interpretations be reconciled? Both versions agree that the Bill, as finally passed, received only one reading in the Commons. D'Ewes blames this on the Committee, Clarendon on the House. It is quite possible that Clarendon was confused; indeed, the two dates given in the margin against his description of the Parliamentary proceedings, 30 March and 2 April, are respectively the days for the first reading of the second Bill, and of the instruction to the Committee to take over the earlier Bill also. It may be conjectured that the speech by the member, about whose identity Clarendon weaves a wholly irritating and quite unpenetrable circumlocution, was made in Committee, and not in the full House.

Nevertheless, two facts emerge. First, the Star Chamber was abolished by proceedings that were as unusual as they were precipitate. Secondly, its irregularities had been extreme. The latter conclusion is expanded in the Preamble to the final Act, which indicts the judges of the Court for not limiting the jurisdiction of the Star Chamber to the points laid down in the Act 'Pro Camera Stellata' of Henry VII. They have 'undertaken to punish when no harm doth warrant and to make decrees for things having noe such authoritie and to inflict heavier punishments than by any Law is warranted'.[2] To the opinion of D'Ewes and to that of Clarendon's anonymous orator we are now able to add the official expression of opinion as enunciated by a common lawyer such as Prideaux, the leading light on the Star Chamber Committee.[3]

[1] *The History of the Rebellion* (ed. W. Macray, 1888), i. 374.
[2] *Statutes of the Realm*, v. 110.
[3] He was the spokesman of the Commons in later conferences with the Lords on the subject of the Star Chamber Bill. Cf. D'Ewes' Diary, ff. 747, 748*v*.

These various opinions have been accepted too much at their face value by later historians of the Court. During the period under review, the historian tends to proceed by strides from one outstanding case to another, with scarce a glance at what lies between. Even Gardiner is not entirely guiltless in this matter. But Gardiner was writing a general history of the period; he was, moreover, seated on the daïs of Liberty, watching and encouraging the less fortunate men of all epochs in their struggles to attain freedom. The outstanding cases were repugnant to his sensibilities; and, as he did not set out to write a history of the Court of Star Chamber, the many other cases that occupied its attention were not of interest to him.

G. M. Trevelyan, however, a successor of Gardiner in the historiography of the period under consideration, does admit, albeit rather grudgingly, that 'a careful study of the non-political cases in the Star Chamber in the time of Charles I shows good work being done by an unnecessarily powerful instrument of State'.[1] It is perhaps a pity that the author does not define his term 'non-political', and that his remarks seem to be based almost entirely upon the reports of cases in 1631–2, which his predecessor had so ably edited and published for the Camden Society.[2] Trevelyan, however, like Gardiner, was more intent on fitting the Court into the more general picture of Stuart despotism.

Miss Elfreda Skelton is the most recent authority on the Court. There is as yet no published work to her account; but her thesis on the Elizabethan Star Chamber, which is deposited at the University of London, is invaluable.[3] She shows quite conclusively that the Court was not only beneficial in the sixteenth century, but that it was also popular. But even she, visualising only the outstanding cases in the later period, seems quite convinced that under the Stuarts the Court deteriorated to the extent that it became a mere instrument of tyranny.

It is of course essential to examine the outstanding cases, and to dwell

---

[1] *England under the Stuarts*, p. 165.

[2] S. R. Gardiner, *Reports of Cases in the Courts of Star Chamber, and High Commission* (Camden Soc., 1886).

[3] Elfreda Skelton (now Lady Neale): 'The Court of Star Chamber in the reign of Elizabeth,' 1931, available at the Institute of Historical Research, London.

upon the cruel judgements therein; it is equally necessary to determine exactly what were the causes at issue in these cases; but completely to ignore the many other cases which occupied the Court's attention during this period is to do less than justice to the subject. What must be determined is whether the outstanding cases are the exception or the rule in the annals of the Court. Once this is done, it will be possible to attempt a resolution of the intriguing problem set by the action of the Long Parliament.

At first sight, a consideration of the proceedings of the Court between 1630 and 1641 seems an almost impossible task. The Public Record Office has not been able to calendar more than twenty-six sets of proceedings for the years 1625–41, as against nearly ten thousand for the reign of James I. But there are happily other aids. The State Papers Domestic in the Public Record Office can boast of a good collection of cause-lists, originally the property of Secretary Windebank, who has, more often than not, added some invaluable notes.[1] There are also the less official reports, of which many figure among Rushworth's *Historical Collections*.[2] Others are to be found in manuscript form, and two of these have been admirably transcribed by Gardiner for the Camden Society.[3] Official records are also available in the shape of the various

[1] The cause-list, presumably drawn up by one of the clerical officials of the Court, contains the names of all the plaintiffs and defendants in each hearing set down for the day. In addition, there is always added a brief statement of the cause at issue. Windebank's notes are in the form either of marginalia or of addenda on an attached sheet. These important documents are to be found in the following volumes of the State Papers Domestic for Charles I (P.R.O. Ref. S.P. 16). Arabic numerals are used for convenience. Vols. 159, 167, 224, 225, 231, 239, 242, 248, 250, 251, 259–60, 266–7, 275–7, 283, 299–302, 314, 320–1, 344–6, 361–2, 369–70, 372, 379–81, 388–9, 391, 420, 443, 461, 535 *passim*.

[2] To be found either in Vol. II or in the Appendix to Vol. III. It should be noted in this connection that Rushworth is not always very accurate. The Attorney-General's case against Overman and others, for using fish-oil in soap-making, is quoted in ii. 252, as having been heard in the Trinity term of 1634. In iii. App., p. 54, it is down under Easter 1633. The State Papers bear out the latter date as being the more correct. Cf. *Cal. S.P. Dom., 1633–4*, p. 30.

[3] Reports are to be found for this particular period in the following British Museum manuscripts: Add. MS. 11764, ff. 1–29*v*., Harl. MSS. 4022 and 4130, Hargrave MSS. 404 (the reports begin at the back of this volume) and 489, ff.

Receipt Books of the Exchequer and the Memoranda Rolls for a study of the fines imposed by the Court.[1]

Two other sources remain for comment. Neither has as yet been used in historical writing. Only two years ago there was presented to the Public Record Office a series of process books, formerly the property of the Clerk of the Writs and Processes, in which every writ issuing from the Star Chamber office has been meticulously entered.[2] The books are continuous from the middle years of Elizabeth's reign until the beginning of 1632. In the most tantalising manner they then stop, just when they might have shed a most important light upon the last years of the Court. They are, however, invaluable for the period which they do cover.

The second source is in the Bodleian Library. It is a book which is a most detailed report of each day's session in the Court, covering the period from the Hilary term of the twelfth year of Charles's reign to the Trinity term of the fourteenth year.[3] The writer has not contented

---

9–15*v*. There are also reports in the following Bodleian manuscripts: Rawlinson MSS. A.128 and D.720 ff. 49*v*.–51. The two documents transcribed by Gardiner for the Camden Society are Harl. MS. 4130 and Rawl. MS. A.128.

[1] Fines, after review in the Star Chamber, would be estreated into the Office of the King's Remembrancer, and are therefore enrolled on the Memoranda Rolls. In the Auditor's Receipt Books of the Exchequer (P.R.O. Ref. E.401), each auditor has a heading 'Star Chamber Fines'. I am much indebted to Mr. Mathias for drawing my attention to these most valuable sources of information.

[2] Presented by Sir Giles Sebright, Bt., a descendant of Thomas Saunders, Clerk of the Writs and Processes, 1631–41. The P.R.O. Class No. is P.R.O./30/38. The books appear to have been compiled as follows. A warrant for process would be issued by the Clerk of the Council to the Clerk of the Writs and Processes. The latter would make out the requisite writ and either enter up a record in his book at the time, or else allow warrants to accumulate until the end of the day when he entered them *en bloc.* (Cf. Hudson, *Treatise on the Court of Star Chamber* in F. Hargrave, *Collectanea Juridica*, ii. 47.) Every writ issued carried with it a fee, and accordingly the book could also be used as a check upon fees. The Public Record Office has indeed classified the volumes as Fee Books, but the title of Process Book is the more appropriate. Lists of fees exigible for the issuing of process are to be found in P.R.O./30/38/27 (ii), or in Skelton, *op. cit.*, i, App., p. cxviii.

[3] Rawl. MS. C.827.

himself with reporting the hearings of cases. He has also recorded so many motions and orders, even on the most trifling of subjects, that there is no ground for looking upon his reports as being in any way selective. They can therefore be considered as forming a record of unusual importance.

Many treatises on the Court are extant. William Hudson and Isaac Cotton write at great length about the Star Chamber with which they were intimately connected. In addition, there is an anonymous book among the Harleian manuscripts entitled 'A New Discovery of the Singular Jurisdiccon of the high Courte of Starre Chamber . . .'.[1] All these treatises are of great value, and Hudson's work is particularly exhaustive.[2]

With all these sources at command, it is now possible to consider the various questions arising out of the Parliamentary action of 1641. The alleged differences of procedure and extensions of purview may be examined, while it will also be possible to determine whether excessive punishments were the rule or the exception during the last years of the Court.

For matters of procedure, reliance has to be placed on the contemporary treatises. But Cotton and Hudson were both writing in the later years of the reign of James I, and therefore not far away from the period under discussion, while the 'New Discovery' appeared in 1636. An examination of the proceedings of the period is not, therefore, calculated to reveal much that does not appear in these works. The process books, however, and the pamphlet literature of the later period are quite illuminating in this matter, and, from an examination of these sources, it is possible to observe three general tendencies which lend colour to possible differences of procedure in the last years of the Court.

The first is, perhaps, the least impressive of the three, because its

---

[1] There are numerous manuscript copies of Hudson in private hands as well as in public repositories. It has also been printed in F. Hargrave, *Collectanea Juridica*, Vol. II. A copy of Cotton's Treatise is in Lansdowne MS. 639. The 'New Discovery' is in Harl. MS. 6448, and has also been transcribed by Miss Skelton, *op. cit.*, i, pp. xli *et seq.*

[2] Miss Skelton has made a careful examination of the copies of Hudson in the British Museum, and has noted some discrepancies. *Op. cit.*, i, p. 6.

resolution must remain in the realm of conjecture. Yet it is of very great interest, for it concerns the discrepancy which exists between the number of cases initiated during the period of a single year, and the number of cases eventually brought to a hearing. This can scarcely be looked upon as a feature peculiar to the Stuart period, but what had been perhaps a grave difficulty in the latter years of Elizabeth must have become wellnigh an impossibility under James and Charles. The number of cases heard during the course of a single year averaged rather less than fifty.[1] There might be as many as fifteen during the course of a single term, as in the Easter term of 1634.[2] But, on the other hand, the Bodleian manuscript gives evidence of the amazing fact that only twenty-four cases received a hearing in the four terms commencing with the Easter term of 1637, a year which was exceptional in that twenty-seven of its sitting days were occupied by three outstanding cases.[3] As against these figures, we have the indisputable fact that the number of cases initiated was steadily increasing. Miss Skelton was able to list 732 cases as having entered their first stages during the forty-fourth year of Elizabeth.[4] The process book, which covers the second regnal year of Charles, gives evidence that the number of plaintiffs initiating procedure during the course of a single year had increased to a thousand, and, by the seventh year of the reign, had increased still further. Moreover, a careful investigation over a period of six years ending with the Trinity term of the eighth year of the reign discloses the fact that scarcely 4 per cent of the cases initiated in the Court arrived at a hearing, while only 20 per cent appear to have advanced at all beyond the earliest stages.[5]

[1] This figure is obtained by computing the number of entries of writs *ad audiendum judicium* in the Process Books over a period of several years.

[2] Harl. MS. 4022.

[3] Rawl. MS. C.827. The three cases were Lord Mohun *v.* Sir James Bagg, which occupied nine days, Attorney-General *v.* Bishop Williams, which took up ten days, of which seven were in vacation, and Attorney-General *v.* Lord Saville, which required eight days of the Michaelmas term.

[4] *Op. cit.*, pp. 196, 197.

[5] The number of plaintiffs is obtained by computing the number of entries of writs *ad comparendum*. A large number of the entries have *ren* or *vet* entered against them. Experiment shows that these terms signify that the particular writ

The question that one is tempted to ask is whether the Stuarts had devised any particular procedure to meet this enormous increase in the business of the Court. When Bills lapsed in their early stages, this was due, more often than not, to a failure to proceed on the part of the plaintiff. But it is also just possible that the attorneys of the Court had a certain control in the matter. It is Hudson who tells us that the Lord Keeper delegated a certain power of selection to the attorney in charge of the case,[1] and it is conceivable that so powerful an officer would be in a position to compound cases in order to save their Lordships the trouble of sitting at times other than on their normal Wednesday and Friday during term-time. That cases were compounded is also apparent from a remark by Thomas Saunders in his 'Rules for my Clerkes on taking fees', a document which is to a certain extent a key to the Process Books and which is preserved with them.[2] He exhorts his deputies to 'enquire in the Star Chamber office with the deputy or Register when anie case is compounded'.

---

was being renewed, or that it was a writ to another defendant in a case where one warrant for *subpoena* had already been issued. Such entries have therefore been discounted. It was possible for the plaintiff to issue several other writs, e.g. *ad reiungendum replicacioni* and to sue out various commissions, e.g. *ad examinandum testes*, before the definitive writ *ad audiendum judicium* was issued. It is on an examination of the entries of these later writs that the percentages in this section are based. Mr. Mathias, who has been using these process books in a period anterior to that covered by the present Essay, is in substantial agreement with me over the evidence forthcoming from this important source and over the method of using the books to obtain that evidence.

[1] Hudson expresses himself in this matter as follows: '. . . *lord Egerton*, conceiving that the attorneys best knew the client's cause, gave liberty to them to prefer such causes as their clients which most urged them, which were most earnest, and solicited them to prefer; and those, after the cause required by the king's attorney, were always set to hearing. But because it is his [the Lord Keeper's] charge to set fitting causes for the lords judgment, he many times required those which were of counsel in the cause upon whose judgment he durst rely, to certify him whether the cause were fit to he heard . . .' *Collectanea Juridica*, ii. 216. Hudson goes on to say that the attorneys seldom used their power to decide on the fitness of cases, because, provided that a case were heard, a fine could always accrue to the King, payable by the plaintiff if the hearing were dismissed. Nevertheless this important privilege presumably still remained.

[2] P.R.O./30/38/27 (ii).

This, however, must remain a conjecture, but, if it be accepted that the majority of suits were disposed of before they had an opportunity to reach a hearing, it is easy to explain one of the more puzzling features in the history of the Court, namely the absence of contemporary criticism of the Star Chamber on the grounds of undue delays between the inception of a suit and the hearing of a cause.

The second tendency to be observed is in the prosecution of Crown suits. Miss Skelton suspects that, in the time of Elizabeth, the Attorney-General's cases were given precedence no matter how many other suits were pending.[1] During the period under discussion, this is certain. On 13 November 1633 the Crown's case against Lodovick Bowyer, for libelling the Archbishop of Canterbury, was heard,[2] although it does not appear upon a list of causes to be heard during that particular term;[3] nor does a case, heard on the 16 October, in which the Attorney-General sued Richard Coxe for transporting forty tons of fuller's earth.[4] But the Crown, in certain cases, did more than hasten the hearing; it also tended to abuse its privilege of procedure by *ore tenus*. Normally, it was allowed to proceed thus only *super confessionem*, if the defendant confessed, or *pro confesso*, if he persistently refused to answer the information laid against him. The answers of Burton, Bastwick and Prynne, in 1637, were all, on various pretexts, declared insufficient; they were not given a fair chance to remedy this before they were summarily arraigned.[5] Lilburne, in 1638, would not take the oath

---

[1] *Op. cit.*, i. 96, and cf. passage from Hudson, quoted p. 99, note 1.

[2] S.P. Dom. Charles I, ccl. 58.

[3] *Ibid.*, ccxlvii, 66. There are two such documents among the State Papers, the other being in ccxci, 123. They are examples of the terminal cause-list. It would seem that a long list, in this particular instance amounting to fifty-three cases, would be drawn up prior to the Michaelmas terms, and that this would be worked off in the shortest possible time, not necessarily during the particular term. The *ore tenus* cases would not appear on such a list, but would be taken as soon as they arose. The second of these two documents is, however, a cause-list for the Trinity term, and the assumption here would be that the cause-list for the preceding, Michaelmas, had been worked off.

[4] *Ibid.*, ccxlviii. 6.

[5] The answers had to be signed by one of the attorneys of the Court. Bastwick put in an unsigned answer. Prynne's answer was materially altered by the

without being told the reason for his taking it. In his case also, the Attorney-General proceeded *pro confesso*.[1]

A third tendency which must now be observed is the Stuart practice of increasing the ecclesiastical representation on the bench of the Court. Elizabeth had been careful to allow only one bishop at a time to sit as a judge. During the period under discussion, there were three: the two archbishops and the Bishop of London, who, after 1636 in the person of Juxon, was also Lord Treasurer.[2]

Thus three tendencies can be discerned whereby Stuart procedure could be said to differ from that under the Tudors. The number of original writs of *subpoena* appears to be growing without a proportionate increase in the number of hearings. Again, and this is far more important, procedure by *ore tenus* was being abused. Finally, the ecclesiastical representation had increased markedly.

Is it now possible to discern any general tendency on the part of the Court either to inflict over-severe punishments or to deal with matters outside its competence? In order to examine this, it is necessary to piece together, not always very satisfactorily, the various fragments of evidence of its official proceedings.

The collation of the evidence to be gained from the State Papers with that obtained from the Bodleian manuscript, from Rushworth, and from the other reports at our disposal, provides some interesting facts. From these sources it is possible to extract at least 308 cases as having been up for hearing in the Star Chamber between the sixth and the sixteenth years of the reign of Charles. In 284 of these cases the general nature of the cause at issue may be determined;

Attorney after it had been drafted. Prynne disowned the amended copy and the attorney refused to sign the original. Burton's answer was signed by attorney, but the Court declared a large portion of it to be scandalous. Burton refused to be examined upon what remained of his answer after the offending portion had been expunged. *A new discovery of the Prelates Tyranny in their late prosecutions of Pryn . . . Bastwick . . . and Burton . . .* (1641), pp. 27, 28, 40–5.

[1] *The Christian Man's Triall, or a true Relation of the first apprehension and several examinations of John Lilburne* (1641), pp. 6, 7.

[2] Rawl. MS. C.827 shows that the three ecclesiastics were frequent attenders at the Court.

while, on 236 occasions, there is some note about the judgement delivered.

An examination of the subject matter of these 284 cases gives some very striking results. One of the official reasons for the ultimate fate of the Court was that its competence had extended beyond the limits of the Act of Henry VII.[1] Miss Skelton, drawing on Hudson and on Coke for her theory, and on her own researches for her evidence, devotes a very interesting portion of her treatise to this very important question of jurisdiction. One emerges from a study of her conclusions with the feeling that, already by the end of Elizabeth's reign, the Court was almost omnipotent in cases involving violence, perjury, fraud, conspiracy, libel, oppression, official corruption and contempt of Proclamations.[2] Her figures, like those for the period under discussion, must not be taken absolutely at their face value. For there was scarcely a case in the Court that was not tried on two, three or more counts. Conspiracy might well be accompanied by riot, and supported by perjury; but, as such a case owed its inception to a charge of conspiracy, it is under this heading that it is listed. Miss Skelton's figures are more complete since every Bill that was put in during the period which was covered by her researches is available, whereas for the later period the facts are confined to the cases that were actually heard.[3]

In no fewer than 334 out of her 732 cases in the forty-fourth year of Elizabeth's reign violent outrage was the main issue; out of the 284 cases between 1630 and 1640 in which the subject-matter of the cause is known, only sixty-six come exactly under this category. Where libel

[1] Professor Pollard has effectively disposed of any belief that this Act laid down any limits to the jurisdiction of the Court. *English Historical Review*, xxxvii. 522 *et seq.*

[2] Miss Skelton gives a tabulated list of Bills filed in the forty-fourth year of Elizabeth. *Op. cit.*, i. 196–7.

[3] Miss Skelton's figures throw an interesting light upon social history in the sixteenth century and upon the types of cases which were considered, in popular belief, worthy of the Court, rather than upon the cases which the Court itself deemed worthy of a hearing. In the latter connection, figures based upon the actual hearings are more relevant. It is, therefore, with a certain diffidence that the two sets of figures are compared and percentages established, and the limitation should be borne in mind when they are being considered.

or scandal was the main issue, there are eighteen cases in the earlier year, forty-one in the later period; this represents a rise of nearly 12 per cent. Some 5 per cent of the total are assigned by Miss Skelton to the heading of fraud; during our period the proportion has risen to 10 per cent. Only sixteen cases, or slightly over 2 per cent are traceable to a conspiracy in the Elizabethan year. During the Caroline period, there were fifty-three, that is 18 per cent. But whereas there were ninety-six charges against corrupt officials among the cases for the earlier period, the percentage of such cases has dropped in the later period by as much as 9 per cent, although it is fairly certain from the State Papers that between 1636 and 1641 many sheriffs were brought before the Court for refusing to levy ship-money.[1]

There remains one other class of cases for consideration. Between the sixth and the sixteenth years of Charles's reign, there were some seventeen cases arising out of contempt of royal Proclamations and Orders. Miss Skelton makes an interesting comment on this subject. 'Extension of the jurisdiction,' she says, 'was possibly a factor making for the unpopularity of the Court under the Stuarts. Yet the widening of the scope of the Court was begun under Elizabeth. Contempt of proclamation was heard and punished here.'[2] Proclamations against erecting buildings in London, against the engrossing of corn, against the cornering of tin and coal were all punished by the Star Chamber; so also was any abuse of the Proclamation against the printing of seditious literature. The increase from the two cases which Miss Skelton lists for the forty-fourth year of Elizabeth to the seventeen in the later period can be easily accounted for. The period under consideration is remarkable for the fact that during its course the country was virtually governed by Proclamations and Orders in Council. Nor is it possible to challenge the competence of the Court in the matter. An Order is made by the King in Council, very often by the Council after its judicial session in the Star Chamber. It is not surprising that the Council *qua* judicial body should devise and apply sanctions for its own legislative measures.

[1] E.g. *Cal. S.P. Dom.*, *1635*, pp. 481, 498. The bill of the Attorney-General *v*. Lumley for such an offence is in Add. MS. 25266, ff. 21–48.

[2] *Op. cit.*, i. 144.

An examination of the subject-matter leads to two conclusions. First, the number of overt acts of violence was diminishing before a rise in the number of conspiracies and practices. This is well borne out in a statement by Bishop Williams during the course of a hearing in the Star Chamber in 1626. The Lord Keeper remarked that 'whereas in ancient time the records of the Court are filled with battayles and ryotts soe outrageous whereas now wee here not of one in our age. The justice of this Court hath bin to lett justice flourish in her proper coloures & now our labour is only to suppresse those that bring grist to the mill, Conspirators and Barretors'.[1] Williams was a little euphemistic, but his statement is none the less interesting.

The second conclusion is that the Court had a very wide jurisdiction and was the great rival of the Common Law Courts. The official reason for the abolition of the Court as embodied in the preamble to the definitive Act was an almost absurdly one-sided attempt by common lawyers of the calibre of Prideaux to restrict the activities of the Court to the terms of the Act of Henry VII.

It is now possible to turn to another charge which was levelled against the Star Chamber in its latter years, that it would be satisfied only with 'cropped ears and slit noses', and that its fines were impossibly exorbitant.

It is a fact of extraordinary interest that out of our 236 known judgements during this period, only nineteen involved the corporal punishment of any of the parties to the suit. On seventy-five occasions a fine of more than a thousand pounds was imposed. Moreover no fewer than 109 cases were dismissed.

To find that more than 60 per cent of the undismissed cases involved a fine exceeding a thousand pounds seems rather startling; but it is the fact that very rarely did anyone pay the full amount. Twice a year, at the end of Hilary and Trinity terms, the fines came up for review.[2] They might be confirmed; they might be respited pending further consideration; or they might be mitigated. There are three very interesting documents among the State Papers which show how the system worked.

[1] Lansdowne MS. 620, f. 3*v*. (Star Chamber Reports 1–3, Charles I.)
[2] 'The New Discovery . . .' in Skelton, *op. cit.*, i. App., p. lix.

At the end of Hilary term, 1632 (O.S.),[1] four fines, imposed during the course of that term, came up for mitigation. In two cases, the fines were respited until the next day for mitigation; in another, fines of three hundred pounds were abated to sixty pounds, and fines of two hundred pounds to thirty pounds. In the fourth case, the fine was neither respited nor mitigated. It was confirmed. The same document records fines imposed in Michaelmas term, 1632, that is, since the previous day of mitigation. But it also records a fine imposed in Michaelmas term, 1629, and, in this particular case, Attorney-General *v.* Sir John Stowell, for assaulting and abusing a sheriff at an election, the fine of two hundred pounds was given a further respite. In fact, one gains the distinct impression that the Court purposely forbore to pronounce on fines. For the fines imposed in two cases heard during the Michaelmas term of 1632, which are respited in this particular document, appear in similar lists for mitigation drawn up at the end of Trinity term, 1637 and at the end of Trinity term, 1640.[2]

These particular cases were both at the suit of the Attorney-General, one against William Torkesey, and twelve others, for riotous destroying of the fen works in Lincolnshire, the second against William Steward and six others for riotous throwing down of enclosures in the forest of Feckenham. It is thus possible to see the Court witholding its judgement as a guarantee of the good behaviour of the defendants, an excellent device.

Not only were fines mitigated; they were also pardoned or 'estalled'. The State Papers give several examples of such royal pardons;[3] while the entries in the books of receipt show exactly how common it was for fines to be paid in instalments. A typical half-yearly entry, selected at random from the Auditors' Receipt Book for Michaelmas 1641,[4] records the names of eight people, all of whom are paying instalments of their fines. One, Thomas Wright, is represented as paying thirty shillings in part payment of a fine of thirty pounds imposed in Trinity term, 1631. Moreover, in 1638, a certain John Wotton is

---

[1] S.P. Dom. Charles I, ccxxxii. 43.
[2] S.P. Dom. Charles I, ccclxii. 103; ccccl xi. 95.
[3] E.g. *ibid.*, cxciv. 22, 23; ccclxii. 103.
[4] P.R.O. Ref. E.401, 2466.

still paying an instalment of a fine imposed in the fifth regnal year of James I![1]

In the face of these facts it is hardly possible to sustain the generalisation that the Star Chamber habitually insisted on crushing fines. On the contrary the evidence suggests that the general, one might say average, tendency was in the direction of leniency.

Yet it must be admitted that occasionally the fines were crushing and were not respited. Burton, Bastwick and Prynne were fined five thousand pounds each in 1637, and their fines were neither mitigated nor respited until the Long Parliament quashed their sentences in 1641. John Williams, Bishop of Lincoln, was fined ten thousand pounds; it was not respited. An interesting case is that where the City of London was cited for failure to carry out the terms of its charter in connection with the plantation of Ulster. A fine of seventy thousand pounds imposed in the Hilary term, 1634 (O.S.), was meant, according to Gardiner, to be pardoned, but, because twelve thousand pounds had already been granted to the Queen's use, some arrangement was come to whereby the City paid over the smaller sum directly to the Queen, and was pardoned the remainder.[2] The Exchequer therefore received nothing, but the fine remains the largest to be levied during the period under consideration.

Speaking generally, the insistence on heavy fines is as rare as the award of corporal punishment. One's first impressions of the Star Chamber are so greatly influenced by mental pictures of the whip and the hangman's knife that it is revealing to find that only nineteen out of the 236 cases involved corporal punishment. An analysis of these cases, interesting in itself, is essential to a due appreciation of the true position.

In the very first year of our period, Dr. Leighton was sentenced to

> be committed to the prison of the Fleet for life, and pay a fine of 10000 l., that the high commission should degrade him from his ministry; and that then he should be brought to the pillory at Westminster while the Court was siting, and be whiped. After whiping, be set upon the pillory, a convenient time; and have one of his ears cut off, one side of his nose slit, and be branded in his face, with a double S.S. for Sower of Sedition. That then he should be carried

[1] P.R.O. Ref. E.401, 2460.   [2] *History of England*, vii. p. 148 *n*.

back to prison; and, after a few days, be pilloried again in Cheapside; and be there likewise whiped, and have the other side of his nose slit, and his other ear cut off; and then be shut up in close prison, for the remainder of his life . . .[1]

This sentence is quoted *in extenso* because it is at once a pattern for most of the outstanding cases of the period, and because it is the most ghastly of them all. The reader of the case is horrified; the Long Parliament, to which Leighton addressed a petition, was moved to tears.[2] There is nothing that can excuse the appalling cruelty of the sentence and the ruthlessness with which it was carried out. Leighton was arraigned for publishing his book entitled *Sion's Plea against the Prelacie* in which he vituperated against bishops in general and Laud in particular. This dreadful censure was the price of his scandal of the episcopacy.

Another libel was heard in the following term. This time it concerned the Lord Keeper, and was instigated by one Bonham Norton.[3] His sentence is light in comparison: three thousand pounds fine to the King, and three thousand pounds damages to the Lord Keeper. He himself did not suffer corporal punishment. Two of his confederates, however, had their ears nailed to the pillory.

We descend the scale a little farther in Hilary, 1630 (O.S.), when one Morgan, a Popish recusant, had to suffer for slandering two justices.[4] His fate was to lose his ears and pay a fine of one thousand marks. To libel an ordinary minister of the Church seems to have been an offence of even less importance. In Dalton cler. *v.* Beck, in Michaelmas, 1631, the defendant had to pay a trifling fine, and undergo a whipping.[5] Libels against ordinary folk never appear to have been punished by anything but a fine, although, if the libeller was himself a man of substance, the fine might be very heavy. Thus, in 1631, Sir Richard Greenvile was fined four thousand pounds for slandering the Earl of Suffolk.[6]

But anyone who dared to speak disrespectfully of Laud, the leading

---

[1] 'Brief account of . . . treatment of . . . Leighton' in G. Benson, *Collection of Tracts*, pp. 220–1.

[2] *Ibid.*, p. 224. [3] Rushworth, Appendix to Vol. III, p. 30.

[4] *Ibid., idem*, p. 33. [5] *Ibid., idem*, p. 40.

[6] *Ibid., idem*, p. 43, and see Gardiner, *Reports of Cases . . .*, p. 108.

man of the time, or of his hierarchy, suffered for his temerity. On 13 November 1633 Lodovick Bowyer was sentenced to a fine of three thousand pounds, to life imprisonment, to lose his ears and to be stigmatised for publishing false tales and scandals about the Archbishop of Canterbury.[1] He was followed to a similar fate on 7 February by William Prynne, now appearing for the first time, who, by sneering at the Queen as well as at the episcopacy, laid himself open to severe censure.[2] Mephistosheth Robyns, appearing in Michaelmas term, 1634, selected the Archbishop of York as his particular butt and was ordered to pay one thousand pounds and undergo whipping.[3] John Bastwicke and Henry Burton joined Prynne in a more concerted outcry against the ecclesiastical system in 1637 and were summarily inflicted with all corporal punishments and a fine of five thousand pounds each.[4] John Lilburne, who, at the age of nineteen, had the temerity to publish books containing similarly seditious material, albeit published abroad, was perhaps spared by his age from the hangman's knife. He was nevertheless whipped.[5]

When it is found that William Pickering, in 1638, lost his ears for 'speaking and publishing lewd and insolent speeches to the scandall of his Majestie and the true Religion established in this kingdom', libel appears to have a very general interpretation.[6] But no general interpretation was needed a week later when Sir Richard Wiseman was before the Court for slandering the Lord Keeper by accusing him of taking bribes.[7] Although his fine of ten thousand pounds was respited on the day for mitigation of fines at the end of Trinity term, 1640,[8] he had to pay prodigious sums of money in damages, was degraded from both knighthood and baronetcy, and deprived of his ears. All were treated alike who slandered men in high places.

Libel was not the only offence for which corporal punishment was

---

[1] S.P. Dom. Charles I, ccl. 59, and Rushworth, *loc. cit.*, p. 65.

[2] Rushworth, ii. 220 *et seq.*   [3] *Ibid., idem*, p. 269.

[4] *A brief relation of certaine speciall . . . passages . . . in the Star Chamber . . . at the censure of Bastwick . . . Burton . . . and Pyrnne . . .*, p. 32.

[5] Rushworth, ii. 463.

[6] S.P. Dom. Charles I, cccxci. 85, and Rawl. MS. D.720, f. 49*v*.

[7] Rawl. MS. D.720, f. 49*v*.   [8] S.P. Dom. Charles I, cccclxi. 95.

deemed fitting. It was also used for conspiracy, and the remainder of the nineteen cases come under this heading. Conspiracy might range from the attempt of Dorothy Blackburn to accuse one Monk of treason, as a result of which he was sent unjustly to the rack,[1] to the case where a certain Baker falsely accused Sir Edward Seabright for the rape of his daughter.[2] The most notorious of such cases was where George Walker accused Freegift Stace of stealing wool. He was adjudged to lose his ears. Even Windebank is constrained to add the remark to his cause list: 'the villanous Judgement'.[3]

It is apparent, however, that the gravest censures were for libel, and that the gravest libels were those directed against the hierarchy of the Church.

It is now possible to draw together the various threads. Procedure under the Stuarts varied from that of former times, principally in those cases where the Attorney-General was the plaintiff, and then only when the defendants were charged with seditious libels against ministers of state or against the hierarchy of the Church. Jurisdiction in the time of the Stuarts cannot be said to have materially altered. But emphasis must be laid on the practice of taking special cognisance of offences against the Church. Finally, punishment, during the period under consideration, was, in the great majority of cases, by no means severe; yet in certain cases, which have been noticed, it was nothing short of ferocious.

It may be well said, therefore, that there was room for reform. It cannot, however, be averred that the court merited complete abolition. What has to be discovered is whether there was not some underlying tendency common to these cases which would make the Star Chamber especially unpopular.

The pamphlet literature of the period gives the decided impression that there was such a deep-seated grievance.

Already attention has been drawn to the fact that the gravest censures of the Court were for libels against the Episcopacy. It was these cases, moreover, that represented a departure from precedent by the

---

[1] Rushworth, Appendix to Vol. III, p. 33.
[2] Hargrave MS. 404. The reports are at the back of this volume.
[3] S.P. Dom. Charles I, ccxlii. 35.

Court both in matters of procedure and in matters of purview. When Prynne suffered the first time, for his *Histrio-Mastix*, no one came to cheer him on the pillory. Yet when he and his friends suffered, three years later, for having libelled the bishops, a huge crowd assembled to give encouragement to them in their ordeal, and to listen to the words which fell from their lips.[1] The malefactor of 1634 had become the martyr of 1637.

It is 'an ill-willer to the Romish brood' that translates this different atmosphere into words. In a pamphlet published in 1641, entitled *England's Rejoycing at the Prelate's downfall*, he expresses himself in no uncertain terms.

> Consider how most barbarously [he says] [the Bishops] persecuted God's people, in dismembring, and disfiguring and whipping, and Pilloring, and Fettering, and Imprisoning, and Banishing and Silencing, &c. At first, in cutting off those Three Worthy mens Eares, Mr. Burton, Dr. Bastwicke and Mr. Pryn and then Fining them and Banishing them to Perpetuall Imprisonment, which was against the Laws of God and men. O it was most cruell dealing, not like Christians, but as dogs. And also good Dr. Layton that hath bin both branded and whipt, and his nose slit, and Imprisoned. And Mr. John Lilburne, that hath bin whipt and gagged, and Fettered, and Pillorisied, [*sic*] and Imprisoned. And so many others of Gods children did the Lordly Prelates prosecute and tyrannise over . . .[2]

Here at once the keynote is struck. The chord echoes and re-echoes throughout the sessions of the Long Parliament. It is to the bishops that the paramount objection is taken. Rushworth, in a short treatise, culled mostly from Hudson, remarks that 'nothing would satisfie the revenge of some Clerymen but Cropt Ears, slit noses, branded Faces, whipt Backs, gag'd Mouths . . .'.[3] His use of the word 'clerymen' is significant. When W. H. Terry, in his *Life and Times of John Finch*, misquotes 'members' for 'clerymen',[4] he causes this significance to be lost.

There are many examples of the objection to the presence of bishops

---

[1] Gardiner gives a good account in *History of England*, viii. 231–3.
[2] *England's Rejoycing at the Prelate's downfall*, p. 5 of text.
[3] II. 475.
[4] W. H. Terry, *Life and Times of John Finch* (1936), p. 189.

in the Star Chamber. 'It is both against Gods Laws and mans,' thunders Prynne, 'that Bishops and Clergie should be Judges over any Subjects within this Realm, for it is no part of their office . . .'[1] Leighton's trial was the subject of another pamphlet. The title speaks for itself: *A brief account of Archbishop Lauds cruel treatment of Doctor Leighton.* In it is a statement of how 'that pious, merciful, and truly Christian Bishop Dr. Laud, pulled off his cap, when (the) horrible sentence was pronounced, and gave God thanks for it'.[2]

One is beginning to sense more and more the presence of Laud. The treatment of John Williams, Bishop of Lincoln, is illustrative of this. The bishop had succeeded to the Lord Keepership after the disgrace of Bacon, and had retained it up till 1626, when Charles I, by a device, got rid of him. The hand of Laud was in this. Later, Williams was brought before the Star Chamber for betraying official secrets, and, in his over-eagerness to prove his innocence, appears to have tampered with witnesses. It was on the latter count that he was fined ten thousand pounds in 1637. If Laud had done nothing else but introduce Kilvert to carry on the prosecution after the death of Attorney-General Noy, his attitude to Williams would have been obvious. For Kilvert, who really had no right to prosecute a Crown case, was perhaps the most unscrupulous person ever to undertake a prosecution in the Court. He was well paid for his pains.[3]

Something of the almost universal fear of Laud is reflected in Prynne's speech from the pillory, in which he makes reference to Williams.

I had thought [he says] they would have left alone those of their own Rochet and not have medled with any of their own Sacred Order. And yet the next (for ought I know) that is to follow us and

[1] W. Prynne, *A Terrible Outcry against the Loytering exalted Prelates*, p. 3.
[2] P. 221.
[3] John Hacket, in his biography of Williams, *Scrinia Reserata*, is very bitter gainst Kilvert, whom he accuses of bribing witnesses and falsifying evidence, ii. § 112. Even when due allowance has been made for Hacket's obvious prejudices Kilvert still appears as a most unpleasant figure. There is a reference to the fact that he was paid fifteen hundred pounds for his services in *Cal. S.P. Dom., 1637*, p. 356.

receive a Censure in the Starre-Chamber, is like to be a Bishop. You see they spare none of what society or calling soever, none are exempted that crosse their owne ends. Gentlemen look to yourselves, you know not whose turn may be next.[1]

The hand of Laud was everywhere. In spite of his cloth, and in contradistinction to Williams when the latter, as Lord Keeper, had presided over the Court,[2] he thought nothing of the shedding of blood. His power was formidable. Elizabeth's decree against printing seditious books was revitalised at his command. He sat on the Board of Licensers in his dual capacity of Archbishop of Canterbury and Chancellor of Oxford University, controlling an additional vote on that board of four by his influence over the mild Juxon, and dragging all offenders into the Star Chamber or High Commission.[3] His membership of the Court before which such offenders were brought was never deemed incompatible with his deep interest in the matter at trial. After heavily inveighing against Prynne, he could, with seeming magnanimity, refrain from formally passing judgement — the influence of his presence sufficed. Windebank was an appointee of his;[4] Juxon also owed his position to the Primate.[5] Chief Justice Finch, later the Lord Keeper, was his friend. Richard Neile, Archbishop of York, was of the same circle.

Very interesting are some remarks by Bishop Williams in the margin of a copy of Laud's speech at the censure of Burton, Bastwicke, and Prynne.[6]

> All your life [he notes] is but a diversion from your calling. . . . This very act of yours to neglect all Christian mildness, and fall upon the killing and massacring of these poor flies in the Star Chamber, to draw malice and hatred upon all your coate and

---

[1] *A brief Relation* . . . pp. 43, 44. [2] Cf. Hacket, *op. cit.*, p. 83.

[3] Cf. R. P. T. Coffin, *Life of Archbishop Laud* (1930), pp. 156–7.

[4] Laud's Diary, quoted in P. Heylyn, *Cyprianus Anglicus*, p. 225.

[5] W. H. Marah, *Memoirs of Archbishop Juxon* (1869), p. 20.

[6] This speech was printed, with a foreword by Laud, at the command of Charles. Williams annotated his copy, and there is a copy of the speech in the British Museum, which has been printed together with these marginalia.

calling, was unto the Church of England a most unfortunate diversion . . .[1]

In another place, Williams refers to the severity of the sentences as bringing 'scorn and contempt upon the Ministers', and a 'generall odium upon the prelates of this Kingdome beside the universall resentment now conceived against the High Court of Starr Chamber'.[2] Now Williams does not say that the proceedings of the Court were without precedent or that its jurisdiction was too far extended; nor does he say that the Court had outlived its usefulness. His remarks are concerned with the severity of the sentence, and he links this with the Archbishop. So did some person unknown, who, on 30 June 1637, pasted a libel on the Cross in Cheapside 'that the Archbishop had his hand in persecuting the Saints and shedding the bloud of the Martyrs'.[3] The saints and martyrs were more especially Burton, Bastwicke, and Prynne. It was as well for the perpetrator that his anonymity was not pierced.

If it be objected that the greater part of the evidence examined above proceeds from biased sources and should be offset by evidence from the opposite side, the answer must be that the attempt is being made to assign a reason for the summary action of the Commons in 1641, and that that body was itself biased. It was as virulent in its attacks on the episcopacy as are any of the pamphlets which have been quoted. Without any compunction a Bill was prepared to remove bishops from their seats in the Upper House, a privilege as old as Parliament itself; to sweep them too from the Council board.[4] But this was not enough. Parliament, in its prevailing temper, was not a prop of the episcopacy; the Courts were. The High Commission went as a matter of course. The Star Chamber followed.

Indeed it was the misfortune of the latter Court often to be confounded with the Commission for Causes Ecclesiastical, a confusion which might nevertheless be called co-operation. The Star Chamber

[1] P. 2 of Foreword.
[2] P. 6 of Foreword.
[3] From Laud's Diary, quoted in W. Prynne, *Breviate of the Life of Laud*, p. 21.
[4] *Commons Journals*, ii. 101.

could convict John Traske, in 1618, for judaical practices;[1] it might logically be expected to arraign Theophilus Brabourne in 1634 and Mary Chester in 1635, who were accused of similar offences. Yet these cases went before the High Commission.[2] In return for the help of the Star Chamber in trying riot committed within the sacred precincts of a church,[3] the ecclesiastical body might relieve the secular court of some of its trials for offences against the committee for licensing books.[4] Prynne and Leighton were both in the first instances before the High Commission; while it was often the custom of the Star Chamber to hand over clerics to the Commissioners so that they might be degraded prior to the execution of sentence.

And so the scene shifts again to the Parliament of 1641. One by one the great men of the Court vanished, if not by order of the Parliament, then through fear. One by one they disappeared, Windebank and Finch abroad, Laud into prison. Neile was already dead. Juxon, the mild Juxon, was left in peace. The Court simply fades away. The State Papers are almost empty of documents relating to it during the early months of the Long Parliament. Reports are absent, and the total of fines drops from close on two thousand pounds in 1640 to under one thousand pounds in 1641.[5]

During this time also, the Commons were considering the petitions of the 'martyrs'. Bastwicke was pardoned on 25 February, Burton on 24 March. But the cases of Prynne, Leighton and Lilburne were all under review while the Committee was considering the Bill for regulating the Court. Lilburne, the last of them, received his pardon on

[1] Cf. Historical Manuscripts Commission, *Calendar of MSS. of Marquess of Bath*, ii. p. 67.

[2] *Cal. S.P. Dom.*, *1634–5*, p. 126; *1635–6*, p. 32.

[3] The most outstanding example is the Attorney-General *v.* Henry Sherfield in February 1632 (o.s.) for riotous breaking of a stained glass window in St. Edmund's Church, Salisbury. He was fined five hundred pounds. This case is of especial interest in that the charge of riot seems to have been only the excuse for bringing Sherfield before the Star Chamber. He was really punished for an offence against the existing ecclesiastical system. *v.* Rushworth, ii. 152 *et seq.*

[4] Cf. *Cal. S.P. Dom.*, *1638–9*, p. 213.

[5] F. C. Dietz, *Receipts . . . of the Exchequer*. Smith College Studies in History, xiii. no. 4, p. 213.

4 May.[1] Fresh from the examination of these causes, the Commons must have been very ready to administer the *coup de grâce* to the Star Chamber.

But the Lords were not so ready. In spite of Clarendon's assurance that the Bill passed easily,[2] contemporary evidence goes to show that the Peers wanted to retain the Court 'with a limitation'.[3] Indeed there were no fewer than three conferences between Lords and Commons on the subject.[4] The Lords quibbled on small points of terminology as if to gain time. Their attitude is extraordinary in view of Lord Andover's speech in the Upper House which Rushworth quotes.[5] Andover's chief objection to the Court was that it was too dangerous to those in high places. Perhaps he was thinking of the information laid by the Attorney-General in 1635 against the Earl of Clare, Viscount Newark and many other men of standing, for residing in London contrary to the Proclamation against such an action.[6] But Andover was presumably the son of the Earl of Berkshire,[7] therefore a young man of twenty-five. It is easier, therefore, to picture him as one of a youthful minority than as representative of the feeling of the Upper House.

But the obstructionist policy of the Lords was of no avail. The Bill passed the Upper House on 2 July[8] in almost as strange circumstances as those in which it had already passed the Commons. In the various reports which are at our disposal, there is no mention of its having been passed, and, had we not the testimony of the Journals, we should be tempted to think that it had been shelved. The Act received the King's reluctant consent on 5 July.[9]

The sudden reaction against the Star Chamber may be considered a

[1] *Commons Journals*, ii. 92, 112, 124, 134.

[2] *Op. cit.*, i. 375.

[3] *Diurnall occurrences in Parliament* . . . p. 165 (28 June 1641), and also in Add. MS. 36829, f. 38 (1 July 1641).

[4] *Commons Journals*, ii. 189, 194.

[5] Rushworth, iv. 298.   [6] *Ibid.*, ii. 288 *et seq.*

[7] The Earl of Berkshire's eldest son was called by his father's second title, Viscount Andover. But he was summoned to Parliament, during his father's lifetime, as Lord Howard of Charlton. G.E.C. *Complete Peerage*, ii. 151. No doubt he continued to be known as Lord Andover.

[8] *Lords Journals*, iv. 298.   [9] *Ibid.*, *idem*, p. 299.

phase of the general movement against the episcopacy. Individuals might object to the sentences which they incurred in the Court; lawyers might inveigh against its omnipotence; but the power to punish can be limited, and competence may be restricted. The complete abolition of the Court argues a deeper enmity, a hatred which finds expression in the popular manifestations against the savage excesses with which ecclesiastical authority was wielded in temporal affairs. It is not far from the truth to say that the Star Chamber perished in a burst of fanatical frenzy.

For the Court was really serving a purpose. D'Ewes, in his reply to Coventry in the House on 31 May, had been careful to add to his comment that they had really destroyed only a branch of the Council table, which itself would still remain.[1] Hacket seems quite surprised at its fate. 'I am not so bold with Providence, to determine why God caused or permitted this great Court to be shut up like an unclean place; or why Divine judgment was so severe against their persons especially that inflamed the censure against our Bishop . . .'[2] He adds 'a Pot that boils over may be taken from the fire and set on again . . .' a beautifully expressed sentiment which Clarendon re-echoes: 'the taking it away was an act very popular; which, it may be, was not then more politic, then the reviving it may be thought hereafter, when the present distempers shall be expired'.[3]

It is Sir Philip Warwick who tells us a delightful story, for which we have only his authority. The absence of the Court, it appears, prompted Judge Hales 'to say quite openly at an Assize at Cambridge (as a Gentleman of great quality, who was then on the Bench, assured me), that he believed since the pulling down of that Court, there had bin in few years more perjuries and frauds unpunished, than there had bin in an hundred years before'.[4]

The Star Chamber did not pass unmourned.

Henry E. I. Phillips

[1] D'Ewes's Diary, Harl. MS. 163, f. 635.
[2] J. Hacket, *Scrinia Reserata*, ii. 120.   [3] *Op. cit.*, i. 375.
[4] Sir Philip Warwick, *Memoirs of the Reign of King Charles*, 1702, p. 175.

6 The Raising of the Ironsides

The term 'Ironsides' was a nickname, originally conferred upon Cromwell by Prince Rupert, which was afterwards applied to the regiment as well as to the man who commanded it. Popular usage has come to employ it as a designation for Cromwell's troopers rather than for Cromwell himself, and in its popular sense it is employed in the title of this paper.[1] In this paper, therefore, I shall attempt to trace the history of Cromwell's regiment of horse from its origin in 1643 to its incorporation in the New Model in 1645, and to show how it was raised, equipped and organised, and by whom it was commanded.

The nucleus of Cromwell's regiment was the troop of horse which he raised at the beginning of the Civil War. In the list of the army under the Earl of Essex in 1642 there are seventy-five troops of horse, and the 67th troop is that of Oliver Cromwell. It must not be supposed that the troops enumerated in this list were raised entirely at the expense of the persons commanding them, though no doubt some few of them were. Cromwell was not rich, and, like other leading Parliamentarians, he had subscribed liberally to the loan for raising Essex's army. He contributed £500 for that purpose, which was probably not much less than

---

[1] 'Lieutenant General Cromwell, alias Ironside, for that title was given him by Prince Rupert after his defeat neere York' (*Mercurius Civicus*, 19–26 September 1644).

'News being brought them, as a countryman told the General next day, that Ironsides was comming to joyne with the Parliament's Army' (*A more exact and perfect relation of the great victory in Naseby Field*, 1645). Heath, in his *Flagellum*, 1663, speaks of Cromwell at Marston Moor as 'gaining here the title of Ironsides from the impenetrable strength of his troops, which could by no means be broken or divided' (p. 29). Lilly, in his *Autobiography*, written about 1667, says of the same battle: 'The honour of that day's fight was given to Manchester, Sir Thomas Fairfax's brigade of horse, and Oliver Cromwell's ironsides; for Cromwell's horse in those times usually wore headpieces, back and breastplates of iron' (p. 144, edn. 1774). The last passage, is, I believe, the first instance in which it is directly applied to Cromwell's soldiers. For a discussion of the term, see also W. G. Ross, *Oliver Cromwell and his Ironsides* (1889), p. 19.

a year's income.[1] From the fund obtained by these subscriptions and from loans procured in London the Parliament defrayed the cost of equipping its troops. A captain who was given a commission to raise a troop of horse received a certain sum from the Treasury to enable him to mount and arm his troopers and his subordinate officers. This sum was called 'mounting money', and Cromwell's name appears in a list of eighty captains who were each of them paid the sum of £1,104 for this purpose.[2]

Cromwell's officers consisted of Lieutenant Cuthbert Baildon, Cornet Joseph Waterhouse and Quartermaster John Desborough, and his men were probably volunteers enlisted in Huntingdonshire and Cambridge.[3] The business of raising the troop was completed in August 1642, and in September it was ready to take the field. The first notice of it to be found in the accounts is a payment, dated 7 September 1642 for a month's pay due to Captain Oliver Cromwell's troop of sixty men, mustered on 29 August, and the receipt is signed by John Desborough.[4] A week later, on 13 September 1642, 'the Committee

---

[1] Cf. T. Carlyle, *Oliver Cromwell's letters and speeches*. Letter XVII. 'The business of Ireland and England,' writes Cromwell, 'hath had of me in money between 1,100 and 1,200 pounds.' Cromwell promised £500 for raising an army, 5 June 1642 (J. L. Sanford, *Studies and Illustrations of the Great Rebellion* (London, 1858), p. 491). For the reduction of Ireland he subscribed another £500 (Rushworth, v. 564).

[2] *Exchequer Papers*.

[3] A pamphlet published in 1652 contains a passage which doubtless refers to Cromwell's exhortations when he was collecting his volunteers. 'Hear, my Lord Oliver Cromwell,' says the author, 'I claim protection from you by virtue of the path you have sworn unto the people, and confirmed by many reiterations, vows and protestations, as that protest at Huntington in the Market House, myself there present, and these words I challenge you to make good which you declared, the words are these: you sought not ours but us and our welfare, and to stand with us for the liberty of the gospel and the laws of the land' (*Theauro John his Disputive Challenge to the Universities of Oxford and Cambridge*, March 165½, p. 6. On Cromwell's doings at Cambridge, see A. Kingston, *East Anglia and the Great Civil War* (London, 1897), pp. 50, 56, 57, 68, and R. Tangye, *The Two Protectors: Oliver and Richard Cromwell* (London, 1899), p. 59.

[4] *Exchequer Papers*. Desborough was paid £210, a month's pay for sixty troopers, but nothing for the officers.

appointed to settle the affairs of the kingdom' ordered that Captain Cromwell and two other officers named 'should forthwith muster their troops of horse, and make themselves ready to go to his Excellency the Earl of Essex', who had set out three days before for the head-quarters of his army at Northampton.[1] Cromwell accordingly joined Essex, and his troop was put into the Lord General's own regiment of horse, under the command of Sir Philip Stapleton. Under Stapleton's command Cromwell and his troop fought at Edgehill, though there is some evidence that Cromwell was not on the field at the time when the battle begun, but arrived later.[2]

After Edgehill Essex retreated to Warwick, but about the beginning

[1] Sanford, *Studies and Illustrations*, p. 519.

[2] Nathaniel Fiennes, in his account of the battle of Edgehill, says at the end: 'These persons underwritten were of the right wing, and never stirred from their troops, but they and their troops fought till the last minute.' Then follows a list of the regiments of the Lord General and Sir William Balfour, and in the list of the general's regiment which was commanded by Sir Philip Stapleton occurs the name of Captain Cromwell. On the other hand, in a letter to Lord Say, which serves as a preface to the same pamphlet, Nathaniel Fiennes gives a long account of the doings of his brother John, who, having been detached to Evesham a couple of days before the battle, did not arrive at Keynton till between three and four o'clock on the afternoon of the day when the battle was fought. There he met the flying cavalry of the Parliamentary left, and did his best to persuade some of them to stand. In time he 'gathered a pretty body upon a hill together, and with them (there being Captain Keightlye's and Captain Cromwell's troope at length came to them also) he marched towards the town.' Finally, says Fiennes, his brother joined Hampden's brigade, and they came to the army together. This statement is obviously very difficult to recon-cile with the other statement about Cromwell and his troop which the same pamphlet contains. The only solution seems to be that Cromwell and his men, though not on the field when the battle began, yet came up in time to take part in the final struggle with the Royalists.

His absence at the beginning of the battle would to some extent explain the Royalist stories to the effect that he took no part in it at all. Holles, for instance, writing in 1647, accuses Cromwell of 'base keeping out of the field at Keinton Battle; where he with his troop of horse came not in, impudently and ridicu-lously affirming, the day after, that he had been all that day seeking the army and place of fight, though his quarters were but at a village near hand, whence he could not find his way, nor be directed by his ear, when the ordnance was heard, as I have been credibly informed, 20 or 30 miles off' (*Memoirs*, p. 17).

of November his army was quartered about London. The next notice of Cromwell's troop is a warrant from Essex, dated 17 December 1642, for a fortnight's pay to Captain Cromwell's troop. In it Cromwell is described as captain 'of a troop of 80 harquebusiers'.[1] The meaning and use of the term harquebusiers are explained in a later part of this paper; at present it is enough to say that harquebusiers were a class of cavalry less heavily armed than cuirassiers. The fact that Cromwell's troop of sixty had now become a troop of eighty is also worth noting, though it is not easy to explain.[2]

[1] 'Theis are to will and require you forthwith out of the Treasure remayning in yo hands to paie unto Captaine Oliver Cromwell Captaine off a Troope of Eightie harquebuziers for one halfe monthes paie of the saide Troope commencing from the tenth daie of this instant December inclusive, the some of Two hundred and four Pounds and thirteen shillinges, and for soe doing this shal be yo\u02b3 Warrant.

'Dated this XVII\u1d57\u02b0 daie of December 1642.

'ESSEX.

  'To Sir Gilbert Gerrard, Baron\u1d57.
   'Trear. of the Army or his Deputie.
      'RO: CHAMBERS.'

Chambers was the secretary of the Earl of Essex, and the sum mentioned represented the pay of the officers of Cromwell's troop as well as the men. A letter from Cromwell to Captain Vernon, one of the paymasters of the army, follows:

'Capt. Vernon: I desire you to pay this bearer George Barton my servant the monie accordinge to this warrant from his Excellency due to mee and my troupe, and I shall rest your lovinge freind,

'OLIVER CROMWELL.

  'Dec. 17, 1642.'
[On back]. 'To Captayne Vernon—present theise.'
NOTE.—The Warrant No. 1 has at foot the following receipt:—

'Rec\u1d48 this 19\u1d57\u02b0 December 1642 by' ['virtue' or 'force,' a little indistinct] 'of this Warr\u1d57 Two hundred and four Pounds XIII shillings £204 13.

      'GEORGE + BARTON (Mark).
        'By order of Capt. Cromwell.'
    Notes and Queries, second series, xii. 285.

[2] In the spring of 1644 the normal size of the troop in 'the army under Essex' was fixed at eighty. It is possible that the change may have begun at the end of 1642, or it may be that some weak troop of horse (of which there were many

Less than a month later Cromwell left the army under Essex to return to the eastern counties. At the close of 1642 the need of united action for defensive purposes led to the formation of little local leagues among the counties supporting the Parliament. On 22 December 1642 the counties of Norfolk, Suffolk, Essex and Cambridge established what was known as the Eastern Association. On 16 January 1643 eight midland counties, including Huntingdonshire, formed a similar association, but, unlike the former, it soon broke up.

Cromwell, as member for Cambridge, was appointed one of the committee for that county, and being a person of influence in Huntingdonshire, was one of its committee also. In both capacities, therefore, he was wanted in the eastern counties, and obtained leave from Essex to repair thither, and to take his troop with him, as soon as the first campaign was over. There Cromwell hoped to carry out the scheme which he had discussed with Hampden — to raise men that 'had a spirit that would do something in the work', a spirit that was likely to go on as far as gentlemen would go — such men as had the fear of God before them and made some conscience of what they did.[1] With this object before

---

under Essex) had been reduced into Cromwell's after Edgehill. Possibly fresh recruits from the eastern counties may have swollen the numbers of Cromwell's troop.

[1] 'I had a very worthy friend then; and he was a very noble person, and I know his memory is very grateful to all — Mr. John Hampden. At my first going out into this engagement I saw our men were beaten at every hand. I did indeed; and desired him that he would make some additions to my Lord Essex's army, of some new regiments; and told him I would be serviceable to him in bringing in such men as I thought had a spirit that would do something in the work . . . Your troops, said I, are most of them old decayed serving men, and tapsters, and such kind of fellows. Their troops are gentlemen's sons, younger sons and persons of quality: do you think the spirits of such base and mean fellows will ever be able to encounter gentlemen, that have honour and courage and resolution in them? . . . You must get men of a spirit. . . . that is likely to go on as far as gentlemen will do, or else you will be beaten still. . . . He was a wise and worthy person; and he did think that I talked a good notion but an impracticable one. Truly I told him I could do somewhat in it. I did so. . . . I raised such men as had the fear of God before them, as made some conscience of what they did, and from that day forward . . . they were never beaten.' (Carlyle's *Cromwell*, Speech xi.) Cf. Gardiner, i. 40.

him he set out from London about the beginning of January 1643. On his way down, about 14 January, he seized the Royalist high sheriff of Hertfordshire, as he was proclaiming the King's Commission of Array at St. Albans, and sent him up to London to answer for his conduct to Parliament.[1] On 23 January or thereabouts, he was at Huntingdon,[2] and three or four days later at Cambridge.[3] Cromwell brought his commission to raise a regiment in his pocket. He is described as colonel in the proceedings of the Norfolk Committee on 26 January 1643,[4] and in a letter written by Lord Grey on 6 February, though it is not till March that he is mentioned as a colonel in the newspapers. His commission was probably not derived from Essex but from Lord Grey. William Lord Grey of Wark had been chosen Commander-in-Chief of all the forces to be raised in the Eastern Association, with the rank of major-general, and Essex had been desired to grant him a commission empowering him to appoint colonels, captains and other officers. It was from Lord Grey, therefore, that Cromwell's commission as colonel was probably derived.[5]

---

[1] *Kingdom's Weekly Intelligence*, 10–17 January. Cf. A. Kingston, *Hertfordshire during the Great Civil War* (London, 1894), p. 31.

[2] See Letter iv. in Caryle's *Collection*, from Cromwell to his neighbour Barnard. The place is added by Carlyle, but there is little doubt it is correct.

[3] See Carlyle's *Cromwell*, Appendix iv, two letters signed by Cromwell about 27 January from Cambridge.

[4] *Tanner MSS.*, lxiv. 125.

[5] 'Gentlemen, — Having been requested by divers of the Deputy Lieutenants of the Associated Counties, members of the House of Commons and others, to be present this day at their committee, the cheife matter in debate was the subject of a letter verie lately received from Collonel Cromwell concerning some present supply of forces, but, because none of the County of Hertford were present, and they not knowing what propositions would be made at your meeting or what proceedings other counties have made upon the order of the Association, have with my advice thought fit to desire Sir William Rowe and Sir Thomas Honywood to give you a meeting on the behalfe of the Essex Committee, to the end they may give you an account how far that businesse is advanced in Essex, and to receyve your resolutions therein, as you shall be pleased to offer them, and upon hearing (at their returne) what shall be propounded in any particular, we shall speedilie fall to a positive, conceyveing that

As soon as he was established at Cambridge, Cromwell set to work to convert his troop into a regiment. The principle upon which he selected his officers and enlisted his men was that set forth in his conversation with Hampden. He had already put it into practice in the formation of his original troop.

At his first entrance into the wars [writes Baxter] being but a captain of horse he had special care to get religious men into his troop. These men were of greater understanding than common soldiers, and therefore more apprehensive of the importance and consequence of war; and making not money but that which they took for the public felicity to be their end, they were the more engaged to be valiant; for he that maketh money his end doth esteem his life above his pay, and therefore is like enough to save it, when danger comes, if possibly he can: but he that taketh the felicity of Church and State to be his end, esteemeth it above his life, and therefore will the sooner lay down his life for it. And men of parts and understanding know how to manage their business, and know that flying is the surest way to death, and that standing to it is the likeliest way to escape; there being many usually that fall in flight for one that falls in valiant fight. These things 'tis probable Cromwell understood; and that none would be such engaged valiant men as the religious. But yet I conjecture, that at his first choosing such men into his troop, it was the very esteem and love of religious men that principally moved him; and the avoiding of those disorders, mutinies, plunderings, and grievances of the country, which deboist men in armies are commonly guilty of. By this means he indeed sped better than he

---

the secureing of those passages mentioned by Collonel Cromwell and others, is of greate importance for the safetie of these five counties.

'His Majesty hath this day sent up propositions which fills both houses with businesse that denyes the absence of any member, otherwise divers gentlemen of the House of Commons would willinglie have attended this service, whose absence there from I know you will excuse, thus recommending the successe of your good intentions and endeavours to supreme blessing I rest

'Your verie affectionate friend,

'GREY of WARK.

'London, the 6th of Feb. 1642.

'To my worthy friends the Deputye Lieutenants of the Associated Countyes of Northfolke, Suffolke, Cambridge, and Hartford,' — *Tanner MSS.*, lxiv. 157.

expected. Aires, Desborough, Berry, Evanson and the rest of that troop did prove so valiant, that as far as I could learn they never once ran away before an enemy.[1]

Whitelocke briefly confirms Baxter's statement, describing the regiment as 'most of them freeholders and freeholders' sons, and who upon matter of conscience engaged in this quarrel and under Cromwell. And thus being well armed within, by the satisfaction of their consciences, and without by good iron arms, they would as one man stand firmly and charge desperately'.[2] Cromwell's opponents among his own party complained bitterly of the method in which he selected his officers.

> Col. Cromwell raysing of his regiment [wrote one of them in 1645] makes choyce of his officers, not such as weare souldiers or men of estate, but such as were common men, pore and of mean parentage, onely he would give them the title of godly pretious men. . . . I have heard him oftentimes say that it must not be souldiers nor Scots that must doe this worke, but it must be the godly to this purpose. . . . If you looke upon his own regiment of horse see what a swarme there is of thos that call themselves the godly; some of them profess they have sene visions and had revelations.[3]

But in spite of the fact that Cromwell's officers were most of them men of no great local position, and that his men were selected with far more care than was usual, the development of his troop into a regiment

---

[1] *Reliquiæ Baxterianæ*, p. 98.

[2] Whitelocke's *Memorials*, i. 209, edn. 1853. A contemporary biographer gives the following fantastic account of the method in which Cromwell picked out his soldiers. It is a good example of the stories which grew up: 'In listing, he picked out such only as he judged to be stout and resolute. But lest he might have been mistaken in his choice, as soon as he had filled up his troop he used this stratagem to try them, upon the first muster of them, he privily placed twelve resolute men in ambuscado (it being near some of the King's garrisons) who upon a signal or at a time appointed, with a trumpet sounding a charge, galloped furiously to the body, out of which some twenty instantly fled for fear and dismay; from these he took their horses, and got them mounted with others more courageous.'—Henry Fletcher, *The Perfect Politician*, 1660, p. 3.

[3] *Manchester's Quarrel with Cromwell*, p. 72.

was astonishingly rapid. In March 1643, when Cromwell suppressed the intended Royalist rising at Lowestoft, he had with him, according to a contemporary letter, 'his five troops'.[1] In September, when Lincolnshire was added to the Eastern Association, the ordinance authorising the addition states that 'Colonel Cromwell hath ten troops of horse already armed, which were heretofore raised in the said Associated Counties'.[2] Baxter states that Cromwell's regiment became in the end 'a double regiment of fourteen full troops, and all these as full of religious men as he could get'.[3] Baxter's statement has been called in question, on the ground that six troops was the usual number in a regiment,[4] but the fact that Cromwell's regiment did actually contain fourteen troops is proved by the existence of a pay roll for Manchester's army showing the sums paid by his treasurer, Gregory Gawsell, to different troops and companies between 29 April 1644 and 1 March 1645.[5] Taking this list as a basis it is possible to show who the commanders of these fourteen troops were and when they were raised.

THE FOURTEEN TROOPS AND THEIR OFFICERS

The existence of the fourteen troops is proved, as has been stated, by the accounts of the paymaster of Manchester's army, and by the explicit statement of Richard Baxter. The names of the officers themselves can be collected from the accounts, from Cromwell's letters, and from the newspapers and correspondence of the period. The lives of all the more important officers can be traced from the time when they joined the regiment to the Restoration, and even in some cases later.

1. Cromwell's own troop claims the first place. Lieutenant Cuthbert Baildon and Cornet Joseph Waterhouse, the two officers named in the list of the army under Essex as belonging to Cromwell's troops, are not heard of again in connection with the regiment. The command of the

---

[1] Letter of John Cory to Sir John Potts, 17 March 1643, printed in Carlyle's *Cromwell*.

[2] Husband's *Ordinances*, etc., ii. 331, 20 September 1643.

[3] *Reliquiæ Baxterianæ*, p. 98.

[4] W. G. Ross, *Oliver Cromwell and his Ironsides*, p. 29.

[5] *Exchequer MSS.*

colonel's troop or company in any regiment was during the civil war practically vested in his lieutenant, who bore the title of captain-lieutenant. Cromwell's captain-lieutenant in 1643 was James Berry, who had been before the war (according to Richard Baxter), a clerk in some ironworks in Shropshire. At the battle of Gainsborough in July 1643, Berry slew Charles Cavendish, the Royalist general, 'with a thrust under his short ribs', as Cromwell's despatch relates (Carlyle, Letter XI). And in August 1644 he became captain of a vacant troop in the regiment. Berry was succeeded as captain-lieutenant by John Glad-man, who held that rank in 1645, when the regiment was incorporated in the New Model.[1] Berry passed into another regiment as major in 1647, and became colonel in 1651. His subsequent career is traced in the *Dictionary of National Biography*.

2. The second troop in the regiment was that of Edward Whalley, Cromwell's cousin. He is styled captain in the ordinance of 25 April 1643, empowering Cromwell to seize the horses and plate of malignants. In Cromwell's despatch on the battle of Gainsborough, Cromwell describes Whalley as his major, and in narrating the retreat after the battle he says 'Major Whalley did in this carry himself with all gallantry becoming a gentleman and a Christian' (Carlyle, Letter XII). In 1644 Whalley became lieutenant-colonel of the regiment. Cavalry regiments in general at this period did not possess lieutenant-colonels, which was a rank confined to infantry regiments.[2] In the New Model no cavalry regiment had a lieutenant-colonel, but Cromwell's regiment, with the fourteen troops it finally numbered, was so large that an additional field officer doubtless seemed necessary, and for that reason Whalley was made its lieutenant-colonel. There was another regiment

---

[1] Berry is first mentioned as a captain in the accounts under August 1644, and Gladman as captain-lieutenant in September 1644. Cromwell's cornet in September 1644 was — Gething or Gethings.

In Cromwell's troop one of the corporals was a certain Peter Wallis, who was ordered on 2 March 1643-4, to be paid £30 for discharging the quarters of the troop. He subsequently became major of Henry Cromwell's regiment of horse in Ireland.

[2] Whalley is described as lieutenant-colonel on 25 July 1644, and earlier. He became colonel on the formation of the New Model, and his life is contained in the *Dictionary of National Biography*.

also in the army of the Eastern Association — viz. Manchester's own regiment of horse — which contained in 1644 no less than eleven troops, and in consequence it also had a lieutenant-colonel, in the person of Nathaniel Rich.

3. The third troop to be formed was pretty certainly that commanded by John Desborough.[1] Desborough, the husband of Cromwell's sister Jane, began the campaign of 1644 as quartermaster to his brother-in-law's troop. His commission as captain dates from April 1643 or earlier. A warrant for the pay of a trooper named Lewis Browne of Cambridge states that he entered the troop of Captain John Desborough on 12 April 1643, and Desborough is mentioned as a captain in the sequestration ordinance of 25 April 1643. When Whalley was promoted to be lieutenant-colonel of the regiment Desborough became its major, and held that rank when it was incorporated in the New Model in 1645.[2] He became a colonel in 1649, and lieutenant-general in 1659. An account of his life is contained in the *Dictionary of National Biography*.

4. The fourth troop was that commanded by Cromwell's son, young Oliver. Baptised on 6 February 1623, he was now just over twenty years old, and had entered Essex's army in 1642 as cornet to Lord St. John's troop of horse. A curious letter from him to the Steward of Norwich, dated 15 August 1643, about some deserters from his troop, is printed in *Notes and Queries*.[3]

[1] The proper spelling of his name is apparently Disbrowe, but the form given above is that generally used and that by which he is known to fame.

[2] He is described as major in Gawsell's account of pay due to Manchester's army from 29 April 1644 to 1 March 1645.

[3] 'Worthie Sir, — I am sorry that I should have an occasion to write to Norwich concerning those which say they came from that noble Cittie, which hath furnished our armies (I can speak by experience) with Godly men, but indeed I suppose them rather spurious offspring of some ignoble place. Sir, thus it is that among many honest men some knaves have been admitted into my troope, which coming with expectation of some base ends, being frustrated of them and finding that this cause did not nourish their expectations, have to the dishonor of God, my discredit, and their own infamie, disserted the cause and me their Captayne, therefore Sir, looke upon them as dishonorers of God's cause, and high displeasers of my father, my selfe, and the whole regiment, in breife I would desire you to make them severe examples by takeing and returning the armes and horses of all that have not a Tickett under my hand and to

According to the author of the 'Squire Papers,' young Cromwell was killed at a skirmish near Knaresborough just before the battle of Marston Moor, but it is now ascertained that he died of smallpox in his quarters at Newport Pagnell about March 1644. 'A civil young gentleman, and the joy of his father,' says the newspaper which relates his death.[1]

On his death the command of the troop went to Captain John Browne, who still held it at the formation of the New Model.[2] Browne became major in 1649, left the army after the battle of Worcester, re-entered it in 1658, and played a small part in bringing about the restoration of Charles II.

5. Like its four predecessors, the fifth troop was commanded by one of Cromwell's relatives. Its captain was young Valentine Walton, son of Cromwell's sister Margaret and of Colonel Valentine Walton, the Governor of Lynn.[3] This was the young officer whose death at Marston Moor Cromwell relates in Letter XXI in Carlyle's collection. 'A gallant young man, exceeding gracious,' writes his colonel, and 'exceedingly beloved in the army of all that knew him', who died

---

clapp them upp into prison and inflicting of such punishment as you shall think fitt, especially I desire you would deale severely with one Robert Waffe and Symon Scafe. Pray Sir cause to returne speedily all that had libertie from me to go to their freinds. And likewise, I desire you would secure a good horse from some of your malignants to mount one of my souldiers John Manyng now at Norwich, who was lately taken prisoner by the Enemy, and by that means destitute and pray doe me the favour to mount such men as this bearer Richard Waddelow my Clerke shall procure and so I rest

'Yours to command

'OLIVER CROMWELL.

'From my quarters at Peterborough 15th of August 1643.

'To the right worp[ll] and worthie freind Samuell Smythe Esq[re] Steward of the Citty for Norwich these.'

[1] *The Parliament Scout*, 15–22 March 1644; cf. Gardiner, *Great Civil War*, i. 314.

[2] The troop is mentioned as Captain Cromwell's in the account for January 1644, and as Cromwell's and Browne's in the account for the period for March 1644 to April 1645. Browne's cornet in January 1645 was Alexander Akehurst.

[3] Walton became Governor of Lynn in September 1643. When his son's troop was raised he was a prisoner at Oxford, having been captured at Edgehill.

lamenting that God had not suffered him to be any more 'the executioner of his enemies', and bidding his men 'open to the right and left that he might see the rogues run'.

Walton's troop passed to William Packer, formerly, I believe, its lieutenant,[1] who continued with the regiment after its incorporation in the New Model, becoming a major about 1652, and colonel in 1659. His life is given in the *Dictionary of National Biography*.

6. The sixth troop was that of Captain Ayers, or Ayres. Who Captain Ayres was it is difficult to say. He may perhaps be identical with a certain William Eyres, a friend of Harry Marten's, and a leading spirit among the Levellers.[2] At all events, whoever he was he left the regiment about June 1644, and his troop was given to James Berry, who has been already mentioned as the captain-lieutenant of Cromwell's own troop.[3] Berry kept the command of the troop until 1647, when he became major of Colonel Twisleton's regiment, and obtained the command of a regiment himself in 1651. Subsequently he became one of Cromwell's major-generals, and his life is to be found in the *Dictionary of National Biography*.

7. The seventh troop was Captain Patterson's. It was raised before the end of 1643, as a bill for its quarters during January 1644 proves.[4]

---

[1] Gawsell's account for 1644–5 proves that Walton's troop went to Packer. William Pickering was the cornet of the troop in 1644. Walton's troop is mentioned in the accounts for January 1644.

[2] Colonel Eyres was arrested in November 1647 for inciting the soldiers to mutiny at the rendezvous at Corkbush Field. Rushworth, vii. 875. He was imprisoned again in 1649 for complicity in the mutiny which was suppressed at Burford. *The Moderate*, 7–14 August 1649. In January 1655 he was a third time under arrest as an accomplice in Wildman's plot. Thurloe, iii. 124, 126, 146. In January 1660 the restored Long Parliament gave him command of the regiment, late Major-General Lambert's. *Commons Journals*, vii. 815, 817, 818, 828. See also *Clarke Papers*, ii. 57.

[3] On 12 August 1644, William Newman was paid £12 as lieutenant of the troop formerly commanded by Captain Ayres, but now by Captain Berry. On Newman see *Clarke Papers*, ii. 276; *Scotland and the Protectorate*, p. 249; *Somers Tracts*, vii. 532, ed. Scott.

[4] On 14 October 1643, Lieutenant Russell was paid £14 16s. for the completing of forty horses and saddles for Captain Patterson's troop. This was evidently the balance of an account of which the rest had been paid earlier, so

Captain Robert Patterson[1] left the regiment about the spring of 1644, and was succeeded in command of the troop by Captain Robert Horsman.[2] Horsman had been governor of the garrison established at Rockingham Castle, but, quarrelling violently with the Rutlandshire Committee, and being complained of by them to Parliament, he resigned or was forced to resign.[3] His troop is mentioned as quartered in Huntingdonshire in April 1644. Horsman left the regiment when it was incorporated in the New Model.

8. The eighth troop was that of Captain John Grove. It is mentioned in the accounts for January 1644, and throughout the year. John Grove continued to command it until the regiment was incorporated in the New Model. He became major of Colonel Francis Hacker's regiment about 1652, and continued in the army until the Restoration. Grove was an exile on the Continent in 1666.[4]

9. The ninth troop was Captain Samuel Porter's. It was raised in 1643, during the summer or early in the autumn.[5] Captain Porter continued with the regiment up to the time of its incorporation in the New Model, and then seems to have left the army. In 1650 he took service again, and was a captain in Ireton's regiment of horse in Ireland.

10. The tenth troop was that of Captain Adam Lawrence, and was

---

that the troop must have been raised in the summer, or at latest the autumn of 1643.

[1] In the bill for quartering Patterson's troop at Ripton Abbotts in January 1644, he signs 'Ro. Patterson', and on April 1644 Robert Gethings was paid as cornet to Captain Robert Patterson's troop. There was also a Captain William Patterson of Norfolk in the army of the Eastern Association, commanding a troop of horse. It was doubtless this Captain William Patterson who is mentioned as an opponent of Cromwell's. — *Manchester's Quarrel with Cromwell*, p. 60.

[2] Horsman's lieutenant in 1644 was Francis Lambe.

[3] See *Tanner MSS.*, lxii. 610.

[4] *Memoirs of Edmund Ludlow*, ed. Firth (2 vols., Oxford, 1894), ii. 393, 490.

[5] An account of monies collected and paid by the constables of the Isle of Ely contains, under 19 September 1643, a payment of £10 to Capt. Sam. Porter, captain in the regiment of Col. Cromwell, towards one month's pay for his troop.

raised by the autumn of 1643.¹ Lawrence was a friend of Richard Baxter's, and when Baxter became chaplain to Whalley's regiment, in the summer of 1645, he found Lawrence the only orthodox officer in the regiment.² Lawrence commanded the troop when the regiment was incorporated in the New Model, and was killed at the siege of Colchester in 1648.³

The cornet of this troop in August 1644 was Edmund Rolfe — once Cromwell's servant — an officer who became notorious in 1648 because he was accused of a plot to kill Charles I during the King's captivity at Carisbrook.⁴

11. The eleventh troop, Captain Swallow's, is one of special interest. Letter XIII in Carlyle's *Cromwell*, dated 2 August 1643, is a letter from Cromwell addressed to a gentleman at a place not named, where the young men and maids had raised £240 to equip a company of foot. Let them turn their proposed foot company, says Cromwell, into a troop of horse, 'which indeed will by God's blessing far more advantage the cause than two or three companies of foot'. It was true that £240 was not enough to buy pistols and saddles for a troop of horse, but he himself would provide horses to mount the men if they provided arms. 'Pray raise honest godly men,' he concludes, 'and I will have them of my regiment. As for your officers, I leave it as God shall or hath directed to choose.'⁵

Norwich, as the comments of a Royalist newspaper show, was the town in question, and its young men and maidens did as Cromwell

---

¹ This is proved *inter alia* by a bill for quartering his troop at Cambridge during the winter. 'Due to the tapster at the Red Lyon for Capt. Lawrence's troopers, as followeth, from October 13 till February 12, 1643, 5l. 8s.2d.' The signature of 'Adam Lawrence' is appended. See also Tangye, *Two Protectors*, p. 101.

² *Reliquiæ Baxterianæ.*

³ *Report on the Duke of Portland's MSS.*, i. 459.

⁴ 'November 30, 1643, paid to Edmund Rolph, Colonell Cromwell his man, towards his charges, being sent by his colonell in the state service, 2l.' Rolfe is mentioned as cornet in August 1644. On the accusation brought against him in 1648 see the old *Parliamentary History*, xvii, 243, 259, 268, 274, 401; xviii. 293; xxii. 354, 357.

⁵ In this letter Cromwell evidently calculates the troop of horse as eighty men.

requested.[1] A troop of horse was raised, and Captain Robert Swallow became its commander, with Joseph Sabberton as his lieutenant, two officers who continued to serve in the army right up to the Restoration.[2] In December 1643 the troop was in the field, doing good service in Lincolnshire. A newspaper says 'Captain Swallow, the captain of the Maiden troop raised by the maids of Norwich, hath lately done some service, and surprised some of the enemies horse which were formerly of the garrison at Gainsborough.'[3]

In 1644, or earlier, the men being men of the kind Cromwell had desired, the troop was incorporated in Cromwell's regiment, and it is paid as part of it throughout that year. Swallow became a colonel in 1659, succeeding Whalley when the latter was turned out by the restored Long Parliament, on account of his connection with the Cromwell family.

12. The twelfth troop added to the regiment was that of Captain Christopher Bethell.[4] The bills for horses and saddles for the troop which occur in the accounts of the Eastern Association for April 1644, show it was raised during the spring of that year.[5] Bethell and his lieutenant,

---

[1] See *Mercurius Aulicus*, 3 August 1643.

[2] Captain Swallow borrowed £184 17s. for the use of his troops from a relative Richard Swallow. There was also paid on 18 October 1643, by the treasurer of the county of Norfolk. 'To Capt. Ro. Swallow and Mr. Sol. Camby his lieutenant by warrant of the deputy lieutenants at the request of Col. Cromwell.' *Tanner MSS.*, lxvi. 9 G.

[3] 'Occurrences of Certain Special and Remarkable Passages,' 5–12 January 1644. Another paper, 'Certain Information,' for 29 August 1643, says that on 23 August, the 'Virgin Troop', raised by the maids of Norwich, went out upon some design, 'a brave company of about 80 men, honest men and good soldiers, their captain one Master Swallow' (quoted by Mason, *History of Norfolk*, p. 292).

[4] There were two other Bethells in the Parliamentary army, Walter Bethell, a major in Col. Horton's regiment in the New Model, and Col. Hugh Bethell, who served under the Fairfaxes in the army of the Northern Association, and assisted Monck in bringing about the Restoration.

[5] John Pitchford as Bethell's lieutenant, and Thomas Watkinson as his quartermaster, attest bills for the purchase of horses in April 1644. In *Cal. State Papers Dom. 1655*, pp. 284, 332, a petition of Captain Richard Pechell is calendared which states that he served under Bethell in Cromwell's regiment, and was his executor. Pechell was perhaps Bethell's cornet.

John Pitchford, were great favourers of sectaries, and the ranks of this troop, according to Richard Baxter, were filled with Anabaptists and Levellers of the worst kind.[1] Both officers continued with the troop till the regiment was incorporated in the New Model, and also after that event took place. Bethell was mortally wounded at the storming of Bristol in 1645;[2] Pitchford retired about 1648.

13. The thirteenth troop is also a troop with a history. It was raised in the latter part of 1643, apparently in Suffolk. Its commander was Captain Ralph Margery, whose character and doings form the subject of Letters XVI and XVIII in Carlyle's *Cromwell*. In September or thereabouts Cromwell wrote to the Suffolk Committee urging them to haste in raising their quota of cavalry and to care in choosing their commanders. 'I understand,' he says, 'Mr. Margery hath honest men will follow him;[3] if so be pleased to make use of him; it much concerns your good to have conscientious men. . . . I beseech you give countenance to Mr. Margery. Help him in raising his troop; let him not want your favour in whatsoever is needful for promoting this work.'

The defect of Captain Margery was that he was a man of small estate, and of no position in the county — not a gentleman, it seems to have been said. Cromwell had answered this objection by anticipation in his letter to the Committee: 'I had rather have a plain russet-coated captain, that knows what he fights for and loves what he knows, than that which you call a gentleman, and is nothing else.' A week or two later he had to argue the same point again, and did so equally forcibly:

> It may be it provokes some spirits to see such plain men made captains of horse. It had been well that men of honour and birth had entered into these employments, but why do they not appear? Who would have hindered them? But seeing it was necessary the work must go on better plain men than none; but best to have men patient of wants, faithful and conscientious in their employment. And such I hope these will approve themselves to be.[4]

[1] *Reliquiæ Baxterianæ*, p. 53.

[2] *Ibid.*, p. 55; J. Sprigge, *Anglia Rediviva*, pp. 126, 153.

[3] Margery certainly had. In February 1645 his troops contained 112 men, and was the largest in the regiment.

[4] Letter XVI mentions Cornet Boalry as one of Margery's officers.

There were, as we shall see, other complaints against Margery, with respect to the manner in which he proceeded in equipping his troop. The upshot was a general desire in the Suffolk Committee to get rid of him and his troopers, to which Cromwell answered with promptitude: 'If these men be accounted troublesome to the country, I shall be glad you would send them all to me. I'll bid them welcome.' Sent to him they accordingly were, and before the close of 1643, or early in 1644, they were incorporated in his regiment. Margery seems to have given satisfaction as an officer, since he remained in the army till 1653, but he never rose higher than captain.

14. The fourteenth and last troop in the pay list of 1644–5 is that of Major Ireton. This was probably the troop which Ireton had raised in 1642. When the Civil War began, says Mrs. Hutchinson, Henry Ireton, being zealous for the cause of the Parliament, and finding the county of Nottingham generally disaffected to it, gathered a troop of those godly people which the Cavaliers drove out, and joined the army under Essex. At the end of 1642 a Parliamentary Committee was established in Nottinghamshire, and began to raise forces. Essex at their request sent Ireton's troop back to defend their own county, and Ireton became major of the regiment of horse raised for Sir Francis Thornhaugh. In July 1643 the three or four troops of horse forming this regiment were drawn off from Nottingham by Sir John Meldrum to assist in raising the siege of Gainsborough. Ireton, and probably Ireton's troop, did not return to Nottingham. 'Major Ireton,' says Mrs. Hutchinson, 'quite left Colonel Thornhaugh's regiment and began an inseparable league with Colonel Cromwell.'[1] On 28 July 1643 Parliament had appointed Cromwell Governor of the Isle of Ely, and about August he appointed Ireton his deputy, and the latter at once established himself at Ely.[2]

Ireton's troop being part of the garrison of the Isle of Ely, and therefore under Cromwell's command, came naturally to be part of Cromwell's regiment, and served with it in the field throughout 1644.[3] It

---

[1] *Life of Col. Hutchinson*, edn. 1885, i. 168, 199, 232.

[2] *Manchester's Quarrel with Cromwell*, p. 73; cf. Carlyle's *Cromwell*, Letter XXII.

[3] A warrant for the payment of Ireton's troop is among the papers of the Ely Committee:

fought at Marston Moor, and about three weeks after that battle Ireton was appointed quartermaster-general in Manchester's army.[1] He left the regiment at the formation of the New Model, when he was made colonel of a regiment of horse raised in Kent, in place of Sir Michael Livesey.[2]

The next question to be considered is the question of the numerical strength of the troops whose history has been traced and of the regiment as a whole. At the commencement of the civil war, as has been seen, the ordinary strength of the troop in Essex's army was sixty men. Afterwards it was fixed at eighty. In the Eastern Association the

---

'These are to require you forthwith out [of] the treasure in your hands to pay to Sarj.-Maj. Henry Ireton the summe of seventye pounds upon accompt towards the paye of his troope and officers, and also the summe of thirtye pounds to bee by him payd over to Capt. Gervase Lomax upon accompt towards the pay of his foote company and officers: Hereof fayle not at your perill, and this shall bee your warrant.

'Given under my hand this 3rd daye of October 1643.

'OLIVER CROMWELL.

'To Robert Brown, Deputy Treasurer of Ely.'

The letter is endorsed with a receipt showing that the money was paid on 6 October. It is only signed by Cromwell, and apparently was written by Ireton.

[1] In an account of the pay due to himself for his services in Manchester's army Ireton gives the date of his commission as 25 June 1644.

[2] It is a question whether there may not have been another troop attached to the regiment. In the *Calendar of State Papers* for 1654 appears a petition presented on behalf of a Major William Poe to the Protector (p. 421). It recites that by commissions from Cromwell, the Earl of Manchester, and Lord Grey of Wark, William Poe and his brother Anthony served in Cromwell's regiment in the Associated Counties as captain and lieutenant from 21 February 1642-3 to 19 April 1646, and disbursed therein £3,201 14s. 4d., which they pray to be paid. They refer to an order of Parliament of 10 December 1646.

The accounts of the County of Norfolk show that Poe collected £401 in that county during 1643, 'which if it were for the use of his troop the County of Suffolk is to answer that sum out of their treasury' (*Tanner MSS.*, lxii. 348). Poe was ordered to be arrested and his troop disarmed in February 1645 (*Commons Journals*, iv. 64). It is evident that by that time his troop was not part of Cromwell's regiment, whatever it may have been originally. See also on Poe, *8th Rept. Hist. MSS. Comm.*, ii. 62.

strength of the troop originally seems to have been also fixed at eighty. In Cromwell's letter to the young men and maids of Norwich he says, 'employ your twelve score pounds to buy pistols and saddles, and I will provide four score horses'.[1] A year later, on 12 July 1644, it was declared, by an ordinance for raising additional forces in the Eastern Association and elsewhere, that no troop of horse should consist of less than one hundred men.[2] The order was not rigidly observed, but the troop of horse in the army of the Eastern Association frequently rose to one hundred men, inclusive of officers, and the average number of a troop in Cromwell's regiment was over eighty. A muster of eleven troops out of the fourteen taken on 20 February 1645 shows a total of 914 troopers, besides commissioned and non-commissioned officers, so that the whole regiment must have contained over 1,100 troopers.[3]

[1] Carlyle's *Cromwell*, Letter XIII.

[2] Husbands, ii. 526. The strength of the troop of horse in the New Model was fixed at one hundred originally.

[3] The following is a summary of the strength of eleven troops of Cromwell's regiment on 20 February 1644–5, and the sum paid each troop as a fortnight's pay:

Lieut.-Gen.'s own troop, lieut., cornet, 2 corporals, 81 troopers: paid 164*l.* 14*s.* 4*d.*

Capt. Bethell's troop, capt., lieut., cornet, quartermaster, surgeon, 1 trumpet, 1 corporal, 79 troopers: paid 189*l.* 4*s.*

Capt. Lawrence's troop, capt., lieut., cornet, quartermaster, 3 corporals, 2 trumpeters, 95 men: paid 220*l.* 8*s.*

Capt. Margery's troop, lieut., cornet, quartermaster, 2 trumpeters, 3 corporals, 112 troopers: paid 239*l.* 15*s.*

Capt. Swallow's troop, capt., lieut., quartermaster, 3 corporals, 2 trumpeters, 70 troopers: paid 168*l.* 18*s.* 4*d.*

Capt. Browne's troop, lieut., cornet, quartermaster, 3 corporals, 2 trumpeters, 88 troopers: paid 208*l.* 9*s.* 4*d.*

Capt. Packer's troop, lieut., cornet, quartermaster, 3 corporals, 1 trumpeter, 80 troopers: paid 192*l.* 7*s.* 4*d.*

Capt. Horsman's troop, lieut., quartermaster, cornet, 2 corporals, 2 trumpeters, 51 troopers: paid 141*l.* 12*s.* 4*d.*

Major Desborough's troop, lieut., cornet, quartermaster, 3 corporals, 1 trumpeter, 97 troopers: paid 203*l.* 4*s.* 8*d.*

Lieut.-Col. Whalley's troop, lieut., cornet, quartermaster, 2 corporals, 1 trumpeter, surgeon, marshall, 88 troopers: paid 214*l.* 13*s.* 0*d.*

The officers who are not included in this computation consisted of four commissioned officers for each troop — captain, lieutenant, cornet, and quartermaster; while there were also three corporals and about a couple of trumpeters per troop.

ARMS AND EQUIPMENT

The Ironsides are frequently described as cuirassiers, but that is a mistake.[1] A few cuirassiers were raised at the beginning of the war, but as it went on they were superseded by another species of cavalry.[2]

Capt. Berry's troop, lieut., cornet, quartermaster, 2 corporals, trumpeter, surgeon, 73 troopers: paid 180*l.* 16*s.* 4*d.*

Three other troops of horse belonging to Manchester's army were mustered with Cromwell's men, viz. those of Capts. Huntington, Hammond and Sir John Norwich, numbering 67, 62 and 77 troopers respectively. — *Exchequer Papers.*

[1] Heath, in his *Flagellum*, p. 29, describing Marston Moor, speaks of 'Cromwell with his Associated horse, most of them cuirassiers.' Fletcher, in his *Life of Cromwell*, describes him as arming his men, '*cap a pe*, after the manner of the German crabats'. But both used technical terms very loosely. Colonel Ross argues that 'when first raised, Cromwell's own troop was a body of cuirassiers proper', that the horse of the Association, following this pattern, were most of them of this class of horse, but that when incorporated in the New Model they were transformed into a species of modified cuirassier horsemen, who, offensively armed as cuirassiers, no longer retained the heavy armour of cuirassier proper (*Oliver Cromwell and his Ironsides*, p. 24). But, as stated above, Cromwell's original troop were not cuirassiers proper, and there is no evidence for this supposed change in the armament of the horse at the formation of the New Model.

[2] The lifeguards of general officers were usually cuirassiers; cf. *Ludlow Memoirs*, i. 44; Haslerig's regiment consisted of cuirassiers (*Clarendon Rebellion*, vii. 104, 118; viii. 13). In the first passage it is said of Haslerig's regiment, 'they were called by the other side the regiment of lobsters, because of their bright iron shells with which they were covered, being perfect cuirassiers, *and were the first seen so armed on either side*'. Cuirassiers, according to *Brief Instructions for the Exercising of the Cavalry*, by J. B. 1661, were 'neglected in our late English wars', though 'some few troops of cuirassiers were in use at the first, but afterwards reduced, and the charge saved'. (Quoted by Col. Ross on p. 22 of *Cromwell and the Ironsides*.)

Cromwell's original troop consisted of what were technically termed 'harquebusiers', as the warrant for its payment in December 1642 proves.[1] Harquebusiers were a lighter kind of cavalry than cuirassiers, wearing defensive armour, but much less of it, and taking their name from the harquebuse or carbine with which they were originally equipped.[2] The Ironsides accordingly, like Cromwell's original troop, belonged to the class of harquebusiers.

The defensive arms of a trooper in Cromwell's regiment consisted of an iron head-piece, or 'pot', and of a 'back and breast', which was a sort of cuirass. The price of these arms was in all about 30s. In one bill I find 'two harquebusiers armes, backs, breasts, and pots', charged £2 4s.

In another '20 back, breast, and head pieces lined with leather', cost 34s. each.[3]

The offensive weapons of Cromwell's troopers consisted solely of a sword and a pair of pistols. The cost of the sword is a little difficult to ascertain, because the accounts do not generally distinguish between cavalry and infantry swords.[4] It may be computed as costing 5s. or 6s.

Pistols were a much more expensive item in raising a troop of horse. Two hundred and fifty case of pistols, that is pairs of pistols, bought for Manchester in 1644 cost 38s. apiece, while holsters for the pistols came to 3s. 4d. per pair. On the other hand, in July 1645 80 pairs of pistols for the New Model cost, with holsters included, 26s.[5]

In addition to this there was the cost of the saddle and other furniture

---

[1] *Ante*, p. 137, note 1.

[2] On the origin of Harquebusiers, see Sir James S. D. Scott, *The British Army: its origin, progress, and equipment* (3 vols., London, 1868), ii. 267. The mounted harquebusier, according to Cruso's *Military Instructions for the Cavalry*, 1632, 'must have the harquebuse of two foot and a half long (the bore of 17 bullets in the pound), resting in' [hanging on] 'a belt by a swivell, a flask, and touch-box'.

[3] *Exchequer Papers.*

[4] On 19 July 1645, 3,100 swords and belts were bought for the New Model at 4s. 6d. apiece. In 1644, 1,000 swords and belts for Manchester's army cost 6s. apiece. These were probably in both cases for infantry.

[5] *Exchequer Papers.* On 14 January 1643-4, Col. Valentine Walton contracted with three London merchants for armour for 800 harquebusiers, consisting of 'a breastplate (high pistol proof), a backe, and a pott headpeece with three barres,' at 33s. per head. *Hist. MSS. Comm.*, 8th Rep. ii. 66.

which completed the horseman's outfit. The saddle alone cost 16s. or more,[1] so that it cost not less than £5 to equip each of Cromwell's troopers.[2] An officer's outfit was naturally much more expensive. In 1642 I find the sum of £280 paid to Captain Thomas Lydcote for the equipment of himself and his officers, which he was instructed to divide in the following proportions — for himself as captain £140, for his lieutenant £60, for his cornet £50, for his quartermaster £30.[3] This sum, however, was meant to include their horses as well as their arms.

It should be noted that Cromwell's troopers carried no fire-arms except pistols. Though nominally harquebusiers they had no harquebuse, for that weapon had now entirely gone out of use.[4] Nor was it in their case replaced by the carbine.[5] Neither in the bills for arms supplied to the troops composing the regiment nor in the narratives of their services is there any sign that the Ironsides and the cavalry of the Eastern Association in general (excepting, of course, the dragoons) were armed with anything but pistols.[6] And that fact must have exerted

[1] A bill for arms for Manchester's army dated 6 April 1644, includes 170 saddles and furniture at 20s. apiece, and 50 troop saddles with furniture for the New Model on 2 July 1645, cost 16s. 6d. apiece (*Exchequer Papers*, 31). On the other hand, in May 1643 the Norfolk Committee paid £20 for 10 great saddles for Captain Wild.

[2] A Parliamentary ordinance passed 10 May 1643, authorising Col. James Maleverer to raise a regiment of harquebusiers, estimates the cost of the soldiers' arms at £315 per troop of 63, *i.e.* at £5 per trooper. Husbands, *Ordinances*, ii. 163.

[3] *Cal. State Papers Dom. 1641–3*, p. 363.

[4] Markham in his *Souldier's Accidence*, writing in 1643, speaks of 'harque-bushes, which are now out of use with us'.

[5] In the account for arms supplied for the use of Manchester's army, carbines are hardly ever mentioned: and though the Norfolk Committee bought forty-one in April 1643, it is evident that the purchase was exceptional. Perhaps a single troop in Manchester's army, or an occasional officer, may have had carbines, but they were evidently not in ordinary use. Among the English army in Ireland, where cavalry was employed more to perform the functions of dragoons, firelocks, carbines or musketoons were frequently used.

[6] As to Cromwell's regiment there is an entry in the *Commons Journals* for 4 October 1644: 'Ordered that 300 pair of pistols with holsters, 100 heads, 100 backs, and 100 breasts be forthwith provided and sent to Lieut.-Gen. Cromwell to arm his regiment.' No mention is made of carbines. As to the Association

an important influence on the tactics adopted by Cromwell as a cavalry leader.

HORSES

Next to the question how Cromwell's regiment was armed comes the question how it was mounted. The cost of mounting a regiment of harquebusiers was estimated in May 1643 to be £10 per head, but that sum doubtless included saddles and other necessaries, and it is probable that Cromwell mounted his regiment for a good deal less.[1] In the first place a certain proportion of his men provided their own horses. There is evidence that some of the soldiers of the New Model did so, and even later during the Protectorate recruits sometimes brought their horses with them when they enlisted. Much more so was this likely to be the case with volunteers who entered the Parliamentary service at the beginning of the war.

But a great number of horses, of course, had to be bought for Cromwell's regiment, as the accounts of the Eastern Association show. The price of a troop horse in a regiment like Cromwell's ran from £5 to £10. In 1644 forty-nine horses were bought at Huntingdon fair for Cromwell's regiment at an average of a little over £6 apiece.[2] Recruiting Lieutenant-General Cromwell's regiment with 110 horses in July 1644, just after Marston Moor, cost £1,100, which seems to show either that horses were very scarce just then, or that Cromwell insisted on having the very best that could be got.[3]

In addition to direct purchase in the market, there were two other

---

cavalry in general, see the description given by Symonds in his *Diary* (p. 231) of the armament of the horse encountered in a skirmish at Huntingdon in 1645, who all had 'back and breast, headpiece, and brace of pistols', but no other fire-arms are mentioned. Colonel Ross, commenting on this passage, says, 'Defensively, therefore, they carried no more armour than harquebusiers should wear, and yet in offensive arms they lacked the carbine which was a distinguishing feature of that trooper's armament' (*Cromwell and his Ironsides*, p. 24). This is true not only of the particular body of horse referred to by Symonds, but of Cromwell's regiment and Manchester's cavalry in general.

[1] Husbands, ii. 73; see p. 139, note 2.
[2] *Exchequer Papers.*   [3] *Ibid.*

ways of mounting a regiment, both extensively practised. One was to rely upon the well affected in the associated counties, who at the invitation of Parliament contributed their horses for the public service, which horses were duly valued by proper officials, and repayment promised the owners, with interest at the rate of 8 per cent on the amount, just as if they had subscribed loans of money. After the first flash of zeal was over this source of supply proved insufficient, and Parliament ordered that if the owners of horses neglected or refused to bring them in the county committees should be empowered to take them at a valuation, giving certificates for future repayment to their owners.[1] A third step taken by Parliament was to levy a certain number of horses on a particular district, and order it to provide that number for military use by a certain date, leaving the task of enforcing this requisition to the local committees. On 25 July 1643, for instance, Parliament ordered 6,500 horses to be raised in some fifteen different counties, and delivered to certain colonels named by a given date.[2] Cambridge and Ely were to find two hundred horses, and Huntingdon a hundred, while both contingents were to be under the command of Colonel Cromwell.[3] It is uncertain whether this ordinance was generally carried out, but if it was carried out anywhere it must have been in the district in which Cromwell was entrusted with its execution, and having got his authority

[1] Husbands, i. 339, 358, 456, 773.

[2] *Ibid.*, ii. 275. The horse so raised were to be under the command of Manchester, and the ordinance of 10 August, appointing him to raise a distinct army, may have superseded this.

[3] 'And it is also Ordained, that the respective Deputy Lieutenants, Committees, and persons imployed by them of the Counties of Huntingdon, Cambridge, and Isle of Ely, doe deliver the Horses of their severall Counties, unto the said Earl of Manchester, or in his absence to Collonell Oliver Cromwell, appointed hereby to command the said Horse under the said Earle of Manchester, and to Train and Exercise them, and to imploy them for the defence of the said Counties as cause shall require, untill such time as further Order shall be taken by the Lords and Commons now assembled in Parliament. And it is further Ordained, That the said Earle, or the said Collonel Cromwell, shall give in writing under his hand a perfect List of the number of Horses and Armes hee receives of the severall Counties; for the which Horse and Armes, the severall Counties and persons who furnish the same, shall have the Publique faith for repayment and satisfaction.' Husbands, *Ordinances*, ii. 277.

there can be little doubt that he insisted on getting his three hundred horses.

In general, however, horses were procured by a much less elaborate and formal process. The horses of persons opposed to the Parliament were taken with very little ceremony, under colour of 'disarming the malignants', even before Parliament legalised the system.[1] Later on, 1 April 1643, Parliament passed its sequestration ordinance, by which the property of delinquents — that is, of persons who had in any way assisted the King in the war — might be seized and used for the maintenance of the Parliamentary forces by committees appointed for the purpose. Cromwell was a member of the committees appointed for the counties of Cambridge and Huntingdon. A month later, on 25 April 1643, a special ordinance was passed giving Cromwell, Whalley and Desborough power to put this sequestration ordinance into execution by seizing the arms, money and horses of Royalists in the eastern counties.[2]

---

[1] Cromwell's letter to Mr. Barnard (Letter IV in Carlyle's *Cromwell*) refers to this when speaking of sending a party to visit Barnard, and, hinting his suspicions of Barnard's loyalty to the Parliament, he concludes: 'Be assured, fair words from me shall neither deceive you of your *horses* nor of your liberty.' Carlyle prints 'houses', missing thus the point of the postscript.

[2] 25 April 1643.

An Additionall Ordinance for seizing horses and goods of Malignants according to a former Ordinance.

Whereas Authority was formerly given by Ordinance of both Houses of Parliament to Collonel Oliver Crumwell and others for the seizing of the Persons, Horses, Armes, Money and Plate, of Malignants and ill affected persons, within the County of Cambridge, the Isle of Ely, and other Counties, Cities, and places in the said Ordinance mentioned. It is now further Ordeyned by the Lords and Commons in Parliament, that the said Collonel Crumwell, and other the Committees and Deputy-Lieutenants in the said Ordinance mentioned, as also Captain Charles Fleetwood, Captaine Edward Walley, and Captaine John Disborrough, or any two or more of them, together with any of the said Committees or Deputy-Lieutenants formerly appointed, shall have the like power and authority for the seizing of Horses, Armes, Money or Plate, the same to be disposed of, used and employed to the same uses, as in the said Ordinance is specified, upon accompt thereof to be made to both Houses of Parliament, or such as they shall appoint; And that they and every of them for

These different ordinances, of 1 April, 25 April and 25 July 1643, naturally much reduced the expenditure which the mounting of Cromwell's regiment would otherwise have entailed.

But the drawbacks of the system were very obvious. In the first place, horse stealing on a large scale was somewhat demoralising to the soldiers employed, and sometimes led them to horse stealing on their own account. In the second place, as it was not always easy to determine whether a man was or was not 'a malignant', the officers employed were involved in frequent disputes. Whalley, for instance, got into trouble with the House of Lords for seizing a horse belonging to the Earl of Carlisle.[1] The difficulties caused are still more clearly shown in the case of Captain Margery. 'If he can raise the horses from malignants,' Cromwell had written to the Deputy-Lieutenants of Suffolk, 'let him have your warrant; it will be of special service.'[2] Then came trouble.

> I hear [wrote Cromwell] there hath been much exception taken to Captain Margery and his officers for taking of horses. I am sorry you should discountenance those who (not to make benefit for themselves but to serve their country) are willing to venture their lives, and to purchase to themselves the displeasure of bad men, that they may do

so doing shall be protected and saved harmlesse by the Power and Authority of both Houses of Parliament. Husbands, *Ordinances*, ii. 44, 155.

[1] On 21 March 1643 Captain Whalley was called into the House of Lords, 'being sent for to know why he seized the horses of the Earl of Carlisle, and spoke words that his lordship was a *malignant*. He said ,"Coming to Newmarket, he was told by a constable that the Earl of Carlisle was a malignant, and that he had horses there. Upon this he seized the horses of the Earl of Carlisle, which he acknowledged he was too hasty in, and craved their lordships' pardon for the same, and professed his good affection to the Parliament." The Earl of Carlisle moved the House, that what concerns him their lordships would please to remit; but desired that the constable that told him his lordship was a malignant, may be sent for, and the witnesses that heard him say so. Which the House ordered accordingly. The said Captain Whalley was called in, and told, in regard of his good service done to the Parliament, and upon the mediation of the Earl of Carlisle, this House is willing to pass by what he hath hastily done; but do enjoin him to deliver in the name of the constable and the witnesses to this House.' — *Lords Journal*, v. 656.

[2] Carlyle's *Cromwell*, Letter XVI.

a public benefit. I undertake not to justify all Captain Margery's actions, but his own conscience knows whether he hath taken the horses of any but malignants, and it were somewhat too hard to put it upon the consciences of your fellow Deputy-Lieutenants, whether they have not freed the horses of known malignants? A fault not less, considering the sad estate of this kingdom, than to take a horse from a known honest man, the offence being against the public, which is a considerable aggravation. I know not the measure everyone takes of malignants. I think it is not fit Captain Margery should be the judge; but if he, in this taking of horses, hath observed the plain character of a malignant, and cannot be charged for one horse otherwise taken, — it had been better that some of the bitterness wherewith he and his have been followed had been spared.

Cromwell himself was involved in a like difficulty, and the same letter shows how he dealt with the situation:

> I understand there were some exceptions taken at a horse that was sent me, which was seized out of the hands of one Mr. Goldsmith of Wilby. If he be not by you judged a malignant, and that you do not approve of me having of the horse, I shall as willingly return him again as you shall desire. And therefore I pray you signify your pleasure to me herein under your hands. Not that I would for ten thousand horses have the horse to my own private benefit, saving to make use of him for the public; for I will most gladly return the value of him to the State, if the gentleman stand clear in your judgments. I beg it as a special favour, that if the gentleman be freely willing to let me have him for my money, let him set his own price. I shall very justly return him the money, or if he be unwilling to part with him, but keeps him for his own pleasure, be pleased to send me an answer thereof. I shall instantly return him his horse, and do it with a great deal more satisfaction to myself than keep him.[1]

Cromwell, who was throughout his life a great lover of horses, was careful to see that his men were well-mounted, and that their horses were kept in good condition. Cromwell, says a Royalist historian (as if it were something exceptional), 'accustomed them daily to look after, feed, and dress their horses'.[2] Contemporary pamphlets mention two

[1] Carlyle's *Cromwell*, Letter XVIII.   [2] Bates' *Elenchus*.

examples of his solicitude for the horses of his troopers. In October 1643, just before Winceby fight in Lincolnshire, when the Earl of Manchester ordered his officers to prepare to give battle, Cromwell alone among them opposed his proposition. 'Colonel Cromwell was in no way satisfied that we should fight, our horse being already wearied with hard duty two or three days together.'[1] Again, in November 1644, after the second battle of Newbury, when Charles returned to fetch away his guns from Donnington Castle, the Earl of Manchester, who had previously refused to advance when opportunity offered, ordered Cromwell and the cavalry to check the King's march. Cromwell, who had been eager to advance three days earlier, held it impossible to carry out the plan now. Manchester's chaplain heard Cromwell earnestly dissuading his general. 'My Lord,' he said, 'your horse are so spent, so harassed out by hard duty, that they will fall down under their riders if you thus command them; you may have their skins, but you can have no service.'[2] At the close of the Newbury campaign in November 1644, the cavalry of the three armies of Manchester, Essex and Waller was completely worn out by hard service and bad weather. 'Many hundreds of our horses be already dead, and the living very weak,' wrote Manchester, Waller and Balfour to the Committee of Both Kingdoms. In such cases the dismounted men, if other horses could not be procured, seem to have been sent home. Under 20 January 1645 there is a memorandum among the accounts of the Eastern Association that ten men of Swallow's troop, eight of Berry's and one of Packer's were 'sent homeward for want of horses', and 'given 25s. apiece on accompt' to enable them to get there. No doubt others were dismissed in the same way. In other cases horses seem to have been taken from farmers, and the sick animals left to replace them.[3]

---

[1] Vicars, *God's Ark*, p. 45.

[2] Simeon Ashe, *Relation of Newbury*, 1644, p. 6. I have quoted these passages before in an article on *Cromwell's Views on Sport*, published in *Macmillan's Magazine* for October 1894, but it seems necessary to cite them once more, at the risk of repetition, in order to show Cromwell as a cavalry officer.

[3] At the Committee for the Association. 'These are to certifie that John Barfoote of Eltisley had a horse taken from him by Captain Jenkins for the

PAY AND MAINTENANCE

Having equipped and mounted his men the riddle which Cromwell had to solve was how to pay them. Though the eastern counties had agreed to co-operate for mutual defence, each county remained a separate financial entity, and maintained its own troops. Each county had its distinct collectors, paymasters and treasury. Not till the establishment of Manchester's army in August 1643, or rather not till January 1644, was a common financial organisation and a central treasury for the payment of all the forces of the Eastern Association finally established. Hence the constant want of money which is the burden of Cromwell's letters during 1643. The respective counties did not even pay their own contingents. Cromwell's seventh letter is an appeal to the Mayor of Colchester to send money to pay Captain Dodsworth's company of Essex foot quartered at Cambridge for the defence of the headquarters of the Association. His eleventh letter is addressed to the same dignitary, begging for money for the payment of the Essex foot and dragoons then with him at Nottingham.[1] Cromwell's own regiment seems to have been originally regarded as a Huntingdonshire regiment, and that county did not even belong to the Eastern Association till 26 May 1643. Consequently, Cromwell was at first obliged to depend exclusively on what he could get from Huntingdonshire, which was the poorest of all the eastern counties. Even after Huntingdonshire had joined the Eastern Association Cromwell still found it very difficult to get the other counties to contribute anything towards the maintenance of his regiment. His seventeenth letter, dated 11 September 1643, is a bitter complaint of this difficulty.

---

service of the King and Parliament, and left with the said John Barfoote two poore horses in his sted, which hee is quietly to enjoy. But if in case that one of the said poore horses doe chance to dye of the disease he is nowe sick on, then wee thinke fitt that 30 shillings of lawful money shall be paid to the said John Barfoote toward the recompense of his losse.' This is dated 22 March 164¾, and signed by Manchester and eight other Committee men. Appended is a certificate that the horse is dead, and that Barfoote was paid his thirty shillings on 11 May 1644 (*Exchequer Papers*, Bundle 223).

[1] Cromwell eventually borrowed £100 or £115 at Nottingham for the payment of these Essex men. T. Bailey, *Annals of Nottinghamshire* (4 vols. [1852–5]), ii. 682; cf. *7th Rep. Hist. MSS. Comm.*, p. 557.

Of all men I should not trouble you with money matters [he wrote to his friend St. John] did not the heavy necessities my troops are in press me beyond measure. I am neglected exceedingly. . . . Many of my Lord of Manchester's troops are come to me: very bad and mutinous, not to be confided in — they paid to a week almost: mine noways provided for to support them, except by the poor sequestrations of the county of Huntingdon.

In its gratitude after the relief of Gainsborough Parliament had ordered on 4 August 1643, that £300 already levied in the Associated Counties and sent to Cambridge should be paid to Colonel Cromwell for the support of his forces.[1] Most of his money, however, he never succeeded in getting. Essex sent their part, or near it, Cromwell told the Suffolk Committee, and Suffolk, after some delay, seems to have followed the example of Essex. But the other counties apparently did not. 'If I took pleasure to write to the House in bitterness I have occasion,' wrote Cromwell. 'Of the three thousand allotted to me I cannot get the Norfolk part, nor the Hertfordshire, it was gone before I had it.'[2] Norfolk never seems to have paid this money at all. In November 1643 the Norfolk Committee drew up a statement of the moneys paid by them towards the common purposes of the Association, explaining that they had paid more than their share to Cromwell earlier in the year. 'We have sent him' said they, 'at two several times the sum of 827*l*., besides the sums of money he received in this county.'[3] (The last clause refers to voluntary subscriptions of the well-affected in the

---

[1] *Commons Journal*, iii. 193.　　　　[2] Letter XVII.

[3] An account appended to this gives the following items as received by Col. Cromwell in Norfolk and from Norfolk Committee:

Colonel Cromwell had of Sir Richard Berney, March 19.	48*l*.
Colonell Cromwell had of Mr. Heyward, March 25	20*l*.
Wee paid Colonell Cromwell at Boston	500*l*.
Colonel Cromwell received of Mr. Roger Castle, March 19	50*l*.
Paid more to Col. Cromwell by Coll. Pagrave (*Tanner MSS.*, lxii, 348)	50*l*.

In another account (*Tanner MSS.*, lxvi. 1) the Committee mention a further payment made to Cromwell later, making a total of 1,068*l*.

1643, May 22, to Col. Cromwell wch was sent by Major Sherwood 400*l*. I cannot explain this discrepancy in the totals.

county paid to Cromwell by the subscribers when he was in the county.) 'There is no reason,' they continue, 'why this county should bear any part of the charges of Colonel Cromwell's eight troops unless they had bin reputed a part of their forces, and [they had] not have bin enjoined to raise their full proportion of horses, which they have done according to the order of the 9 of August, being 500.'[1]

The defence might be excellent and the logic of the Committee conclusive, but in the meantime Cromwell and his regiment were *in extremis*.

I have minded your service [concludes Cromwell's letter to St. John] to forgetfulness of my own and soldiers' necessities. I desire not to seek myself. I have little money of my own to help my soldiers. My estate is little. I tell you the business of Ireland and England hath had of me in money between 1,100 and 1,200 pounds, — therefore my private can do little to help the public. You have had my money; I hope in God I desire to venture my skin. So do mine. Lay weight upon their patience, but break it not. Think of that which may be a real help. I believe five thousand is due. If you lay aside the thought of me and my letter I expect no help.

Happily the response to his appeal was not long delayed. Already, on 10 August 1643, in appointing a general committee for the government of the Associated Counties, Parliament had ordered 'That all forces raised before this ordinance in the Associated Counties shall be paid their arrears, if any be unpaid, by money raised out of the Associated Counties and the City of Norwich according to their proportions.'[2] Furthermore, in the ordinance of 20 September 1643, adding Lincolnshire to the other six counties, a general tax of £5,660 per week was ordered to be levied for the maintenance of Manchester's army. It contained, moreover, a special provision for Cromwell's forces mentioned by name:

And whereas Colonell Cromwell hath ten Troopes of Horse already Armed, which were heretofore raysed in the said Associated Counties, It is Ordained that all the now Associated Counties shall discharge their pay till this time, and so long as the said Troopes shall

[1] *Tanner MSS.*, lxii. 349.   [2] Husbands, *Ordinances*, ii. 285.

be thought fit to be continued together as one intyre Regiment, they shall be payd equally by all the said Counties. And for as much as the preservation of the Isle of Ely, Holland, and Marshland, in respect of the Avynewes and passages leading to them, doth mutually depend each of them upon the other, and that Colonell Cromwell is already appointed Governour of the Isle of Ely, but no speciall Provision is yet made for the parts of Holland and Marshland, the same is hereby recommended to the Earle of Manchester, who by vertue of this Ordinance is authorized to place such Governour or Governours in Holland or Marshland aforesaid (with the approbation of the Lord Generall) with such directions for the mutuall preservation of them and the Isle of Ely, as in his judgement he shall conceive to bee most effectuall for their joynt preservation.

From this date, therefore, Cromwell's difficulties about the payment of his regiment were practically at an end. They were as well paid as the rest of the forces of the Eastern Association, and if their pay fell into arrears, it was no more than happened to the rest of Manchester's army. They were not the only ones to suffer, and as a matter of fact they were paid, all things considered, with tolerable regularity.

Turn now to the subject of the pay received by individual officers and men. An ordinary trooper was paid 2s. 6d. per diem, a corporal or a trumpeter 3s. From this sum, however, the trooper was expected to defray the cost of his clothes, his food, and his lodgings, and to find shoes and provender for his horse. The general method of payment for quarters was that the commander of the troop gave the man at whose house the trooper was quartered a certificate, or 'ticket' as it was called, for the amount owing, and the recipient obtained payment of the sum due from the treasurer of the Association at Cambridge.[1] The

[1] There are hundreds of bills for quarters and provisions in existence, but the following petition illustrates the subject discussed and is of more personal interest:

'Petition of Robert Coulson of Sleaford, co. Lincoln, to Lieutenant-General Cromwell.

'At your worships last coming against Lincoln, Major Moore, Captain Bury, Captain Swallow, Captain Walton, and others, with their troops, were quartered in and about Sleaford, and 14 waggon loads of petitioners hay were eaten up by the horses. Your worship gave order that the hay should be prized

same process was followed in paying for the forage required for the trooper's horse. The money thus expended on behalf of a troop or regiment, was finally deducted by the paymaster from the pay due to the said troop or regiment, and the soldier got the remainder, or rather was entitled to get it. With such a complicated system of accounts, it took naturally months or years to work out exactly the sum due to any particular soldier or officer. The general practice in consequence was to pay the regiment a fortnight's full pay from time to time, so that the soldiers and officers might have some ready money in hand for their daily needs, and to charge the cost of their quarters and other expenses against the arrears due to them. When the accounts of the regiment were finally made up, or when the soldier was discharged, he obtained a certificate entitling him to the balance of pay due after the deductions referred to had been paid.

In the general want of ready money to pay the soldiers and enable them to pay for their lodging and food, the practice of free quarter received official sanction. On 4 August 1643, the House of Commons ordered 'that Colonel Cromwell shall have the like order for free quarter upon his march that the Lord General hath'.[1] Free quarter, however, was rather a misnomer. It did not mean that the quarters and food taken were not eventually to be paid for. They were paid for by the ticket system already mentioned, and by an ordinance dated 20 January 1644, it was enacted:

> That if any of the Associated Forces have taken or shall take free quarter within the said Association, every officer is then to have but one third part of the present pay due to him by this ordinance for so long a time as he or they have had or shall have free quarter. And every common foot soldier but half-pay, and every common horseman or trooper 14 pence a day, and the residue of their pay is to be reserved for payment of their quarters.[2]

---

and paid for, and accordingly it was valued at 7*l.*, yet petitioner is ordered to pay 7*l.* to the [County] Committee.'

Endorsed. — 'The within mentioned 7*l.* to be charged on Colonel Cromwell's troop.'

Cal. 1625–49, Addenda, p. 689.

[1] *Commons Journals*, iii. 193.   [2] Husbands, *Ordinances*, ii. 414.

The cost of a day's quartering for one of Cromwell's troopers and his horse was therefore estimated to be 1s. 4d.

Commissioned officers were paid on a somewhat similar system. The captain of a troop of horse got £1 19s. a day, a lieutenant of horse 18s. 6d., a cornet 13s. 6d. and a quartermaster 9s. The pay of higher officers was calculated on a much more complicated system. A major or a colonel received pay as captain of a troop of horse, and a certain additional sum as major or colonel. The major, for instance, besides his £1 19s. a day as captain, received 12s. a day as major; while a colonel, in addition to his £1 19s. as captain, got £1 10s. as colonel of horse. A major-general or lieutenant-general had £2 additional or more. Besides this the higher officers had allowances given them for extra horses, two, four or six in number according to rank, to the amount of 2s. 6d. per diem for each.

On paper, therefore, the officers were liberally and even extravagantly paid, but as a matter of fact, they did not generally get anything like their full pay. By 1644 Parliament had adopted the plan of putting all the higher officers on half-pay during the war, and promising to pay the other half after the war was ended. This system of payment by results relieved the Treasury for the moment, but it had great disadvantages, political and other, in the long run.

The system of deferred payment was applied to Manchester's army by an ordinance passed on 20 January 1644. Henceforth every officer in it above the rank of captain was to get only half his pay in cash, and to respite the other half on the public faith till the war ended. For this second half he received a 'debenture' stating the sum owing to him, a practice which had been adopted still earlier during the war, but was now made general. An account for pay due to Cromwell at the end of 1644 illustrates these various points.[1] It states that there was due to him on a debenture for services prior to 1 January 1644, the sum of £528. For his services during the year 1644 a further debenture for £1,626 9s. was now owing, which would make up a total of £2,154 9s. to be paid him when the war ended. As to the half pay for his services during 1644 which he was entitled to receive in cash, he had received £1,455 out of the £1,626 9s. which was due.

[1] *Exchequer Papers.*

The separate items of Cromwell's pay are set forth in an account drawn up by him for the year 1644.

There was owing to him:

From the 22th of January to the 23th of December, 1644,
  being 48 weeks half pay att 50s. per diem as Lieutenant
  Generall of horse and foote .   .   .   .   . £840 0s.
For the same tyme as Colonell and Captain of horse, with
  allowance for 6 horses at 42s. half pay per diem .   . £705 12s.
Making a total of £1,545 12s.

Before being appointed lieutenant-general he had been major-general, and there was due to him from 1 January 1643 to the 22nd of the same, being three weeks' half-pay at £1 15s. per diem as major-general of horse and foot, £36 15s.

A note explains that of this £1 15s., £1 represented half-pay for the foot, and 15s. half-pay for the horse. To this was to be added his half-pay as colonel and captain of horse for the same three weeks, which at £2 2s. per diem came to £44 2s. Thus the total due for his services in these fifty-one weeks amounted to £1,626 9s., towards which he had received £1,335 1s., leaving a balance due to him of £291 8s. He received on account at the time this was delivered £120.

MEDICAL ORGANISATION

After the question of the payment and maintenance of Cromwell's troops, another question of interest is the treatment of the sick and wounded. Each regiment of horse had its surgeon, and two assistants termed his mates. The surgeon received 4s. a day (just half the pay of the chaplain) and the two mates 2s. 6d. a day each, the pay of a trooper. The surgeon of Cromwell's regiment was Thomas Fothergill.

Besides the regimental surgeon outsiders were frequently employed, who were paid by the job, as the following warrant, signed by the committee of the Eastern Association, shows: 'Whereas William Reynolds hath spent eight weeks in curing Matthew Gibson of Captain Lawrence his troop, we are content to allow the said William Reynolds the sum of 3l. in recompense of his cure.' Dated January 9, 1644⅘.[1]

[1] *Exchequer Papers.*

There seem to have been no general hospitals, and soldiers who were seriously ill or severely wounded were generally left behind at their quarters. Among the State papers there is a note from Cromwell to some local magistrate, dated 5 October 1644, saying, 'Sir, I would desire you to let these sick soldiers have convenient quarter in your town until they be recovered of their sickness.' Appended is a note that £1 12s. was paid for quartering these men.[1] Another piece of evidence of the same kind is a bill running as follows: 'Due to Clifford Weedon at the Angell in Cambridge for quartering of Will. Cleaton under the command of Lieut.-Gen. Cromwell, being very sick, for his diet, horse meat, and looking to him, the 21 of Jan. 1644 to the 6 of Feb., being sixteen days, one pound three shillings.'[2] Soldiers left behind in this way were often ordered a fortnight's pay to maintain themselves till cured, but as their pay was usually much in arrear, a man who was long ill found himself often in great distress. On behalf of one such soldier, belonging to his own troop, Cromwell wrote the following letter:

> Gentlemen, — This soldier of mine (Mr. Frane) is a man whoe on my knowledge hath very faythfully served you, his arreeres are great, his sicknesse much and longe, by occasion whereof hee is brought to great lownesse, and is much indebted. If now upon my recommendation of his person and condition unto you, you will please to help him with some competent summ of monie to discharge his debt, and relieve himselfe, I shall take it for a great favor, and bee ready to repay such a respect with a thankfull [acknow]legment and ever [be]
>
> Your real and faythfull [servant],
> OLIVER CROMWELL.[3]

Jan. 21, 164[4], London.

This is endorsed with the note ('pd 25 January'), and a warrant, dated 24 January describes the recipient as 'George Frane trooper in Lieutenant General Cromwells owne troope', and orders the £5 to be charged 'upon the Lieutenant Generall's accompt'.[4]

---

[1] *Cal. State Papers Dom., Addenda, 1625–1649*, p. 667.
[2] *Exchequer Papers.*   [3] *Ibid.*
[4] The following account shows the cost of burying those of the wounded who did not recover:

Religious Organisation

As to the religious organisation of the regiment, each regiment in Manchester's army, whether horse or foot, had its chaplain whose pay was 8*s*. a day. The colonel of the regiment seems to have had the choice of the minister, and according to his taste chose Presbyterian or Independent as he thought fit. Cromwell and his officers offered the chaplaincy of the regiment originally to Richard Baxter. 'When he lay at Cambridge,' says Baxter, 'with that famous troop which he began his army with, his officers purposed to make their troop a gathered church, and they all subscribed an invitation to me to be their pastor.' Baxter attributed this invitation specially to his old friend James Berry, Cromwell's Captain-Lieutenant. But Baxter disapproved of Congregationalism, and so, he continues,

> I sent them a denial reproving their attempt, and told them wherein my judgment was against the lawfulness and convenience of their way, and so I heard no more from them. And afterwards meeting Cromwell at Leicester he expostulated with me for denying them. These very men that invited me to be their pastor, were the men that afterwards headed much of the army and some of them were the forwardest in all our changes; which made me wish I had gone among them however it had been interpreted; for then all the fire was in one spark.[1]

Who became chaplain of Cromwell's regiment when Baxter refused is uncertain. The names of the chaplains of several of Manchester's regiments are known, but the name of that of Cromwell's does not appear in the accounts, which are unfortunately very imperfect. It is possible that it was William Sedgwick, on behalf of whom, together with an-

---

'Money expended by Anthony Solomon, a trooper in Lieut.-Generall Cromwell his troope, by him expended and ordered to be audited by the Committee:

'For the burying of William Molbert	.	.	.	.	. 17*s*.
'For the burying of William Hill	.	.	.	.	. 1*l*.

both of Lieut.-Generall Cromwell's owne troope.'

[1] *Reliquiæ Baxterianæ*, pp. 51, 57.

other minister, Cromwell wrote in January 1645 a pressing appeal to the Sequestrators of the Isle of Ely.[1] But there are reasons for believing that Sedgwick was more probably chaplain to the Governor of Ely. In any case, whoever the chaplain was, a good deal of preaching and exhorting was conducted by the soldiers themselves. John Lilburne mentions in one of his pamphlets that about October 1643, Colonel King, the governor of Lincoln, 'imprisoned divers of his officers, and divers of the townspeople, and some of Lieut. Gen. Cromwell's troopers for assembling together at a private meeting, in a most despite-full and disgracefull manner'. The result of this was a quarrel, which Lilburne, who was King's Major, had to appease. 'I rid to Sleaford,' says he, 'to Lieut. Gen. Cromwell, with whom and his officers and soldiers I used the best of my interest to make peace, which I accordingly did, though divers of the soldiers in Lieut. Gen. Cromwell's regiment were so exasperated that they were resolved either to lay down their arms or to get him punished for abusing them.'[2] In spite, however, of this propensity for attending conventicles, and of all that Baxter and other Presbyterians say against Cromwell's troopers, it must not be supposed that all, or even the majority of them, belonged to the extremer sects of Independents. 'They are no Anabaptists but

---

[1] 'Gentlemen, — If I have found any respect or favour from you, or may any wayes seeme to deserve any, I intreate you most earnestly and as for myselfe, that you will pay to Doctor Wells, and to Mr. William Sedgwick the money which the Earle of Manchester hath given them a warrant to receive. I am inform'd that moneyes are not very plentifull with you. Howbeit I intreate you to doe that for my sake, and for their sakes that should have it. For let me speake freely, whatsoever the world may iudge they doe fully deserve what I desire for them. I have not been often troublesome to you, I have studyed to deserve the good opinion of honest men, amongst which number, As I have cause to account you, Soe I hope I have the like esteeme with you, which I desire you to testify by fulfilling this my request, giveing you the assurance of his unfained friendship, who is,

'Yo^r very loveing freind,
'OLIVER CROMWELL.

'London, Jan. 17th, 1644.
'*Dorso.* — To the Sequestrators of the Isle of Ely, these.' — State Papers Dom., Chas. I., vol. 539, No. 256.
[2] *Lilburne's Innocency and Truth Justified,* 1645, p. 40.

honest sober Christians,' says Cromwell of his regiment in general.[1] There were, of course, Anabaptists among them, and some of the officers who held those views can be named. For instance, William Packer. 'In the spring of 1644,' says Major-General Crawford, 'one lieutenant Packer, a notorious Anabaptist, disobeyed Major-General Crawford's orders near Bedford, whereupon the head of the army gave the said Packer a sore check, and put him in arrest.'[2] It is probable that Packer's offence was of a religious rather than a military nature, for the narrator goes on to say that 'the said Packer complained to the said Cromwell, who upon my return to Cambridge sent Lieutenant-Colonel Rich to signify unto me that I did exceeding ill in checking such a man, which was not well taken, he being a godly man'. Letter XX in Carlyle's *Cromwell*, which is addressed to Crawford, is taken by Carlyle to refer to this incident, but wrongly. It refers to Crawford's lieutenant-colonel, as Cromwell expressly states, an officer whose name was Warner.[3] Moreover, Packer was at this time only a lieutenant, and never at any period in his life held the rank of lieutenant-colonel. It refers to him only so far as Cromwell's defence of the employment of Anabaptists in general may be supposed to allude to his case as well as Warner's.

DISCIPLINE

In conclusion, a few words must be added on the discipline of Cromwell's regiment. Just as the army of the Eastern Association as a whole had its provost marshal and his assistants, so each particular regiment of horse or foot had its marshal, who was specially charged with disciplinary punishments. The concurrent testimony of contemporary writers and the absence of complaints prove the excellence of the discipline Cromwell maintained in his regiment, but not much information can be gathered about it so far as the years 1643–5 are concerned. A newspaper called *Special Passages* describes Colonel Cromwell in April 1643 as being then at Huntingdon with some five troops, and adds: 'The Colonell exercises strict discipline, for when two troopers

---

[1] Carlyle's *Cromwell*, Letter XVII.
[2] *Manchester's Quarrel with Cromwell*, p. 59.
[3] His name is given in the accounts for 1644.

would have escapt, he sent for them back, caused them to be whipt at the market place in Huntingdon, and being before dismounted and disarmed, he turned them off as renegadoes.'[1] Next month the same paper contains the familiar account of the discipline Cromwell maintained not only in his own regiment but among all forces temporarily under his command: 'No man swears but he pays his twelve pence; if he be drunk he is set in the stocks or worse; if one calls the other "Roundhead" he is cashiered; insomuch that the countries where they come leap for joy of them, and come in and join with them.'[2]

An incident which took place in the spring of 1645 supplies some curious illustrations of the temper and state of discipline of the regiment. On 15 January 1645 the House of Commons determined that six thousand horse and foot should be sent into the West under Waller. As his own diminished army was not sufficient for the purpose it was to be supplemented by detachments from the armies of Essex and Manchester. On 12 February the order was again repeated, for Weymouth was in urgent need of relief.[3] Waller's delay in setting out was caused by want of money, by the general disorganisation of the Parliamentary forces at the moment, and by the reluctance of the forces to start till they were paid and recruited. Essex's cavalry shared the antipathy which existed between their commander and Waller, and refused to march, saying that 'they would rather go under any commander the Lord-General should appoint without money, than with Sir William Waller with all the money in England'.[4] Manchester's cavalry, which included eleven troops of Cromwell's regiment under Whalley, showed a better spirit, and the newspapers were loud in their praise. At a conference between the two Houses at the end of January letters were read from the army 'of the mutinous and disobedient carriage of the soldiers refusing to march into the west to relieve poor Weymouth in great distress'. At the same time, however, 'the letters did further certify, that at the muster no men appeared so full in number, well armed, nor

[1] Quoted in Kingston's *Civil War in East Anglia*, p. 110.
[2] Quoted in *Cromwelliana*, p. 5.
[3] *Commons Journals*, iv. 20, 46. See also Gardiner, *Great Civil War*, ii. 128, 178.
[4] *Cal. State Papers Dom.*, 1644–5, 278, 291.

more civil in their carriage, nor less complaint of than Col. Cromwell's horse'.[1] Another paper was still more enthusiastic:

> This day there came Letters from the Commissioners of our Army which certifie of the state thereof, thus: &c.
>
> That they have received divers complaints against some of our Officers of Horse, wherein was reckoned up, such and such horse to plunder, and among the country-people, others to mutinie at the motion of going with Sir William Waller, in his advance for the West, others complaining that they wanted saddles, and others things, as pistolls, and the like, and for Col. Cromwell's souldiers, it was informed, that in what posture soever they were, that (were it at midnight) they were alwaies ready to obey any Ordinance of Parliament, and that there was none of them knowne to do the least wrong by plunder, or any abuse to any country-people where they came but were very orderly, and paid onely for what they had, and were ready to advance with Sir William Waller. Now let us consider, and lay these things to heart, for (as a person of note then said) these are the men (meaning the Independents, as we call them) that the other day many would have had to have been turned out of the Army, you see how they submit to authority, and to be obedient, and how orderly they are, and readie to do service for the publicke. And we had more need to fall downe upon our knees to pray them to stay in the Army, then to go about to put them out; and truly for my part, I never tooke them for friends that went about to make divisions between us and them in the Army, for however they differ insomething in judgement from us, yet we cannot be ignorant that they have been as active for the Parliament both in purse, person, and prayers, as any in the kingdome.[2]

Cromwell's men accordingly set out with Waller, but by the time he reached Portsmouth they too began to be mutinous. Parliament had ordered them all a fortnight's pay on 5 February, but the money had not been forthcoming, for the Eastern Association was reluctant to provide money when the forces it had raised for its own defence were sent so far from its borders.[3] On the 22nd, letters came to the Speaker of the

---

[1] *Perfect Diurnal*, 30 January 1645.   [2] E. $\frac{270}{5}$ p. 131. *Perfect Passages*.

[3] *Commons Journals*, iv. 42, 56. The order to pay Cromwell's regiment was repeated on February 20, showing it had not been obeyed. On the same day

Commons from Waller and other commanders 'relating how the Earl of Manchester's forces did now refuse to go with Sir William Waller westward as well as the Lord-General's, because they had hitherto received no money as was promised, and yet they were ordered to carry with them four days' provision for horse and men, by reason the countries into which they were to go were so wasted that they were like a wilderness, and had no provision for them; besides all this they were to be recruited and furnished with pistols, which they were in great want of'.[1] Another letter, dated from Portsmouth on 22 February, added 'that 700 of Cromwell's horse, do what their officers could, had left them that afternoon, and were returned with colours to former quarters, pretending they had received great injuries and affronts'.[2]

In this difficulty all the Commons could do was to order Cromwell, who was then in London attending to his Parliamentary duties, to accompany Waller, and to reduce his troops to obedience. The order was voted on 27 February 1645, and Cromwell was voted at the same time £1,000, half for himself and half for his regiment, and was told to take with him Ireton's troop and two other troops of his regiment which were at Henley.[3]

The situation was a curious comment on Cromwell's words when he proposed the Self-Denying Ordinance:

I am not of the mind [he had told the Commons] that the calling of the members to sit in Parliament will break or scatter our armies. I can speak this for my own soldiers, that they look not upon me but upon you, and for you they will fight and live and die in your cause; and if others be of that mind that they are you need not fear them; they do not idolise me, but look upon the cause they fight for; you

---

the money was paid to Captain Berry on behalf of the regiment, but as the payment probably took place at the headquarters of the Association at Cambridge, the news could scarcely have reached either the House or the regiment.

[1] Whitacre's *Diary*; Add. MSS. 31116, f. 195; cf. *Commons Journals*, iv. 60.

[2] *Diary of Sir S. D'Ewes*; *Harleian MSS.*, 166, f. 179.

[3] *Commons Journals*, iv. 63; cf. *Cal. State Papers Dom. 1644–5*, pp. 323, 331.

may lay upon them what commands you please, they will obey your commands in that cause they fight for.[1]

It seemed now as if his soldiers had set themselves to give the lie to their colonel's professions, and he had to prove the truth of his statement. Getting together his three troops as quickly as he could Cromwell set out to overtake Waller, and both marched westwards.[2] On 12 March they defeated Colonel Long's regiment of Royalists in Wiltshire, capturing over three hundred out of his four hundred men. When Cromwell announced this success, he at the same time was able to announce that his regiment was once more as obedient as he had promised.

A letter came this day to the House of Commons [says the 'Perfect Diurnal' for 19 March] from Colonel Cromwell, a worthy and valiant member thereof, and one of the Saviours (as God hath miraculously manifested him to be) of this Israel, informing the House that since his coming to his regiment, the carriage of it hath been very obedient and respectful to him, and valiant, a good testimony whereof they gave upon the late service against Long's regiment; and for their late mutinous carriage to the Parliament they had expressed their hearty sorrow for the same, and had desired him to send their most humble petition to the Houses, that they might be again received into their former favour, and have their pardon fully for their late offence; and for the quite removing the cloud of jealousy over them, they doubted not to clear it by valiant testimony, as occasion should require. The House, upon reading the same, received much satisfaction, and accepted it affectionately from them.[3]

Still more curious is an advertisement which appeared in one of the newspapers about the same time:

'There being many of Lieut.-General Cromwell's regiment who were gone into the country to visit their friends, and could not have

[1] 'Perfect Occurrences,' 9 December 1644, reprinted in *Cromwelliana*, p. 12.
[2] It is difficult to see how Cromwell could have been much quicker, seeing that his three troops had to be got together, and preparations made for the expedition, but the Committee of Both Kingdoms and the House of Commons alike thought he was unnecessarily slow. — *Cal. State Papers Dom., 1644–5*, p. 334; *Commons Journals*, iv. 67.
[3] *Perfect Diurnal*, 17–24 March; *Cromwelliana*, p. 13.

timely notice of his going west, by reason of the unexpectedness of that command: it's desired by the colonel that all such will repair to a rendezvous near Barking in Surrey, where they shall have further order by the officers left for that purpose.[1]

Six weeks later Cromwell, having returned from the expedition into the West, and successfully effected its object, came back to headquarters at Windsor to resign his command and to take leave of the new general-in-chief. During his absence the Self-Denying Ordinance had been passed, and the New Model Army organised.[2] The regiment he had raised was now incorporated into the New Model, and as no regiment in that body was to consist of more than six troops, the fourteen troops were necessarily separated. 'So,' says Baxter, 'Cromwell's old regiment, which had made itself famous for religion and valour, being fourteen troops was divided; six troops were made the Lord Fairfax's regiment; and six troops were Colonel Whalley's regiment; and the other two were in Colonel Rich's and Sir Robert Pye's regiments.'[3] A glance at the list of the officers of Fairfax's and Whalley's regiments confirms Baxter's statement.[4] There are no new names in Fairfax's regiment, and the new troop commanders in Whalley's regiment, Cannon and Evanson, were probably both of them subalterns in those troops when they formed part of Cromwell's regiment.[5] Captain Margery and his troop appear in Pye's regiment, and in Rich's appears the name of Captain Ireton, that is, of Captain Thomas Ireton, Henry Ireton's younger brother, who had no doubt been lieutenant of his brother's troop.[6]

---

[1] *The Moderate Intelligencer*, 13–20 March 1645.

[2] Cf. Sprigge, *Anglia Rediviva*, p. 11, edn. 1854.

[3] *Reliquiæ Baxterianæ*, p. 49. In Cromwell's letter to Fairfax, 24 April 1645, in relating his victory near Islip, he says: 'I drew forth your Honour's regiment lately mine own against the enemy . . . and commanded your Honour's own troop therein to charge a squadron of the enemy.'

[4] Sprigge, *Anglia Rediviva*, p. 331.

[5] Henry Cannon and William Evanson. The latter is mentioned by Baxter as one of Cromwell's original regiment, *Reliquiæ Baxterianæ*, pp. 51, 98.

[6] Thomas Ireton was severely wounded at the siege of Bristol, became in 1647 Quartermaster-General, and died governor of Landguard Fort in June

Cromwell's connection with his old regiment came to an end in April 1645, but only for a time. He had no command in the New Model Army as it was first organised, but just before Naseby Colonel Vermuyden resigned his commission, thus creating a vacancy in the command of a cavalry regiment which Fairfax at once appointed Cromwell to fill. In June 1650 Fairfax resigned all his commissions, and the six troops of Cromwell's own regiment, which had composed the commander-in-chief's regiment since 1645, returned at last to the command of the man who had originally raised them.

In conclusion I wish to point out that in the foregoing pages I have taken no account of any statements made in the so-called 'Squire Papers'. The 'Squire Papers' are a forgery from beginning to end.[1] The dates of the letters, when there are any, are frequently impossible. The military details they contain are flagrantly absurd.[2] Their English is the English of the nineteenth century, clumsily disguised by affected archaisms. The list of officers supposed to have commanded troops in Cromwell's regiment does not agree with the names of its officers as given in the regimental accounts.[3] The list of names of privates supposed to have belonged to the regiment is purely fantastic and grotesque.[4]

1652. — Sprigge, *Anglia Rediviva*, 118, 121; *Clarke Papers*, i. 223; Leslie, *History of Landguard Fort*, p. 92.

[1] The criticisms of the 'Squire Papers', published by Dr. Gardiner and Mr. Walter Rye in the *English Historical Review* for 1886, pp. 517, 744, conclusively disprove their authenticity.

[2] Lieutenant-Colonel W. G. Ross in his pamphlet on *Cromwell and his Ironsides*, proves this at length. Among other things he shows (p. 12) that no such officer as an 'auditor' was attached to any English regiments of the Civil War period: a statement which is fully confirmed by the army accounts.

[3] This list is 'scrap 2' in Carlyle's appendix on the *Squire Papers*. 'The names of the original Ironside captains, well worth preserving indeed!' adds Carlyle. Of the forty-two names given in the list only eight (or possibly nine) are identical with the names of officers who actually served in Cromwell's regiment. The names of three of these eight were derived from Baxter's account of the regiment, the names of the other five were provided by Cromwell's genuine letters, already printed by Carlyle.

[4] 'Scrap 4' in Carlyle's appendix.

No officer of any rank bearing the name of Squire appears in any of the existing lists, pay rolls, or accounts relating to Cromwell's regiment. A document recently published by Sir Richard Tangye throws some new light on the history of the Squire imposture.[1] He possesses a 'Life of Cromwell' containing certain notes written in what experts say is an eighteenth-century hand, concerning 'a certain Capt. H. Squire'. 'This H. Squire,' says one of the notes, 'joined a Stilton troop, 1641, and was cornet, and rode as Lieutenant at Naseby, where he was wounded, and fought all through the Civil War, but gave up when they killed the King,' &c. Among these notes is a 'copy of a letter respecting Cromwell's attack upon Lowestoft'. It is addressed:

'*For Capt. H. Squire, at his quarters, Oundle.*'

'Dear friend, — We have secret and sure hints that a meeting of the malignants takes place at Lowestoft in Co. Suffolk on Tuesday. Now, I want your ayd, so come with all speed on getting this, with your troop and tell no one your route, but lett me see you ere sundown.

'From your friend and commandant,

'O. CROMWELL.'

Sir Richard Tangye justly observes that the notes and letter are evidently a portion of the 'Squire' correspondence dealt with by Carlyle. In this he is quite right, for the volume must have been once in William Squire's possession. He opened his correspondence with Carlyle by sending him a copy of this very letter, on 29 January 1847,[2] but he omitted the address to 'Capt. H. Squire'. Carlyle naturally wanted to know to whom the letter was written. William Squire answered on 11 February, 'The letter I sent you is addressed to Capt. Berry', quoting in confirmation 'an extract relating to that affair' from his ancestor's journal, and also saying 'that letter is copied in my prayer-book from the original verbatim, for the MS. is all in fragments'. In the same letter he described his ancestor, the owner of the

---

[1] *The Two Protectors*, p. 66.

[2] *English Historical Review*, 1886, p. 313. There are some variations in the spelling and signature of the two versions.

notebook and letter, as 'auditor' and afterwards 'cornet Samuel Squire'.[1]

It is clear that if Sir Richard Tangye's document is genuine, the statements of William Squire to Carlyle were false. But there can be little doubt that the eighteenth-century handwriting in the 'Life of Cromwell' is a forgery of the same kind as the entries purporting to be in a seventeenth-century hand written in a prayer-book of 1627, which Mr. Rye exposed.[2] 'Captain H. Squire' of Cromwell's regiment is as mythical a personage as 'Auditor Sam Squire'. He was an earlier version of Sam Squire, just as the letter to 'Capt. H. Squire' was an earlier version of the letter to Captain Berry.[3] The value of Sir Richard Tangye's book consists in its revelation of the first stage in the history of this imposture.

I have added in an appendix a few documents relating to this portion of Cromwell's career.

C. H. Firth

APPENDIX I

FIVE NOTES OF CROMWELL'S, FROM THE 'EXCHEQUER MANUSCRIPTS' IN THE RECORD OFFICE

(I)

Dr. Staines, — I desire you doe me the favor to let the bearer have five pounds of my money for his Captain, Captain Coleman, his want is great and I should be loathe he should be sent away to him empty. You must not fayle me herein.

I rest,
Your very loving father,
Oliver Cromwell.

Jan. 6 [1644].

---

[1] *English Historical Review*, 1886, pp. 317, 318. The letter appears in its third state in Carlyle's appendix on the 'Squire Papers' as letter No. xi., with the omission of the suspicious phrase 'in Co. Suffolk'.

[2] *Ibid.*, 1886, p. 752.

[3] Berry was not a captain in March 1643, when this letter is supposed to be written.

Addressed apparently to Richard Stane, Treasurer for the Isle of Ely. In the New Model William Coleman was a captain in Fleetwood's regiment of horse.

(II)

Gentlemen, there is a boate framinge for the defence of theise parts, I beleive it's of consequence, I therefore desire you to lett the officer that directs the framinge of itt to have twenty markes for the perfectinge of itt and I shall rest,

Your true servant,
OLIVER CROMWELL.

Jan. 10, 1643.

To my very noble freinds the Committees of the Isle of Ely present these.

Lieutenant Thomas Selby was accordingly paid £13. Probably he is to be identified with the Captain Selby, afterwards of Fleetwood's regiment, who was killed at Naseby in 1645.

(III)

To the Right Honourable Leiftenant Generall Cromwell the Petition of John Disbrowe, showeth

That wheras he was commanded by my Lord of Manchester to conduct a company of prest men out of the Isle of Ely into Lincolne with the promise of satisfaction for the said service which he never could obtaine, he hath since repayred to the Committee of the Isle of Ely for pay for the said service. But they informed him they could pay nothing without expresse order from your Honour May it therefore please you to order the said Committee herein, and your petitioner shall upon all occasions be ready to serve you.

Gentlemen, I desire you to take this petition into consideration, and to doe therein as to your judgments shall seeme meete, and what you please to doe heerein shall content mee.

Your servant,
OLIVER CROMWELL.

Jan. 30th, 1644.

To the Committee for the Isle of Ely.

(IV)

April 11, 1644.

Mr. Browne, what monies you have in hands of the last three months tax I desire you to pay to Leift^nt Bolton, to Captaine Wests uses for the payment of his cumpanie, which I now order him to receave upon account. If you have not soe much yett lett him have what is in your hands And for soe doeinge this shall be your warrant. Given under my hand the day and yeare above written.

OLIVER CROMWELL.

(Countersigned by William Marche and Miles Sandys, and addressed to Robert Browne, Deputy-Treasurer for the Isle of Ely.) The officers referred to, Lieutenant Roger Bolton and Captain Nicholas West, belonged to a company stationed at the Hermitage, in the Isle of Ely.

(v)

Dr. Stane, — I do hereby require you to pay my wife 5*l.* a weeke to beare the extraordinary charges. This shall be your warrant. Take her hand in your noates.

OLIVER CROMWELL.
MILES SANDYS.
April 13, 1644.   WILLIAM MARCHE.
[To Richard Stane, Treasurer for the Isle of Ely.]

On this order see the comments of an opponent of Cromwell's, in the Camden Society's volume on Manchester's quarrel with Cromwell, p. 74.

APPENDIX II

PAPERS RELATING TO THE SIEGE AND RELIEF OF GAINSBOROUGH

Sir John Meldrum to the Speaker of the House of Commons[1]

Mr. Speaker, — By a resolution taken to disingage my Lord Willowby by the best meanes that could fall within the compasse of my judgment or resolution, there was a bodie of seaventeene hundred troopers, dragooners, and commaunded musketeers, without ordinaunce or foote, with the which wee marched from our last quarter at North Scarle to within two miles of Gainsborrow, where wee had some skirmish with the forlorne hope of the enimie, but with disadvantage by the unworthy carriage of the dragooners on our side,

[1] *Tanner MSS.*, lxii. 205.

which made the officers of the horse to advance with their wholl bodie, and drive them to a shamefull retreat, first to their quarter where they were encamped, and from thence in an absolute rout. Three hundred went towards a bridge where their ordinaunce were, and where my Lord of Newcastle his secourse did passe, and the rest were dispersed severall wayes. In their retreate they lost many colours of horse and foote, amongst the rest the Earle of Kingstone's. Upon this retreate I tooke the opportunitie to passe through to the towne with two hundred horse, which I did for the better incouragement of my Lord Willowby and his soldiers, and for a greater terrour to the enimie seeinge his reeleife, and to drawe forth the foote out of the towne for further prosecution of the victorie, all which succeeded as could have been expected; and whilst with horse and foote wee had resolved to fall upon their ordinaunce my Lord of Newcastle his secourse did passe the river, drawinge himselfe up in a bodie, and with their ordinaunce did strike such a terrour amongst both horse and foote that it was impossible to keepe them together, nothwithstandinge all the vehement purswacions of the cheefe officers, by whose endeavours and example there was an honorable retreate made with as much saftie as could have been expected on such an occacion. The enimie hath lost divers of their cheefe commaunders, as is reported Lieutenaunt Generall King, Colonel Cavendish, Lieutenaunt Colonel Markham. There is none of note lost on our side.

Upon a consultation taken after the secourse had passed the river, and havinge noe ordinaunce, noe foote, noe safe quarter, wee resolved to forsake the place, to leave all the ammunition that could bee spared in the towne, and to withdrawe my Lord Willowby, which could not bee soe quickly done in regard of the enimies sudden mocion. A soldier by a longe and continewed practise in warlike acciones may supply the defect in his profession, but cannot supply the defects of nature, which is to make cowards valient. Soe that to bee shorte our horse carried themselves valiently, but a great part of the dragooners most basely. If there bee a sudden course taken to advance Sir Miles Hubbard his regiment with that of Sir John Palgraves, which are allreadie soe far upon the way towards us, and that the Committee of Derbie may bee ordered to mount Sir John Gell's regiment of foot on horseback, which if it bee done there is very good hope that all the north parts of England may bee freed from the trouble and terrour of my Lord of Newcastle his armes, and that within a very few dayes: which otherwise cannot but run an extreame great hassard by a victorious armie, there beeinge here soe few of able commaunders. There are many other particulars left to the relacion of Colonel Cromwell, whose carriage hath beene discreet and valient. Soe haveinge noe further for the present to impart to you I shall bee glad of any occacion wherein I may expresse my affeccion and zeale to the publicke cause, and that I am,

Your affectionate freind and servant.

Endorsed

'From Sir John Meldrum: read July ultimo.'

Lord Willoughby of Parham to the Speaker of the House of Lords[1]

My Lord, — I knew thire Lordships had soe many searious affaires to take upp thire time as it hath diverted me all this time from troubling them with the trifeling things which hath past heare; besides my Lord, I have beene heere but in a mixt way, soe as I have had nothing to act but my share, and of that I hope I shall be able to give a good account to the House that they will not have cause to blame me for a[2] . . . . but that I have ventered to farr having[2] [no commi]ssion; it was out of my zeale to serve the P[arliame]nt and kingdome which I hope will mitti-gate[2] [their] sensure of mee; my Lord I have indeavoured what I could of my selfe, for I must confess I hade noe command for it, to suppress and stop the violence of the enimy in this cuntry of Lincolneshir, and had of late the fortune to beate upp one of thire garrisons called Gains-borrow, wheare I tooke my Lord of Kingston thire Generall, and divers others prissoners to the number of 400, many of them of good quality; but the strength of the enimy was soe greate by some forces which weare come from my Lord Newcassell which I knew not of, that the same day I tooke it I was beseeged before night, and there kept itt som ten dayse before I had any relife, till Sir John Meldrum and Collonell Crumwell came and relived me: but the relife was soe short, as that morning they came my Lord Newcastell with a greate part of his army beate them away, and did new beseege it, he planted 16 peeces of ordenance and some morter peecess. For all that we stood it out till by his long shooting and his grannadouse he sett fyer to part of the towne, which when the townse people saw they threatned to give upp the towne, and did soe deboyse our soulgiers as many of them could not be gott to stand to thire workes, soe as we weare forsed to come to a parly,

---

[1] *Tanner MSS.*, lxii, 208.   [2] Hole in MS.

and to accept of these condisions, which weare verry hard, but we could not healp it, for we had these thrown uppon us, wee had noe vittles, our men would not stand to it, and there was noe hopes given us of any relife within 14 dayse; wee held out three dayse in that condition. My Lord Newcastell's army is now at Gainsborrow, and will advance to Lincolne, and soe wheather he pleaseth, without some speedy course be taken for his stopp; for he is heare with 6000 horse and foote, and hath 2000 more uppon thire marsh to him. I am heare at Lincolne where Sir Jhon Meldrum is; the greatest strength that is in the towne is but 100 foote, some 4 broaken troopes of horse, wee want armes for many of these, and they run away verry much for they know[1] .   .

.   .   .   .   [Lincolnshire] will be wholly att the enimyes devotion; as it is soe malignant as I belive he may raise as menny men as he hath now with him, if he hath armes for them. I must further acquaint you, and hide nothing to make things better then they are, for that hath beene and is a greate ruine, without some speedy assistance by some forces drawing downe these people are soe coued as they will not defend the place; they must likewise have a supply of mony, for it is not possible this cuntry should raise any, when the enimy is soe powerfull and we soe weake. I must needs say this for this cuntry, that it hath neather reaceaved mony nor armes from the Parliament since I came into it, and if you expect any service from them or that you hould it of any consequence, it must be supplyed with both, and that with speed, or else it will be too late. There is noe way to hould it but by sending a speedy forse to assist them. I heald it my duty to write this, which I beseech your Lordship to acquaint the House with. Sir Jhon Meldrum is now heare whoe I believe hath acquainted you with the state of these parts before now; I could not soner because I had noe means to doe it, being soe close kept in as I could not send a boy but he was taken. My Lord I have beene two teadious, I crave your pardon, and remaine,

Your Lordships most humble servant,

F. WILLUGHBYE.

Lincolne, this 1 of August 1643.

[1] Illegible through folding of the paper.

APPENDIX III

The Speaker of the House of Commons to Colonel Cromwell[1]

Sr, — The house hath taken into consideration your letter: they have commanded mee to send you these enclosed orders, and to lett you know that nothing is more repugnant to the opinion and sence of this house, and dangerous to the kingdome, then the unwillingnesse of theire forces to march out of their severall countys: they hope now the miserys of other places will be a warning to this Association, and an encouragement rather to endevour with honour and ease to keepe the enemy out of theire confines, then with extreame hasard and danger to expell them, and for those that are negligent herein, they will not fayle to proceed against them with all severity. For your selfe, as they doe exceedingly approve of your faythfull endevours for god and the kingdome, soe they have commanded mee to assure you that noe power they have shall be wanting to improve the good affections of these Associated countys to the publick advantage. Whereunto they beseech god to give a blessing.

Your assured loving friend,

[unsigned]

Endorsed.
'Read Aug. 4[to], and assented unto and ordered to bee sent to Colonel Cromwell.'

APPENDIX IV

Lord Willoughby of Parham to the Earl of Essex[2]

May it please your Exellence,

My obligations are soe infinite for the favours I have reaceaved from your Exellence in the care you have beene pleased to have of mee in this time of my misfortune and distress, that I cannot tell how to goe about to make the expressions of my acknowledgments; fortune hath brought me soe low now by the baseness and cowardlyness of this cuntry, that I cannot say I have any thing in my power to serve you with but my life, which ever was and shall be att your command; a month agoe I could have saide more, but the fortune of warr hath taken it from mee. I reaceaved your Exellence' letter by the returne of

---

[1] *Tanner MSS.*, lxii. 224.   [2] *Ibid.*, 232.

my servant, which direction I was fitt to observe, and noe other, for the garisson was soe weake by the running away of the men, that I did not carry out of towne above two hundred foote. I gott away the litest peecess of ordenance and all the amunition, the bidgest I was forced to leave; for when that it was understood that I would leave the towne, every one did leave me, soe as Sir Jhon Meldrum and my selfe was forsed to hand many things on else they had beene left behind. I was forsed to doe it in the night and suddainely, lest the enimy should gett intelligence, and soe we should loose all, who was not long out of it, for the towne sent immeadiately for him. My Lord I am now at Boston, but I find the people soe out of hart, that without some speedy supply I think they will all give them selves up to the enimy, for they are just as the tide goese, and truly this place Boston is of that importance, that if the enemy gett it he will have the sea by it, and a passage into Norfuck and Suffuck, which will be verry dangerouse as the affaires of the Parlament now goese, and if they be noe quicker nor resoluter they will not long keepe thire heads upp, [nor] I believe on. If a force be speedely sent into this cuntry my Lord Newcassell will be little better for having Lincolne, and except there be a speedy course taken to attempt the beating of his army drawne into this cuntry, he will not easily be beaten; for as I heare our cuntrymen have agreed to give him 33000^{li} and to raise 6000 men, Nottingamshire 11000^{li} and to raise 2000 men. I shall indeavour what I can to hould up thire spirritts till [by] the returne of this messinger I heare what your Excellence' pleasure is, which I shall ever obay as,

Your Excellence' most humble and obedient servant,

F. WILLUGHBYE.

Boston, this 6 of August.

7 Economic Aspects of the Negotiations at Ryswick

The treaty of Ryswick has been neglected by recent historians. No satisfactory account of it exists in English, for no one has touched it with serious intent since Lord Macaulay wrote his sketch during the last years of his life. Its economic and colonial aspects have been ignored by French and German historians.[1] Yet this treaty plays a fundamental rôle in European diplomacy between the treaties of Nimeguen (1678) and Utrecht (1713). It is, in fact, a commentary upon the former and a

[1] J. C. Neuhaus, *Der Friede von Ryswick und die Abtretung Strasbourg an Frankreich* (Freiburg in Breisgau, 1873), as its title indicates, is concerned almost exclusively with what went on at Ryswick with reference to the Rhine frontier. It is obviously now out of date, and is but slightly concerned with the Dutch phase, and with the English aspects of it scarcely at all. A. Gaedeke, *Die Politik Oesterreichs in der Spanischen Erbfolgefrage* (Leipsic, 1877), deals only incidentally with the negotiations at Ryswick, although he does print some valuable documents bearing on them. Little attention is paid to the Anglo-Dutch affairs, in any case, and the abundance of material that has become available in the last quarter century. Onno Klopp's *Der Fall des Hauses Stuart* (Wien, 1879) contains an excellent account from the dispatches of the Imperial and Brandenburg archives, but it makes little use of the Dutch or French archives. On the other hand, A. Legrelle's *La Diplomatie française et la succession d'Espagne* (Paris, 1888–92; 2nd edn., Braine-le-Comte, 1895–9) is based very largely upon French archives. The best account (and latest) of the treaty from the Anglo-Dutch aspect is that of G. Koch, *Die Friedensbestrebungen Wilhelms III von den England in den Jahren 1694–7* (Tubingen und Leipsic, 1903), although it is only an outline of what might have been a definitive work by this young scholar, had death but spared him a few more years. Even this excellent fragment is mainly concerned with the recognition of William III, rather than the questions of commerce and colonies, although Dr. Koch ranged far and wide in European archives for his materials. For a brief discussion of the colonial aspects of the treaty and an exhaustive bibliography, see Frances G. Davenport, *European Treaties bearing on the History of the United States* (Washington, 1929), ii. 350–60. In addition should be mentioned Sirtima de Grovestins, *Guillaume et Louis XIV, Historie des luttes et rivalites politiques* (Paris, 1868).

prelude to the latter. The negotiations themselves are not without interest, as the procedure ranks among the most undiplomatic in modern history; for nothing (except the Emperor's interminable delays) passed off according to expectations.

The first chapter in the Second Hundred Years War extends from the formation of the Grand Alliance to the treaty of Ryswick. This alliance resulted from the territorial aggressions of Louis XIV. By the War of the Devolution, the Dutch War and the Courts of Reunion he had aroused the fears of his continental neighbours; by his revocation of the Edict of Nantes he had earned the loathing of the Protestant groups; by his hospitality to James II, he brought England into the war in conjunction with Holland under the leadership of their joint ruler, William of Orange, his bitter rival. The alliance included, besides the maritime powers, Spain, the Emperor, Savoy, Bavaria, Saxony and the Palatinate, with some lesser German princes. These nations aimed at the reduction of the power of France that she might not weaken the Dutch barrier, nor strengthen her Rhine frontier, nor seize the Spanish inheritance at Charles II's death, which was imminent. For five years the war was decidedly a humdrum affair, relieved occasionally by naval battles, which proved to be more decisive than those on land. The despatch in 1694 of an Anglo-Dutch fleet to winter in the Mediterranean brought a new note into the conflict, just as both sides were rapidly reaching the point of exhaustion. This move was inspired by the desire to keep the wavering Duke of Savoy and the imbecile King of Spain true to the Allies, and to challenge the vexatious activity of French privateers, which had led to some blistering reflections upon the Admiralty in Parliament.

Although Louis XIV made earlier overtures for peace, the presence of the allied squadron around Toulon increased his desire for it. In 1690 Charles XI of Sweden offered himself as mediator, and in the next two years Louis attempted to seduce Spain and Savoy. By 1693 he was seeking peace through advances in Sweden and Holland. Both moves interested William III as promising a peace based on the treaties of Westphalia and Nimeguen, with liberal concessions as to the Dutch Barrier and the left bank of the Rhine. This was, according to M. Henri

Martin, 'the first retrograde step France had taken' since the days of Richelieu.[1] France employed as her secret agent, Peter Daguerre, a merchant from Bayonne, but a naturalised 'bourgeois d'Amsterdam', who went to Brussels to sound out the Dutch as to Luxembourg, and the recognition of William as king. Louis XIV's ambiguous proposals led William to suspect his sincerity.[2]

The Grand Monarque was still more active in 1694. His new intermediary was François Mollo, Polish Resident to the States-General of Holland, and diplomatic 'assistant' to William III and Antoine Heinsius, Grand Pensionary of Holland. The Polish minister had established while in Paris a close friendship with François Callières, a French littérateur, and by his tact had managed to gain the attention of the Court. On his return to Holland, Mollo communicated with Heinsius and Jacob Boreel, bourgomaster of Amsterdam, and spokesman of the merchants. As a result, he soon returned to Paris with a secret commission from the States-General.[3] Some weeks later he, together with Callières and Nicolas Auguste Harlay, Seigneur de Bonneuil et Comte de Cely, were at Maestricht secretly negotiating with Everard van Weede van Dijkveld, William's confidential agent. Three questions monopolised the time of these diplomats: Luxembourg, Strasbourg and the recognition of William. Bound up with Luxembourg were the questions of the Dutch Barrier and the protection of the frontier of the Spanish Netherlands, which were to plague

[1] *History of France* (Boston, 1865), ii. 167; H. J. van der Heim, ed., *Het Archief van Raadpensionaris Antonie Heinsius* ('s Gravenhage, 1867–80), iii. 6–45 *passim* (cited below as Heim); Hist[orical] MSS. Com[mission], *Portland MSS.* iii. 515; A. Legrelle, *Notes et documents sur la paix de Ryswick* (Lille, 1894), pp. 7–26, *passim*; G. Burnet, *History of Our Own Time* (Oxford, 1833), iv, 214–17. See also [Archives des Affaires Entrangères]: C[orrespondence] P[olitique]: Rome, 341, f. 126.

[2] C.P., Hollande, 158, f. 184; 394; 160, ff. 20–6; *Receuil Hollande*, i. 380, 414; Heim, *op. cit.*, iii. 7–72 *passim*. Louis XIV felt that there were no difficulties in the way of an accommodation between him and the English. 'Qu'elle n'a d'ailleurs rien a demeler avec les Anglais, en sorte que le seul retablissement du commerce de Part et d'autre et la restitution de ce qu'ils ont occupé dans les iles et continent de l'Amerique peut fair la paix.' C.P., Hollande, 158, ff. 260–8.

[3] Heim, *op. cit.*, iii. 49–59, 90–2, 129; Legrelle, *Notes et documents*, p. 44. *Receuil, Hollande*, i. 442–71.

European diplomats from that day till 1914. Strasbourg was probably the most strategic point on the left bank of the Rhine. As the gateway to the German States it had been seized by Louis XIV in 1681, as indispensable in consolidating French possessions in the Alsace-Lorraine area. To Louis XIV, William of Orange was only the Stadtholder of Holland, which made formal English negotiation with France impossible as England could not negotiate except through her king. So much wrangling occurred over these three matters that scholars have neglected other points fully as fundamental.

Louis XIV, being convinced by Mollo that the Dutch merchants were eager for peace, offered the Dutch a bribe, by promising the abolition of the duty of fifty sols per ton levied upon imports into France, in case they would secure a peace. Dijkveld, however, insisted upon a strong barrier, and negotiations broke down because Louis refused a satisfactory equivalent for Luxembourg.[1] Meanwhile France continued her overtures at Stockholm, where the discussions centred around the equivalent for Strasbourg. Austria naïvely proposed that negotiations be carried on at Stockholm, with the Imperial Chancellery acting as a clearing-house for allied demands.[2]

The year 1695 found French, English and Dutch even more anxious for peace than a year earlier. Louis believed that the Allies were badly divided, and that the English and Dutch people demanded peace, which had been denied them by Dijkveld's intransigeance. Mollo, after feeling the public pulse at Amsterdam, was so certain of the good will of the merchants, and particularly of Boreel, son-in-law of John Dewitt, that Louis XIV sent Callières back to Holland with offers,

[1] C.P., Hollande, 159, ff. 209–90 *passim*, 364; 160, ff. 213, 218, 347; Heim, *op. cit.*, iii. 46–129 *passim*; *Bath MSS.*, iii. 42; Legrelle. *Notes et documents*, pp. 45–8; *Correspondentie van Willem III en van Hans Willem Bentinck* (ed., N. Japikse, 's Gravenhage, 1927); Burnet, *op. cit.*, iv. 231. Prior did not doubt the sincerity of the French. *Bath MSS.*, iii. 17. Robert Harley reported in the summer: 'All talk now of peace and that the King will not fight.' Hist. MSS. Com., *Portland MSS.*, iii. 552.

[2] Copies of intercepted letter from Avaux to Louis XIV are found in Heim, *op. cit.*, iii. 46, 63, 103. See also one from Callières to Mollo and those exchanged by William III and Heinsius with the minister-resident of Hesse-Cassel, *ibid.*, iii. 82, 113 *passim*.

intended especially to attract Amsterdam.¹ Conditions meanwhile were changing for the worse in England and France. The allied fleet in the Mediterranean paralysed Louis's military projects, and he lost Luxembourg, his only able marshal. William III was also borne down, not only by the death of his queen but by the lack of allied co-operation, astonishing revelations of English political corruption, glaring administrative inefficiency in the Admiralty and a dangerous fall in credit as Parliament essayed to reform the currency. Moribund Spain expected the Allies not only to protect her possessions in Italy but bear besides the burden of the war in Catalonia, which on account of its proximity invited French attacks. French overtures for peace from various quarters, especially Sweden, worried the Duke of Shrewsbury, leading secretary of state, lest some allied diplomat might proceed without expressly providing for William's recognition, which could not be permitted under any condition.²

France agreed to recognise William in a secret article, if the Dutch would approve the equivalent she offered for Luxembourg and declare themselves neutral in case their allies, opposed peace. Upon Dutch economic enterprise and greed Louis counted much, and upon their trade jealousy of England still more. He was soon undeceived. Dijkveld again demanded a stronger barrier. The mediation of Boreel and Mollo produced no compromise. Callières wrote emphatically to the French Court, however, that if Maubeuge were added to the barrier, negotiations would succeed. 'Instructions additionnelles', ceding either Maubeuge or Condé, as the French might choose, were rushed to him.³ These French concessions came just too late. Before they could be made use of, William had surpassed himself in taking Namur, which brought

¹ Heim, *op. cit.*, iii. 122, 137, 140, 144; C.P., Hollande, 161, f. 1; 160, *passim* (folios unnumbered); Heinsius Papers (Rijksarchief, Den Haag), 10B; [Charles Sevin] de Quincy, *Histoire Militaire du Regne de Louis le Grand* (Paris, 1726), iii. 194.

² The Imperial and Spanish plenipotentiaries agreed to insist upon the recognition of William III. *Lexington Papers*, pp. 79, 133; Heim, *op. cit.*, 133, 141–4.

³ Additional Instruction for Callières, July 25/August 4; Callières, to Croissy, July 10/30; C.P., Hollande, 161, ff. 100–11, 162, 180, 253; *Receuil, Hollande*, i. 472–3, 480; Legrelle, *Notes et documents*, pp. 48–52.

in its train so much hard feeling that further parleys seemed futile. The cruel irony of fate decreed that what was probably the most considerable military achievement of William's career should prove a definite obstacle to the making of a peace that he desired. It served, nevertheless, to increase the Dutch demands for the barrier at the moment when Louis XIV's pride was touched to the quick by the only serious military reverse France had suffered in half a century, and by the bombardment of the French coast. Boreel, however, corresponded directly with Callières until the latter returned on a third peace mission in the summer of 1696.[1]

By that time the French position was becoming desperate. William gained great prestige by capturing Namur, and allied naval activity ruined French commerce, particularly in the Mediterranean. The financial stringency caused Louis to turn towards Spanish America to secure some of its treasure, with the additional hope that peace negotiations might find him with some valuable pawns in his hands. Meanwhile more ambitious efforts must be made nearer home as a reply to Namur and the activity of the allied fleets. France, therefore, planned to make a separate treaty with Savoy and invade the British Isles. The former would weaken the alliance, the latter would occasion great alarm in England, and even divert her attention from the main theatre of war.[2]

Louis felt that the English financial situation was so bad that Parliament would not vote sufficient funds for continuing the war. Spain was a steadily increasing liability to the Allies, yet in her helplessness

---

[1] Japikse, *op. cit.*, i. 270–4; C.P., Hollande, 161, ff. 236–337 *passim*; *Downshire MSS.*, i. 544; *Lexington Papers*, i. 99, 104, 135; *House of Lords MSS.*, 1695–7, No. 959; Hist. MSS. Com., *Buccleuch MSS.*, ii. 191–213; Heim, *op. cit.*, iii. 173; W. Coxe, *Correspondence of . . . Shrewsbury* (London, 1821), p. 266; Burnet, *op. cit.*, iv. 269. A Paris News Letter said, 'I am assured that at the commencement of the siege, M. de Callières had almost succeeded in concluding a peace, but the detention of the garrisons of Dixmude and Deysne [by the French], the bombardment of Brussels, and the dispute concerning the wounded at Namur, have carried so much bitterness of feeling that it now appears more distant than ever.' *Lexington Papers*, i. 125.

[2] J. Macpherson, ed., *Original Papers* (London, 1775), i. 538; Capefigue, *op. cit.*, i. 470; [Public Record Office], S[tate] P[apers, Foreign], 77/57, f. 6.

she insisted on the Peace of the Pyrenees as a basis of negotiations. The Imperialists always neglected their obligations on the western front, and selfish German princes held out eager hands for subsidies that could come only from the maritime powers, who found that great commercial losses from war and the pestiferous activity of nimble French privateers, were heavier than they could bear. Both William and Louis might well welcome peace on almost any terms that would afford them relief from the ever-increasing expense of war. Heinsius wrote the Dutch minister in Sweden that William was very anxious for peace, but that it was to be kept a profound secret. The Emperor, however, prevented progress, although Jean Antoine Esmes, Comte d'Avaux, French ambassador at Stockholm, laboured hard to secure the mediation of Charles XI.

In Holland, Callières resumed secret conversations, mainly with Boreel, for Dijkveld was too closely watched by the jealous ministers of Spain and Austria. France offered more satisfactory equivalents for Luxembourg, arrangements for recognising William at the signing of peace, mutual restitution of conquests in America and the re-establishment of Dutch commerce on the basis of the treaty of Nimeguen with the abolition of the fifty sols duty. The Dutch seemed content with these offers. Strasbourg proved a greater difficulty: Louis wished to keep it; the Emperor Leopold desired as great an equivalent for it as possible; the Dutch agents sought to deal fairly with both.[1]

Meanwhile the danger of an invasion of England was averted by the Anglo-Dutch navy, though only by the recall of their Mediterranean fleet. The Dutch informed the Emperor that the maritime powers must move directly towards peace, and were broaching the subject of a truce to Callières, when suddenly news came that Savoy had made a separate peace. Allied diplomats were stunned. William feared that he might be forced to accept such terms as France should offer. Before he could rally his courage, the second blow came. Despite his opposition,

---

[1] C.P., Hollande, 163, ff. 1–119 *passim*; *Mémoires et documents, fonds France*, 435, ff. 83–95; Add. MSS. 28941; *Lexington Papers*, p. 204; Lord Mahon [Stanhope], *Spain under Charles II* (2nd ed., London, 1844), p. 93; *Receuil, Hollande*, i. 477. See also Add. MSS. 34504, ff. 215–25, and the letters of Boreel to the Pensionary, Hensius Papers, 13B.

the Hapsburgs, at the suggestion of France, accepted a neutrality in Italy, automatically releasing for service elsewhere thirty thousand French troops under the ablest French marshal, Catinat.[1] William felt unable to continue the war, 'without exposing ourselves to total ruin'. Under such circumstances the Emperor and the German princes should have made peace, or protected the line of the Rhine with a greater force. They did neither. Austria was in a bad way financially, the pay of Prince Eugene's army being two years in arrears.

Since it seemed impossible for England and Holland to finance their own efforts, William was anxious to arrange the preliminaries for a general peace. He was 'more melancholy than I have ever seen him', reported one of his agents. To Shrewsbury the king wrote, 'if we do not soon receive some remittances, the army will be disbanded'; and a week later, 'I see no resource which can prevent the army from mutiny or total desertion . . . if you cannot . . . send contributions, or procure credit, all is lost, and I must go to the Indies.'[2] That he did not exaggerate is shown by the letters of Richard Hill, Assistant Paymaster of the Forces in the Low Countries, who wrote, 'We must be allowed here to desire a peace, since all our sinews of war are shrunk . . . When I stop payment for one day only, I fear there is an end of our war, and of our peace also.'[3] Shrewsbury believed that credit from Amsterdam was the 'only expedient left to preserve them from immediate ruin'. Even as he wrote, the bankers of that city were protesting English

[1] Archives de la Marine, Serie B. 7/531; C.P., Hollande, 163, ff. 119–44, *passim*; S.P., 77/57, f. 63; 81–87, f. 224; 105/56, f. 31; Brit. Mus., Lansdowne MSS. 1153E, f. 22; Coxe, *op. cit.*, pp. 126, 297. For the provisions of the treaty with Savoy, see Marine, B. 7/531; H. Vest, *Les Grands Traités du Regne de Louis XIV* (Paris, 1893), pp. 171–89. See also *Buccleuch MSS.*, ii. 353–5, 359, 366; Add. MSS. 28941; Petit fonds français (Bibliothèque Nationale), 24983, f. 7.

[2] Coxe, *op. cit.*, pp. 126–9. See also Resolutions of the States-General, August 24/September 3, C.P., Hollande, 162; 163, ff. 254, 342; Add. MSS. 34504, ff. 223–6; *Buccleuch MSS.*, ii. 355; *Receuil, Hollande*, i. 478; *Lexington Papers*, p. 209. L'Hermitage, Dutch secretary in London, to Heinsius, July 17/27, Heinsius Papers (Rijksarchief), 11B.

[3] *Buccleuch MSS.*, ii. 349; A little later Hill could see no way 'to subsist our army to the end of the Campaign'. *Ibid.*, ii. 364.

commercial paper. Both William and the English bankers were forced to appeal to Jewish financiers; the king even considered pawning his jewels.[1] In this great emergency, William despatched William Bentinck, Duke of Portland, to England on a special mission to bolster up finance, and perhaps to prepare the public for a poor peace.

Of the financial conditions in London and Amsterdam Louis was aware, and that, coupled with his treaty with Savoy, made him less conciliatory as to Strasbourg. Englishmen feared his designs on the Spanish inheritance, for if he be 'left at liberty to make himself master of Spain, . . . by adding Cadiz to Toulon and Brest, [he could] give laws to all the trading parts of Europe'.[2] Enterprising English merchants were competing with the Portuguese for the Asiento, and the Dutch were following their usual course of making a profit out of war by trading privately with the enemy.[3] With Strasbourg the most important point in dispute, William felt that it was essential to put pressure upon the Emperor, and warned his ministers that the maritime powers intended to make peace if concessions were made to Lorraine. The Imperial representatives insisted upon sending to Vienna for instructions. Fortunately for the diplomats, the delay was not entirely dull, as they could gossip about the probable place for the peace con-

[1] Japikse, *op. cit.*, i. 179, 184; Add. MSS. 34514, f. 87; *Bath MSS.*, iii. 81; C.P., Hollande, 163, ff. 218–23, 304. Hill pessimistically summarized the situation: 'I think it impossible for the King's own army to subsist there till another campaign; the Hollanders will not lend us a stiver; and the king is going to pawn his jewels for about 300,000 florins, and Schuylenbourg (Secretary of the king's council) will help us with 100,000 more, which is altogether fourteen days' subsistence, after which we must depend entirely upon Providence, and my Lord Godolphin.' *Buccleuch MSS.*, ii. 373. See also S.P., 105/56, f. 45; S.P., 87/1, f. 330. Shrewsbury confessed that he was discouraged 'from the ruyne of all creditt, and the scarcity of money, the deficiency in the supply for restoring the coin and other anticipations'. Heim, *op. cit.*, ii. 226.

[2] 'Observations', June 22/July 2, *Downshire MSS.*, i. 674. The English envoy to Spain felt that England and Holland must have peace, by which they would recover their great trade, 'as soon as the French, who if we may credit common fame, or judge by their present sueing, are at this time much lower than we are', Mahon, *op. cit.*, p. 95. For the misery in France, see *Downshire MSS.*, i. 642.

[3] S.P., 94/74, f. 95; Hist. MSS. Com., *Hastings MSS.*, ii. 288.

ference, the probable bride of William III, the election of a new Polish king, a truce, Louis XIV's agonies from boils and the reported death of the Spanish queen from a surfeit of eels and lemonade.[1]

William availed himself of this breathing spell to study the economic implications of a peace with France, especially as to English commerce, and the status of his West Indian possessions. Meanwhile he must protect the Spanish treasure fleet because of the great financial stake in it of English and Dutch merchants. The English trading classes, too, demanded a commercial treaty, with the preservation or restitution of conquests in the Caribbean, and they watched with jaundiced eye the possibility of a Franco-Dutch reciprocity agreement, as Callières emphasised the stimulus Dutch trade would receive if the fifty sols duty were abolished. Such rumours were fully capitalised by recalcitrant Tories. The whole question of tariffs, indeed, together with their bearing on Anglo-French and Franco-Dutch commercial treaties was brought up.[2] One John Nelson presented a memorial concerning the Hudson's Bay and Acadia. By October 1696 it was generally understood, despite the unsatisfactory replies of Austria, that a peace conference would soon begin. The preliminary terms offered by Callières now became known. Sweden was to mediate, with the treaties of Westphalia and Nimeguen as the basis of negotiations, Luxembourg

---

[1] S.P., 105/56, f. 53; Add. MSS. 28898, f. 402; Marine B. 2/117, f. 646; Petit fonds français, 24983, ff. 21, 25; *Buccleuch MSS.*, ii. 382, 403; *Portland MSS.*, iii. 528, 578. One writer noted that Louis XIV 'stinks above ground', another that he would 'not hold out this winter', S.P., 87/1.

[2] Add. MSS. 28898, f. 378; 34505, f. 1; Add. MSS. 28921, f. 102; Coxe, *op. cit.*, p. 331; *Bath MSS.*, iii. 88; C.P., Hollande, 164; Petit fonds français, 24983, ff. 31–46; S.P., 87/1; 105/56; f. 55; *Calendar of State Papers, Colonial: America and the West Indies, 1696–7*, pp. 134–5; L'Hermitage to Heinsius, October 6/16, 13/23, Heinsius Papers, 11B. An intercepted despatch found in King William's Chest from the Danish ambassador in Paris, noted that Callières and the Dutch had already started 'à régler les partes d'un traitté de commerce entre la France et la Hollande, le quil mesure estsit desja fort advancé'. S.P., 8/16, No. 77. Some weeks later Callières suggested to the Dutch that they should settle their commercial difficulties without the meditator. A. Legrelle, *La Diplomatie française et la succession d'Espagne* (2nd edn., 6 vols., Braine-le-Comte, 1895–99), i. 473. See also Coxe, *op. cit.*, p. 331. Landsowne MSS., 1153E, f. 4.

to be restored as it now was, and Strasbourg as it was when the French seized it, or generous equivalents should be given for each place.

The English king, knowing that his rival believed him unable to finance another campaign, informed Parliament that 'the only way of treating with France is with our sword in our hands'.[1] England's needs were great, five millions for current expenditures and nearly three millions more to cover the existing deficit. Shrewsbury felt that a cheerful voting of this money would 'forward the peace' as it was folly to imagine 'the French will think of a peace with us, when they know we are no longer able to make war'.[2] For many weeks, French and Dutch ministers alike waited not only for the Emperor to moderate his demands but more particularly to see how Parliament met the situation. William was exceedingly irritable, fearing that the Dutch bourgeoisie would refuse to continue the war to secure satisfaction for such an arrogant, dilatory ally as the Emperor. France meanwhile earnestly prepared for another campaign. Yet Marshal Boufflers felt that peace was imminent, and an English agent in the Netherlands wrote that if the Allies would 'make as much haste as our enemies, . . . the peace might be signed this winter, supposing our Parliament puts His Majesty in a way to make another campaign'. If the Commons 'could but make good what they promise, and redress the coyne', wrote another well-informed diplomat, ''tis certain we should have a good peace before the year has gone about'.[3] Fortunately, Parliament adopted a strong attitude, although the greatest scepticism existed, even in England, as to its ability to raise the sums appropriated.[4] Realising the

[1] Cobbett, *Parliamentary History* (London, 1810), v. 995. See also C.P., Angleterre, 173, f. 132; S.P., 8/16, No. 70; S.P., 94/74, f. 106; C.P., Hollande, 164, ff. 1, 28. The English secretaries of State had difficulty in finding any data on Anglo-French relations in America except the treaty of neutrality of 1686. S.P., 104/69, f. 62; *Buccleuch MSS.*, ii. 398; Add. MSS. 28898, f. 378.

[2] Coxe, *op. cit.*, p. 155. Petit fonds français, 24983, f. 78; S.P., 105/56, f. 80.

[3] *Buccleuch MSS.*, ii. 415. See also Add. MSS. 34505, f. 3; S.P., 105/56, f. 114. Louis XIV believed that last year's deficit indicated that England was impoverished. S.P., 8/16, Nos. 102–3.

[4] S.P., 105/56, f. 83. L'Hermitage to Heinsius; October 13/23, 23/November

weakness of Spain and the supineness of the Emperor, William was despondent and feared an invasion of England, to meet which, 'ready money was indispensable, which he absolutely lacked'.[1]

Peace negotiations now gradually assumed a rosier hue, and a half-dozen powers vied with each other for the honour of acting as mediator, an honour that eventually went to Sweden through Nils (Nicolaus) Eosen, Count Lillieroot, her ambassador at The Hague. Louis XIV appointed two additional plenipotentiaries, Harlay and Louis de Verjus, Comte de Crécy. Before their arrival, Callières agreed to negotiate more definitely as to the barrier, but maintained that France could not restore Luxembourg without compensation for the expense of fortifying it. Further embarrassment arose through the report that Avaux at Stockholm had recognised William as king. This episode not only served to delay the preliminaries but brought up a fundamental point, because Callières had refused to state in writing that France would recognise William at the conclusion of peace. Eventually Callières agreed to dictate the preliminaries to the mediator in the presence of witnesses; furthermore that Dijkveld and Boreel might say to the mediator in his presence that Louis would recognise William, and he would confirm the statement.[2]

Early in December 1696 William appointed the Earl of Pembroke, Lord Villiers and Sir Joseph Williamson as his plenipotentiaries, with Matthew Prior as secretary. At the same time he confessed to Heinsius his desperation. 'I cannot close,' he said, 'without adding that the more I consider our state and that of the allies, the more I am convinced that it is absolutely necessary to make peace, . . . before the opening of the campaign.'[3] Louis XIV hoped that this situation would cause the

---

3, November 3/13, Heinsius Papers 11B. L'Hermitage paid a tribute to the steadfastness of the merchants in insisting upon a continuation of the war.

[1] Add. MSS. 34505, f. 5. See also S.P., 105/56, f. 92; 94/74, f. 15.

[2] Stepney to Trumbull, November 17/27, S.P., 87/1. See also S.P., 105/56, f. 102; S.P. 8/16, No. 90; Heim, *op. cit.*, iii. 216; *Buccleuch MSS.*, ii. 419; C.P., Hollande, 164, f. 229.

[3] Add. MSS. 34505, f. 13. 'Sir, the people of England do amuse themselves if they think to make war only by votes and resolutions to restore credit.' Hill to Vernon, S.P., 77/57, f. 140.

maritime powers either to force the Imperialists to join in a peace, or conclude a separate treaty.[1]

William III recognised that the Emperor felt the Spanish Succession could be settled more advantageously while the Grand Alliance remained intact, so he 'would be glad to have all the world in arms' at Charles II's death. The Anglo-Dutch leader realised that this was not 'for our advantage, and . . . I persist in believing, . . . that a prompt peace is absolutely indispensable for us'.[2] Meanwhile, English economic conditions seemed to mend, because the Bank and rich men of the highest social rank placed their resources at the command of the government.[3] During the financial stringency of 1696, England tightened her belt, as is shown by the establishment of the Board of Trade, a new Navigation Act and currency reform.

Callières and the Dutch ministers agreed upon Ryswick Castle for the general negotiations. Many weeks later it was accepted by the Emperor, who suggested at various times Aix-la-Chapelle, Stockholm, Hamburg, Bremen and Brussels. The year 1696 closed, therefore, with good prospects for peace, although there were still many clouds upon the horizon. During the year Louis XIV had to his credit only the treaty with Savoy, but he manifested an increasing desire to tap the treasure of Mexico and Peru. He had sent three small expeditions to the Caribbean in 1696. The projects were more elaborate for 1697. A large squadron was to be sent to the same area, a second to Hudson Bay, and a third against the English in Newfoundland. During the opening weeks of this year, England was mainly concerned in protecting herself against this first fleet under Baron de Pointis.

In drawing up instructions for the plenipotentiaries the English Cabinet said little about either commerce or Colonies. It was poorly

[1] C.P., Hollande, 164, f. 404; Petit fonds français, 24983, f. 136. There was also a fear that Austria might be treating separately with France. This rumour received more credence from William III than it would otherwise have received because Austria was making no preparations upon the Rhine, although France was massing troops there. Add. MSS. 34505, f. 18; *Buccleuch MSS.*, ii, 430.

[2] Add. MSS. 34505, f. 16. See also C.P., Hollande, 165, f. 196.

[3] G. P. R. James, editor, *Letters Illustrative of the Reign of William III* (London, 1841), i. 135; Petit fonds français, 24983, f. 147; *Hastings MSS.*, ii. 271.

informed and felt it must wait for the report of the new Board of Trade on these subjects. Until the recognition of William at the conclusion of peace, moreover, the English representatives could have no formal meeting with the French, and whatever treaty might be arranged must be referred to Parliament. George Stepney, one of England's leading diplomats, realising the importance of a commercial treaty, and fearing that the Dutch had already made their own arrangements (despite the angry disclaimers of the Pensionary), felt it 'high time we got busy on our own treaty of commerce'.[1] Louis XIV empowered Callières, while discussing a Franco-Dutch commercial treaty, to sound out the Dutch on their attitude as to the Spanish inheritance. The French king was avowedly trying to bribe the Dutch to compel the Emperor to choose the equivalent instead of Strasbourg, and at the same time drive an economic wedge between the English and Dutch. 'If we are not certain of peace before the beginning of the, campaign,' William wrote, 'we will fall into such confusion that the French will dictate the terms.' He had, therefore, little time to think of an Anglo-French treaty of commerce, although English merchants were educating the Board of Trade as to their needs, and the Hudson's Bay Company was presenting its case to the English plenipotentiaries.[2] William was exasperated with Callières, both because he seemed

[1] Add. MSS. 9719, f. 112; S.P., 8/16, No. 145; *Downshire MSS.*, i. 726; C.C. 1696-7, p. 299. The Board of Trade was particularly concerned with the Hudson's Bay area. Stepney hoped to be appointed one of the special commissioners to confer with similar French representatives. S.P., 105/56, f. 134; [Public Record Office] C[olonial] O[ffice], 388/6. For an interesting project for the establishment of direct trade between France and Spanish America *via* Buenos Ayres, see Marine B. 7/221. It included a suggestion that if six thousand troops were ready at Charles II's death, they could capture all Spanish America. A second stressed the importance of Pondicherry. A third one on commerce and colonies, found in Marine B. 2/121 (f. 132), was a memorial sent to the French plenipotentiaries. See also C.P., Hollande, 166, f. 120.

[2] C.C., 1696-7, No. 947; C.O., 388/6; Add. MSS. 34505, f. 23. See also S.P., 8/16, Nos. 118, 130; Marine B. 7/498, ff. 350, 447; Callières to Louis XIV, January 10/20; Louis XIV to Callières, January 18/28, C.P., Hollande, 165. The French felt that they could settle the outstanding Anglo-French colonial difficulties 'en moins de deux heures'.

unfriendly towards suggestions for a truce, and unwilling to make any concessions to Lorraine. The feeling was spreading among the English and Dutch, however, that they had nothing to lose and everything to gain by a peace. Dijkveld quarrelled with the Imperial ambassador, and William III was sorely tempted to ask the Emperor what forces he was ready to place upon the Rhine. Callières constantly stressed England's economic weakness and military unpreparedness, and the great strength of France, for Louis imagined himself incomparably stronger than the Allies. William continued pessimistic. Both rulers desired peace before the campaign opened. Louis XIV, moreover, made it clear that the abolition of the fifty sols duty was to be a special favour to the Dutch for their aid in securing peace. This pleased Boreel, who referred to the English as the national and perpetual enemies of the Dutch, seeking to raise themselves on the ruin of Holland. He held the Admiralty responsible for the great losses to Dutch shipping through waiting for convoys in English ports.[1] In planning the conference at Ryswick Louis and William both desired to expedite matters by reducing ceremonials to a minimum, but the ministers of Austria and of some German princes insisted upon all of their perquisites, assuming that diplomats should be both seen and heard.

The Spanish ambassador opposed any moves towards peace, yet bewailed in the same breath the almost certain loss of Catalonia if the war continued. English and Dutch diplomats were fearful lest Spain, in her defenceless condition, might agree to the French proposal to neutralise that area. To prevent this, William agreed to send an Anglo-Dutch squadron into the Mediterranean. Hill repeatedly lamented the condition of the English army in the Low Countries for lack of pay, and Heinsius thought 'our present want of money may be the only reason that France can find to stand off'.[2] When Callières' preliminaries

---

[1] C.P., Hollande, 165, ff. 215, 248, 261; 166, ff. 68, 74, 112, 131; 172, f. 34; Add. MSS. 34505, f. 24; S.P., Foreign: Treaty Papers, 95; S.P., 105/56. The necessity of co-operating in sending a squadron to relieve Barcelona was another fancied grievance of the Dutch. S.P., 104/69, f. 77.

[2] *Bath MSS.*, iii. 103; *Buccleuch MSS.*, ii. 447–451; C.P., Hollande, 165, ff. 261, 272, 333; 166, f. 74; S.P., 92/26; Add. MSS. 34505, ff. 27–28; *Receuil, Hollande*, i. 528.

became known, the French were amazed at their liberality, for they understood that the Allies were practically bankrupt, whereas in France money seemed more plentiful than before the war. Louis XIV, therefore, refused a truce except on the basis of a treaty actually agreed to by Spain and the maritime powers in case Austria refused to make peace.[1]

Stepney became indignant over the Emperor's policy of waiting expectantly for Charles II's death. 'It would be a shorter way,' he wrote, 'to knock him on the head downright rather than all Europe should be kept in suspense with the uncertain state of his health.'[2] Treasure from the Spanish flota or customs duties from merchant shipping seemed to be England's only hope of financial salvation. 'Ye world sayes you have not money enough to send ministers of peace, and those of war are much dearer,' wrote Hill, who despaired of any speedy relief, for 'I am sure I am broke here, [Antwerp] unless I receive large supplies to-morrow'. A fortnight afterward he was still more pessimistic over French military preparations, as they 'are pretty sure to live upon their enemies during the campaign, or upon the countries which they must restore ... pray consider whether the people of England does not amuse itself, when they think to get service from an army which has seven months pay due em'.[3] At Ryswick some progress was made in clarifying the Franco-Dutch commercial treaty. William was inclined to distrust French sincerity, partly because they would not discuss the questions of English colonies and commerce, ostensibly because they could not confer directly with England. He felt himself definitely at the end of his resources, and instructed Heinsius to ne-

[1] C.P., Hollande, 166, f. 30; 172, ff. 12–58. See also *Ibid.*, 165, f. 240; 167, ff. 58–167, *passim*; S.P., 8/16, Nos. 117A, 124, 164; Add. MSS. 34505, ff. 34, 40. Daguerre, who went upon a mission to the Hague, learned that English people were very desirous of peace on account of the insufferable burden of taxation, Marine B. 7/221 (Cipher).

[2] *Lexington Papers*, p. 252. See also *Calendar of State Papers Domestic, 1697*, p. 57; Prior to Vernon, March 16/26, S.P., 84/223. Prior heard a rumour that the Spanish treasure fleet had arrived in safety, 'so we hope and fear in perfection'.

[3] March 18/28, S.P., 92/26. He justly feared lest the army disintegrate for lack of money. *Buccleuch MSS.*, ii. 454.

gotiate secretly with France for a general peace, as he had not felt bound to Austria since the neutralization of Italy.[1]

Anglo-Dutch pessimism was measurably increased by the serious losses of their Bilboa fleet. William noted that 'this news will cause a great sensation at Amsterdam', and Daguerre prophesied that it would have the same effect on Rotterdam. Louis XIV now urged his ambassadors to agree to a treaty of commerce[2] with the Dutch if by so doing they could settle the question of Strasbourg, which still appeared insoluble. Little was accomplished, however, despite the persistence of the two leading Dutch ministers, who carried on, although one had the gout and could not move, while the other had lost his voice and could not speak. The mediator, Charles XI, also died suddenly. Fortunately, Lillieroot was tacitly accepted as mediator by all parties, but the other difficulties remained to harass William's soul as he began another military campaign. 'I have written also in all confidence to M. van Dycvelt,' he noted. Although he never despaired in the face of obstacles, William perhaps faced the most difficult situation of his career in May 1697, for he had no weapons except his craft to use against the French and the Allies.

Too much attention has been paid to the formal negotiations at Ryswick. They meant little. The mediator conducted the formal proceedings, and the ceremonies so dear to the heart of the professional diplomat were carefully observed. Lord Macaulay need not have wasted so much sarcasm upon diplomatic ceremonies, for they served as a screen behind which the real play went on. The real mediator was not Lillieroot but Boreel or Dijkveld; occasionally it was Heinsius or Portland, and on certain critical occasions William himself. This was due to the ambiguous position of the English plenipotentiaries, whose interests William found it necessary to protect. The true key to this

[1] Add. MSS. 34505, ff. 31–3; C.P., Hollande, 166, f. 56. William believed Catalonia was already neutralised.

[2] C.P., Hollande, 166, ff. 149, 216, 226; Daguerre to Pontchartrain, April 1/11, Marine B. 7/221; Prior to [Vernon?], April 1/11, S.P., 84/223. Boreel suggested reciprocal rights of fishing for whale and herring, but thanks to Bart's exploits against Dutch fisheries, France paid little attention to it. Marine B. 2/125, f. 143.

diplomacy is found in the correspondence of the French and Dutch plenipotentiaries, and in the private letters of William. Nothing could be more exhausting than to follow in detail the formal negotiations, and nothing more useless. By the time the first formal session was held Louis XIV had offered to cede Luxembourg or an equivalent, on condition that after Spain had decided on the equivalent he could make his choice. In the case of Strasbourg, however, France would offer the equivalent, and the Emperor must choose. Over these points they quibbled four weary months. While the Emperor waited for Charles II to die, thousands of men laid down their lives in that solemn, serious farce called war.

In other spheres, the French and English were busy. France sent Pointis to the Caribbean with a powerful squadron, and the maritime powers eventually despatched a stronger one in pursuit; England organised an expedition to regain her Newfoundland settlements, France matched it by a larger one with a roving commission against Boston and New York, and sent the redoubtable d'Iberville against the English in Hudson's Bay. Early in the campaign France captured Ath, and Barcelona seemed at her mercy. Louis XIV championed the claims of his obnoxious cousin, Prince de Conti, to the Polish throne. The Dutch sought as best they could to protect their valuable Baltic trade from the ubiquitous Bart.[1] These things had far more influence upon negotiations than the artifices of the Austrian and Spanish ambassadors or the intrigues of petty German princes.

The English king, that he might carry on his campaign, next attempted, with indifferent success, to borrow money from the Dutch. He learned at that moment that French privateers had badly handled the convoy of his West Indian merchant fleet, with heavy losses for the merchants.[2] William's uneasiness, however, was also due to the plight of Barcelona, because a breakdown in the Admiralty administration rendered it impossible to co-operate efficiently with the Dutch in

[1] Marine B. 4/18, f. 242; C.P., Hollande, 174, f. 16; W. T. Morgan, 'The Expedition of Baron de Pointis against Cartagena', *American Historical Review*, January 1932; *Camden Soc. Pubs.* (N.S.), xv. 187.

[2] C.P., Hollande, 167, f. 154; 174, ff. 22–4; *Portland MSS.*, iii. 583; *Downshire MSS.*, i. 743.

sending relief. Barcelona was without provisions, England without money.[1]

As negotiations lagged, the Dutch, English and French ministers paid increasing attention to questions of commerce and colonies. France was willing to treat on the basis of a mutual restoration, and even suggested a treaty of neutrality in America, which William considered 'tres disadvantageuse'.[2] The Dutch and French proceeded slowly with their commercial treaty. The fifty sols duty on direct trade of the Dutch with France was to be taken off, and the plenipotentiaries even discussed returning to the low tariff schedules of 1664 in France. Louis XIV seemed willing to concede a favourable treaty to the Dutch, though he was rather tenacious as to Pondicherry in India, which they had captured. Negotiations were not concluded, however, despite Louis XIV's strenuous endeavours to secure support in Amsterdam, where commerce languished partly because of the continuous attacks of French privateers.[3]

During the month of June 1697 four factors influenced negotiations: the candidacy of Conti, the siege of Barcelona, the expedition of Pointis, and the decline of Anglo-Dutch credit. Conti's enormous supply of money gained for him an initial advantage, but the Elector of Saxony with his 'convoy of 9,000 troops and £600,000 St.' eventually proved the stronger. Had Conti won, it would have enhanced French

[1] C.P., Hollande, 174, ff. 32, 50; *Buccleuch MSS.*, ii. 470. A Hollander wrote Heinsius that the continuation of the war in the manner 'que nous faisons, nous ruynira sans resource'. Heim, *op. cit.*, ii. 150. Daguerre reported English Bank stock at 21 per cent discount. C.P., Hollande, 174, f. 20. John Ellis, undersecretary of state, felt that if Louis offered peace to Spain and the Empire, England would be much inclined to take it 'upon almost any terms'. *C.D.*, 1697, p. 166.

[2] Memoranda: Archives des Colonies (Paris), Serie C/11, E/9, ff. 58–203; Memoires for Tallard and Phelypeaux, Marine B. 7/221. See also C.P., Hollande, 167, ff. 212–7; Add. MSS. 34505, ff. 37–43; S.P., 104/69, f. 82; English plenipotentiaries to Trumbull, May 25/June 4, S.P., 84/223; Marine B. 2/121, ff. 122, 128, 171. French colonial interests, however, extended beyond North America, especially to the Caribbean area, and even to the East Indies, f. 291.

[3] C.P., Hollande, 165, f. 183; 167, ff. 25, 194, 223, 275, 295; 168, ff. 16, 67; Daguerre to [Pontchartrain], June 24/July 4, July 9/19, Marine B. 7/221. See also Marine B., 2/121, f. 204.

prestige at Ryswick. The siege of Barcelona was carefully followed by the French and allied ministers. English observers said repeatedly and emphatically that France negotiated with one eye on Barcelona and the other on Pointis.[1]

Most attention was paid to Pointis, who was in quest of the Spanish flota, estimated to be worth £15,000,000. So great indeed was the fear for its safety that merchants financially interested, secured insurance at 20 per cent to 30 per cent premium. A false report that Pointis had captured Jamaica caused consternation among the merchants at Amsterdam, particularly the English. Heinsius accused France of marking time until she could hear from Pointis, and similar complaints came from other quarters. Williamson minimised the influence of Conti's candidacy and the fate of Barcelona: 'We want only to be secured in the other hazard; the galleons . . . which God grant us.' The fears for them is 'universelle' in Holland and England, wrote Daguerre, 'if Pointy has taken them or a part, it is certain that an infinite number of bankruptcies will occur, causing great disorder'.[2] The secretary of state's office reported the rumour that the galleons had escaped, hoping that it might speed negotiations, whereas Mme de Maintenon said that the 'capture of Barcelona, Ath and Cartegena will allow the king to convince the allies of his love of peace'.[3]

Early in May William had felt that he could not continue hostilities

[1] S.P., 82/19, f. 81; Daguerre to [Pontchartrain], June 7/17, July 1/11, Marine B. 7/221; *Portledge Papers*, p. 261; Lansdowne MSS., 1153E, ff. 51, 54; James, *op. cit.*, i. 306. Avaux felt that the fall of Barcelona would force the Allies to a peace. A Dutch friend of William thought it would cost the Allies Luxembourg. Wijnne, *Les Negociations d'Avaux* (Utrecht, 1882), ii. 198; Heim, *op. cit.*, ii. 151.

[2] C.P., Hollande, 174, ff. 59–66; Williamson's letters of June 15/25, July 5/15, 6/16; S.P., 84/223; Japikse, *op. cit.*, ii. 445; S.P., 82/19, f. 77; Williamson 'Journal', June 30/July 10, S.P., 103/95; *Bath MSS.* iii. 130–1. Daguerre even suggested that such economic disorder might bring on a revolution at least in Amsterdam, if peace did not come quickly. He reported the republicans there as saying that William did not desire peace, and if he could secure control of the treasure from the galleons he would continue the war. June 21/July 1, Marine B. 7/221.

[3] Add. MSS. 28898, f. 267; C.D., *1697*, p. 207; H. Brongniart, *Les Carsaires et la guerre maritime* (Paris, 1904), p. 52.

and conditions had steadily worsened in the weeks that had passed, although English people were bringing their plate to the mint. The Duke [Elector?] of Bavaria, stadtholder in the Spanish Netherlands, pawned all his jewels, and was still unable to provision his troops.[1] Mollo and Daguerre were both positive that Amsterdam either could not, or would not advance William any money. 'Peace is absolutely necessary for us, and I have written in all confidence to M. van Dycvelt,'[2] wrote William to Heinsius. The only important point of dispute remaining between England and France arose because Louis XIV refused to promise that he would not aid James II directly or indirectly. Having exhausted the ordinary channel of diplomacy by the mediator and the less regular avenue of the Dutch plenipotentiaries, William shortened negotiations, by instructing Portland to approach Boufflers and promise him that if Louis would agree to withhold aid from James II William would compel the Hapsburgs to accept terms.[3] *Pourparlers* were arranged, and after several meetings the two men succeeded where the professional diplomats had failed. Louis yielded reluctantly but gracefully, and the negotiations at Ryswick thereafter proceeded apace despite the unrelenting hostility of the Imperialists.

[1] C.P., Hollande, 174, ff. 36, 45; *Downshire MSS.*, i. 749. Louis wrote his plenipotentiaries: 'J'aprens également de tous côtés qu'il est également impossible à l'Angleterre et aux Provinces Unies de soustenir plus longtemps les despenses de la guerre.' C.P., Hollande, 167, f. 33.

[2] Add. MSS. 34505, f. 34; 22031, f. 1. C.P., Hollande, 168, f. 16; 174, f. 67; *Buccleuch MSS.*, ii. 459. Vernon reported a rumour that William would get 'a great supply of money from Holland, and that Amsterdam will furnish him five million guilders on the credit of our parliamentary funds at 5 per cent. I wish it were true on many accounts.' James, *op. cit.*, i. 283. 'Le Prince d'Orange témoigne vouloir la paix parce qu'il en a besoin et que l'Angleterre et la Hollande la demandent et ne sont plus disposées a luy fournir toutes les sommes qui lui sont necessaires pour continuer la guerre.' Plenipotentiaries to Louis XIV, C.P., Hollande, 168, f. 42. At the same time the Lords of the Treasury in England found it difficult to get even £10,000 for the Victuallers. *Ibid.*, p. 295.

[3] Archives Historique (Depot de la Guerre), 1402, f. 74; C.P., Hollande, 167, f. 322; 172, f. 183; Prior to Vernon, June 22/July 2, S.P., 84/223; S.P., Foreign Archives, 257, f. 61; *Downshire MSS.*, i. 750; P. Grimblot, *Letters of William III, Louis XIV and their Ministers . . . 1697 to 1700* (London, 1848), i. 8.

The Anglo-French and the Franco-Dutch commercial treaties, involving the question of colonies, were also to be concluded. Little official progress had been made with the former, because the French plenipotentiaries pleaded lack of power, but the latter was nearly ready. The English Cabinet now abandoned the idea of a separate commercial treaty in favour of a provision in the peace treaty for the appointment of commissioners to meet within a reasonable time to adjust any conflicts.[1] Consequently, there remained no difficulties except as to Hudson's Bay, on which William finally agreed to give way rather than break the negotiations.[2] While the English and Dutch arranged the final details of their treaties, the Spanish and Imperialists made increasing trouble over Strasbourg and Luxembourg, which caused France to threaten to recall her preliminaries unless agreed to by 22 July/1 August, although she later extended the date.

[1] Meetings of the 'Foraigne Committee' (Cabinet Council), January 5/15, February 14/24, S.P., 103/95. They felt that the Hudson's Bay question was the only urgent one. The changes in what seems to be the final draft from that of an earlier one are indicated by italics and are significant in that they stress the importance of commerce, restitution of colonies, and particularly compensations for French depredations in Hudson's Bay. '3 But y[t] w[wh] principally imports us wth relacon to ye French is to have a fair and equall regulation of trade by a mutual treaty of commerce and navigation, *w[ch] is a thing we found could never be obtained from ye French during ye late reignes, notwithstanding ye most intimate and close termes of Allyance ye two crowns otherwise stood united in.* This, therefore, must be chiefly taken care of as being indeed ye great point in which our subjects are concerned in a peace with France. *Although as ye point of trade with France now stands upon ye late acts of Parliament wee doubt much how such a treaty at present can be reasonably expected, or indeed how it could be possibly preceded in our Parliament till after ye peace be made, when ye reason for ye making these acts will be changed. Yet this is a matter ye must early have in your thoughts, and with ye best care you can prepare a way for, by inserting at least an article in your treaty, for ye final settling this matter,* of commerce and navigation within some reasonable time by Comissioners to be appointed by each party.' These extracts are taken from a very rough draft in the inexecrable writing of Sir Joseph Williamson, as the final instruction to the English plenipotentiaries at Ryswick seem to be lost.

[2] See W. T. Morgan, 'A Crisis in the History of the Hudson's Bay Company 1694–1697', *North Dakota Historical Quarterly*, 29 July 1931. See also Japikse, *op. cit.*, i. 203; Archives des Colonies, C/11.E/9, ff. 25–31.

Even as Portland and Boufflers negotiated, the influence of the siege of Barcelona, the expedition of Pointis and the Polish election could be observed. Conti's failure lowered French morale, while the lack of news from Pointis and the stubborn resistance of Barcelona wore down French opposition. In July, Blathwayt wrote that the French 'make sure of Barcelona, despair of Poland, and are in great fear for Pointis'.[1] Premature rumours that Pointis had reached home with five million sterling preceded the news of Barcelona's surrender, but Boufflers and Portland had concluded their fruitful labours before any accurate information was received about either. Barcelona surrendered 31 July/ 10 August, but not until 18/28 August did Pointis creep into Brest with his booty from Carthagena. Fortunately for the allies the galleons and Allied merchant fleets escaped him.

The negotiations now proceeded to their conclusion. The Emperor refused to sign upon the appointed day, and France, sustained by the booty from Carthagena and buoyed up by the capture of Barcelona, refused to abide longer by the preliminaries and insisted upon keeping Strasbourg.[2] Louis XIV had his way. England and Holland signed their treaties on the final day without the Emperor, who was allowed until November to accept or reject the terms that had been offered. For the maritime powers Ryswick was not a brilliant peace, although the Dutch secured a valuable commercial treaty and a stronger barrier. Curiously enough the two provisions for which England had striven hardest, the recognition of the king and her rights in Hudson's Bay, proved least enduring. Almost as they were signing the treaty, d'Iber-

---

[1] Letter to Williamson, July 12/22, S.P., 87/1. A fortnight earlier he more optimistically noted the arrival of the Virginia and Barbados fleet, which they feared had fallen into Pointis' clutches. S.P., 84/23. See also S.P. 82/19.

[2] *A. & M.*, iii. 48; William had anticipated this and feared France would break all negotiations, 'after these two important successes, the taking of Barcelona and the sally from Pointis', Grimblot, *op. cit.*, i. 99. Stepney prophesied that the French would be insufferable if Pointis reached home with his booty, Letters of July 28/August 7, August 10/20, August 24/September 3, S.P., 105/57. Villiers noted that the news of Barcelona and Pointis came very untimely. Shrewsbury feared the Allies would never get better terms since the 'misfortune of Barcelona and Pointis'. Coxe, *op. cit.*, p. 367.

ville was sweeping the bay, and four years later Louis XIV's recognition of the Old Pretender turned the other article into a scrap of paper. Nevertheless Ryswick marks the beginning of the end for Louis XIV: Ryswick laid the egg of his destruction, and Utrecht hatched it.

W. T. MORGAN

8 The Causes of the War of Jenkins'[1] Ear, 1739

Both Burke and Coxe have said that Jenkins never lost his ear from the stroke of a Spanish 'cutlash'; a modern historian has shown it to be likely that he did. What, however, is more important than the establishment of this truth is the decision as to the exact amount of influence it had upon producing the war which followed. Jenkins' ear may be said to typify the feelings of the English public in their broad sense, their hatred for the Spaniards as cruel Papists, their insular detestation of the foreigner and the like. The question is how far did these feelings influence the declaration of war; what were the main motives of the diplomats on either side? Did the English statesmen first truckle to Spain and then to England? The great interest of such an enquiry lies in the fact that the year 1739 was a turning point of history. It was, perhaps, the first of English wars in which the trade interest absolutely predominated, in which the war was waged solely for balance of trade rather than for balance of power. But it is not alone memorable on this account; from this war issued, in a clear and undeviating succession, the series of wars which were waged between England and France during the eighteenth century — wars in which Spain was sometimes a passive spectator, oftener an active enemy, never the friend of England. Spain's alliance with France produced grave complications for England in 1743, contributed to the fall of the greatest of English ministers in 1761, and to the loss of the greatest of English colonies in 1783. The danger of this union was only averted in 1791 by the use of the most

[1] *Bibliographical Note.* — Lord Acton once said that on most European events the historian could consult the diplomacy of ten governments. For the New World, however, three are usually sufficient. The archives of France and Spain on this incident have been well explored by H. M. A. Baudrillart, *Philippe V et la cour de France*, vols. iii and iv (Paris, 1893); and by Edward Armstrong, *Elizabeth Farnese* (London, 1892). This article endeavours to present fresh evidence from the English diplomatic records.

196

skilful diplomacy; it induced the younger Pitt to coquet with Spanish-American revolutionists in 1797, to plan military expeditions to Buenos Ayres in 1805, and it brought Canning to recognise the Spanish-American republics in 1823. Between 1739 and 1823 the cause and effect are clear and unmistakable, the danger of the Bourbon Alliance giving France an empire in the West hovers ever before the eyes of English statesmen, until Canning baffled the Spanish and French monarchies alike by his recognition of republican South America, when

> Debating despots hemmed on either shore
> Shrank trembling from the roused Atlantic's roar.

The immeasurable consequences of the decisions taken by the English Ministry and people in 1739 are therefore clear. To drive Spain into the arms of France was to imperil the future of English predominance in the New World. To make an ally of Spain was, on the other hand, to assure it. The following narrative will show that England, during the negotiations of 1738–9, had at times a real possibility of securing the second alternative. It will attempt to show that, though a decision for war was certainly intelligible, it was not inevitable, and that, like the Roman of old, the English Minister carried peace or war in the fold of his mantle.

In foreign policy the personal factor is always important; it was never more so than in the years 1737–9. Elizabeth Farnese was the real ruler of Spain at almost any time during the life of her indolent and hypochondriacal husband. She was more the ruler than usual during 1738–9, because King Philip V was beset with a fit of mania, which showed itself, wrote Keene, in imitating Farinelli's singing (very badly) and in howling at dinner. Patiño, the great commercial minister, who had sometimes dominated even Elizabeth, had died in 1736, and his chief successor, De la Quadra (afterwards Marquis of Villariàs), was a mere clerk in comparison with him. 'More dull and stubborn than I could well conceive.' Beside him was Quintana, Secretary of Marine and for the Indies, 'a more difficult, tenacious, disputable antagonist never was met with'; and Ustariz, first Commissioner of the War Office, said to be all-powerful with La Quadra. Montijo, President of the Council of the Indies, 'the most reasonable and the most instructed

person I meet with'; but during 1738-9 said to have been set aside by
the influence of Ustariz. In brief,

> 'this country [Spain] is at present governed by three or four mean
> stubborn people of little minds and limited understandings but full of
> the Romantick Ideas they have found in old Memorials and Specula-
> tive authors who have treated of the immense Grandeur of the Spanish
> Monarchy, People who have vanity enough to think themselves
> reserved by Providence to rectify and reform the mistakes and abuses
> of past ministers and ages.'[1]

Even if Don Quixote had not been revived in the Spanish Ministry,
Queen Elizabeth needed no stirring for her impetuous temper. Generally Keene's sketch is etched in with somewhat too biting an acid, but
none the less the insignificance of the Ministers, combined with the
humours of Elizabeth, constituted a danger to peace in Spain quite as
great as the violence of parliamentary discussions or the venom of
popular pamphlets in England. To this there was added 'a superstitious
delicacy' and an almost incredible slowness and carelessness on the part
of Spanish diplomacy. 'Can you well believe that such is the infatuation
here that more serious moments have been spent in choosing Patterns
for lacing and embroidering the Uniforms they have given to all the
Officers of the Household, than in thinking of our affairs. . . . This is
properly Negotiating by inch of candle like our Auctions.'[2] But
though this mixture of dilettantism, sleepiness, and caprice must have
been trying enough, it had a certain advantage. There may have been
a good deal of inattention shown to the negotiations, but there was also
a good deal of inattention shown to the wishes of the Spanish people as
a whole. The personal caprices of Spanish queen or courtiers may have
irritated the English people, but they guarded against a good deal of
danger from the anger of the whole Spanish nation. The conciliation of
a few persons at the Spanish Court was the real way to arrive at a

---

[1] Keene to Newcastle, 'private and particular,' 13 January [Public Record
Office], S[tate] P[apers] F[oreign], Spain, vol. 133; Keene to Newcastle, 'most
private' 13/24 April 1739; (*vide* also for above touches — S.P.F., vol. 131,
Segovia, 18/29 August 1738).

[2] Keene to Couraud (Under Secretary to Newcastle). January (apparently 13
or 14) 1739, S.P.F., Spain, vol. 133.

satisfactory settlement, and Keene had only to cajole the Court to secure everything he wanted.

For this purpose the negotiators on the English side were well chosen. Sir Robert Walpole was easy, good-natured and strongly desirous of peace, as was Horatio Walpole the elder, Ambassador at the Hague, who was frequently consulted by the Ministry.[1] Lord Harrington, the second Secretary of State, followed suit. Benjamin Keene — the Ambassador at Madrid, and the chief negotiator throughout — was good-natured, easy, fat and agreeable, but yet resolute and adroit enough when occasion served. He was at times a little sharp in criticism and repartee, but conspicuous for the real moderation of his views, and if he occasionally displayed an ignorance of his Government's actions which was a little too diplomatic, or a knowledge of his opponent's aims which was the reverse, he succeeded where the best French and Austrian diplomats had failed. He was never out of favour with their Spanish Majesties, who specially signified their genuine personal regret on his departure in 1739. His position was, however, difficult throughout, because he acted in a double capacity and in two respects. He was not only the representative of the English Crown, but the agent of the South Sea Company, a private and comparatively irresponsible business firm which had special transactions with the Spanish King; he not only received instructions from Newcastle but private letters from Walpole throughout his negotiations.[2] In England the negotiations which took place in London with the Spanish Ambassador, Sir Thomas FitzGerald (Don Geraldino), in June–July 1738,

---

[1] He was the author of a secret memoir, January 1738, *vide* below, p. 205. This Memoir is referred to by Coxe, and contains most valuable matter. I hope to publish it in full at a later stage.

[2] I have found no trace of the Keene–Walpole correspondence, but the fact is substantiated by Coxe, *Walpole* (3 vols., London, 1798), vol. 3, pp. 520–2. Keene writes, p. 522, that he intends to burn all Walpole's letters and papers before leaving Madrid. This is the only letter of the series that appears to have escaped this English *auto-da-fé* on Spanish soil. There seems to be a reference to the fact of this Correspondence in Keene to Stone, 12/23 February 1739, S.P.F., Spain, vol. 133. There is some unpublished correspondence of Keene to the Duke of Leeds calendared, *Hist[orical] MSS. Comm[ission] Rep[ort]*, xi. App., pt. vii. p. 47, but it appears to refer to the years 1751–6.

were managed chiefly by Sir Robert Walpole, and had a very important bearing on all later transactions, although the diplomacy proper
was in the hands of the Duke of Newcastle, the Principal Secretary of
State and chief negotiator throughout. The obligation of serving two
public masters and one private company undoubtedly increased Keene's
difficulties as well as anxieties. But it was Newcastle who represented
the real danger — Keene and Walpole at bottom hated the prospect of
war, but Newcastle feared unpopularity at home even more than he
feared the enemy abroad. Evidence will show over and over again how,
at the critical moment, he wished to yield to the public, and how he
allowed the violence of the street to overcome the prudence of the
council.

The causes of dispute between Spain and England may be succinctly
stated; their merits deserve a longer relation. After 1731 the old disputes
about Gibraltar and Minorca ceased to have force, though not to cause
irritation; as for the other great cause of dispute, the claims of English
merchants for vessels seized by Spanish *garda costas*, and for depredations
and ill-treatment, it was referred to a Commission in the same year. This
Commission met in a good spirit, but was interrupted by fresh depredations, in especial by the assault upon Robert Jenkins. Whether his
account that he had his ear cut off by a Spanish pirate, and was bidden
take it to King George, was true or no, the Ministry assumed that it
was. Expressions referring to it like 'immediate satisfaction for this cruel
and barbarous act' occur on 18 June 1731,[1] while apology for it is to be
'particularly' demanded on 3 August 1731.[2] Even at this period, however, the double note, half of defiance, half of humility, which is so
often subsequently to recur, is pre-eminent in English diplomacy.
Delafaye, Newcastle's under-secretary, writes to Keene on 1 October

[1] Drafts Newcastle to Keene, S.P.F., Spain, vol. 109. The letter of 18 June
has annexed to it the deposition of Jenkins, 17 June 1731, made to a government official (Delafaye) and signed and attested by his chief mate and boats-
wain. The Admiralty side of the matter (the first revelation of the truth) was
given to the world by Professor J. K. Laughton, *English Historical Review*, iv
(London, 1889), 741–9. There is a good discussion of the matter in Hertz,
British Imperialism in the Eighteenth Century (London, 1908), pp. 32–3. Cf. also
Newcastle to Keene, 10 January 1731, S.P.F., Spain, vol. 113.

[2] See note 1 above.

1731 in the humblest strain, perhaps under the influence of Walpole. On 8 November and 9 December, respectively, Harrington and Newcastle write in a style which resembles the haughtiness of Pitt.[1] But though the voice of Newcastle (presumably in deference to public opinion) was bellicose, he was not as yet prepared to support complaint by action. This fact is clearly revealed by his letter to Keene of 14 July 1732,[2] where he describes the West Indian Seas as 'spread with British ships': many go from hence to the coast of Guinea to buy Negroes and carry them to Barbadoes and Jamaica, where cargoes are very valuable; others trade directly

> between this country and the British Islands in the West Indies, and many are continually traficking between these islands and His Majesty's Plantations on the Continent of America; all these are, generally speaking, vessels built and fitted out meerly for trade, and not provided or equipped in a military way, and become an easy prey to Spanish Privateers; and besides this advantage the Spaniards have over us, *in case of a rupture*, the South Sea trade necessarily leaves constantly in their power ships and effects of a considerable value belonging to that Company, which they never fail to seize upon in every dispute we have with them.

For the reason, then, that our shipping was vulnerable, Newcastle was not anxious for war, though he did not mind trumpeting our grievances loud enough to the Spanish Government, or even writing as on 29 June 1733, that 'such enormitys for the future' (as some of the late outrages) 'could not fail of bringing on a war between the two nations'.[3]

Fortunately enough, just at this time, the question of the Polish Succession began to absorb the attention of France. Spain became her ally in continental warfare and the obligation was extended to the New

---

[1] See p.200, note 1.

[2] S.P.F., Spain, vol. 113. Cf. also Horatio Walpole's Secret Memoir, January 1738, B[ritish] M[useum] Add. MSS. 9131, ff. 236 *sqq.*

[3] S.P.F., Spain, vol. 118, Newcastle to Keene; Patiño was rather bellicose also about this time, *vide ibid.* Newcastle to Keene, 9 October 1733, 'Private' and in cypher; and *vide id.* to *id.* 5 February 1733/4, addition 'most private', *ibid.*, vol. 121.

World; and the two Bourbon Courts concluded, in great secrecy, the famous treaty of the Escurial (7 November 1733). This was the earliest of those three famous *Pactes de Famille*, which so profoundly influenced the history of the New World. This, the first of them, however, appears to have had little influence, though some think that it pledged Spain irrevocably to fight with France against England. The exact contrary is the case — Elizabeth remained the bitter enemy of the French Cardinal Minister Fleury, neither Queen nor Cardinal felt bound by the 'eternal and irrevocable union', of 1733, and in 1736 and 1737 their irritation with one another was extreme. The substance of this treaty of 1733 was known to Newcastle in February 1734, and this knowledge was to exercise a sinister effect upon the negotiations of 1739.

Meanwhile the depredations went on despite Newcastle's remonstrances, and it was not until five years from this date (1737) that he demanded satisfaction in a peremptory manner. It is probable that even Newcastle was sensible that some of the British tales of outrage, injury and the like may have been exaggerated. At any rate, as the subsequent diplomacy will show, the British Government were willing to abate some of the claims of their merchants in return for a cash payment. That there were some grievances may be readily admitted; the Spanish governors could not be adequately supervised from Madrid, and, in any case, had great difficulty in controlling the privateers with which the Spanish Main swarmed. The Spanish *garda costas* sometimes acted as pirates towards Englishmen while posing as official vessels, very much in the same way as a clever thief now robs a law-abiding citizen by impersonating a tax collector. Again, the Spanish governor sometimes had a share in the profits of the privateer, and therefore winked at his actions. Montijo, the most moderate of the Spaniards, put the case in a nutshell to Keene, 'If Spain would accumulate all her grievances against us, she might make as much to do as we did . . . that there were Faults on both Sides; our [*i.e.* England's] Contrabandists ought to be punished, and some of their [Spanish] Governors hanged.'[1]

---

[1] Keene to Newcastle 'private', 12 April 1738, S.P.F., Spain, vol. 130 (*vide* also *id.* to *id.* 16 March 1739, *ibid.*, vol. 133); *vide* Horace Walpole to Trevor, 21 July/1 August 1738, *Hist. MSS. Comm. Rep.*, xiv. App. pt. ix. p. 20 (Buck-

The illicit trade, which Englishmen pursued with the Spanish colonies, was the real secret of the Spanish fury against English vessels.[1] A certain amount of this smuggling was conducted through the annual ship sent by the South Sea Company to trade with Spanish America, in accordance with a provision of the Treaty of Utrecht.[2] But, apart from this, the illicit trade of private individuals was very considerable, and England's record in this matter, both official and unofficial, compares unfavourably with that of other nations. We hear, for instance, of the Dutch, that

'their trade in the West Indies, in general, is much more confined than ours, and that which they carry on to the Spanish Colonies is altogether an illicit one, and therefore the Dutch Merchant Ships are generally of sufficient force to be an overmatch for the *garda costas*; and wherever they are not, the Dutch know they have no pretence to trade there, and never complain when their Ships are taken.'[3]

---

inghamshire Papers, Trevor MSS.), on the advantages for illicit trade which the Assiento gave; *vide* also Horatio Walpole's Secret Memoir, January 1738, B.M. Add. MSS. 9131, f. 209, ff. 222 *sqq.* The judgement of Montijo is precisely that of the foreigner; cf. Vaulgrenaut's instructions from Paris, 11 April 1749, *Recueil des Instructions*, xii. *bis. Espagne*; Morel-Fatio et Léonardon, p. 316, Paris, 1899.

[1] Cf. Duke of Bedford to Keene, 11 May 1749, S.P.F., Spain, vol. 135, 'The contraband trade with the Spanish West Indies, the great bone of contention between the two nations, and the cause of most of the wars that have happened betwixt them.'

[2] According to the King of Spain's Memorial, 17 April 1732, received by Keene from Stert, 23 September 1738, S.P.F., Spain, vol. 131, this 'unlawful trade' was 'carried on by the directors themselves . . . under the shadow of the ship of permission and of the Assiento of negroes.' There was also, there can be little doubt, a very large private trade among the Company's servants without the directorial cognizance. Consult the most instructive contemporary pamphlet on this subject, *Considerations on the American Trade before and since the Establishment of the South Sea Company*, 1739.

[3] Newcastle to Keene, 14 July 1732, S.P.F., Spain, vol. 113; and 16 March, *ibid.*, vol. 133: 'Mor de la Quadra has insinuated to me more than once, as well as to the Dutch Ambr., that the principal remedy (for grievances) . . . lyes in our own hands, by imposing penalties on Contrabandists, and he gave this as a reason why France never had any occasion to pass offices on this subject, not-

Again, if we take the case of France, we find her trade conducted in an unexceptionable manner —

> we have been informed that France obliges Her Captains, when they receive their Expeditions at any of their Ports either in Europe or America, to give Security not to trade in any Port or on any Coast belonging to His Catholick Majesty in the West Indies. By this method they have not only put an effectual stop to those illicite practices, but have secured thereby a free and uninterrupted Navigation to the fair and innocent trade. But [as England's Plenipotentiaries ingenuously add] how far any Regulation of this nature, or any other equivalent to it, may be consistent with our *Constitution*, *or with the sense of the trading part of our nation, we must leave to better judgments than our own to determine.*[1]

If England had shown the same zeal in suppressing her illicit trade as France, Jenkins would probably not have lost his ear, the British public their temper, and Newcastle his head.

But, while the illicit trade of Englishmen was certainly felt as a most serious grievance in Spain, there can be no doubt that the Spaniards sometimes confounded innocent English traders with the guilty. It was impossible to line the Spanish-American coasts with troops, and consequently, when the *garda costas* did search anyone, they stuck at little in order to prove them to be guilty. If pieces of eight, cocoa, or logwood were found aboard a British vessel it was held that contraband was proved. Yet this contention, though a natural sophistry, was still a real one. Carteret pointed out that cocoa might come from Jamaica,

---

withstanding the proximity of their Possessions in St. Domingo.' This letter shows Keene to have been much afraid that the Dutch would agree to provisions suppressing their illicit commerce which would not be 'agreeable to our constitution or the present temper of our [England's] people'.

[1] Keene and Castres to Newcastle, 2/13 October 1738, Segovia, S.P.F., Spain, vol. 131. For France, *vide* also Armstrong's well-known work *Elizabeth Farnese*, p. 286; references to English illicit trade may be found in Newcastle to Keene, 7 January 1738, S.P.F., Spain, vol. 132; Keene to Newcastle, 7 May 1738, 'secret and private', 26 May 1738 (enclosure in same of translation of La Quadra's letter), *ibid.*, vol. 130; Keene to Couraud, (13?) January 1739, *ibid.*, vol. 133; Keene to Newcastle, 16 March 1739, *ibid.*

logwood from Domingo, while pieces of eight were a usual tender throughout the West Indies. Newcastle had frequently pressed this point in his despatches,[1] and Keene reported to Newcastle that 'a friend of mine in the [Spanish] Admiralty' was ingenuous enough to confess ... that 'as We had now a permitted commerce to the Spanish possessions in America by the Assiento Contract, and consequently neither the Spanish Coin, nor the Fruits of their Countries could pass as proof for condemning an English Vessel of having been guilty of Illicite Commerce'.[2] But, though we may readily admit that England had real and serious grievances, there can be no question that her illicit trade was enormous. Even the moderate Montijo, whose knowledge and judgement were equally worthy of respect, speaks of 'the immense prejudice Spain receives from unlawfull [i.e. private] traders'.[3] The South Sea Company conducted an illicit trade of their own in connection with their annual ship, yet it is uncertain whether they ever really made any considerable profits. Undoubtedly one of the causes of their failure was the enormous number of private individuals, interlopers and adventurers, whose successful smuggling produced an unfair competition with which the Company could not contend. Contemporary pamphlets tell us that the interlopers sold slaves and goods at a price with which the Company could not compete, that New Spain and Cuba derived half their provisions from illicit sources, and the like.[4] The prices of the Company were cut, their goods undersold, and even their existence

[1] Carteret, 2 May 1738, *Parl. Hist.*, x. 745–54. Cf. also the same contention by Newcastle to Keene, 10 January 1733, S.P.F., Spain, vol. 118; *vide* also Horatio Walpole's Secret Memoir, B.M. Add. MSS. 9131 f. 131, ff. 221–2. The author of *Popular Prejudices against the Convention* (1739) pointed out, however, 'there is indeed some cocoa growing in our Colonies, but very different from Spanish cocoa.'

[2] 3 February 1738, Madrid, S.P.F., Spain, vol. 130; cf. Armstrong's *Elizabeth Farnese*, p. 246.

[3] Keene to Newcastle, Casa del Monte, 7 May 1738, 'most private'. S.P.F., Spain, vol. 130.

[4] Most of the valuable contemporary pamphlets on this subject are referred to in G. B. Hertz, *British Imperialism in the Eighteenth Century*, London, 1908, pp. 15 *sqq.* While not dealing with the diplomacy of the period, this work is of great value, owing to the patience and care with which the printed pamphlets and works of the period have been ransacked for information.

endangered. As Spain had inflicted considerable losses on the Company not only through the *garda costas*, but by seizing all their effects in Spanish ports in 1719 and 1727, it is easily intelligible that the Company should have been the most bitter opponents of the Spaniards and the most earnest advocates of the war.

But though the English peaceful traders between one British West Indian isle and another, as well as the South Sea Company, may have had some real grievances against Spain, there was another side of the question. If English ships were exposed to Spanish pirates, if Englishmen were chained in Spanish dungeons, or tied to labouring oars in the galleys, Spain had her own list of outrages also to unfold. One well-informed pamphleteer declared that he had seen Spaniards publicly sold as slaves in British Colonies, and that the seas swarmed with English pirates, often including British logwood cutters from Campeachy Bay.[1] The latter, at any rate, was a notorious fact proved by the Instructions to British war vessels[2] as well as by various other testimonies.

Thus there were plenty of grievances on both sides, though the main key to the bitterness clearly is that, while the English could complain of many, and the Spaniards of some outrages, the former continued their profitable illicit trade unchecked. The latter, being no traders and severe monopolists, resented this practice intensely, and tacitly intimated that the *garda costas* would not be checked by Spain until the

---

[1] *Popular Prejudices against the Convention*, p. 21, quoted by Mr. Hertz, p. 52. This particular statement as to seeing Spaniards sold as slaves in British colonies is hotly traversed in *A New Miscellany for the Year 1739*, pp. 25–6.

[2] *Vide* Instructions to Captain Reddish, *Anglesea*, Plymouth, 15 February 1738, P.R.O., Admiralty Secretary Out Letters, vol. 55, pp. 194–8; and, Instructions to Captain Sir Yelverton Peyton, *Hector*, Portsmouth, 9 May 1738, *ibid.*, pp. 231–5. 'And whereas we have received information that the pirates do frequently infest the island of Providence' . . . 'and the coast of Virginia'. . . . 'the ships under your command shall be constantly kept in a good condition for service'. The instructions state that the service during recent years had been very slack, and that British captains had allowed their vessels to lie in harbour. It is significant that the instructions say nothing of stopping illicit commerce, though they make it clear that the captains must not themselves be concerned with any kind of private trade, etc.

smugglers were checked by England.[1] To a commercially minded Minister like Patiño nothing could have been more irritating than that England, while imposing the severest penalties on smugglers in her own country, was gentle enough towards them, as long as they only tried to smuggle in Spanish America. Hence until Patiño's death (1736) matters did not improve. Montijo even told Keene that Patiño's efforts to obtain compensation for unlawful captures of English ships in the West Indies were so languid that 'many of the [Spanish] Governors . . . have not thought fit so much as to acknowledge the Letters and Orders sent to them in his time'.[2] Whatever be the truth of this, little or nothing was done, despite remonstrances of a serious nature. A British memorandum records that between 1732 and October 1737 there were captures of over a dozen British sloops, four ships, four brigantines and a schooner; and Keene presented twenty-eight bundles of claims and depositions in 1738.[3] It was clearly impossible that this situation should continue, remonstrances in 1732-3 had failed to do anything but hasten the signature of the *Pacte de Famille*. That instrument, though regarded lightly by Spain, had tended to deepen England's distrust and uncertainty. In 1737, however, Fleury and Elizabeth were on such exceedingly bad terms that even Newcastle could not suspect a danger from a joint Bourbon coalition, and this fact probably influenced the British Ministry in pressing during this year for a redress of grievances, which should be at once speedy and final. The voice of the British public was beginning to be heard with no uncertain note, and Newcastle, never inattentive to it, thought that a good opportunity had at last arrived to enforce upon Spain his somewhat empty threats of five years before.[4] A Petition of West India Merchants on the Spanish Depredations of 11 October (o.s.), 1737, was heard 'before the Lords of the Cabinet

[1] Cf. Sorel, *L'Europe et la Révolution Français* (Paris, 1908), i. p. 338.

[2] Keene to Newcastle, Casa del Monte, 'most private', 7 May 1738, S.P.F., Spain, vol. 130. There may be exaggeration here, for Montijo had reason to hate Patiño.

[3] S.P.F., Spain, vol. 113 [no date given].

[4] On 1 October 1731, Delafaye wrote to Keene (S.P.F., Spain, 109): 'In short, my dear friend, unless we do something to stop the Clamours of people, all we have done will be of little service here at home.' This terror of the home public is the consistent note throughout.

Council' on the 15th (o.s.) and was sympathetically answered by King George, and during the remainder of the year Keene pressed the Spanish Court for immediate redress of grievances in a spirited manner. The atmosphere began to grow dark, the thunder to mutter, and the storm seemed on the point of breaking.

On 2 March 1738 Newcastle wrote to Keene that 'His Majesty has thought fit to declare, that he will grant Letters of Reprisal, to such of His Subjects, whose Ships, or effects, may have been seized on the High Seas by Spanish *garda costas*, or ships, acting by Spanish Commissions; which is what His Majesty thinks, He could not, in Justice, any longer Delay'.[1] As a matter of fact, His Majesty's name and sentiments were used rather in vain, for no letters were issued even till as late as 28 April.[2] But the information was a threat of action to frighten Spain, and a thunderbolt is sometimes formidable, when brandished, even if it is not discharged. As such, it was speedy and effectual.

> The Resolution of granting Letters of Reprisal seems to have struck them in a particular manner, since they presume that even after an accommodation of the present Differences, the commerce of the Indies will continue to be disturbed for years to come, by People, who may neglect their sovereign's orders, when used to a Licentious way of living. This, at least, they say, is what is to be apprehended from experience of past times, both with regard to the English and Spanish.[3]

This declaration reveals naïvely how great must have been the extent of piracy and smuggling, if the official grant of Letters of Reprisal could produce such gloomy apprehensions of future licence.

[1] S.P.F., Spain, vol. 132; *vide* also postscript of 3 March.

[2] Newcastle to Keene, Whitehall, 28 April 1738, 'secret and private'. S.P.F., Spain, vol. 132. The reason was not due to diplomatic caution, 'in Fact, not one Merchant has applied to the King for Letters of Reprisal'. *Vide* also *Hist. MSS. Comm. Rep.*, xiv. App. pt. ix; Earl of Buckinghamshire's Papers (Trevor MSS.), p. 13, 1738, 7/18 March. *Ibid.*, p. 24. 'The merchants would not, when it came to, take Letters of Reprisal, they required the Government to engage', etc. Horatio Walpole's Secret Memoir had recommended taking out Letters of Reprisal, B.M. Add. MSS. 9131, ff. 244 *sqq.*

[3] Keene to Newcastle, 24 October, 4 November 1738, S.P.F., Spain, vol. 131.

But, while the Spaniards were appalled by this threat, there wanted not advocates — one of brass and one of iron — to clinch the English argument. On 17 March 1738 the inimitable Captain Jenkins is believed to have presented to a sympathetic House of Commons his tale of woes together with his ear in a bottle. On 30 March Captain Clinton, Commander-in-Chief in the Mediterranean, was ordered to repair from Gibraltar to Minorca, and the tenor of his instructions[1] left no doubt that the prospect of war was already in contemplation. His orders were secret, but Jenkins and his grievances were public property; and parliamentary orators denounced the truckling and subservience of the Government, without suspecting that it had at last become bellicose. Seldom had English indignation swelled higher — one speaker talked of Englishmen in chains, another of Englishmen crawling with vermin in Spanish prisons. Every artifice of malice or ingenuity was used — the Spaniards were cruel, the Spaniards were proud, the days of Elizabeth were remembered with regret, the days of Cromwell were appealed to with pride. Let there be an end of the haughtiness and cruelty and tyranny of the Spaniard by the assertion of the freedom of the Protestant Briton and the like. Such strains were jaunty and popular, and they beat insistently and not in vain, upon the ears of Newcastle. On 12 April (o.s.) 1738 he wrote to Keene making the usual demands for the security of navigation and redress for injuries, and referring to his Majesty's desire to make a last effort for peace and to the strong resolutions of the House of Commons.[2] The Spanish Court had been threatened by the thunderbolt of the Letters of Reprisal, the popular agitation was now used by Newcastle and Keene to drive the lesson home: 'I have omitted no occasion of setting this Court right in its notions about the Motives of the present general dissatisfaction in England, and of convincing them that it does not arise from any Intrigues of Party, but from the just resentment of the whole Nation occasioned by the cruel treatment His Majesty's subjects have received from the Spaniards.'[3] La Quadra, like a true Spanish Grandee, was

[1] P.R.O., Admiralty Out Letters, 55, Instructions to Clinton, p. 208.
[2] S.P.F., Spain, vol. 132.
[3] Keene to Newcastle, Casa del Monte, 7 May (N.S.) 1738. S.P.F., Spain, vol. 130.

inclined to be haughty and obstinate, but Keene had already judged that he was not in a condition to resist.[1] On 26 April/7 May after reading to him Newcastle's despatch 'in a tone that did not diminish any part of its spirit', Keene suddenly made a frank appeal to La Quadra: 'As yet the whole matter was *dans son entier*, and it was absolutely in the hands of Spain to put a happy conclusion to it.'[2]

La Quadra was impressed, the Spanish treasury was unusually empty, the fleet was small, and concession therefore desirable. So on 26 April/7 May he sent orders to the Council of the Indies, 'drawn up in a manner to let them perceive that His Catholick Majesty's Intentions were to cultivate a good Understanding with the King of Great Britain and to render justice to such of his subjects as had been injured by the *garda costas*'. Orders sent to the Fiscal, however, with regard to monetary compensation, etc., instructed the officials to make out the best case for Spain.[3] Concession was in the Spanish air, and La Quadra only reflected the desires of Montijo, the most moderate and impartial of Spanish diplomats, and the wishes of the Spanish people as a whole.[4] Montijo, as usual, gave Keene the neatest summary of the situation: 'If you ... have a mind to regulate our disputes in the Indies, you can never wish for better Intentions and Dispositions than ours now are, and if you have a mind to take advantage from our bad situation and fall out with us, you can never look out for a better oportunity [*sic*].'[5]

[1] Keene to Stone (under-secretary of Newcastle), Casa del Monte, 4/15 April 1738, S.P.F., Spain, vol. 130. 'It is pretty plain they would not fall out with us at present, notwithstanding their late Blustering about Georgia.' This was *à propos* of an angry memorial of La Quadra's of this same date (4/15 April) on the subject of the Letters of Reprisal.

[2] Keene to Newcastle, Aranjuez, 26 April/7 May, S.P.F., Spain, vol. 130.

[3] Keene to Newcastle, Casa del Monte, 26 April/7 May 1738, 'most private', *ibid*. The information given was on the authority of Montijo, President of the Council of the Indies. Other information was sometimes secured by Keene from the Cardinal Nuncio, 'my purple friend'.

[4] S.P.F., vol. 224 (Reports of Spanish Consuls 1737–9). Report of J. B. Parker (Consul at Coruña) to Newcastle, 4 June, 1738. 'I cannot express to your Grace the concern and Consternation the Inhabitants of all this coast are under with the apprehension of a War with England, which they very much dread, and heartily wish to see it prevented.' *Vide* also under 13 June 1738.

[5] S.P.F., Spain, vol. 130, in Keene's 'most private' letter to Newcastle of

While La Quadra was conceding, Newcastle was arming; for, in point of fact, he seems to have been influenced less by a desire to take advantage of the Spaniard than by a resolve to yield to English popular opinion. Despatches ordered Admiral Haddock to the Mediterranean and to Minorca, with a squadron of nine ships and two fireships, and with instructions which obviously contemplated an immediate outbreak of war.[1] At the same time (9 May)[2] Captain Peyton was ordered to convey Oglethorpe's regiment to Georgia, in order to defend that newly founded colony against Spanish encroachments. By 15/26 May some rumours of warlike preparations reached Spain, their concessions vanished, and work on their fortifications began to be pushed on.[3] La Quadra addressed a lengthy letter (15/26 May) to Keene, which was haughty, almost defiant in tone, and which contained several flat contradictions of the English 'spirited' despatch. The real sting of La Quadra's reply lay, not so much in the force of his expressions, as in the superiority of his argument. The logic of Newcastle's despatch had been unequal to its spirit, for he had made a bad slip. In asserting the right of free navigation and prohibition of search he had tried to prove that the treaty with Spain of 1667 related to the West Indies, whereas it was concerned with Europe alone.[4] La Quadra had already pointed out

---

26 April/7 May 1738; Montijo continues in the warmth of his assurances, 'that there never were, nor ever can be, better dispositions in his Court, than its present ones to do us justice, and to settle matters of this nature on a known and sure footing'.

[1] P.R.O., Admiralty Out Letters, vol. 55, pp. 230, 242–5. 9, 15 May.

[2] *Ibid.*, pp. 231–5.

[3] Keene to Newcastle, 15/26 May, 'Secret and private'. S.P.F., Spain, vol. 130.

[4] Keene to Newcastle, 7 May 1738 (N.S.) *ibid.*; Newcastle to Keen, 2 and 17 March 1738 (O.S.), *ibid.*, vol. 132. The extent of the error was fully realised by the Ministry, *vide Hist. MSS. Comm. Report*, xiv. App. pt. ix., Papers of Earl of Buckinghamshire (Trevor MSS.), p. 13, Horace Walpole to Robert Trevor, 28 February (O.S.) 1738: 'The council is divided with respect to the sense of the treaty of 1667 as to the West Indies, and his Grace must support what he has wrote and signed, and Lord Chan[cello]r, between you and me, must support his friend'; also p. 13, 7 March (O.S.); and p. 14, 14/25 March 1738, Horace Walpole to Robert Trevor 'We have been a good deal embarrassed in having

the error, and he now insisted on it again, to the confusion of the Ministry. Nothing is more irritating in a negotiation than to be proved to be in the wrong, and it was tempting to reply to a Spanish diplomatic victory on paper by an English victory on the sea. In acknowledging the receipt of La Quadra's memorial on 1/11 June, Newcastle clearly intimated to Keene that war was almost inevitable. The English merchants were to be told immediately to withdraw their effects from Spanish harbours. Meanwhile orders for impressment on a large scale — the sure sign of immediate action — were sent out by the Admiralty.[1]

War, which was now within a hairsbreadth, was averted by a sudden and a new influence, probably by the hand of Sir Robert Walpole, who now for the first time assumes importance in the negotiation. Very fortunately for the peace party when La Quadra handed Keene his Memorial, he added certain verbal expressions, 'which he called a proof of his master's pacific intentions', a proof indeed by no means deducible from the written word.

> He told me [reported Keene[2] . . .] that his Catholick Majesty would readily agree with the King, in following any amicable means that may be thought of, for finishing all the Disputes in general between the two Crowns, in such a manner That all past motives of Complaint may be adjusted and buryed in oblivion: and that such Rules may be fixt on for the future as may prevent any fresh un-easiness and dissatisfaction between England and Spain.

This short speech was to prove at once the refuge of the peace party in the English Ministry, and the *fons et origo* of all subsequent negotiation.

Very fortunately Don Geraldino, the Spanish ambassador in London, and Stert (formerly British commissary for the Treaty of Seville) had

---

laid, altho' we don't care to own it, the foundation of our arguments upon a wrong treaty. We scramble out of it as well as we can, and connect the treaties of 1667 and 1670 together, on account of the last having confirmed the first, and the full powers for making the last being founded upon the necessity of explaining the first.'

[1] P.R.O., Admiralty Out Letters, vol. 55, p. 270, 27 June 1738; *vide* also pp., 296, 304, etc.

[2] Keene to Newcastle, Casa del Monte, 18/29 May 1738, S.P.F., Spain, vol. 130.

been amicably discussing the financial claims of each Power since the middle of April, and had arrived at a basis of agreement.[1] The transaction had been considered private, and Keene was not informed of it, but Geraldino had communicated the matter to the Spanish Court. Immediately after the receipt of Keene's letter, containing La Quadra's interminable Memorial and an account of his verbal expressions, the financial project was taken up with vigour. Walpole was present at two further interviews between Stert and Geraldino — 1/12 June, 14/25 June. On the latter date the Lords of the Council met and suspended any immediate resolution on La Quadra's Memorial, and extended their blessing to the Stert–Geraldino negotiations. These were pushed on rapidly under the guidance of Walpole, who, as supreme financial official, was now really master of the situation. Proposals which offered a fair basis of settlement were temporarily accepted by Geraldino, with some anticipatory sanction from Madrid, and sent home on 20 June/ 1 July. Walpole might long for peace, but he also liked to get the best of a bargain, and there can be little doubt that he drove Geraldino a little hard.[2] The reception of these overtures at Madrid was therefore not at first very favourable. La Quadra complained that the British Ministry had one proportion for estimating English financial pretensions, another for Spanish, and suspicions as to our arithmetical good faith were ominous.[3] Haddock's squadron cruising grimly in the Mediterranean

[1] All this is described in Newcastle to Keene, 21 June 1738, and enclosures thereto, S.P.F., Spain, vol. 132, 'The Lords' mentioned below were Lord Chancellor, Lord Privy Seal, Duke of Devonshire, Earl of Pembroke, Earl of Scarborough, Earl of Islay, Lord Harrington, Sir C. Wager, Duke of Newcastle. I do not use the word 'Cabinet' to describe them, because, strictly, that phrase was applied to a larger and more formal body, corresponding more nearly to the modern Privy Council, to which reference is made on pp. 207–8.

[2] Keene to Newcastle, Segovia, 18/29 August 1738, S.P.F., Spain, vol. 131.

[3] 22 July/2 August, *ibid.* 'Montijo says he (Geraldino) ought to be hanged for his *crassa ignorancia*, in letting himself be imposed on by such an account.' . . . 'La Quadra, more moderate . . . wonders how he could have engaged himself so far . . . says that he has let himself be blinded by his good intentions.' Keene here suggests that the whole negotiation may have been to delude England, while a secret treaty of alliance was being signed with France.

gave both irritation and alarm to Queen Elizabeth Farnese.[1] On 18/29 August 'she appeared in a bad humour after mass, and was beginning a discourse with the Nuncio in the following terms "*on a envie de nous faire peur*", but the King going out of the Oratory she followed him and had not time to vent her passion'. These, however, were but passing clouds: there was bluster but there was concession. By October the whole business of adjustment of financial claims seemed in a fair way of settlement, and this result owed not little to the iron arguments of Haddock. After much haggling Spain agreed to pay England £95,000, and this arrangement was to be preliminary to a general adjustment of disputes. Everything seemed to be settling down in the winter of 1738; the British Parliament with its noisy declaimers was prorogued, Elizabeth was quiescent, Newcastle moderate, the star of Walpole in the ascendant. On 13 October 1738,[2] Castres wrote to Couraud (Newcastle's under-secretary) that a short time before 'I would have given my Plenipotentiary-ship for half a crown. It has risen in value considerably since.' The impression of tranquillity was general throughout Spain, and the relief and jubilation corresponded. Even on 2/13 August Alicante was (a little prematurely) 'in a state of profound tranquillity'.[3] The fortifications, which had been rising at Cadiz, Ferrol, and Coruña, were stopped, and on 19/30 October at Coruña, 'The happy turn which

[1] 29 August 1738 *ibid.*; *vide ibid.* Keene to Newcastle, 13 October 1738, 'Most private': 'I am persuaded They (the Spanish Court) have now gone all the Lengths they will go, towards avoiding a War, and bringing on a Reconciliation between the two Crowns.' How much Haddock's fleet had counted as an argument in bringing Spain this length is revealed in a letter from R. Trevor to Sir E. Fawkener, from the Hague (a copy), B.M. Add. MSS. 23802, f. 86, verso, 6 September (N.S.) 1738. 'You ought not to be surprised at these pacifick appearances, when I tell you, England has at present 107 Ships of War, of different Force, and Denominations, actually in Commission.'

[2] British Consul-General at Madrid and Commissioner Plenipotentiary for the adjustment of British claims in conjunction with Keene. Segovia, S.P.F., Spain, vol. 131.

[3] Consuls' Reports, S.P.F., Spain, vol. 224, 13 August (N.S.), Report of A. Stanyford. For a local English view at Chichester, 9 September 1738, of the affairs, cf. Hare MSS. p. 241. *Hist. MSS. Comm. Rep.*, xiv. App., pt. ix. London, 1895.

Publick affairs have taken, hath caused a general joy in this Province, which is attended with the wishes of everyone for a lasting Peace' (except perhaps the Pretender's supporters — a number of hard-drinking Irish captains in the Spanish service).[1]

After infinite delays, due less to ill-will than to the caprice of Elizabeth and to the snail-pace of Spanish diplomacy, Keene eventually prevailed, and signed with La Quadra the famous Convention of the Pardo on 3/14 January 1739. This arrangement had for its main provisions the agreement that all outstanding claims to 10 December 1737, as between Spain and England, should be reckoned to be discharged by the Spanish payment of £95,000 within four months. Plenipotentiary commissioners (Castres and Keene on the English side, Quintana and Abaria on the Spanish) were to meet for the speedy settlement of outstanding disputes. There can be no question whatever that the signature of this convention was regarded on both sides as preliminary to a final adjustment of difficulties. So clearly was this recognised by both sides that on 26 January/6 February Newcastle instructed Keene to sound La Quadra as to the possibility of an English alliance with Spain;[2] and on 29 January (o.s.) the Admiralty issued orders to Haddock (whose fleet had done much to secure Spanish compliance with English terms) 'forthwith to repair to England'.[3] So much for English sincerity; Spanish is even more capable of proof. The Spaniards at once abandoned their warlike preparations; on 13/24 April 1739,[4] Keene could

---

[1] Consuls' Reports, S.P.F., Spain, vol. 224, 13 August (N.S.), Report of J. B. Parker, *vide* also 19 November 1738, 'all the apprehensions which this People had of a Rupture with England are entirely vanished.' Cadiz was specially important as an index of feeling, because the British interest was so strong there; 'we have seldom less than a hundred sail of Vessels in that Bay, there being by this post above one Hundred and Twenty'. Keene to Newcastle, 31 March 1738, S.P.F., Spain, vol. 130.

[2] Newcastle to Keene, 26 January, S.P.F., Spain, vol. 134. Newcastle had previously hinted at this possibility in a letter to Keene of 21 August/1 September 1738, *ibid.*, vol. 132.

[3] P.R.O., Admiralty Out Letters, vol. 55, p. 370.

[4] S.P.F., Spain, vol. 133. 'Apart.' Mr. Leadam (*Political History of England*, vol. ix (London, 1909), p. 363) traverses Mr. Armstrong's statement (*Elizabeth Farnese*, p. 355), that 'till within a month of the declaration of war, October

write to Newcastle: 'They have unarmed the greater part of their Ships, given liberty to their Officers to leave their Regiments, and their Destinations,' etc. For the rest it is obvious that both Powers had made real concessions for the sake of peace. Spain, which was nearly bankrupt, had agreed to make a speedy cash payment, and England, which was afraid of its merchants, had made considerable reductions in the amount of their original claims for compensation.

That results like these were secured should alone be quite enough answer to the countless criticisms which the Convention has evoked in those, and in later, times. For, whatever else may be thought of it, it cannot be maintained that the Convention was not sincere, or that one result which it secured, viz. the disarmament of the Spanish fleet, was a vague one. Even apart from this the English Ministry had scored a considerable diplomatic advantage, which could be used in subsequent negotiation. In an informal note, which Andrew Stone (Under-Secretary of Foreign Affairs) was ordered by Newcastle to write to Keene previous to the signature of the Convention, this point is made exceptionally clear. 'As Spain has consented to pay a considerable Balance due to our Merchants, for Vessels and Effects, taken from them, by Spanish garda costas, etc., *it is evident, that they thereby acknowledge those Vessels, and Effects, for which They have thus consented to give Satisfaction, to have been unjustly, and wrongfully taken.*'[1] He goes on to say that this admission can be made use of to get rid of the obnoxious right of search. It is quite evident, therefore, from this letter that the British negotiators themselves would be privately convinced that they had gained important advantages, when the payment of the £95,000 was

---

1739, no serious preparations were made.' This is putting it too strongly, but the fact of the Spanish disarmament till the end of May is proved by the MSS. over and over again. Mr. Leadam quotes from H. Walpole, *Hist. MSS. Comm. Rep.*, xiv. App., pt. ix (Trevor MSS., p. 33), a letter to Trevor 8/19 June to show that the Spaniards were arming. But, as will be seen below, on 29 May (o.s.), Spain refused to pay the £95,000, and this was known in England on June 7, after which war was inevitable and arming began.

[1] Stone to Keene, 'private', 21 August 1738 S.P.F., Spain, vol. 132 (italics my own). Horace Walpole took the same line of argument in Parliament; *vide* also *The Convention Vindicated*, pp. 11 *sqq.*

subsequently made the principal point of the Convention.[1] They had, as they believed, evidently gained an admirable basis for securing their own points in the future Treaty.

The disputes likely to be discussed in the new Treaty, to which the Convention was a preliminary, touched three points — the boundaries of Georgia and Carolina, the British right to cut logwood in Campeachy Bay, the British right to Free Navigation or exemption from search by Spanish *garda costas*. All of these may be very briefly dismissed, though all were subjects full of difficulty. The dispute about Georgia was doubtful; the British right to cut logwood, though probably not established by treaty, was perhaps established by custom; on the right to Free Navigation there can be no doubt whatever that England was in the wrong.[2] Newcastle first tried to establish the latter right by Treaty and, when that proved ineffectual, fell back on that last refuge of bankrupt diplomatists in that age, 'the Law of Nations (which is a Rule for all Countries, where particular treaties do not in-

[1] This point is argued very forcibly in *The Convention Vindicated, etc., from the misrepresentations of the enemies of our Peace,* sold by J. Roberts, London, 1739. This pamphlet has been plausibly attributed to Horatio Walpole, but it is not in the catalogue of his works in B.M. Add. MSS. 9131, ff. 1-5, which is in his own handwriting. Other pamphlets in favour of the Convention, Bordon's *Appeal to the Unprejudiced concerning the present Discontents* (1739), *Popular Prejudices against the Convention with Spain* (1739), the *Grand Question whether War or no War with Spain* (1739), are all worth reading and perhaps quasi-official. *Vide* Hertz, pp. 51 *sqq.*

[2] In its extreme form the cry 'No Search' appears to have been intended to mean no search of British vessels by Spaniards on the high seas. Even the most ardent British patriots (e.g. Carteret, *Parl. Hist.,* x. 745-54) appear to have admitted that Spaniards should be allowed to search and to seize British ships found in Spanish ports or really near their coasts. The question of the right to search on the high seas was full of difficulty, because contrary winds frequently blew perfectly honest vessels (which were trading between British colonies), to some point near the Spanish coasts. It is easy to see how mistakes could thus arise, and how extremely difficult it would be to frame equable conditions. Even Sir Robert Walpole seems to have been quite firm in the resolve to oppose the right of search, except when British ships were lurking near the Spanish coasts; *vide* Newcastle to Hardwicke, 25 August 1738, B.M. Add. MSS. 35406, f. 39, A well-informed and sober contemporary view may be found in Hare MSS. *Hist. MSS. Comm. Rep.,* xiv. App., pt. ix. pp. 243-4.

tervene).'[1] Unfortunately the Law of Nations, as held at this time and later expounded by Vattel, was not much more favourable to his claims than was the treaty right.[2] But it took much to shake Newcastle's confidence in this or any other British claim. Thus he wrote on 7/18 January 1738, of the right to cut logwood in Campeachy Bay 'to which they (British subjects) are entitled by Right and Custom, as very fully appears by the Report of the Board of Trade in 1717'.[3] Unhappily the calmer judgement of Keene was not convinced or even impressed by this. 'As to the cutting of logwood, I find that *at last* He [Colonel Bladen] is of the same opinion which some others I could name were always of, upon that article. But' [as Keene naïvely confesses] 'the Report of the Board of Trade in 1717 is become publick and who will venture to yeild [*sic*] a Tittle from it.'[4] Newcastle had himself some doubts about Georgia, but here as elsewhere no doubts as to the course he was to pursue. 'I fancy however the right may be, it will now be pretty difficult to give up Georgia.'[5] Thus, in brief and on the whole, practical judgements were simple, if theoretical solutions were difficult. Keene and Castres had left Newcastle to determine what portion of right or of justice 'our Constitution and the sense of the trading part of our nation might allow' (*vide* p. 204), and the Duke was satisfied with a

[1] *Vide supra*, and also Newcastle to Keene, 12 April (o.s.) 1738, S.P.F., Spain, vol. 132. 'The Freedom of Navigation and Commerce, which the Subjects of Great Britain have an undoubted Right to, by the Law of Nations, and by the Treaties subsisting between the two Crowns.' etc.; *vide* also B.M. Add. MSS. 35406, ff. 55–6.

[2] Vattel's *Law of Nations* (ed. Chitty, 1834, p. 39), quoted by Mr. Hertz, p. 16; *vide* also p. 35.

[3] Newcastle to Keene, S.P.F., Spain, vol. 132. On the whole question *vide* B.M., Stowe MSS. 256, ff. 305–7, 308–18; Add. MSS. 33117, ff. 25–36 (Memoranda of Thos. Pelham), which give all the relevant documents or copies of them.

[4] Keene to Couraud, Madrid, 9 June 1739, S.P.F., Spain, vol. 133.

[5] Newcastle to Hardwicke, Claremont, 25 September 1738. B.M. Add. MSS. 35406, f. 50, Add. MSS. 35909, ff. 74–5; *vide A New and Actual Account of the Provinces of South Carolina and Georgia* [London, 1732] for interesting details. Pulteney, in *A Review of all that passed between Great Britain and Spain, 1721–1739* [London, 1739], writes: 'The giving up of Georgia will be esteemed very dishonourable to the Legislature, which hath passed so many acts for maintaining it.'

modest remnant. Not the rights of the question, but the might of the British public, was the real measure of concession and negotiation for England, and the most slavish servant of mobs could hardly have truckled more to public opinion than did Newcastle, the aristocrat of aristocrats.

At first glance it might seem that the noisy declamations of a few unscrupulous and irresponsible politicians might upset the acutest and most delicate of negotiations, but, in reality, there were real hopes of arriving at a settlement, by way of mutual concession. Behind the three questions above-mentioned was a more important one for Spaniards, that of illicit trade. This was the point on which they felt most deeply, and it was here that an English concession could be made.[1]

> In all my conversations, as well with M. Montijo, as M. La Quadra, from the very beginning of our Disputes, I have always found this constant Condition expected from us, Namely that England should do something on her part towards stopping an illicite commerce. What would it avail, says Monsr. Montijo, if we should hang up a Dozen of our Governors in America to please You, or because they deserve it, if you, the English, do not treat your Contrabandists with equal Rigour; You only hear of your Ships being taken, but you give no attention to the Damages we suffer by Interlopers [quotes La Quadra as of the same view, *vide supra*, note 3, p. 203] . . . Besides, My Lord, no one who has any experience of this Court will ever believe they will come to any solid agreement, or any favourable extension of the American Treaty, on their side, if they have not some apparent condescension on ours. The art and Difficulty will be to know where to yield, in order to get an advantageous Bargain.

In brief Keene's idea was that the promise to suppress the illicit trade might be used so as to extort concessions in other directions from Spain. Newcastle was quite sensible of the value of this suggestion, and seems to have been willing to adopt it. The first and second articles of a Project of a Treaty sent by him to Keene and Castres on 8/19 May contained provisions for suppressing the illicit trade, apparently so far as it related to private persons, but not touching that in connection with

[1] Keene to Newcastle, 5/16 March 1739, S.P.F., Spain, vol. 133.

the South Sea Company.[1] Hence, if the South Sea Company would only be compliant in other directions, there was a real chance of final agreement.

A study of the documents does not confirm the popular view that England's desire to maintain the illicit trade of the interlopers and private individuals weighed deeply with the Ministry.[2] Their tenderness was reserved for the South Sea Company — that body so closely connected with the Government by financial ties, which was to repay Walpole for saving it in 1720 by ruining him in 1739. The kind of way in which the interests of merchants in general, and South Sea directors in particular, were beginning to be of Parliamentary importance is very strikingly illustrated by Delafaye's letter to Keene on 1 October 1731: 'These gentlemen [the Merchants] upon this have assumed a quite different air from what I have formerly known. They used in times past to come Cap in Hand to the Office praying for Relief, now the second word is *You shall hear of it in another Place*, meaning in Parliament. All this must be endured, and now in our turn we must bow and cringe to them.'[3] When the 'trading sense of the nation' was thus growing in power, and when Newcastle was in office, the reasons why the Government showed such deference to the South Sea Company are not far to seek. Trade by companies, as Bacon had said, was natural to England,

[1] 8 May, S.P.F., Spain, vol. 134; *vide* also Hardwicke, Debate in the Lords on the Convention, 1 March 1739, x. 1151–3; Horatio Walpole's Secret Memoir, January 1738, B.M. Add. MSS. 9131, f. 249, points out the impossibility of getting Parliament to pass, or subjects to keep, legislation of this kind.

[2] The main part of Newcastle's remonstrances seems to have been throughout against the *garda costas* for confiscating vessels carrying a few pieces of eight or a little logwood or cocoa (all of which *might* come from British colonies) *not* against obvious smugglers. That the above construction is his real meaning is proved from Newcastle to Keene, 'Private', 9 December 1731, S.P.F., Spain, vol. 109, where he declares that restitution must be made in all cases 'provided there be no collusive trade'; *vide* also in the same strain Horatio Walpole's Secret Memoir, B.M. Add. MSS. 9131, ff. 246 *sqq.*; and references *supra*, note 1, p. 205. A passage in Newcastle to Keene, 10 January 1733, S.P.F., Spain, vol. 118, indeed, seems at first against this view — Keene is instructed to 'prevail with the Court of Spain not to be so tenacious of their old laws, or jealous of facilitating an illicit trade', but the meaning appears to be that above mentioned.

[3] S.P.F., Spain, vol. 109.

and all Englishmen still believed in the dictum. This Company had been undercut by the interlopers, and would benefit by their suppression. An Englishman at home had money in the South Sea Company and the West Indies, and not in New England (whence most of the interlopers came), hence many London merchants would not have suffered much by the prohibition of private smuggling. The suppression of the illicit trade would indeed have occasioned considerable loss to various West Indian islands, but it would certainly have operated to the advantage of the South Sea Company. It was in the latter that the Government was most interested, and it was its refusal to put any sort of pressure upon the Company that was to be no slight occasion of the eventual rupture.

From the first to the last the action of the South Sea Company and its manner of advancing its claims hampered the Government, increased irritation, and exercised a sinister and disastrous influence on negotiations. In particular, the exclusion of their concerns from the Convention of the Pardo was fraught with serious disaster. The South Sea Company owed the King of Spain £68,000 as a fourth share in the proceeds of the annual ship sent to Spanish-American shores. But the South Sea directors, being often near insolvency, were not seldom impatient with the King of Spain, from whom they had suffered severe confiscations in the wars of 1719 and 1727. They declared further that the damage they had sustained from the *garda costas* amounted to three times the £68,000 (though they could not produce proofs for the whole of that sum), and would not produce their accounts though obliged to by treaty. In 1738 contention had already run so high that La Quadra had excluded their business from the Convention, and had made a declaration on 31 December/10 January 1738-9 to Keene that his Majesty might suspend the Assiento, unless the South Sea Company paid the £68,000 at once. The South Sea Company replied by a defiant refusal to pay the sum in question or to produce their accounts. Eventually on 6/17 May 1739, this attitude produced a declaration from La Quadra (Villariàs) that the Assiento was suspended. Nothing contributed more to the eventual wreckage of all negotiation than this affair, and the complication of the business of a private company with the interests of the two nations was extremely objectionable.

The King of Spain, being very poor, wanted to get the £68,000 in order to use it to discharge some of the debt of £95,000 to the English Government. When he could not get the money from the private company he suspended the Assiento (which was a national treaty) and thus irritated the English Government by suspending a national treaty in deference to his private quarrel with the merchants of the South Sea Company. But the blame certainly did not rest wholly with the Spanish King. Keene, at least, who had once been an agent of the South Sea Company, and was now their representative in Spain, thought their conduct wrong, short-sighted, and even dishonest.

> Other Countries and Companies would have given as large a sum as what is askt [£68,000] for the goodwill of a Court to let them carry on a winkt-at Commerce, but our Directors would not so much as bribe the Court of Spain with its own Money, as They might have done some time ago. Tho' now all is over, and Spain is now so disgusted at the *crambe repetita* They (South Sea Company) sent me, when Geraldino told them I had full Powers, that she will never lend an ear to any further Representations till she hears the money chink.[1]

He thought 'this affair would bring us into an unlucky scrape'; and complained to Newcastle that the South Sea Company would make no concessions.[2] He confided to Stone on the same day, 13/24 April, that he expected 'a thundering answer to my offices in favour of the S. Sea Company'.[3] He got it on 6/17 May, when La Quadra suspended

---

[1] Keene to Couraud January 1739, S.P.F., Spain, vol. 133 (cf. Mr. Armstrong, p. 286). A letter of Horace Walpole's, 21 July/1 August 1738 (*vide supra*, note 1, p. 202), Trevor MSS., p. 20, makes it clear that in the case of an Assiento, illicit trade in connection with it was inevitable, even though it might be entirely suppressed elsewhere. The point is, then, that Newcastle was willing to suppress the illicit trade of interlopers, but knew that some such smuggling was inevitable in the case of the Company, cf. Carteret, Speech, 1 March 1739, *Parl. Hist.* x. 1104. The dangers of relying too much on this argument are forcibly pointed out by Hoadley, Bishop of Salisbury, *ibid.*, p. 1127. For general details about the South Sea Company's affairs, etc. at this time *vide* B.M. Add. MSS. 33032, ff. 218–28, 277–82, etc.

[2] Keene to Newcastle, 'Apart', S.P.F., Spain, vol. 133; cf. also Keene to Newcastle, 13 January, 'Private and particular', *ibid.*

[3] Keene to Stone, 13/24 April, *Ibid.*

the Assiento, as above described. A last hope that the English Ministry might put pressure on the fire-eating directors flickered out, and Newcastle on 8/19 May wrote that the 'Resolution of the South Sea Company' was one of the causes of the Spanish refusal to pay the £95,000 to the National Government of England.[1]

Having dealt with all the points of dispute — including that connected with the South Sea Company — we can now appreciate the value of the opposition criticism, which was heaped upon the Convention. The real point of the innumerable petitions and the like (which poured in upon a harassed Government) was that the Convention had concluded nothing, had resulted in nothing, that all wrongs of British subjects were still unredressed. But the Convention had in fact brought us a promise of payment of £95,000, and that in itself was an admission by Spain of the wrongs done to British subjects, and an augury of future peace.[2] As a basis for negotiation the Convention had great merits, and offered every prospect of a speedy and sincere settlement of all outstanding difficulties. The contention that the Ministers were truckling to Spain was untrue, because it was owing to Haddock's fleet as much as to Keene's diplomacy that La Quadra's signature had been affixed to the Convention. The arguments that the Right of Search and other subjects were not touched upon in the agreement were utterly beside the point, because the Ministers had in no way abandoned these claims, but had in fact signed the Convention, as the best mode of securing their future acknowledgement.[3] This fact, the Opposition could not

[1] Newcastle to Keene 8 May, 'Private and particular to be opened by himself.' S.P.F., Spain, vol. 134.

[2] *Vide* the admirable speech of the Earl of Cholmondley in the Lords, March 1739. *Parl. Hist.*, vol. x, pp. 1091–1102. It is difficult to know how far to give confidence to these Parliamentary utterances, but in these debates independent testimony occasionally confirms the opinions of the speakers, e.g. Hare MSS. *Hist. MSS. Comm. Rep.*, xiv. pt. ix, pp. 242 *sqq.*

[3] *Vide* the papers of this period *passim*, but especially Newcastle to Hardwicke, Claremont, 22 October 1738, B.M. Add. MSS. 35406, ff. 55–6,: 'the instructions should go at the same time that we send back the Treaty, that it may appear that tho' we consented to their *alterations* as immaterial, we still intended to insist upon the freedom of navigation in a proper manner'; *vide* also Keene and Castres to Newcastle, 23 April 1739, Add. MSS. 32800, f. 280.

understand, and it may be admitted that it was difficult to explain it. None the less, the appeals to the fame of Elizabeth, to the great name of Oliver, to the passions of England and the barbarities of Spain — were so much empty beating of the wind. A government which had coerced Spain was not humiliated; a Convention which announced the concessions of Spain, and which was but the prelude to a definite treaty, could not be treated as a surrender of British rights. The real evil did not lie with the Spanish Convention, but with the English Constitution. As long as British liberty prescribed that incomplete negotiations of the most delicate character should be submitted to a noisy and ill-informed assembly, British policy could hardly prosper. Nations are as sensitive about the criticism of treaties as individual writers about the criticism of their works, and the situation might not inaptly be compared to that in the *Critic*. An author produces his play before a row of critics, who interrupt it as it proceeds, and wither it with their sarcasms. In the play which Walpole's Ministry now produced for the benefit of Parliament, Carteret and Pitt occupied the places of Dangle and Sneer.

Debates began in February 1739, but the issue was not really joined till March. It then became violent enough, and Francis Hare spoke of it as the greatest party struggle there had been since the Revolution. Carteret in the Lords displayed a large grasp of the whole question; Argyle was violent and rhetorical; in the Commons Pitt was ardent, Pulteney vehement and Wyndham venomous. Their views have already been outlined, as appeals to British honour, to British justice and to British interests, and are too well-known to need discussion here. It will be more to the point to reproduce the opinions of the English plenipotentiaries upon them, and to show how far they produced an effect on Spanish policy. De Castres, Keene's brother-plenipotentiary, treated the Opposition with great contempt, and thought that the Patriots were infinitely surprised and displeased to find the Convention no worse. Keene, having regard to Spain, took a graver view.

> They (the Spanish Ministers) [wrote he] are but too well informed of all that passes (the delay in our full powers, etc.) thanks to our Patriots who by bawling for the honour of our nation strip it of its

weight and dignity as I too sensibly [*keenly* erased] feel to my sorrow. Every scurrilous Pamphlet and Paper is sent hither translated, and you may judge how pleased they must be at seeing themselves treated so *cavaliérement*. Dⁿ la Quadra, as he is called, has condoled himself with Dⁿ Keene on this doleful occasion.[1]

Seven months later Keene assured Sir Robert Walpole that 'the Opposers make the War'.[2] None the less, despite all these protestations, it is conceivable that the Spanish Court might have overlooked irresponsible utterances of the Opposition, if only Newcastle had been able to do so. It is almost certain that the measures (which the Duke now took) were directly due to the influence of popular opinion; it is quite certain that they caused the war. Spanish sincerity had been proved by the disarmament of Spanish ships, English by the significant act of 29 January 1739, when Admiral Haddock was ordered 'forthwith to repair to England with the Squadron of His Maj. ships under your Command'.[3] On 10 March, this order was deliberately revoked. '*You are hereby required and directed, (Notwithstanding any former orders) to remain with the Squadron of His Majesty's Ships under your command at Gibraltar.*'[4] The date of this order is highly suggestive, it is that of the last day of the Convention debate in the Commons. As early as 24 February, Newcastle had written to Hardwicke, 'We must yeild [*sic*] to the times',[5] and his subsequent action did not belie his words. The whole

[1] Keene to Stone, 24 April, S.P.F., Spain, vol. 133; cf. also Francis Hare's description, Hare MSS., *Hist MSS. Comm.*, *Rep.*, xiv. App. ix., pp. 240 *sqq.* 'The Patriots were resolved to damn it, before they knew a word of it, and to inflame the people against it, which they have done with great success.'

[2] Newcastle to Hardwicke, 30 September 1739, B.M. Add. MSS. 35406, f. 158.

[3] P.R.O., Admiralty Out Letters, vol. 55, p. 370.

[4] P.R.O., Admiralty Out Letters, vol. 55, p. 389 (italics my own). The best contemporary discussion of the counter orders question is in Hare's MSS. *Hist. MSS. Comm. Rep.*, xiv. App. pt. ix., p. 249. Hare knew and sometimes talked with Sir R. Walpole (p. 246), and his evidence and judgement are equally entitled to respect.

[5] B.M. Add. MSS. 35406, f. 111: 'as far as is consistent at least with our own point' (i.e. alteration of the forms of the Resolution with reference to the Convention with Spain).

tenor of his policy indeed shows that he turned with every popular breath, but this alone is not sufficient to explain why this grave decision was taken. There were other men in the Ministry besides Newcastle, men not so impressionable or so anxious to yield to the times; even as late as 8 March Walpole had proudly declared 'I am resolved . . . to let no popular clamour get the better of what I think is for my country's good.'[1] The decision, in which he acquiesced two days after this utterance, placed peace in such hazard that perhaps he would have permitted neither popular clamour nor Newcastle to force him into it, had there not been another factor in the situation — and that was France.

Ever since the signature of the *Pacte de Famille* in 1733 (the substance of which had been revealed to England in February 1734), Newcastle had been nervously anxious about French relations with Spain. Immediate danger had been averted, and the hatred of Elizabeth Farnese for Fleury was so obvious that during 1737 even Newcastle realised that the *Pacte de Famille* was waste paper. When on 21 August 1738 (o.s.) Newcastle had hinted to Keene to sound La Quadra as to the possibility of an alliance between England and Spain, he had clearly in mind Spanish estrangement from France.[2] On 26 January/6 February 1739 he renewed these hints to the same purpose, but added as a postscript that his hopes were faint, as he had just heard of the good relations which the new French Ambassador was establishing with the Spanish Court.[3] La Marck, who had superseded Champeaux at Madrid, was a true courtier, difficulties and even impossibilities disappeared before his address; Elizabeth began to think favourably of the Cardinal, France and Spain to approach one another. On 22 February La Marck's politeness had its reward and the negotiation of a match 'between Don

[1] *Parl. Hist.*, x. 1291.

[2] *Vide supra*. Keene had suspicions of French interference between England and Spain so early as 29 May 1738, *vide* letter of that date, 'most secret', Keene to Newcastle, S.P.F., Spain, 130, and more important *vide ibid.*, 131, Keene to Newcastle, Segovia, 2 August, 'most private', where Keene hints at a projected alliance between Spain and France as having taken place in June 1738. B.M. Add. MSS. 19036, f. 1, has a memoir drawn up for the English Government on the state of military force, revenue and gallies of *France and Spain*, June 1738.

[3] Newcastle to Keene, 26 January 1739, S.P.F., Spain, vol. 134.

Phelipe and the eldest daughter of France' was announced.[1] Keene writing to Newcastle the next day announced this intelligence, said that he had 'never had any reply to my Hints on this head that was worth His Majesty's notice', and suggesting that an Anglo-Spanish alliance was now hopeless and a Franco-Spanish one extremely probable. He gave no decisive evidence, but a deduction from a marital union to a diplomatic one was natural. This letter reached London on 4 March, in sufficient time to clinch the Ministerial decision.[2] Hence while fear of the mob in England drove Newcastle, fear of the Cardinal in France appears to have driven Walpole, to this momentous decision of 10 March 1739.

It is possible, though extremely unlikely, that the British Ministry were unaware of the effect that their counter-orders to Haddock were likely to produce upon Spain. If so they were soon undeceived; Don Geraldino remonstrated within ten days from its issue 'upon the Report, that Orders were sent to stop the Fleet, and expressed his apprehension that his Court would be alarmed at it, and imagine that this new Resolution (*as he called it*) might proceed from an Alteration of Measures'.[3] This assumption that the issue of Counter-Orders was an idle rumour, this bashful pretence of ignorance was surprising even for Newcastle. Unfortunately for the ducal innocence, the Admiralty

---

[1] 12/23 February 1739. S.P.F., Spain, vol. 133.

[2] Harrington to Robinson, 6/17 March 1739, B.M. Add. MSS. 23803, f. 121 [interesting as written before the decision of 10 March]. 'What [was] said to you concerning the communication of a French Treaty with Spain proceeds from a mistake, nothing of that kind having past, but I may acquaint you in confidence that His Majesty has certain information of a Treaty of Commerce now actually on foot between those two Crowns, which is intended to be concluded and will no doubt be followed by an offensive and defensive Alliance.' *Vide* also Newcastle to Keene, 20 March, 'Private and Particular to be opened by Himself.' S.P.F., Spain, 134. This letter goes farther than Harrington's, and expresses a keen conviction that a Franco-Spanish alliance *may* already have been signed. Newcastle to Waldegrave, 20 March 1739, 'Private and particular in cypher, to be opened by himself,' B.M. Add. MSS. 32800, f. 215, shows clearly that Newcastle entertained the gravest suspicions as to a Franco-Spanish Treaty, but that, despite disturbing intelligence from Waldegrave, absolutely definite proof of such a Treaty was not to hand.

[3] 20 March (o.s.), Whitehall, 'most private', S.P.F., Spain, vol. 134.

Records already quoted prove that Counter-Orders were issued, and remain to abash him in the eyes of posterity. None the less, on the occasion as on many subsequent ones, Newcastle cheerfully instructed Keene to deny the fact of the Counter-Orders and to give pacific assurances. But unfortunately after such an action pacific assurances were not convincing. Spain had had enough of Haddock's threats in 1738, she had showed her sincerity by disarming her fleet in 1739, and now she was once more menaced. Even Montijo, the truly moderate and reasonable, told Keene he could not understand how the Conferences could begin 'in the capital of Spain, whilst we [England] are upon Their Coasts, with our Matches ready lighted to fall upon them'.[1] La Quadra (now Marquis de Villariàs) said to Keene on 13/24 April that his assurances might be all very well, but 'what air does it carry in publick, and what can the world judge of it, unless it be that Spain is to be fright'ned and menaced into such measures as England shall require of her? . . . Perhaps the [Spanish] King would have been much more inclined to facilitate the future negotiation,' etc.[2] Keene strove to soften him, and wrote plainly to Newcastle that 'They [the Spaniards] will be ashamed either to trust to our word, or to discover their lightness in having altered their military Measures before the departure of Admiral Haddock, by being obliged to renew them.' On 23 April/4 May Villariàs reopened the question to Keene, who vainly sought to appease him. Keene wrote that the Gentlemen of the [Spanish] Admiralty were 'uneasy as they have given Orders for unarming the Ships that were got in a Readiness for all Events, before the Convention was signed', but do not appear yet to have countermanded them.[3] To rearm the Spanish Fleet was for the Spanish Government to confess publicly that they had been duped in negotiation and bullied by Haddock. The situation thus rapidly became impossible, for the Spaniards had a shrewd suspicion that Keene was lying when he denied the fact of the Counter-Orders. The two preliminary Conferences, which took place on 5 and 15 May, were long and stormy, and when the matter of the Counter-Orders was brought forward by Quintana 'in a muttering

---

[1] Keene to Newcastle, 4 May (N.S.), 'private', S.P.F., Spain, vol. 133.
[2] Keene to Newcastle, 13/24 April 1739, *Apart*, S.P.F., Spain, vol. 133.
[3] Keene to Newcastle, 4 May (N.S.), 'private', *Ibid.*, vol. 133.

stammering manner', Keene declared it not to be within his competence as a commissioner. On 6/17 May came the final rupture of the Spanish Government with the South Sea Company — a most unfortunate occurrence which contributed greatly to fan the flame. Neither side could now withdraw from their position with honour or safety, England now feared war and would not recall Haddock, Spain feared war and would not therefore pay £95,000 to England just on the eve of it. On 29 May (o.s.) Villariàs is reported by Keene as having told him that there would be no payment of the £95,000 (due 25 May o.s.) until Haddock's Fleet was withdrawn.[1]

This last communication, which was received by Newcastle on 7 June (o.s.), meant nothing else but war, a fact that must have been obvious to both sides. The Convention had not seemed very glorious to English opinion in any case, but peace became hopeless after the refusal to pay the £95,000, for the payment of which British Ministers had staked their reputations. English Ministers had a real cause on which to appeal to the public — the breach of the Convention — and that public knew nothing of the part the Counter-Orders had played. That war was recognised as inevitable is clear from the sealed orders issued by the Admiralty on 11 June (o.s.) 1739, to Captain Fanshawe of the *Phoenix*, going to South Carolina. They authorised him 'to commit all sorts of Hostilities against the Spaniards'.[2] On 14 June (o.s.) Newcastle wrote to Keene to decline further conferences, and instructed him privately to spy upon the Spanish Military and Naval preparations. Each side masked its intentions as long as possible, for in this age all things moved slowly, and nations even went to war with the decorous dignity of dancers in a minuet, but before the end of July hostilities in effect began. In August Cardinal Fleury made an attempt to intervene and secure the payment of the £95,000 to England, but, for reasons

---

[1] Keene to Newcastle, Madrid (29 May/9 June), *Apart*, S.P.F., Spain, vol. 133. As a proleptic commentary on this *vide* Newcastle to Keene, Whitehall, 8 May (o.s.), S.P.F., Spain, vol. 134, 'private and particular in Cypher to be opened by himself.' Newcastle attributes the evident silence of the Spaniards as to paying the £95,000 to the 'Resolution of the South Sea Co. and the Counter-Orders *supposed to be sent to the Fleet in the Mediterranean*'! ! The italics my own.

[2] P.R.O., Admiralty Out Letters, vol. 55, pp. 445 *sqq.*

which will already be clear to us, England regarded French offers as insidious and rejected the proposal. War was actually declared on 19 October, Heralds proclaiming it at Temple Bar, the Prince of Wales drinking to its success in a tavern, the steeples rocking, and the crowds shouting. Newcastle, approving 'this little yeilding to times', and seeing things 'in a very melancholy light';[1] and Walpole uttering the bitter and immortal sentence that there would soon be a wringing, not of bells, but of hands.

To sum up briefly the results of our investigation. The deepest cause of the war was unquestionably the selfish policy of Spain. It had never been able to conduct its own slave-trade: it had never failed to irritate any nation undertaking that duty by the Assiento. Such a situation was difficult; on the other hand manuscript sources prove decisively that French and Dutch trading in the West Indies was not open to the same objections as the English or, in other words, show that the latter misused the advantages given them by the Assiento. It cannot be denied that the English gave genuine and admitted cause for reprisal to the Spanish *garda costas*; or that the French and Dutch Governments (who kept their smugglers within due bounds) found that Spanish reprisals were fewer and more promptly atoned for. But, though the matter of Spanish reprisals lent itself to most unjustifiable misrepresentation in England, the fact of Spain's agreement to pay £95,000 shows the genuineness of some of England's claims. Against this must be placed the fact that concession was not all Spanish, and that England's Ministers appear also to have been willing to make serious efforts for the suppression of private interlopers engaged in illicit trade. Here again, then, the difficulties of coming to an arrangement, though real, were not insuperable.

Unpublished records prove again and again the absolute genuineness and seriousness of the attempt to settle all the difficulties outstanding after the signature of the Convention. Both sides made real concessions in the Convention, both sides proved their sincerity immediately afterwards. Spain by disarming her fleet, England by projecting an alliance between the signatory Powers. It can further be established that both

[1] Newcastle to Hardwicke, 30 September 1739, B.M. Add. MSS. 35406, f. 159.

sides intended to make real efforts in the near future, in order to settle all
further problems on the basis of this preliminary agreement. Their task
was, however, made much harder by the unfortunate interference of
the South Sea Company. On the abstract rights of the other questions
discussed it appears that Spain was, in the main, in the right. Keene, the
most moderate and best informed of English negotiators, supported
Spain on the right to cut logwood in Campeachy Bay; Newcastle
certainly blundered as to the Treaties with reference to the Right of
Search; about the limits of Georgia even the Duke himself had his
doubts. None the less, there was still a possibility of adjusting these
respective claims, because England could offer a suppression of the
private smuggling trade as an equivalent for concessions from Spain in
other directions. All this proves that the attitude of the English Opposition was mistaken, and that it was untrue to say that England's commercial interests or honour had been sacrificed. Conciliatory England's
Ministers may have tried to be, especially in minute points, but as to
the essentials they stood firm enough, much too firm to enable them to
plead the abstract justice of their cause.

> It was not the proceedings in Parliament, Sir, that precipitated us
> into that War [i.e. of 1739], but the truckling submissions of our
> Ministers for many years before, and the trash of treaties they had
> concluded were such, that a war was become absolutely necessary
> *before* the Parliament interposed. . . . it was apparent that our Minis-
> ters were resolved to sacrifice both our trade and navigation in the
> American Seas, rather than go to War.[1]

So spoke Henry Bathurst in 1750 and none of his statements, considered in the light of documents, appears to be true. The Ministers had
not truckled to Spain, they were not prepared to sacrifice our trade and
navigation; peace appeared to be almost certain until Parliament inter-
vened. Newcastle's deference to Parliament and to public opinion is
too obvious, the fateful despatch of the Counter-Orders coincides too
closely with the date of the Parliamentary Debate on the Convention,
to prevent anyone denying that popular and Parliamentary agitation
was the main factor in causing the War. In the main, therefore, the old

[1] *Parl. Hist.*, xiv. 698.

contention of Burke that the War was unjust, that it was provoked by opposition clamour, and was 'the fruit of popular desire' appears to be true.[1]

None the less, unpublished records usually have a secret or two in their folios to qualify or modify simple explanations and to prevent the ascription of single causes to great events. In this case they clearly prove that fear of France joining forces with Spain at least influenced the decision as to the Counter-Orders, and that dread of a Bourbon *Pacte de Famille*, as well as of an English mob, helped to drive the British Ministry into war. Fear of France may not have been the main factor, but it certainly was an important subsidiary one in causing the war, and England's suspicion of French alliance with Spain is significant of the new age. Until 10 March 1739 it was a possibility that England and Spain might work on parallel lines in America, to the exclusion of France. After 10 March 1739 it was inevitable that France and Spain would eventually work together in America to the exclusion of England. The logic of events associated the two Bourbon Powers, brought them to two more *Pactes de Famille*, to their humiliations in 1763, and their triumphs of twenty years later. The first act of an eighty years' struggle was rung up in 1739, the curtain fell for the last time in the last months of 1823, when the downfall of Franco-Spanish influence in America was finally decreed.

Horatio Walpole was not far wrong when he stated in Parliament that England could hardly contend against the two Bourbons single-handed, and the result was always a balanced contest. England triumphed over the two allies for a moment in 1763, only to fall prostrate in 1783. Between 1793 and 1807 she struggled hard once more,

---

[1] Burke, 'First Letter on a Regicide Peace.' He says that he studied the original documents concerning certain important transactions of those times, but he did not study them enough to convince himself that Jenkins' ear was no 'fable'. He says that many of the principal actors in producing that clamour afterwards conversed with him, and that none of them, no not one, did in the least defend the measure, or attempt to justify their conduct! No doubt he conversed with Pitt, who repented in public in 1751 (*Parl. Hist.*, xiv. pp. 798–803). Compare his more private repentance in 1757, B.M. Stowe MSS. 256, ff. 282–304; of which transcripts are printed in *Hist. MSS. Comm. Rep.*, x. App. i, pp. 212–21.

but failed in her last chance of securing dominion on the South American continent. England could baffle France, but Spain over-weighted the balance, and, if a real equilibrium was to be found, an ally in the New World must be sought. This counterpoise was first found in 1823 — not indeed in an ally, but in an independent helper against Franco-Spanish interference in the New World. In September of that year Canning acting for England, bade France interfere in the New World at her peril; in December Monroe and Adams, on behalf of the United States, gave warning both to France and Spain, and clinched the Englishman's argument. Bourbonism in its two branches was at length met in the New World by Anglo-Saxondom in its two branches, and the result was the entire defeat of the two Latin Powers and the dissolution of that once formidable union, which had first seriously threatened the English dominion in 1739.

H. W. V. TEMPERLEY

9 Fox's Martyrs: The General Election of 1784

> It is on opinion only that Government is founded, and this maxim extends to the most despotic and most military government as well to the most free and most popular.
>
> HUME

The story of the overthrow of Fox and North has often been told. Since the publication of the papers of John Robinson[1] it has been very generally held that public opinion did not express itself at the 1784 election to any great degree. Professor Laprade pillories the view that Pitt was carried into power by a frenzied wave of popular hostility to the Coalition as the incorrect view of every historian from Lecky to Dr. Rose.[2] The landslide theory was indeed unquestioned till the publication of Robinson's papers. Since then it has been generally dismissed.[3] In fact, some writers have accepted the popular hostility theory without consideration of the circumstances of an eighteenth-century election; they were naturally taken for granted by contemporaries to whom they were all too familiar. It is the thesis of this paper that those who have accepted the views of Professor Laprade have fallen into a similar error from an opposite angle. The belief that the election of 1784 was different in kind from other pre-Reform elections is not of course tenable. The parliament of 1761 was 'chosen' by Newcastle, that of

[1] *Parliamentary Papers of John Robinson*, 1774–1784, ed. W. T. Laprade (1922).

[2] 'William Pitt and Westminster Elections', *American Hist. Rev.*, xviii. 253–74.

[3] 'The investigation which has been made into the preparations, calculations, and attitude of John Robinson . . . proves that little, if any, consideration was given to the effect which the views of the electors on any of the public questions of the day might have on the election results. Interest was of much greater importance.' C. S. Emden, *The People and the Constitution* (1933), p. 197.

234

1780 by North.[1] A ministry supported by the Crown could be certain of a majority by the purchase of boroughs in cash or patronage or by Treasury support to ministerial candidates. At least equally potent was the desire of candidates and their constituents to be on the side of the loaves and fishes.

It is also true that the Ministry were always concerned with the state of opinion on the eve of an election,[2] and that members were anxious to conciliate their constituents.[3] Robinson's estimate, made before the defeat of the India Bill, is naturally concerned with the results to be got from negotiation and purchase: it was not his business to discuss the state of opinion, which moreover had not then declared itself. And, before dismissing the 'frenzied hostility' theory, it is worth considering why it was so firmly held by contemporaries, who were well aware, not only of the conditions of an election, but of Robinson's activities, which were the subject of popular prints and newspaper paragraphs.[4] For instance Burke, retrospectively defending the India Bill, said in 1788:

> The people at that time were unfortunately infatuated, deceived, hurried on to madness to the overthrow, to the destruction, of the high priest of their liberties, when exerting himself at the public altar in their support. The leaders of that mob were a thousand times worse than Lord George Gordon, now suffering in his Jewish gaberdine.

[1] A parliament 'chosen by Lord North and occasionally filled by Mr. Fox'. Buckingham, *Courts and Cabinets of George III* (4 vols., 1853–5), i. p. 304. For 1761 see L. B. Namier, *England in the Age of the American Revolution* (1930), pp. 153 ff.

[2] Cf. a letter from Newcastle to Lord Irwin, patron of the borough of Horsham, 11 June 1747; 'Upon all considerations it has been determined to call a new Parliament immediately the Session is ended. The Nation is now in a good humour, no accident has yet happened to make them otherwise, since the happy extinction of the rebellion, and therefore I verily think we cannot fail of getting a good whig Parliament.' Quoted, W. Albery, *Parliamentary History of Horsham* (1927), p. 88.

[3] E. and A. G. Porritt, *The Unreformed House of Commons* (2 vols., 1903, 1909), i. 267 ff.

[4] See below, p. 256. Wraxall, who is explicit, and remarkably well-informed, about Robinson's services, is also emphatic as to the landslide character of the election. *Memoirs*, 1884, iii. 236, 331–8.

Had his mob destroyed the Bank, the country's wealth might have rebuilt it: had they destroyed St. Paul's Cathedral, the piety of the nation would have rebuilt it: but the mob of 1784 destroyed the House of Commons, destroyed their best friends.[1]

But still more weight has been given to the fact that only in a few constituencies did candidates 'have to submit to so much as formal opposition at the polls'. Now opposition at the polls, in large constituencies at least, was never formal, it was opposition at the last ditch when a decision could be reached in no other way. Professor Laprade takes the returns in Stooks Smith[2] and estimates that there were 71 unsuccessful candidates in 1768, 113 in 1774, 92 in 1780, 107 in 1784 and 96 in 1790.[3] These figures do indeed give a remarkable result: contests (so-called) were at a maximum in the interval of political apathy between the Wilkes crises and the heats of the American War. Such calculations, I suggest, are trebly fallacious. First, a contest in a tiny borough is equated with one in Middlesex or Westminster. Secondly, it is forgotten that after the Grenville Act (surely the true cause of the rise in 1774) contests were more than ever undertaken, not on political grounds, but to establish an interest, so that contests in boroughs were often mere preliminaries to an election petition. Thirdly, the criterion of a contested election is contrary to eighteenth-century practice, leaving aside the further point — that it is hard to see why an election in which one side is in a clear majority reflects opinion less than one where the issue is doubtful: contemporaries were impressed when Foxites declined the poll.

The returns in Stooks Smith fall into three classes. First, where votes are recorded, the only ones regarded by Professor Laprade as contests. Second, where the names of the unsuccessful candidates are given in italics, as in the famous Yorkshire election of 1784, when the Foxites withdrew after being in a hopeless minority at the county meeting, on Nomination Day, and on their canvass.[4] If not a contest it was a signal

[1] *Parl. Hist.*, xvii. 134.

[2] *The Parliaments of England from George I to the Present Time* (3 vols., 1844–50).

[3] 'Public Opinion and the General Election of 1784,' *Eng[lish] Hist[orical] Rev[iew]*, xxxi (1916), 224–37.   [4] B.M. Add. MSS. 28060, ff. 121–2.

victory: 'The triumph in Yorkshire is a great one,' wrote Cornwallis.[1]
In the third class are elections apparently uncontested because the names
of the candidates returned only are given. But no one can read eighteenth-century correspondence without coming across instances of
heated canvassing and doubtful issues, which, on reference to Stooks
Smith, are found to be in class III.[2]

This assumption of no contest, and therefore no defeat, without
polling is inconsistent with contemporary election practice and with
eighteenth-century estimates of elections. According to the *Annual
Register* 'upwards of 160 candidates lost their seats' in 1784.[3] Wilberforce estimates nearly 200 victories besides Yorkshire.[4] The pamphlet
called *Fox's Martyrs* enumerates 97 Foxites who lost the seats they had
held in the last parliament; the list does not seem to be complete[5] and a
few were defeated more than once, or having been defeated got in for
a close borough. In the new parliament there were actually 147 members who had not sat in the last one, and there were of course unsuccessful new candidates — for instance, Tarleton at Liverpool and John
Crewe at Chester — who, though defeated, do not appear among the
'Martyrs'. The rejected therefore include those who did not venture to
stand, those who withdrew before the election, either after an advertisement which did not evoke the hoped-for support, or after an unfavourable canvass, or after inadequate support on Nomination Day,
as well as those who were beaten at the election. These last include those

---

[1] *Correspondence*, ed. Ross (3 vols., 1859), i. 165. See below, pp. 265–6.

[2] For instance, the by-election for Staffordshire in 1799. *Private Correspondence of Lord Granville Leveson Gower* (2 vols., 1916), i. 242–4. An election at
which Sir E. Impey was defeated for Stafford after violent electioneering is un-
traceable in Stooks Smith. See E. B. Impey, *Memoirs of Sir Elijah Impey* (1846),
p. 350. Wilberforce excused himself in 1806 to a correspondent on the ground
that 'a contested election for Yorkshire finds a candidate in abundant employment for tongue, legs, and pen'. But this election is in class III. Lascelles had
withdrawn on account of his unpopularity with the clothiers. *Life of Wilberforce*
(5 vols., 1838), iii. 285.

[3] *Annual Register*, 1784, p. 147.   [4] *Life*, i. 64.

[5] Two Foxites disappeared from Leicester: Macnamara, the senior new member, was a strong Pittite; Charles Loraine Smith is known to history only as an
amateur artist (for sporting subjects).

who presented themselves at the place of election with their chief supporters but were in such a minority that they did not venture to demand a poll as well as those who polled and were defeated.[1]

The basis of these contemporary estimates — the numbers of those who failed to secure re-election — shows how strong was the sense that the sitting member should be undisturbed.[2] The same criterion of the influence of opinion on elections, the extent of the change in the composition of the House, was that of Fox in 1797, in a famous speech on Grey's motion for Reform. He demonstrated the lack of such influence in 1780 by pointing out that the new House was much the same as that which it replaced, forgetting his claim for this very parliament in 1784.[3] It is, however, remarkable that in 1780 there were 144 new members as compared with 147 in 1784 and 145 in 1790 — like 1774 a time of political quiet.[4]

Conclusions from the returns in Stooks Smith thus appear to have little validity, and deductions from the mere statistical turnover at a general election, though contemporary, are not much more satisfactory. It is here that Robinson's Papers are of great value, for they enable us to compare his expectations with the results. But before examining them the preliminaries of the election must be considered — the excited state of popular feeling. It has been suggested on the strength of the election addresses for Westminster and Norfolk that the political issue was not put before the constituents.[5] But such addresses were common form:[6] the points at issue, and much else, were to be found in

---

[1] Cf. Namier, *The Structure of Politics at the Accession of George III* (2 vols., 1929), i. 196–7. A Yorkshire squire wrote to Carmarthen on the eve of Nomination Day: 'I am endeavouring as much as I possibly can to make as respectable and numerous a meeting to-morrow in hopes that a Resignation may take place when the opposing party see themselves a second time in so *pitifull* a Minority.' B.M. Add. MSS. 28,060, fo. 121.

[2] See below, p. 254.   [3] See below, p. 248.

[4] These figures are obtained from the annual *Royal Kalendar* ('Red Book') in which the names of members who did not sit in the previous parliament are printed in italics.   [5] C. S. Emden, *op. cit.*, pp. 182, 197.

[6] Cf. Burdett's election address of 1812, in which he speaks of 'the hacknied style of congratulation and profession usual on occasions like the present'. M. W. Patterson, *Sir F. Burdett and his Times* (2 vols., 1931), i. 321.

the bills and advertisements which covered the walls and filled the newspapers. The Westminster election, however, for very good reasons was fought almost entirely on personalities.[1] In Norfolk, Coke stood on his personal connections and stake in the county; his opponent's address was political. The election of 1784 differs from others of the century in the nature and extent of the publicity campaign which preceded and accompanied it: public meetings all over the country to vote addresses to the Crown, pamphlets and election literature of a type then rare in that it was concerned with general and not local issues.[2] Besides this, there was a mass of satirical prints and caricatures, widely circulated and admitted by Fox to have been highly damaging.

And, it may be asked, why were the Foxites so confident in January and even in February, when the nature of Treasury influence in elections was so well known? Their miscalculations are not the less odd when it is remembered that during the Regency crisis they counted on office, notwithstanding the Prince's restricted patronage. Surely because they did not anticipate the wave of popular feeling which strengthened Pitt's hand. The King's action, supported only by Treasury and Court influence, could scarcely have been maintained in face of public disapproval. Ministerial sensitiveness to public clamour, roused and exploited by the Opposition, is one of the basic facts of pre-Reform politics. Pitt, at best, would have been forced to accept the compromise proposed by the country gentlemen of a 'Union' with Fox, the word coalition being avoided. But the cry was all the other way. 'So strong was the tide without doors against Mr. Fox and his majority, that they thought prudent to pass the Mutiny Bill in compliance with the wishes of the Public.'[3] And the King gained a popularity which some thought dangerous to the Constitution.[4]

[1] See Westminster election prints in B.M. *Catalogue of Political and Personal Satires*, vi. 1938, and *History of the Westminster Election*, 1784. See also below, p. 253.

[2] Cf. Lord Holland, *Memoirs of the Whig Party*, ii. 226.

[3] *Political Memoranda of Francis, 5th Duke of Leeds*, ed. O. Browning (1884), p. 99.

[4] E.g. 'The popularity acquired by the Monarch in consequence of this dismission was indeed so great as to efface all memory of former disagreements: and though originating in a cause merely accidental, and on the part of the

The three elements in a stable Ministry were connection, influence, that is patronage, and popularity. In a well-known passage Wilberforce records his belief (surely untenable) that Pitt, by reason of his popularity and the results of the 1784 election could have governed without influence.[1] Fielding in *Amelia* expressed a similar belief, in a passage which can relate only to Pitt's father. The experiment was not tried, but there is no doubt that Pitt, weak in connection, was always concerned with the necessity of preserving popularity.[2] Fox's rapid loss of popularity,[3] while that of Pitt as rapidly progressed, increased the

---

Crown from a sudden and passionate resentment at a supposed invasion of the Prerogative, yet has it not suffered in the sequel any diminution: on the contrary, from an extraordinary concurrence of circumstances, the loyalty of the people has been elevated to a pitch of ardor which court flattery itself will scarcely hesitate to acknowledge at least commensurate with the merits of the Monarch.' Belsham, *Memoirs of the Reign of George III* (1796), iii. 352. Lord Holland calls George III in 1807 'long the most popular man in his dominions'. *Memoirs of the Whig Party*, ii. 226. See Nicholls, *Recollections and Reflections*, 1820, i. 52. The absence of condemnation of the King's action, outside strict Party circles, is remarkable, e.g. Camden did not condemn (see below, pp. 242–3), Bishop Watson excused: 'The King's interference . . . could not be excused on constitutional principles except by the attack which the Commons had made on the Prerogative by passing the Bill. If you will not admit the true principle of the Constitution, which is the exercise of the King's negative, you in a manner compel him to the use of his influence over Parliament, when he conceives either his prerogative to be attacked, or the safety of the country endangered or even his caprices restrained by their proceedings.' *Anecdotes of the Life of Richard Watson, Bishop of Llandaff* (1817), p. 123. The very different judgement of modern historians (even Sir John Fortescue calls the King's action 'absolutely unscrupulous', *British Statesmen of the Great War* (1911), p. 35) seems to derive from the fact that the contemporary interpretation of the patronage aspect of the India Bill (see below, pp. 242–7) has been forgotten. Cf. also p. 246, n. 2.

[1] *Life*, i. 64.

[2] Caricatures and newspaper paragraphs support Pitt's own explanation of his failure to give office to Shelburne — popular prejudice: 'at present it would not be much more alarming to many to bring Lord Bute forward'. Orde to Shelburne, 18 December 1783. Fitzmaurice, *Life of William, Earl of Shelburne* (2 vols., 1912), ii. 284.

[3] Cf. the French Ambassador to Vergennes, 30 March 1783: 'Le Ministre populaire (Monsieur Fox) est un étrange Ministre des Affaires Etrangères; et

drama of the conflict. He was now only in derision 'the man of the people', and this, together with the support given to Pitt by the radicals, reformers and 'dissenting interest' left the oligarchical element in the Whig party starkly apparent, not helped by an accretion of Northites which included Sandwich and Rigby. Indeed, the significance of the loss by the Whigs of their two traditional props, trade and dissent, can hardly be overestimated.[1]

In examining the fate of Fox's Martyrs it will be necessary first to consider trends of opinion and propaganda, and then to compare the election results with Robinson's estimates. Pitt's position largely depended on the supposedly infamous character of the Coalition and on the belief that the India Bill was intended to make Fox perpetual dictator. Such opinions seem crude, the second was dismissed as absurd by Lecky, the first has recently been to some degree discredited on account of the *Robinson Papers*. How far they were justified is here scarcely relevant: the question is, were they strongly held? Undoubtedly they were, not only by the populace and as a result of widespread propaganda, but by those whose opinions command respect. Romilly denounced the 'scandalous alliance', stating and dismissing the apologies for it as 'an insult to the public' and adding, 'Of all the public characters of this devoted country (Mr. Pitt only excepted) there is not a man who has, or who deserves, the nation's confidence.'[2] So ardent a Foxite as Coke of Norfolk called the Coalition (it is said) 'a most revolting compact'.[3] And at the famous meeting in Westminster Hall on 14 February, when an evil-smelling bag was thrown at Fox, Dr. Jebb moved a string of resolutions beginning, 'That the Coalition

---

lorsqu'il aura perdu sa popularité, ce qui s'achemine beaucoup, je ne sais ce qui lui restera.' Quoted, *ibid.*, ii. 269.

[1] The importance of the support of the dissenters at elections was recognised by George III in 1772 (*Correspondence of George III*, ed. W. B. Donne (2 vols., 1867), 101), by Burke in 1789 ('A set of men powerful enough in many things but most of all in elections.' *Memorials and Correspondence of Charles James Fox* (4 vols., 1853–7) ii. 360), by Lord Holland in 1807 ('. . . the Dissenters, upon whom in a contest with the Crown, the Whigs must always rely'. *Memoirs of the Whig Party*, ii. 27, 227).

[2] *Memoirs of . . . Sir Samuel Romilly*, i. 269–70 (21 March 1783).

[3] A. M. D. W. Stirling, *Coke of Norfolk*, i. 213.

... was injurious to the cause of freedom and public virtue.'[1] Later, he wrote to Wyvill, 'I most cordially wish intire rout to the party of Fox, Burke and North. England, if expiring, could never be benefited by such men.'[2] The chorus of dispraise could be widely extended, and Fox owned in the House that his coalition with the noble lord 'had produced to him great unpopularity, great odium and great obloquy'.[3]

As for the India Bill, the vital point was in its patronage provisions, not in the violation of the Company's charter. This violation was of course exploited as a threat to chartered rights, helped by Jack Lee's unlucky phrase when he called a charter 'a mere skin of parchment to which is appended a seal of wax'.[4] But it is what may be called the *Carlo Khan* theme which Fox admitted to have been most damaging to him,[5] and which North said had 'misled the weak part of the country so strangely'.[6] Fox, in squibs innumerable, and in prints, is Emperor of the East, Cromwell, Charles III, Catiline, Milton's Satan; he is 'Belial ... the fleshliest incubus' and he is Beelzebub,[7] so great was the national abhorrence of a dictator. This was owing to the belief that the India Bill would make him irremovable and would bring a vast new field of corruption into politics. Statements to this effect in parliament have been dismissed by Lecky and others as rhetorical exaggeration. But the belief was stated in the correspondence of those whose opinions cannot be disregarded. Camden, who as a lawyer may be supposed to have

---

[1] J. Disney, *Works of Dr. John Jebb with Memoirs of the life of the author* (3 vols., 1787), i. 191–2.

[2] *Wyvill Papers*, iv. 362 (23 May 1784).

[3] *The Parliamentary History*, xxiv. 665 (Lord Mahon, quoting Fox).

[4] Wraxall, *Memoirs*, 1884, iii. 182.

[5] H. Twiss, *Public and Private Life of Lord Chancellor Eldon* (3 vols., 1844), i. 162.

[6] *Parl. Hist.*, xxiv. 744. See B.M. *Catalogue of Political and Personal Satires*, vi. 1938, No. 6473 (pp. 68–9).

[7] *Ibid.*, v. 733–50, vi. 1–130 *passim*, and *History of the Westminster Election*, 1784. It must be remembered that Cromwell had not as yet been rehabilitated. An election squib asks how Fox resembles him, and answers: 'A republican who is in his heart so attached to monarchy as to despise every other form of government — a tyrant, a hypocrite, a notorious enemy to the constitution of his Country.' *Ibid.*, p. 355.

understood the legal position, is explicit. He wrote on the very day of the defeat of the Bill:

> A scene is opened of national disturbance such as I have never yet seen ... Mr. Fox, feeling he had not got his master's confidence, formed a plan for his own security to get possession of the East India Patronage by vesting it in seven of his known friends, by which means the parliamentary influence of a private man would have been almost equal to the great power of the Prerogative which is the common fund of the Minister to manage Parliament. This possession would have made him too powerful to have been turned out and consequently the private being united to the Ministerial influence would have made him perpetual Dictator. The Parliament would have been bought and the King silenced.

He then describes the way in which the measure had been rushed through the Commons, Foxites urgently summoned and Opposition taken unawares, so that 'the Bill came to the Lords with as much expedition as a turnpike bill'. The lack of condemnation of the King's action is striking:

> By this time the Court began to understand the tendency of the Bill and as the Minister had been industrious to collect his friends there as he had been in the other House, and as the time was short, it was necessary the exertion should be uncommon, and accordingly it was reported that his Majesty should tell Lord Temple that he was an enemy to the Bill.

He adds:

> There is something whimsical enough in this Bill being so to unite Whigs and Tories in a just opposition to the principle. The Whigs were against any measure to introduce influence into parliament, either by the subject or the Sovereign, the Tories because it was given to the subject and not to the Sovereign.[1]

Bishop Watson, a Whig like Camden, was even more shocked. Portland wrote to ask him to vote for the Bill, Rutland to vote against it. 'It is impossible for me,' he wrote to Portland, 'who have, on all

[1] H. S. Eeles, *Lord Chancellor Camden* (1934), pp. 155-7.

occasions, opposed the corrupting influence of the Crown, to support the measure which is pregnant with more seeds of corruption than any one which has taken place since the Revolution . . .'[1] To Rutland he wrote: 'I am sick of party. You are a young man and zeal may become you, but I have lost my political zeal for ever: *The Coalition has destroyed it*' (his italics). This was the attitude of the parliamentary reformers and idealists, Wyvill, Mason, Jebb and Cartwright, who all actively supported Pitt at the election. Mason wrote to Wyvill in January that the crisis was more important than Reform itself: 'For what good possible do you think could occur to the nation (was our point actually carried) if Charles Fox had the Indies at his disposal?'[2] This was logical, since the object of the Yorkshire Reformers was 'from a detestation of Corruption as a principle of Government to promote a Reformation of Parliament'.[3] In a canvassing letter Wyvill urged the necessity of supporting those 'who have resented measures that, in my conception, would have introduced corruption to a degree of profligacy which this country has never seen and would in fact have changed our limited Monarchy into a mere aristocratical Republic'.[4]

This view of the Bill was put before the country in pamphlets and at meetings held to vote addresses to the Crown. The contention that it would make Fox dictator calls for examination, since it has been so generally dismissed as absurd, and was yet so generally believed in 1783–4. The point was that the four years of the Bill's duration would cover a general election, in which the Ministry would necessarily be returned, and would then be able to extend the period, together with the fact that the bestowal of patronage constituted a permanent claim on the allegiance of the beneficiary. This aspect of the Bill, 'concerning which the public judgment was at first suspended', was made clear, to quote Belsham, an ardent Whig,

> in a number of able tracts industriously circulated, and . . . it was almost universally condemned as a measure in the highest degree arbitrary and oppressive, and with consummate artifice calculated to perpetuate the power of an administration who were the objects of

---

[1] *Anecdotes of the Life of Richard Watson, Bishop of Llandaff*, pp. 124–5.
[2] *Wyvill Papers*, iv. 352.   [3] *Ibid.*, iv. 354.   [4] *Ibid.*, iv. 387.

the national detestation. It is nevertheless a supposition absolutely inadmissible that such men as the Duke of Portland, Lord John Cavendish and Mr. Fox had concerted a measure insidiously adapted to serve their own purpose, knowing or believing the same to be inimical to the essential interests of their country.[1]

This is self-evident, what Whig, what politician, could think his own uninterrupted office harmful to his country? We know indeed that Fox thought a permanent administration would be 'an amazing advantage' to the country in the 'opinion of Europe'.[2]

The leading pamphlet on the India Bill was that of Pulteney, *The Effect to be expected from the East India Bill upon the Constitution of Great Britain . . .* (1783), though Boswell characteristically thought his own contribution better. It went rapidly through a number of editions. The question of the violation of charters, Pulteney contends, is one that undoubtedly admits of different opinions: it depends on whether the state of India demands so strong a measure. But the patronage question is of much greater importance, and on this, he thinks, opinion could not differ, if the position were understood. Patronage, heretofore divided among twenty-four Directors of differing politics and distributed without regard to party, was to be used as a state engine, either to make Fox irremovable or to increase the power of the Crown. Fox, he says 'took occasion to declare that he never said that at the end of four years the nomination of the seven Directors would be given to the Crown, but that he feared it might'.[3] A politic remark, Pulteney thinks, aimed at quelling fears and creating hopes on both sides of the House. He adds that it is no part of Fox's party to work for an increase in the power of the Crown, 'but they like men of talent of all ages cannot be supposed averse to an independent power in themselves, which they may think it impossible they may ever abuse'. This indeed was the justification of the Bill to those who, like Walpole, thought it a judicious plan for

[1] Belsham, *Memoirs of the Reign of George III*, 1796, iii. 347 ff.

[2] Fox's *Correspondence*, ii. 208 (letter of 9 September 1783).

[3] This is not consistent with Fox's speech of 18 November (Russell, *Life of Fox*, ii. 31–2). Vacancies by death or resignation were to be filled by the King in Council. The Commissioners (at first styled Directors) could be dismissed only by an address from either or both Houses.

combining reform in India with Foxite predominance in Parliament ('Coupling with that rough medicine a desire of confirming the power of himself and his friends').[1] Fox wrote of the Bill as 'a *vigorous* and *hazardous measure* on which *all* depends'.[2]

The patronage question, so closely intertwined with connection, affects the whole of public life in the eighteenth century. The obligation of the beneficiary to give his 'vote and interest' to his patron may be said to correspond to the debt of honour,[3] with obedience to political principle standing for the mere debt of commerce, then so little regarded. Examples will occur to all students of the period, but the case of Dr. Parr deserves remark. Of all Whigs he was the most uncompromising in his defence of the Coalition.[4] He wrote to Lord Dartmouth (a Northite) of the coming election for Cambridge University (for which Pitt and Lord Euston were returned after a contest):

[1] *Letters*, ed. Toynbee, xiii. 138 (30 March 1784).

[2] Fox, *Memorials and Corr.*, ii. 218. Pulteney's view of the Bill is supported by Eden's correspondence: Loughborough to William Eden (n.d., *c.* November 1783): 'That curse of India will be the ruin first of the Administration and then of the Country . . . I have sent you the Paper which was circulated to us. You'll observe the seven Trustees are during good behaviour. That is a very favourite but a very difficult Point . . . I hold it too hazardous to try even if all the rest were safe. If it were carried it is a great Point, but for that reason I think it will fail.' (It was slightly modified, see p. 245, n. 3.) Add. MSS. 34410, fo. 305. Eden wrote to his brother Morton, 21 November 1783: 'Our East India Measure is a very trying one: — undoubtedly it is a very strong proposition and will either knock us down or establish us — I am much mistaken if it will not shew that we have the Confidence and support of at least two-thirds of the House, which is a sufficient Key to my creed as to present politics.' *Ibid.*, fo. 296. In view of Fox's declared intention, on taking office in 1782, of reducing the power of the Crown, the alternative to Pulteney's interpretation of the Bill would seem to be reckless opportunism. (Cf. *Hist[orical] MSS. Comm[ission]*, *Carlisle MSS.*, pp. 599, 604, 623; *Parl. Hist.*, xxii. 1252.)

[3] Cf. the cardinal political obligation: faithfulness to connection, illustrated (e.g.) by Yorke's distress at accepting the Chancellorship in 1770, and by Lord Holland's praise of Grenville for his faithfulness to connection (i.e. in refusing to take office without Fox in 1804). *Memoirs of the Whig Party*, ii. 51.

[4] The dedication of his *Preface to Bellendenus* (1787) is to *tria lumina Anglorum*, Fox, North and Burke.

I wish it were in my power to ask your guidance in both my votes, the one you will command, and in such a manner, I am well assured, as not to violate those feelings of anguish, indignation, and honour, which some late scenes have roused in a mind not quite destitute of penetration of sensibility. To Lord Euston I am bound in honour to give the other vote as his father assisted me in my master's degree . . .

He goes on to promise assistance in Warwickshire 'to the friends of their country at this awful crisis'.[1] Even in an awful crisis personal obligation came before political allegiance (and Euston was returned by a majority of 28 only). It is no wonder that Fox was accused of making in the India Bill 'an immensity of patronage which would follow him to private life'.[2] And Lord Mahon, at the Buckinghamshire meeting at which an address to the Crown was voted, answering Burke on the wrongs of India, said: 'Why, says Mr. Fox, give to me, and seven men named by me, two million sterling of annual patronage, and that shall be your remedy. God defend the Nation from such a remedy as that!'[3]

Addresses 'became at length so universal', writes Belsham, 'that upon no occasion whatever was the sense of the people at large more clearly, strongly, and unequivocally ascertained'.[4] Bishop Watson is one of many who adds his testimony:

The numberless addresses . . . against the Coalition Ministry sufficiently showed the voice of the people to be with Mr. Pitt. Now I consider the voice of the people to be superior, not only to the House of Commons, but to the whole legislature: I hope therefore no harm will come to the Constitution from this example. It was not so much the prerogative of the Crown that kept Mr. Pitt in his place, and set the House of Commons at defiance, as it was the sense of the nation, which on this occasion was in direct contradiction to the sense of the House of Commons.[5]

[1] *Hist. MSS. Comm., Dartmouth MSS.*, iii. 268 (23 December 1784).

[2] *Parl. Hist.*, xxiii. 1402 (Dundas). Cf. below, p. 252, n. 1.

[3] *London Chronicle*, 23 March 1784; *Morning Herald*, same date. See also Stanhope and Gooch, *Life of Charles, third Earl Stanhope* (1914), p. 59.

[4] *Memoirs of the Reign of George III*, iii (1796), 351.

[5] Watson, *op. cit.*, p. 128.

This is the opinion of friends and foes alike. 'The passions of the vulgar made and kept Mr. Pitt Minister,' writes Trotter, Fox's secretary and devotee. Fox in 1799, wrote of the battle 'lost in 1784', when we were 'deserted by the people'.[1] Burke's views on the mob of 1784 have already been quoted; they are consistent with his political philosophy but less so with that of Fox, and he was markedly ill at ease in the controversy which raged in Parliament before the dissolution as to whether the sense of the people was voiced by the Commons or the Addresses.

The claim for Addresses versus unrepresentative House was an old one. Chatham had made it in 1770,[2] Fox in 1780, and was to make it again in 1797, when he based a famous speech in favour of Reform on the unrepresentative character of the House returned in 1780, the very one which he upheld in 1784: 'A device so shallow and barefaced,' he said, 'was enough to ruin the best cause ... Indeed there was no legal way of ascertaining what the general voice was but the sense of that House.'[3] Lord Mahon challenged this inconsistency, which he called habitual, and instanced a resolution of the Westminster Committee in 1780, signed by Fox as chairman, condemning a declaration by North 'That the people of England could only be heard by their representatives in parliament'; this was resolved to be 'unconstitutional and of dangerous import to the country'.[4] The extreme lameness of Fox's rejoinder is significant, since Fox was matchless in debate. First, he often signed resolutions as chairman without agreeing with them. Secondly, he had not been opposed to this one, but though the House had not been the voice of the people in 1780, it had since become so by the Contractors' Bill and 'other salutary laws'. That is, by the reforms of 1782, which could hardly have affected a House returned in 1780.

---

[1] *Memorials and Corr. of Fox*, iii. 152.

[2] *Parl. Hist.*, xvi. 663, 665, etc. (9 January 1770).

[3] *Ibid.*, xxiv. 462–3 (2 February).

[4] *Ibid.*, xxiv. 575–6 (9 February). The parliamentary sequel is interesting: Fox said, answering North: 'When majorities acted wrong, he would both within that House, and out of it, declare his disapprobation of their conduct ... but the noble lord pronounced it as the indispensable duty of a minister to hold the decision of that House in the strictest reverence.' *Ibid.*, xviii. 1094.

A few days later Fox had shifted his ground, and in the course of a long debate on addresses said: 'that he disregarded the opinion of the people no man would imagine, it had been the business of his life to court popularity; but there were circumstances in which the people might err, and under such circumstances it became an act of duty to resist them'.[1] This is the orthodox Whig view of the *débâcle*. Among the many satirical prints on the crisis (some 300 in the British Museum) it is in Foxite prints that Pitt is supported by 'popular frenzy' or 'the breath of popularity'. In one the King, Pitt and Thurlow are held up by bubble-balloons inscribed 'the wishes of the people'.[2] Sheridan spoke contemptuously of 'the arts practised to corrupt the majority'[3] and Fox asserted that he had never appeared as 'the mean candidate of popular approbation'.[4] Fox's attitude was wittily satirised in a West-minster election squib: 'Mr. Fox has upheld the House of Commons against the Freeholders, Electors, and People of Great Britain in the case of the Middlesex Election and in all the late important questions in Parliament'.[5]

By resisting a dissolution, besides strengthening all the imputations against themselves, the Foxites were landed in the awkward position of upholding a parliament which, elected in 1780 to strengthen North's hand, had supported four ministries in turn. Lord Russell, commenting on this, regrets that Fox did not choose rather to attack secret influence and prerogative. The answer of course is that the attempt was made but broke on Temple's resignation (there seems no reason to dismiss Tomline's statement that it was made to appease the public mind),[6] on

[1] *Parl. Hist.*, xxiv. 647.

[2] B.M. *Catalogue of Political and Personal Satires*, vi. 1938, Nos. 6438, 6775, 6486, etc.

[3] *Parl. Hist.*, xxiv. 296 (12 January).

[4] *Ibid.*, xxiv. 449 (29 January).

[5] *Hist. of the Westminster Election . . .*, 1784, p. 95.

[6] The theory that it was because he wanted a dukedom (party gibes apart) seems to derive from a disgruntled letter dated 29 December, clearly relating to Ireland after the Regency crisis and consistent with letters of that date (1789) in the *Dropmore Papers*. It is printed in Buckingham's *Courts and Cabinets of George III*, i. 291–3, and there attributed to 1783, an impossible date: Temple had then no connection with Ireland.

confidence in Pitt's integrity, on the growing popularity of the King's action and the common belief that King, Lords and people were united in defence of the Constitution. Such is the tenor of the addresses. Nevertheless the situation was critical.[1] 'Mr. Pitt could not then [in December] form any opinion of the extent to which that popular cry, of secret influence, might be carried.' Pitt boldly justified the use of the prerogative: 'Prerogative, sir, has been justly called the friend of the people.'[2] Again, at the great Yorkshire meeting of 25 March, Spencer Stanhope declared that Temple had acted openly, and retaliated: 'Secret influence has been the cry since Lord Bute's time . . . yet all his sons vote with the Coalition, Lord North too was called the creature of secret influence.' He maintained that the danger was no longer from the prerogative as in the time of the Star Chamber, or even of North. There was not the immense patronage of the war, Lord North's war, and the civil list had been reduced: 'At present I fear more the tyranny of Venice than that of France.'[3] Indeed, secret influence in the popular imagination was so firmly associated with Bute and North that it was doubly difficult to fix it upon Pitt. Nevertheless, great efforts were made to raise the cry: the 'key of the Backstairs' draped in black as 'Secret Influence Key in Mourning' was an emblem used in Westminster.[4] And the Duchess of Devonshire wrote to her mother, 'There was a new play last night in which the Back Stairs was introduced, it produced an angry riot and they would not allow them to proceed for a long time, however *we* got the better at last.'[5]

The addresses, thanking the King for the salutary use of his prerogative, were agreed to have been decisive. They began, according to seventeenth-century precedent, with one from the City of London presented on 16 January. Its general tenor was that of the other addresses. Explicit and implicit is the declaration that Crown and people were

---

[1] For Pitt's uneasiness, see especially two letters of 23 December to Temple, in Stanhope, *Miscellanies*, 2nd Series (1872), pp. 36–7.

[2] Tomline, *Life of Pitt*, p. 249; *Parl. Hist.*, xxiv. 486.

[3] *Wyvill Papers*, ii. 340–1.

[4] *Full and authentic Account of the Proceedings in Westminster Hall* (1784), pp. 26–7. B.M. *Catalogue of Pol. and Personal Satires*, v. 119.

[5] *Anglo-Saxon Review*, September 1899, p. 73.

united to overthrow a 'corrupt oligarchy' or 'a desperate faction'. The Coalition were charged with denying the constitutional rights of the Crown and the Lords. Confidence was expressed in the new 'able and upright' Ministers. As time went on other points were added: abhorrence of the attempt to cut off supplies and to oppose the prerogative of dissolution. Addresses filled the *Gazette*, they flowed in till the beginning of May, though the high tide was in March. They came from places which were unrepresented as well as from counties and boroughs and from 'inhabitants' as well as electors: the question of Reform underlay the issue between the House of Commons and the Addressers. In Scotland the addresses reflect the movement for borough reform, Glasgow being especially emphatic. In England there were addresses from Birmingham, Leeds, Wolverhampton, Rotherham, Halifax, Doncaster, Wakefield, Sunderland, as well as from smaller places. There were also addresses from Belfast and from the Presbyterian ministers of the Synod of Ulster, who declared that 'in all Revolutions they had been most loyal to the Crown'. Some places, using the old formula, offered their 'lives and fortunes' to the King, and the sense of 'an awful crisis' — to use Parr's phrase — runs through many of the addresses. Appeals for parliamentary reform were made by Yorkshire, Carnarvon, Rotherham and Scarborough. Halifax stressed the right of dissolution as 'the most sacred and salutary branch of the royal prerogative . . . without it the apprehension of a septennial servitude, in a moment like this, would produce alarms, just indeed, but dreadful . . .' Norwich was the second place to address and two strongly worded documents came from Bristol. Other noteworthy towns were Westminster, Southwark, Canterbury, Worcester, Warwick, Coventry, Leicester, Northampton, Bedford, St. Albans, Newcastle, Liverpool, Chester, Hull, York, Beverley, Durham, Colchester, Salisbury, Plymouth, Exeter, Taunton. The merchants and traders of London also presented an address.

The counties which addressed were Middlesex, Berkshire, Cornwall, Northumberland, Leicester, Warwick, Devon, Suffolk, Oxford, Buckinghamshire, Yorkshire, Anglesea, Denbigh, Carnarvon and Glamorgan, with many Scottish counties, and the grand juries of Buckinghamshire, Essex, Surrey and Somerset. There were only (in the *Gazette*) two addresses favourable to the Coalition, Middlesex and

Lancaster, and both places presented counter-addresses. An attempt by Lord Sandwich to promote a Foxite address in Huntingdon failed.[1]

There were some 230 addresses in the *Gazette* and some appear to have been crowded out. That from Yorkshire was by far the most important and was regarded as critical. Its close connection with the Yorkshire election is well known.[2]

In the ferment caused by meetings and addresses the elections began. Election issues were then so local that each place provided its squibs and lampoons, but in 1784 there was a 'celebrated index' to *The Beauties of Fox, North and Burke* which was said to be used at elections with great effect. There were at least two versions of this index, both in the form of a newspaper. One, besides the deadly references to past speeches, contained lists of the House of Commons divided into those who supported 'Mr. Pitt and the Constitution', those who voted against him, and absentees. There were also twelve telling 'points' and a treatise by Dean Tucker on 'The Cardinal Point': the right of the King to appoint Ministers. This Index was sold at the significant price of 6*d*. a copy, a guinea a hundred and eight guineas a thousand.[3] There can be no doubt that the constitutional issues were skilfully, and of course tendenciously, stated and widely circulated. They were cleverly

---

[1] 'Lord S. made some efforts for an Address to the King to dismiss his present Ministry and take in the late, but was told by some of his friends that to be sure many of them would and must sign such a one, but on casting up the numbers privately there was two to one against such a thing, and that the County would be more strong against it, he judged well in Droping it.' Ewin to Lord Hardwicke, 19 March. B.M. Add. MSS. 35629, fo. 20–20b. (I am indebted to Miss H. M. Cam for this and other references to the Hardwicke Papers.) Yet Sandwich was all powerful in the town: 'The interest of the Earl of Sandwich is so powerful, as always to return two members; and this he effects, not by weight of property for his lordship has but one house in the whole town, but by his popularity, and the obligations which he was enabled to confer upon some of his principal friends during his connexion with Lord North's Administration.' Oldfield, *Hist. of Boroughs*, 1794, i. 319–20. In the county 'the Duke of Manchester and Lord Sandwich always return the two members'. *Ibid.*, i. 316.

[2] *Life of Wilberforce*, i. 50–64, 326; A. M. W. Stirling, *Annals of a Yorkshire House* (2 vols., 1911), ii. 191 ff.

[3] Copy in B.M. 1890.e.22, fo. 33 (Banks Collection). See B.M. *Catalogue, ut supra*, vi. 22–3; *Morning Post*, 6 April 1784.

embodied in pictorial satire. Foxite propaganda was also displayed in prints and in Westminster election squibs. Its topics were secret influence, the destruction of the Commons and Pitt's youth. Temple, holding the dark lantern of a conspirator, leads Pitt up the Back Stairs; Pitt and Dundas put up to auction the Rights of the People in 558 volumes.[1]

How is the contemporary belief in a landslide consistent with the character of an eighteenth-century election? For Robinson's papers were not needed to show how completely patronage and custom dominated not only close boroughs but those which were nominally open, and also counties. The inestimable works of Oldfield together with the *Wyvill Papers* conveniently show how all-pervading was patronage. The returns in Stooks Smith, though an unsatisfactory record of 'contests', show how from generation to generation the same families represented boroughs and counties, how a natural progress for the son of a local peer was from a borough to the county and from the county to the Lords. From Oldfield, as well as from memoirs and correspondence, we learn that a contest was not necessarily, or even normally, connected with politics, but was a struggle between rival families for county or borough patronage, which, if interests were evenly matched, generally led to a compromise by which each agreed to nominate one member. Such arrangements were common to avoid the expense and disturbance of a contest. After 1784 they were stigmatised as coalitions. It is scarcely an exaggeration to say that politics occasionally invaded elections because families were by tradition Whig or Tory. That politics should override personal relations was deplored.[2] Even in 1784 Pittite interests supported Foxites and vice versa;

---

[1] B.M. *Catalogue*, vi. Nos. 6417, 6469.

[2] Cf. a letter of Windham, 3 May 1796. *The Windham Papers* (2 vols., 1913), ii. 11. A comment on a by-election for Norwich is significant: 'The contest, which at first promised to be merely a trial of strength between the friends of two most respectable country gentlemen, has now assumed a more important aspect, and seems to involve the great question . . . of the policy or impolicy of the war.' *Morning Herald*, 27 May 1799. Sheridan, M.P. for Stafford, canvassed in 1799 for Lord Granville Leveson-Gower, who was standing for the county. *Private Corr. of Lord G. Leveson-Gower*, i. 242-4.

for instance, Harbord, the Pittite member for Norwich, supported Coke in the County.[1] In counties which by exception were free from aristocratic dominance and therefore considered independent, property and tradition had decreed that certain families had prescriptive rights. A Coke in Norfolk, a Bunbury in Suffolk or a Penruddock in Wiltshire was a predestined knight of the shire. In normal times such members were unshakeable. Added to this was the strong feeling against opposing the sitting member: to do so was to commit that crime of crimes, 'disturbing the peace of the county'. 'You cannot conceive the effect of the magic sounds, disturbing the peace of the county,' wrote Gibbon to Holroyd in 1774, advising him not to stand for Sussex.[2] Mrs. Coke wrote a canvassing letter for her husband in 1784: 'an intention is publicly avowed by Sir J. Wodehouse's friends to disturb the peace of the county by putting him in opposition to the old members'.[3] The phrase is recurrent in election correspondence. The established interest, however feeble, wrote Gibbon, 'always fights with very great advantages'. When a death or resignation occurred, then could a candidate, suitably qualified by landed property and adequately supported by the correct local interests, put himself forward.[4] Such a candidate was not necessarily pledged to either party. For instance, Charles Grey, returned in his absence for Northumberland in 1786, on the Percy interest, was free to choose between Pitt and Fox.[5] Hence the fact that elections were often arranged by correspondence whose tenor suggests a candidate for an academic post, intimately known to a small selection committee already decided in his favour, and this even in constituencies which prided themselves on being free from aristocratic patronage.[6] On the

---

[1] A. M. W. Stirling, *Coke of Norfolk* . . . i. 220–1.

[2] Gibbon, *Private Letters*, ed. Prothero (2 vols., 1896), i. 225 ff.

[3] A. M. W. Stirling, *Coke of Norfolk*, i. 220.

[4] Gibbon, *loc. cit.*

[5] *Journal of Lady Holland*, ed. Lord Ilchester, 1908, i. 100. Grey was returned in place of Lord Algernon Percy, who succeeded to a peerage.

[6] See for instance the letters of Cornwallis on the candidature of his son for Suffolk in 1796. *Cornwallis Corr.*, ii. 303 ff. A letter from George Osborne to Hawkesbury (Liverpool) about his son's candidature for Bedfordshire in 1794 is astonishingly regardless of political connections, B.M. Add. MSS. 38548, fo. 176.

other hand, the contest was welcomed in the frankly corrupt con-
stituency, for example, to cite Oldfield, Colchester 'celebrated in the
annals of controversy and corruption'.

In what ways could popular feeling make itself felt at an election?
First, in the very few constituencies where 'the sense of the people'
was held to reside. 'Fox would often say,' writes Wilberforce, agreeing,
'that Yorkshire and Middlesex between them make up all England.'[1]
They doubtless included London and Westminster, York and possibly
Hull. In much the same category was Surrey, though by no means free
from aristocratic influence, with Southwark, which, says Oldfield, 'was
under no influence of any degree or kind, owing to its great population
and opulence'. Hertfordshire 'had the singular advantage of maintaining its independence'. Norfolk and Suffolk were regarded as pre-
eminently independent counties. Besides these were Kent and Shropshire, and (recently) Northamptonshire, where a violent contest had
exhausted conflicting interests. Some others had a chance of independence, or were independent as to one member. Somerset and Wiltshire
had (by 1792) undertaken not to return the son of a peer. The majority
were under aristocratic influence, and in these the prestige attaching to
county membership was unconnected with 'the sense of the people'.
Some large towns were independent, notably Norwich, Bristol (though
this was compromised after 1784), Exeter, Coventry, Liverpool,
Canterbury, York, Leicester and, after 1789, Gloucester. Others,
though independent, were venal, for instance, Stafford, Hull, Worcester and Colchester.[2]

An election fought on political issues was something to be remembered in the history of a county: such notable elections (before 1784)
were pre-eminently Middlesex in 1768 and 1769, Norfolk in 1734,[3]
Surrey in 1780, when Keppel was invited to stand as a rebuff to George

---

[1] *Life of Wilberforce*, ii. 133 (1795). See below p. 267, n. 1.

[2] This summary is based on Oldfield, *Hist. of Boroughs*, 1792 (2nd edn., 1794)
and *Representative History . . .*, 1816, supplemented by the *Wyvill Papers*. For
the Colchester election in 1784, cf. *Hist. MSS. Comm., Rutland Papers*, iii.
122.

[3] Appealed to as a precedent at the Norfolk election in 1806. *Poll for . . .
Norfolk . . .*, 1806.

III, who had canvassed against him in Windsor, his old seat.[1] The importance of a mandate from the very few populous and open constituencies was such that at by-elections during the American War and at the general election of 1780, although the Ministry had a large majority, money was squandered by North in an attempt to secure favourable results in the City, Westminster, Bristol, Coventry, Surrey and Gloucestershire. He explained to the King that he was 'very unwillingly drawn into the contests . . . but the necessity of strengthening the Government at that time, and weakening the Opposition, and the fair prospect of success prevailed upon him to advise the beginning'. Consequently over £8,000 was fruitlessly spent in Westminster, £4,000 in Surrey, £4,000 in the City.[2] Compared with the price of boroughs these sums are startling.

Such places then had a vast importance. In what other ways could opinion manifest itself? By overthrowing interest in counties and in boroughs; this, even in small constituencies, showed the unusual contagion of political excitement; by defeating the vested interests of established families and old members (this is the basis of the pamphlet called *Fox's Martyrs*); by the proscription of those who had taken a prominent part on the unpopular side. All these things were done in 1784 and to a degree that seemed phenomenal.

Robinson's papers strikingly illustrate the landslide character of the election. He seems to have been over-optimistic in his estimate of the members who, though supporters of the Coalition, would side with Pitt. Those who were suspected of responding to his overtures were called Robinson's Rats; a list of twenty-two appeared in the *Morning Post* (10 February) which it is interesting to compare with his own calculations.[3] Fox's dwindling majority was thus (by the Foxites) attributed to the manoeuvres of Robinson, but the rot had then hardly begun. Robinson was called *Renegado*, because, though North's man,

---

[1] B.M. *Catalogue of Pol. and Personal Satires*, v. 1935, Nos. 5700, 5701, 5708.

[2] *The Correspondence of King George III*, ed. Sir John Fortescue (6 vols., 1927–8), v. 465 ff.; Donne, *Corr. of George III with Lord North*, ii. 425.

[3] B.M. *Catalogue, ut supra*, vi. No. 6431, etc.; *Parliamentary Papers of John Robinson*, pp. 54–5.

he had put his valuable information at the service of the enemy.[1] His defence to North was that this information was due to his official position as Treasury Secretary and that a similar state of the House of Commons had already been given to Shelburne.[2] But he expected few changes in the personnel of the House, except in boroughs which were purchasable or bribable, lists of which he gives, or in the hands of friends, like the Eliot boroughs in Cornwall.

In six counties only did he see any chance of change: in two, Somerset and Monmouth, because of an expected death. In Yorkshire because of the resignation of Savile; he did not expect a second Pittite member. Savile's nephew Foljambe succeeded him unopposed in December, but gave great offence to the Yorkshire Association by his support of the Coalition.[3] In Sussex because there was an old desire for a contest on the part of Lord Surrey, that election buccaneer. Sussex was divided between the Lennox and the Pelham interests; it was no time to challenge the Duke of Richmond and no contest took place. In Cumberland Robinson thought a contest for Sir Henry Fletcher's seat possible. The county, according to Oldfield, was compromised between the Portland and Lowther interests in such a way that a contest was impossible, and none occurred. Robinson expressed doubts as to Buckinghamshire and thought that in Middlesex the members would be '*perhaps the same*'.[4]

Actually, besides the sensational victory of Wilberforce in Yorkshire, there was a number of quite unexpected and noteworthy county martyrs, whose defeat was the main sensation of the election. In Berkshire there were two, but only one, Hartley, ventured to poll. He then,

---

[1] B.M. *Catalogue, ut supra*, vi. No. 6927 (27 February).

[2] *Hist. MSS. Comm., 10th Report*, App. vi (*Abergavenny Papers*), 64. The Treasury State of the House given to Shelburne is in the *Robinson Papers*, pp. 43–8.

[3] *Wyvill Papers*, iv. 382. Wyvill thought he had supported measures 'highly dangerous to the Peace and Liberty of the Country'.

[4] *Parliamentary Papers of John Robinson*, pp. 66–70. The names of the county members, characterised as Abroad, Ill can't attend, Pro, Hopeful, Doubtful, and Con, are given on pp. 51–2, but with the misleading page caption 'the Parliamentary Election of 1780'. He expected Duncombe's Yorkshire colleague to be 'Doubtful'.

if *Fox's Martyrs* is to be believed, contested Gloucestershire, getting only twenty votes, but there is no record of a poll and this must be taken as doubtful. There were two in Buckinghamshire where the Grenville interest was strong. Tom Grenville (who did not poll) was displaced by his brother William, whose canvassing is described by Cowper; Lord Verney was defeated by Aubrey after a close contest,[1] and the victory was achieved despite the influence of the Duke of Portland.[2] Both Essex and Gloucestershire were, according to Oldfield, so compromised between two interests that no contest was possible. Nevertheless, in both counties, the Foxite lost his seat. Robinson managed to be put at the head of a hundred Essex freeholders as an election day demonstration.[3] No polling is recorded for either county.

The defeat of Sturt for Dorset was quite unexpected — the county was one with a chance of independence. In Staffordshire, though the influence of the Pittite Lord Gower was strong, Lord Lewisham's defeat was unexpected. In Middlesex Wilkes remained a strong Pittite, contrary to Robinson's forecast, and lost prestige by doing so, since, as Robinson said, his credit depended on his being in Opposition.[4] His colleague Byng, an uncompromising Foxite, was challenged by Mainwaring, chairman of the Middlesex bench, and a strange knight of the shire. Mainwaring headed the poll, Byng was beaten by Wilkes, but by a small majority. In Hertfordshire Halsey polled and was defeated.

The Surrey election was long remembered. Sir Joseph Mawbey, the Southwark distiller and a butt of the wits, was a Pittite, Sir Robert Clayton a Foxite. He was so confident of keeping his seat that he returned two Foxites for his borough of Bletchingley. But, as Oldfield says, he 'gave so much umbrage to the people and became so unpopular from the support which he gave to the Coalition' that he did not venture to poll. In 1787 Nicholls resigned his Bletchingley seat to his patron.

---

[1] Rose, *Pitt and Napoleon, Essays and Letters* (1912), p. 207. (Letter of George III to Pitt, 12 April; he expected Aubrey to relinquish to Lord Verney.)

[2] Cf. *Hist. MSS. Comm., Dropmore Papers*, i. 363, 590.

[3] See below, p. 264, n. 5.

[4] *Op. cit.*, p. 68. Wilkes was popularly accused of a coalition with the King, see B.M. *Catalogue, ut supra*, vi. No. 6568.

Norfolk and Suffolk were alike in being divided between the two parties, in each case the Foxite was the member whose stake in the county was regarded as making him safe in all circumstances. Robinson had written of Coke, 'his connections, &c. carry him dead'.[1] Nevertheless, he withdrew before election day, but not before having spent large sums on electioneering. He was the Fox's Martyr par excellence — the pamphlet prints his name and attributes within a black border. 'I was rejected,' he wrote long afterwards, 'and I glory in being one of those who were called Fox's Martyrs.'[2] The King wrote 'nothing can be more material than the account of Mr. Coke having declined in Norfolk, as it is as strong a proof as the decision in Yorkshire of the genuine sense of the people'.[3] Coke attributed his defeat chiefly to the dissenters. The Suffolk election was scarcely less sensational. The people, says Oldfield, 'in consequence of the connexion of Sir Thomas Bunbury with the Coalition' proposed Mr. Grigby, because he was 'attached to the cause of liberty'.[4] In Bedfordshire the Duke of Bedford and Lord St. John each returned one member, but in 1784 the St. John influence was challenged, Lord Ongley was one vote behind St. John, was seated on petition but rejected on a second petition.

Such victories, by the defeat of 'the established interest' in Yorkshire, Dorset, Surrey, Norfolk, Suffolk, Hertfordshire and Middlesex, counties which stood out as independent and populous, were great events, though only the last three came within Professor Laprade's category of contest. The position in Cambridgeshire is not without interest; though both members were classed by Robinson as Pittite, Hardwicke, the patron of one seat, was Foxite. 'Robinson and his electioneers' are said to have been present in the shire hall, 'prepared to offer a test', but desisted on assurance that both candidates were 'in favour of Mr. Pitt and a Reform'.[5] Pitt's position as Minister and dispenser of patronage made him very acceptable to Cambridge University. There

---

[1] *Op. cit.*, p. 69.

[2] A. M. W. Stirling, *Coke of Norfolk*, i. 221-9.

[3] Rose, *Pitt and Napoleon*, p. 207.

[4] Joshua Grigby was the 'Association' (Reform) member for Suffolk. *Wyvill Papers*, iv. 407.

[5] B.M. Add. MSS. 35629, fo. 32 (letter of W. H. Ewin, 8 April).

was cross-voting, showing that political issues were little regarded. Hardwicke, the High Steward, gave his interest to Pitt and Mansfield (Solicitor-General to the Coalition). Townshend, as a member of Trinity College, was said to be sure of Trinity support and his defeat by Lord Euston caused surprise.[1] The University thus produced two martyrs.

Two unexpected defeats in counties may have been Foxite successes. In Derbyshire the Curzon interest was defeated and Mundy got in;[2] the Duke of Devonshire always returned the senior member for the county. In Lancashire, Egerton, of whom Robinson had had hopes, was replaced by John Blackburne.[3] No polling is recorded for either county.

It is impossible to go in detail through all the large towns which produced martyrs. Northampton and York were perhaps the most outstanding. Robinson thought that in Northampton the Compton and Spencer interests would combine, each returning one member. According to *Fox's Martyrs*, £100,000 had recently been spent in establishing the Spencer interest, the member being Lord Lucan, Lord Spencer's brother-in-law. The Duchess of Devonshire wrote to her mother, 'at all events St. Albans is a great comfort, other elections go on ill, but let Northampton, Westminster and York succeed, and we shall not be disgraced'.[4] Lucan's defeat by Fiennes Trotman was among the sensations of the election. In York Lord John Cavendish's defeat was unexpected and had a great effect. Robinson had expected both members, one a Pittite, to be returned. Coventry also stands out. Though 'very

---

[1] B.M. Add. MSS. 35629, fo. 26 (letter of 2 April). Ewin writes, 'I go with the stream, Pitt and Townshend of my own College.' See also Add. MSS. 35629, fo. 211, and cf. above, p. 246 (Dr. Parr's letter). Pitt had contemplated contesting Cambridge University at the by-election caused by Mansfield's appointment as Solicitor-General (letter of 16 November 1783). *Hist. MSS. Comm., Lonsdale Papers*, 1893, p. 140.

[2] Cf. *Diaries and Correspondence of James Harris, first Earl of Malmesbury* (4 vols., 1844), ii. 65.

[3] If Blackburne (of Hales, Lancashire) was the nephew of Bamber Gascoyne of whom Robinson wrote on 7 April, the victory was Pittite. *Parliamentary Papers of John Robinson*, p. 123.

[4] *Anglo-Saxon Review*, 1899, ii. 76.

open', Robinson had expected the return of the two coalition members 'for quietness'. Later he writes, the people 'have applied that nobody may be set up for they mean to set up a son of S. Smith of Aldermanbury and another by a union to turn out the present members'.[1] Samuel Smith, a cousin of Wilberforce, actually won a seat at Worcester, but Lord Sheffield and Henry Conway were both defeated after a close contest. Gibbon wrote to Sheffield from Lausanne that he had been

> at first most delighted with your hint that you were setting off for Coventry without any prospect of an opposition ... I am not much surprised that you should have been swept away in the general unpopularity, since even in this quiet place your friends are considered as a factious crew, acting in direct opposition to both King and People.[2]

Worcester was notoriously venal and the Treasury had, it is said, promised £20,000 (?£2,000) towards the expenses of a contest.[3] Smith, however, got in without a contest, thus lending support to Wraxall's remark that 'corruption for once became almost unnecessary'.[4] In Southwark Robinson expected both members to support Pitt and to be re-elected. But Sir Richard Hotham remained a Foxite and was a noted martyr. He had headed the poll in 1780, in 1784 he did not venture to poll, but was turned out by Sir Bernard Turner, a Pittite alderman. Turner died shortly afterwards and in June Hotham stood and was defeated by le Mesurier, another Pittite alderman and an East India Director. In Hull, despite some annoyance at Wilberforce's resignation to sit for the county, Spencer Stanhope was returned unopposed, so that in all three Pittites were returned. Robinson had thought Burke's friends might contest Bristol; there was a contest and the Northite, Daubeny, was a martyr. Burke again sat for Malton, Lord Fitzwilliam's borough.

[1] *Parliamentary Papers of John Robinson*, pp. 78, 117; Rose, *Pitt and Napoleon*, p. 206.

[2] Gibbon, *Private Letters*, 1899, ii. 100 f.

[3] Laprade, 'Public Opinion in the General Election of 1784', *Eng. Hist. Rev.* (1916), pp. 224–37.

[4] *Memoirs*, 1884, iii. 338.

Among places where interest was defeated was Bury St. Edmunds, Grafton's borough: the corporation refused to accept General Conway, who, contrary to expectation, had remained a strong Foxite. Grafton was forced to nominate a Pittite.[1] In Beverley the Pelham interest was defeated in the person of Evelyn Anderson, a prominent Foxite; Robinson had expected the old members to be returned. In Sudbury, a borough which Robinson called 'as open as the day and night too', but which he expected to be hostile, there were two martyrs, involving the defeat of the Crespigny interest. In Bridgnorth (contrary to Robinson's forecast) the electors, to quote Oldfield, gave proof of their independence 'by displacing their old favourite member Admiral Pigot, for voting for the Coalition'. At Wootton Bassett, according to Robinson, one seat could be had for £3,000. The Treasury agreed to spend an equal amount to that spent by the Pittite candidate. Actually they spent £2,500 before the seat was abandoned as hopeless.[2] No polling took place, but North's son, a martyr at Harwich, was returned, together with one of the Conways. This seems to show to what an extent Foxites were thrown back on venal boroughs. Penryn was in the same category, providing two seats out of five which Robinson estimated could all be had for a total of £12,000. Penryn, however, was *a contra*, for which Rose was 'heartily sorry',[3] probably because money had been fruitlessly spent.

The proscription of prominent Foxites, after the county elections, is best illustrated by the fate of the India Bill Commissioners, the Seven Kings as they were called. Sir Gilbert Elliot declined the poll for Roxburgh, his old seat (doubtless the election was managed by Dundas). He tried for Leominster, where Scott, afterwards Lord Eldon, was asked by his barber if it were true that he was one of the Seven Kings: 'because if I might tell the people that you assured me that he was, he has not a chance'. The assurance was given, and Elliot was defeated;[4]

---

[1] *Fox's Martyrs*; Rose, *Pitt and Napoleon*, p. 206. Grafton was presumably pledged to Conway, the old member.

[2] Chatham MSS. 137, 183, cited Laprade, 'Public Opinion in the General Election of 1784', *Eng. Hist. Rev.* (1916), pp. 224–37.

[3] *Parliamentary Papers of John Robinson*, pp. 107, 124.

[4] Twiss, *Life of Eldon.* i. 163.

he tried for Bridgwater and was defeated there. Lord Lewisham was rejected for Staffordshire; Robert Gregory was an unexpected martyr for Rochester. North's son, a martyr for Harwich, got in, as we have seen, for the venal Wootton Bassett. Fitzwilliam was safe in the Lords, Montagu and Fletcher equally so in the Commons, the former as Fitzwilliam's nominee for Higham Ferrers, the latter as Portland's for Cumberland.

The Foxites made no attempt to minimise the disaster, as the account in the *Annual Register* shows. Nevertheless, the character of the defeat is illuminated by an examination of the three chief Foxite 'victories' (in places where 'the sense of the people' could be expressed) summed up in a Westminster Election verse:

> Our Westminster, Norwich, and London successes,
> Are a glorious comment on your boasted addresses.[1]

In Westminster, Lord Hood, the new candidate, was not challenged for the first place. The whole Foxite strength was directed against Wray, very vulnerable from a reputation for parsimony, and because, having originally been brought in by Fox, he could be traduced as Judas. The attempt to make an issue of Reform for which Wray especially stood, failed completely. For his support of Wray Cartwright was pilloried as 'The Drum Major of Sedition'.[2] No one questioned that the Duchess of Devonshire turned the scale, and gave Fox his narrow margin. Walpole goes so far as to say 'she certainly procured the greater part of Mr. Fox's votes for him'.[3] For many days he had despaired. The gross abuse heaped upon her in an attempt to deter her from canvassing is a measure of her achievement. She wrote to her mother: 'I would give the world to be with you for I am unhappy beyond measure here and abus'd for nothing. Yet as it is begun I must

---

[1] *Hist. of the Westminster Election . . .*, 1784, p. 501.

[2] Print by Rowlandson. B.M. *Catalogue (ut supra)*, vi. No. 6474. Wyvill found it impossible in the winter of 1784–5 to get popular support by meetings and petitions for Pitt's Reform Bill. *Wyvill Papers*, iv. 394–409. He attributed the defeat of the Bill to the influence of the aristocracy 'for want of the general support of the people'. *A Defence of Dr. Price . . .*, 1792, p. x. Cf. below, p. 267, n. 1.

[3] *Letters*, xiii. 41 n.

go on with it . . . they insist upon our all continuing to canvass — in short they say having begun and not going on would cause a deal of harm.'[1]

In Norwich there was a vacancy. Sir Harbord Harbord, the old member, was a Pittite and got over a thousand votes more than Windham, who defeated Hobart by 63. In London the tradition that members should be re-elected was particularly strong, as was the custom that they should be aldermen. The old members were in fact returned: the two Pittites at the head of the poll, Brook Watson with 4,789 votes, Watkin Lewes with 4,554. Such totals had never before been reached and were not reached again till 1812. And Watson, who had been re-turned at a by-election in January, did not become an alderman till June. Next came the two Foxites, Newnham and Sawbridge. Robinson had expected this result, 'unless an attack can be made on Sawbridge from present circumstances'.[2] The attack was made in the unpopular person of Richard Atkinson (the 'minor Kinson' of the *Rolliad*), not then an alderman; he was seven votes behind Sawbridge (who was supported by the Pittite Wilkes). The two Foxites were 3,000 votes behind the two Pittites and if the votes given to Atkinson be added the Pittite majority would be nearly 6,000. And 56 votes had been squandered on Pitt, who had not consented to stand, and 287 on the ubiquitous Samuel Smith, who withdrew on the second day.[3] Yet in the circumstances of the election this counted as a Foxite victory. 'The result in the City,' wrote Lansdowne 'is entirely ascribed to mismanagement.'[4]

According to Wraxall, 'never since the accession of the House of Hanover did the Crown or the Treasury make less pecuniary efforts for obtaining favourable returns'.[5] The account in the *Annual Register*,

[1] *Anglo-Saxon Review*, 1899, September, pp. 74 ff. B.M. *Catalogue (ut supra)*, vi, No. 6493, etc.

[2] *Parliamentary Papers of John Robinson*, p. 74.

[3] A. B. Beavan, *The Aldermen of the city of London* (2 vols., 1908–13), i. 281.

[4] *Hist. MSS. Comm., Rutland Papers*, iii. 84–5.

[5] *Memoirs*, 1884, iii. 337. Cf. Robinson's account of his own electioneering in East Anglia. He wrote to Jenkinson from Harwich on 4 April: '. . . I have been hard at work since the Proprietors' list has been fixed upon, for they delayed it so as to straiten me much in time: in the whole I have wrote or arranged about

probably by Burke,[1] is equally emphatic: 'Friendship — gratitude and even dependency gave way ... Power, activity and popularity were exerted on a field, neglected and almost deserted by the adversary.... So complete a rout of what was looked upon as one of the strongest and most powerful parties that ever existed in Great Britain, is scarcely to be credited.' That the results were a surprise to Robinson will be clear to anyone who compares his estimates with the results. 'It exceeds all expectation,' he wrote to Jenkinson early in the election, 'the way in which all the contests turn out.'[2] Two days later, on 6 April, the King wrote to Pitt, regretting Norwich, 'undoubtedly as yet the elections have proved beyond the hopes of the most sanguine friends'.[3] There could be no better judges than Robinson and George III. And on 7 April the Foxite candidates for Yorkshire withdrew. Duncombe wrote to Wilberforce in 1789: 'Many members have confessed to me that

---

220 Persons, having in number 260 Votes. I apprehend from the Treasury they will not stir much, but it was understood at our Meeting that I as an Individual should, and I have accordingly done so — I have been fortunately of more service to them here in the Neighbouring Contests than I could have conceived — Ipswich I clearly managed and carried for them by the weight of 42 Voters from hence — properly kept back, arranged, and at the last Moment declaring — Suffolk we assisted in, as also Sudbury — Colchester very substantially. And the People hereabouts flattered me by proposing to put me at the head of upwards of 100 Freeholders for the county of Essex as *I wished*. ... The People here indeed behave with noble Attachment and Duty to our Sovereign and may be lead to any thing expressive of it — I like them more than before, they are so steady and firm to their principles.' B.M. Add. MSS. 38567, fos. 187–8.

[1] Though he is sometimes said to have ceased writing for the *Annual Register* in 1780, there can be little doubt that he wrote or superintended the account of his quarrel with Fox in 1791, pp. 119 ff. Glenbervie was informed that it was 'perfectly well known in the trade that he wrote the historical part to the end of the year 1792'. *Diaries of Sylvester Douglas, Lord Glenbervie*, ed. F. Bickley (2 vols., 1928), i. 252. Windham had denied Burke's authorship. *Ibid.*, i. 97.

[2] B.M. Add. MSS. 38567, fo. 188.

[3] Rose, *Pitt and Napoleon*, 1912, p. 207. Cf. Carmarthen: 'The Election went far more favourably to Government than its most sanguine friends could have imagined.' *Political Memoranda of the Duke of Leeds*, ed. O. Browning (1884), pp. 101–2.

they owe their success in their own counties to the example set by ours.'[1]
It was the county elections which evoked most comment. In fact, every
one knew and discounted the value of returns for close or venal constituencies. The 1784 election was remarkable, not for an exceptionally
extensive change in the composition of the House, but for the ferment
in which it took place, for the character of the Pittite victories, and for
the way in which Foxites were thrown back on nomination seats or
venal boroughs. Within the limits of the system, a mandate could
scarcely have been more emphatic. One of many tributes to the victory
is that of the member for Bramber who feared that Pitt might be
tempted by its magnitude to the dangerous course of conducting his
Ministry 'on such a narrow system as public virtue'.[2] We know that
Wilberforce thought that he could have done so.

In attempts to explain the disaster the gold of the East India Company[3] played much the same part as the gold of Pitt in later and different
circumstances. It 'conjured up the storm', according to Walpole, that
is, by propaganda, but when we admit propaganda we admit opinion,
and that no contemporary is found to dispute. Opinion was expressed
first and more emphatically in the addresses, then in the elections. And
the appeal was to principles — to the position of the Crown and the
two Houses — and to the personal credit of Pitt and Fox. The crisis was
summed up retrospectively by a Whig as 'Court intrigue and popular
delusion',[4] by a Tory as the discovery and defeat of 'Charles Fox's
plan of governing the nation by an aristocracy with the aid of his India
Bill'.[5] It would seem indeed to have been a political revolution too
deep and too lasting to be explained as a skilful manoeuvre carried

[1] *Life of Wilberforce*, i. 64.

[2] Daniel Pulteney to the Duke of Rutland, 6 July 1784. *Hist. MSS. Comm.,
Rutland Papers*, iii. 122.

[3] Mr. Philips has recently shown that the East India interest was divided and
not wholly Pittite as had been previously believed. 'The East India "Interest"
and the English Government, 1783–4', *Trans. of the Royal Historical Society*,
1937, Fourth Series, xx. 83 ff.

[4] Thomas Green, *Extracts from The Diary of a Lover of Literature* (1810),
p. 113.

[5] *The Autobiography of . . . Alexander Carlyle*, ed. J. H. Burton (Edinburgh,
1860), p. 532.

through by borough manipulation and Treasury patronage, the inevitable basis of every election.[1]

M. DOROTHY GEORGE

[1] Cf. Wyvill's retrospective judgement on the crisis, influenced by his disapproval of the French War: 'The danger apprehended from an oligarchical party in whose hands the immense patronage of India was to be placed, was indeed averted, but hence the Crown was enabled to lull the jealousy of the Public, gradually to recover a more extended influence than it had lost, and finally to obtain that decisive superiority which has annihilated Opposition, and while it preserved the forms has nearly destroyed the substance of the Constitution. The opposition of the public to this obnoxious measure was right and necessary; but their confidence in the new Minister of the Crown was unwary and excessive, and in the course of his long Administration it has been productive of fatal effects.' *Wyvill Papers*, iv. 361. Wilberforce records that owing to the crisis the Yorkshire Association lost sight of its original object — Reform — and stood for opposition to oligarchy in the persons of the great Whig lords, whose influence, combined with the cost of a contest in so large a county, had made Yorkshire the equivalent of a nomination borough. *Life*, i. 51–3, 56–7. Cf. above, p. 263, n. 2.

10 Free Trade in Land: an Aspect of the Irish Question

In 1811 the Solicitor-General of Ireland was prosecuting at Clonmel some members of two agrarian societies of the Ribbon type, the Caravats and the Shanavests.

> What [he asked] is the first object of these savage associations, to enforce the commands of which you are nightly plundered of your arms? It is the regulation of landed property and its produce, it is the vain and idle attempt to fix a maximum for rent and to prescribe the price of labour, it is the frantic project to prevent the transfer of property and to frustrate the exertions of industry. The nature of things, still more than the operation of positive law, has decreed that property should find its own level; and it is the first principle of a commercial country, and the first consequence of national prosperity, that property should be in a state of perpetual transfer and circulation.[1]

This was one view of the Irish agrarian question and it continued to be the view held by the majority of the members of the Houses of Parliament for more than half a century. 'Things will find their level,' Palmerston said in a debate on 27 February 1865; summing up, as he so often did, a commonplace thought in a commonplace phrase.

The opposing point of view was put forward in the resolutions of the Tenant Right conference of 1850.

> That a fair valuation of rent between landlord and tenant in Ireland is indispensable.
> That the tenant shall not be disturbed in his possession so long as he pays the rent fixed by the proposed law.
> That the tenant shall have the right to sell his interest, with all its incidents at the highest market value.[2]

[1] *State Trials*, xxxi. 420.
[2] *Irish Historical Documents 1172–1922*, eds. E. Curtis and R. B. McDowell (1943), pp. 250–1.

These were the 'three F's', derived, in the opinion of their advocates, from the ancient Irish system of land tenure.

Here, then, were two principles which, in their extreme forms, were irreconcilable. One looked primarily to the development of agricultural resources and to the increase of production; the other looked primarily to the protection of the producer. On the one view, the essential needs of Irish agriculture were the free flow of capital and the mechanism of the free market, in which the landlord and the tenant would represent the buyer and the seller, bound by the contract they had made. On the other, the occupancy of land, in itself, gave the occupier certain rights which were not dependent upon and could not be abrogated by contract. If the existence of such rights were admitted, the operation of a free market and the inducements to capital which a free market offered would be gravely checked. It is scarcely necessary to adduce evidence to this effect. If evidence is needed it can be found in the difference which exists today between the price of two identical houses, one sold with vacant possession, the other sold subject to a statutory tenancy at a standard rent.

There was, however, one possible measure which stood not midway but somewhere between these two theories; a measure which would compensate the tenant for improvements carried out by his own labour and capital. Although it formed part of the programme of those who looked primarily to the protection of the tenant, it could also be associated with the demand for the introduction of more capital and for greater productivity. Provided that safeguards were offered to it, the capital which had been quietly accumulating in the hands of the landless Irish Roman Catholic middle class as well as that which existed in England and Scotland could be employed in the improvement of Irish land and the increase of Irish agricultural produce.

The opportunity was not created by any extraordinary zeal for improvement which differentiated the Irish tenant-farmer from the tenant-farmer of other countries. At least, that reading of Irish history which presents hundreds of thousands of tenants virtuously and passionately bent on improving their holdings and only prevented from doing so by the stubbornness and rapacity of their landlords strikes me as nonsensical. The point is not that the Irish tenant was an

269

assiduous improver: it is that the Irish landlord was very rarely an improver at all. Here the Irish system of land tenure differed fundamentally from that of England and Scotland, where the landlord let the land and the fixed capital in the form of buildings and was usually willing, upon payment of interest, to add to that fixed capital by the expenditure of money on additional farm buildings, roads, drainage; in other words, upon improvements. A landlord who did this became in a sense a partner with his tenant, each having an interest in the prosperity of the farm. This element of partnership, which has been the salvation of the landlord-and-tenant system in England, was almost entirely absent in Ireland, where the landlord, even when no middleman stood between him and his tenant, was almost invariably a mere receiver of rent.

However deplorable, it was a relationship arising only too easily from conquests and confiscations, from differences of race, language and religion. These were not, however, the only reasons for it. One was to be found in the densely populated condition of many Irish estates. Improvement, at least in the English sense, could not be begun until a considerable number of the tenants or squatters had been removed. This is no doubt a hard saying, but an estate covered with one-room mud cabins, the land divided and cross-divided and subdivided into tiny plots, could only be improved, agriculturally, by compelling or inducing a large number of its inhabitants to leave it. This might be done humanely or it might be done brutally, but unless it were done there were many estates on which, as Lord Russell said, 'you might as well propose that a landlord should compensate the rabbits for the burrows they have made on his land'.[1] The doing of it, however, was a task from which a kindly man or a lazy man or a timid man might well shrink. The desire for popularity and the desire for personal safety alike suggested a policy of inaction, of compliance with the tendency towards subdivision of holdings.[2]

[1] Spencer Walpole, *The Life of Lord John Russell* (1889), ii. 463.
[2] For a striking warning of what was likely to happen to 'improving' landlords, see W. N. Senior, *Journals, Conversations and Essays relating to Ireland* (2nd edn., 1868), ii. 46–7. And cf. W. S. Trench, *Realities of Irish Life* (1870), pp. 47–8, 206–13.

In consequence, although there were instances of improvements being carried out by landlords (such as those effected by Lord Headley on the Glenbeigh estate in Kerry), there was in Ireland no tradition of the improving landlord. In the vast majority of cases the tenant was the sole agent of such improvements as were made. It was he who had to spend time and money, if they were spent at all, in draining, in the reclamation of waste, in making roads, in erecting farm buildings; and at least by the middle of the eighteen-forties there was a general acceptance of the principle that he ought to be compensated for what he had done and spent.

The acceptance of the principle, however, implied no agreement on the details, which provided matter for acute contention. What was an improvement? There were acts which might increase the comfort and even the temporary prosperity of the tenant without increasing, even if they did not diminish, the value of the holding. Who, then, was to say what constituted an improvement? Should it be the Board of Works or a jury or the assistant-barrister (the stipendiary chairman of Quarter Sessions)? Should there be an appeal to the assize court? The interposition of any intermediary body between the landlord and the tenant was a breach of the principle that their arrangements were best left to themselves. The more precise the system of arbitration and appeal, the more cumbersome and expensive it would become, and time and money were usually on the side of the landlord. What was to be thought of an act of improvement if it had been made in the wrong conditions or in the wrong order; as when a tenant had spent a considerable sum of money on artificial manures without first draining the land on which he put them? How long was the unexhausted benefit of the several kinds of improvements supposed to attach to the land? Above all, was legislation for compulsory compensation, if adopted, to have retrospective effect? It was recognised in the nineteenth century more strongly than it is now that retrospective legislation was undesirable as diminishing the certainty which it is the very business of the law to afford. On the other hand, was it fair to provide compensation for improvements made after a certain date and thus to confiscate all improvements made before that date?

These difficulties were formidable enough, but there was another more formidable still. Whereas compensation for improvements re-presented the limit of the concessions offered by the upholders of the contract or (as Frederick Seebohm called it in an important article in the *Fortnightly Review* of September 1869) the commercial school, it was the least demand of those who represented what was variously called the feudal or the patriarchal system, who stood for status as against con-tract. Apart from theory, moreover, there was great practical difficulty in dissociating compensation for improvements from such other de-mands as those put forward by the Tenant Right League. A landlord might say to his tenant, 'Yes, I shall pay you compensation for the improvements you have made, but I shall at the same time increase your rent and if you do not choose to pay it I shall find another tenant who will.' When Gladstone and Chichester Fortescue were holding their preliminary discussions for the Land Bill of 1870 they realised that any provision for the determination of rents by the State was politically impossible, but they hoped that a provision for compensation for im-provements and for disturbance would deter landlords from arbitrary interference with rent and tenancy.[1] This indirect approach to the question of rents, which worked well enough in England under the Agricultural Holdings Acts, was not sufficient for Ireland, where the demand for compensation for improvements passed very quickly into the demand for the 'three F's'. The result was that English and Scots members of Parliament felt increasingly suspicious of everything which fell under the vague head of tenant-right. They feared, as we might put it today, that they were being 'led up the garden path'. Sharman Crawford, the Ulster landlord who first led the movement for tenant-right in the Commons, was not himself an extremist, and although he sought valuation of rents he declined to go so far as to demand fixity of tenure. Nevertheless he was much influenced in the years 1848–52 by men more extreme than himself, and a Bill which he introduced in 1852 seemed, to English members, to show only too many signs of their influence. It provoked Sir George Grey to say that 'the object of the present agitation was not compensation but a re-duction of rents . . . such a combination must be met by the strong arm

[1] B[ritish] M[useum] Add. MS. 44121 (Gladstone Papers, xxxvi). *passim.*

of the law'.[1] There can be no doubt but that the principle of compensation for improvements suffered badly, in these years, from its association with some or all of the 'three F's', however natural or logical that association might be.

It was an association all the more natural because there existed in the Ulster Custom a system which combined or was held to combine compensation for improvements with these wider demands. Where the Ulster Custom prevailed an outgoing tenant sold his interest, usually to the highest bidder but subject to the veto of the landlord against a particular purchaser. The successful purchaser, who succeeded to the tenancy, had in effect bought two things: the right of succession to what the landlord could let and the right of enjoying the improvements made by the outgoing tenant. This system provided a rough-and-ready method of assessing the value of improvements without creating an elaborate and expensive machinery for arbitration. Such compensation, however, and therefore the total sum realised by the sale, would be seriously diminished if the rent of the holding were markedly raised. Consequently it had come on many estates to be the rule that rents should be fixed by some method of valuation which should prevent the tenant's right being extinguished, while providing the landlord with a proper increase from time to time. Another, but more arguable, rider to the Ulster Custom was to the effect that as long as the tenant paid the 'fair rent' and carried out his other duties under the tenancy agreement he should not be disturbed in the possession of his holding.[2]

Here, then, was a custom firmly entrenched in one Irish province and that admittedly the most prosperous and contented. What was simpler than to give this custom the force of law where it existed and to create a similar custom where it did not exist? This was substantially

---

[1] *Parliamentary Debates*, 3rd ser., cxix. 341 (10 February 1852).

[2] A special bibliography would be necessary for the full references to the Ulster Custom; but see *Digest of Evidence* (Devon Commission, 1847); Isaac Butt, *The Irish People and the Irish Land* (Dublin, 1867); A. G. Richey, *Irish Land Laws* (2nd edn., 1881); C. D. Field, *Landholding and the Relation of Landlord and Tenant in Various Countries* (Calcutta, 1885); W. E. Montgomery, *The History of Land Tenure in Ireland* (Cambridge, 1889); T. H. Maxwell, *An Outline of the Law of Landlord and Tenant and of Land Purchase in Ireland* (Dublin, 1909); G. O'Brien, *The Economic History of Ireland from the Union to the Famine* (1921).

the aim of Sharman Crawford in the forties and early fifties: it was substantially the achievement of Gladstone in 1870. Why was it not achieved earlier? The answers are not difficult to find. The Ulster Custom was extremely hard to define in precise terms. It varied, in important particulars, from district to district and from estate to estate. Even with the best will in the world there was bound to be extreme difficulty in giving legislative force, let alone extension, to a custom so variable. In the second place, in so far as the Ulster Custom embodied the principles of fair rent and fixity of tenure, it embodied principles which were anathema to Parliament as a whole. Parliament did not for a moment contemplate interference with the custom where it existed. Such an attempt would have turned County Down into a second Tipperary. It was one thing, however, to condone the existence of the custom, as a custom; it was quite another to give it formal approval by legislation. Moreover, it was argued that the merits of the Ulster Custom could easily be exaggerated. It suited the outgoing tenant because he obtained a lump sum by the sale of his right: it suited the landlord because he was entitled to deduct from that lump sum all arrears of rent due to him; but it was apt to bear hardly upon the incoming tenant who might have to pay as much as twenty years' purchase and, if he did so, would almost certainly begin his tenancy under a crippling load of debt. A land-agent, writing in 1853, described the Ulster Custom as that of 'one pauper tenant succeeding another, each expending his capital in the purchase of tenant right'.[1]

The foregoing details may serve to explain why no legislation for the protection of Irish tenants, whether along the lines of compensation for improvements or of more ambitious demands, secured the approbation of Parliament before 1860. There was no lack of efforts. Bills were introduced on behalf of the Irish tenants by Sharman Crawford in 1835, 1836, 1847, 1848 and 1852; by Shee in 1852, 1853 and 1854; by G. H. Moore in 1856 and 1857; by Maguire in 1858. In addition to the recommendation made by the Devon Commission in 1845 in favour of compulsory compensation for improvements, bills to that end were introduced by Peel's government in 1845 and 1846 and by Derby's

[1] *Landlordism in Ireland With Its Difficulties: A Sketch of the Tenant-Right Question in Ulster: By One Late an Agent* (Belfast, 1853), p. 18.

government in 1852. The last of these, introduced by Napier, the Attorney-General for Ireland, and forming part of his 'code', was the most ambitious attempt to deal with the question made before 1870, possibly before 1881. The Whig ventures — Somerville's bills of 1848 and 1850 — were more restricted in scope, but it was a Whig government which at last succeeded in passing legislation in the shape of Cardwell's Act of 1860.[1] This act owed its success in Parliament to its innocuousness. So far as it dealt with tenants' improvements it was wholly prospective and it was limited to such improvements as the landlord agreed to. An Irish member, the O'Donoghue, complained that the Government was merely 'prescribing bread pills'; and the act was a complete failure. Gladstone's Irish Land Act of 1870 was a far more ambitious and ingenious measure, but in the opinion of the Bessborough Commission its effect was to lead to an increase in rents and its weakness was glaringly revealed by the situation which developed in the bad years of the later seventies. The fact was that by this time the Irish agrarian question had reached a stage when even an effective measure for compensation for improvements could do little to allay discontent.

So much for what was not done in the years 1845–70. We have now to notice what was done, and on this it is desirable to make one or two preliminary points. The Irish agrarian question was not ignored in Parliament. On the contrary, a very bold and far-reaching measure was adopted for its solution; and this is perfectly in accord with two tendencies which have received, perhaps, less attention than they deserve. Even when it is admitted that England sought to do a great deal for Ireland in the nineteenth century it is usually suggested that she sought to work on conventionally English lines. On the contrary, I should like to see more emphasis on the extent to which Ireland served as a social

[1] There is no complete and accurate account of the legislation and the proposals for legislation in these years, but the subject may be studied in Sir C. Gavan Duffy, *The League of North and South: An Episode in Irish History 1850–1854* (1886); W. Shee, *Papers, Letters and Speeches . . . on the Irish Land Question* (1863); E. Lucas, *The Life of Frederick Lucas* (1886); A. C. Ewald, *The Life and Letters of Sir Joseph Napier* (1892); R. Barry O'Brien, *The Parliamentary History of the Irish Land Question from 1829 to 1869* (1880); M. G. Moore, *An Irish Gentleman: George Henry Moore* (1913).

laboratory, the scene of daring and ambitious experiments. Ireland, after all, had a system of national education before England; it had land purchase; it had, in the Congested Districts Board, what we may recognise as a prototype of the development board today. The most conventional of Englishmen were willing to experiment in Ireland on lines which they were not prepared to contemplate or tolerate at home. They were particularly prepared so to act in the forties. The significance of much of what happened in Britain in the nineteenth century would be plainer if the expression 'laisser-faire' were used in a less comprehensive and inaccurate way than it is. The task of the early Victorians was not primarily that of working a free economy: theirs was the preliminary task of bringing about the conditions in which a free economy could work. This could not be achieved by a policy of negation. On the contrary it needed measures so radical as to be almost revolutionary. None of these measures was more radical than that which aimed at free trade in land.

The demands made on behalf of the Irish tenants were, as we have seen, at odds with the dominating social and economic beliefs of the day; but these beliefs might themselves afford a solution more satisfactory in itself and far more acceptable to Parliamentary opinion. What Irish agriculture needed, it was argued, was capital. If the owner of a Lancashire cotton mill was too much impoverished to run it efficiently, it was in the interests of society that it should be acquired by someone with enough capital to do so. The same argument was applied to Irish land. Of the impoverishment of a great number of Irish proprietors there was no doubt. In the years between the Union and the end of the Napoleonic War something like a 'dance of the millions' had happened in Ireland. Lacking a tradition of agricultural improvement and being prevented from inaugurating one, the Irish landowners had spent their money in other ways, in building on a vast scale; in collecting; in political rivalry; in high living, hospitality and sport. They aspired to live, not merely like gentlemen but like princes; and their example was followed by the petty squireen and the country-town attorney. The basis of this prosperity was the highly precarious one of war-time prices. When those prices fell away the structure erected upon them, with its superstructure of jointures, charges and encumbrances of every kind, was bound to collapse.[1] A Lancashire cotton mill in similar circumstances could be sold. The transference of landed property is necessarily more difficult and the transfer of Irish landed property was unusually difficult because of the complexity of so many of the titles. It had long been customary for an Irish landlord to borrow money on the security of his land by 'confessing to judgement', that is, by executing a deed in which he acknowledged that he was a judgement debtor. These deeds were assignable. Further complications had been introduced by O'Loghlen's Act (1835)[2] which allowed an unsatisfied creditor to appoint a receiver over any and all the land owned by the debtor (including land which he had acquired since contracting the debt) and by Pigott's Act (1840)[3] which extended the lien to chattel interests, leases and terms of lives. A prospective purchaser was therefore obliged to demand the history of every encumbrance which had ever been created on any of the land owned by the vendor. In many instances the mere trouble and expense of tracing the successive assignees was in itself an insuperable obstacle to proving a good title.[4]

That was the situation which the Encumbered Estates Act of 1848[5] was meant to remedy. It was designed, as the Solicitor-General said, 'to make land in Ireland a marketable commodity, which it is not now, or only to a very small extent'. The most important provisions were those which allowed the owner, a first encumbrancer or any encumbrancer who held the deeds, to petition the Court of Chancery to sell the land with an indefeasible, Parliamentary title; distributing the proceeds, so far as they would go, among the encumbrancers and paying the balance, if any, to the owner. This act failed to achieve its purpose, largely because the unreformed Chancery Court of Ireland was too slow, expensive and cumbersome in its procedure. During the prorogation Lord John Russell spent some time in Ireland to investigate

---

[1] W. T. H., *The Encumbered Estates of Ireland* (1850); reprinted from the *Daily News* of August and September 1850.

[2] 5 and 6 Will. IV, c. 55.   [3] 3 and 4 Vict., c. 105.

[4] See Devon Commission *Digest*, p. 1030; J. Pim, *Observations on the Evils Resulting to Ireland from Insecurity of Title* (1847), and *A Letter to Sir John Romilly, M.P.* (1850).   [5] 11 and 12 Vict., c. 48.

the working of the act and on his return instructed the Solicitor-General (Sir John Romilly) to draft a second and more effectual measure.[1]

This was the act which became law on 28 July 1849 under the title of 'An Act further to facilitate the Sale and Transfer of Encumbered Estates in Ireland'.[2] It differed very markedly from its predecessor. In the first place it took away from the Court of Chancery the duties allotted to it in 1848 and placed them in the hands of three Commissioners.[3] The justification for this innovation was stated by Sir Robert Peel in words which would commend themselves to any defender of administrative law today.

> I believe, although the ordinary courts of law are admirably suited for the conduct of ordinary proceedings and for the administration of justice between man and man, without extraordinary courts, yet I must say, when great social difficulties have to be contended with, my belief is that you should step beyond the limits of those ordinary courts of justice and establish some special tribunal, unfettered by reference to technical rules, for the purpose of solving those difficulties.[4]

The powers of the Commissioners were almost absolute. They were empowered to make their own rules of court, subject only to the sanction of the Irish Privy Council; they could decide whether or not to sell and at what price; there was no appeal from them except by

[1] Earl Russell, *Recollections and Suggestions 1813–1873* (1875), p. 195.

[2] 12 and 13 Vict., c. 77.

[3] The Commissioners were Baron Richards, of the Irish Court of Exchequer; Mountifort Longfield (1802–84), who had held the Chairs of Political Economy and of Feudal and English Law in Trinity College, Dublin; and C. J. Hargreave (1820–66), Professor of Jurisprudence in University College, London, 1843–9, and a distinguished mathematician. Longfield was a man of outstanding ability, but his strongly held personal views on the Irish land question may have unfitted him for the performance of judicial duties. See his paper on 'The Tenure of Land in Ireland' in *Systems of Land Tenure in Various Countries*, ed. J. W. Probyn (Cobden Club, 1870).

[4] *Parliamentary Debates*, 3rd ser., civ. 910 (26 April 1849). The Commons debates on the Bill are to be found in vols. civ. 892–920; cv. 344–61, 760–77, 1094–1118; those of the Lords in cv. 1336–67; cvi. 709–14, 1039–42, 960–2.

their own leave. The second great difference between the acts of 1848 and 1849 consisted in the means by which an estate could be brought under the jurisdiction of the Court. The 1848 Act had limited the class of persons who could petition for sale. The 1849 Act allowed the Court to act on the petition of the owner or of any encumbrancer (for howsoever small an amount): an amendment added by the House of Lords limiting the jurisdiction of the Court to estates where the encumbrances amounted to half the net value of the estate was easily avoided, in practice, by means of an encumbrancer securing the appointment of a receiver by the Chancery Court and then having the estate transferred for sale to the Encumbered Estates Court.[1]

The powers of the Court were in the first place temporary but they were extended by successive acts of Parliament until the Transfer of Land (Ireland) Act, 1858,[2] established the Landed Estates Court to carry on (with some additional safeguards) the functions of the Encumbered Estates Court and to extend them to unencumbered estates. By the time this act was passed the success of the policy of free trade in land was a matter of almost unanimous acknowledgement in Parliament and outside.[3] This was the more interesting because in its early years the Encumbered Estates Court had been the object of considerable and indeed virulent criticism. One source of criticism was the Irish Bar, powerfully represented in the Commons by the earnest Napier and the eloquent Whiteside. The Bar, for the most part, regarded the Court as an unconstitutional innovation. This dislike was further heightened by the fact that the Court sat in Henrietta Street (remote from the Four Courts) and that, in the opinion of its critics, its business had fallen into the hands of a small clique of Counsel briefed by a few firms of speculative solicitors. As a pamphleteer of 1852 put it:

The public interest requires — the country is entitled to demand —

---

[1] I have not been able to see R. C. MacNevin's *The Practice of the Incumbered Estates Court in Ireland* (1854) or his *The Practice of the Landed Estates Court in Ireland* (1859). The British Museum's copies of these books, which would have been invaluable to me, were destroyed by enemy action during the late war.

[2] 21 and 22 Vict., c. 72.

[3] See, for instance, *Parliamentary Debates*, 3rd ser., cxl. 184–214, 915–70; cl. 22–44, 1538–69.

that the course of justice shall be turned again and permitted to flow, without further interruption, in its ordinary and legitimate channels.[1]

The other main complaint, in the early days, was that estates were sold at ruinously low figures, so that not merely the owner but most of the puisne encumbrancers received nothing. Figures were quoted to show that land was sold for as little as eight or nine years' purchase. The Commissioners replied that eight or nine years' purchase of rack-rents which had never been fully paid since the famine was equal to twenty years' purchase of the rents actually received. Encumbered landowners whose properties, as they alleged, had been knocked down for a song, voiced their complaints in the House of Lords. Their opponents pointed to other landowners, more alert or more un-scrupulous, who had procured the sale of their own estates and bought them back, at perhaps half their value, at the expense of the encum-brancers.[2]

We may deal with these two complaints at once. The hostility of the Irish Bar gradually disappeared, and it was Whiteside, one of the bitterest critics of the Court in its early days, who clothed it with respectability by the Act of 1858. On the second complaint, it seems very probable that in the first three or four years after 1849 great masses of land were flung recklessly on to a weak market to the loss or ruin of owners and encumbrancers. Before the middle of the fifties the price of land had risen substantially: early purchasers were able to see a profit; and owners who had succeeded so far in preventing the sale of their lands (sometimes as in Kerry, by hiring mobs to drive away the surveyors)[3] were able to sell on reasonable terms. I am prepared to assume, although I cannot prove, that after some bad preliminary

---

[1] *Ireland: The Incumbered Estates Court: Should it be Continued?* (Dublin, 1852), p. 62. This was a reply to *Ireland: Observations on the People, the Land and the Law in 1851, with especial reference to the Policy and Practice of the Incumbered Estates Court* (Dublin, 1851). There is an interesting article on the Court in the *Dublin University Magazine* of September 1850.

[2] See Parliamentary Debates, 3rd ser., cviii. 815–19 (15 February 1850); cx. 100–17 (9 April 1850), 806–42 (25 April 1850); cxi. 932–43 (10 May 1850); cxiii. 910–27 (7 August 1850).

[3] T. M. Healy, *Letters and Leaders of My Day* (1928), i. 27.

mistakes the Court had settled down into its place after a few years and was fulfilling satisfactorily the purposes for which it had been created.

But were these purposes sound? Did they constitute the grand remedy for the ills of the Irish agrarian system? That is a very different matter. It is notable that by 1870 opinion, which ten years before had been almost unanimous in praise of the act, was turning against it. Mill, in the 1871 edition of his *Principles of Political Economy*, could still describe the Encumbered Estates Act as the 'greatest boon ever conferred on Ireland by any government', but he printed in a footnote a letter from Cairnes which spoke of 'a class of men, not very numerous but sufficiently so to do mischief' who had acquired land through the Landed Estates Court and were 'of all classes . . . least likely to recognise the duties of a landlord's position'.[1] W. F. Finlason[2] and Chichester Fortescue[3] were still stronger critics of the operation of the act, and Gladstone's speech, in introducing the Land Act of 1870, showed that he had been influenced by Fortescue's reports.[4] Since that time the act has had many critics and few, if any, defenders.

The chief ground of criticism is that the new purchasers, intent only on securing the highest possible return for their money, treated their tenants far worse than the 'old gentry' had done. This may very well be so in many instances, but until one has followed the history of a number of estates in detail (which I have so far had no opportunity of doing) one is not entitled to accept it as a proved historical truth. For the present I prefer to base my criticism of the Encumbered Estates Act and of the policy of free trade in land on broader grounds. By 1858 the social revolution deliberately inaugurated in 1849 had resulted in the transfer of about a tenth of the total acreage of Ireland to new owners. The policy of free trade in land had had its chance and continued to have it under the Landed Estates Court. As the events of the later

[1] *Principles of Political Economy by John Stuart Mill*, ed. W. J. Ashley (1909), pp. 339 and 338 n. Ashley used the text of the 7th edition (1871).
[2] *The History of the Law of Tenures of Land in England and Ireland* (1870), pp. 113–16.
[3] B.M. Add. MS. 44122 (Gladstone Papers, xxxvii), Fortescue to Gladstone, 17 November 1869.
[4] *Parliamentary Debates*, 3rd ser., cxcix. 343–5.

seventies and of the eighties were to show, it had decidedly failed to provide a solution of the Irish agrarian question.

It is arguable, indeed, that it had done worse than this; that by offering what was in effect a quack remedy it had prevented fundamental treatment of the disease.[1] One great weakness in remedial legislation for Ireland was that of timing. By the time Gladstone provided compensation for improvements in 1870 the Irish tenants were far more interested in the 'three F's'. By the time he provided the 'three F's' in 1881 their minds had turned to land purchase. Suppose — though here one enters the realm of speculation — that something like the Land Act of 1870 had been passed in 1849 when it would have gone a very considerable way towards meeting the demands of the Irish tenants. It is at least arguable that in such circumstances the Irish agrarian question might never have attained its later gravity and dimensions. I have no desire to underestimate the reasons which made it difficult to do in 1849 what was done, and then not without difficulty, in 1870. Indeed, I have dealt with them at perhaps excessive length. But I must add the policy of free trade in land to them. It seemed to provide a remedy when it did not; it allowed statesmen to turn aside from other and more contentious remedies with an easy conscience. Ireland was to have the benefit of the application of the most fashionable and progressive doctrine of the day in lavish measure. How could it ask for more? And when it had received that benefit it must cease demanding others inconsistent with it. Over and over again during the Irish debates in the fifties the point

[1] One notable omission in the Encumbered Estates Acts was that of any provisions facilitating purchases by tenants; and this despite some vague talk during the debates on the 1848 Act about creating a 'middle-class proprietary'. Henley pointed out, with his usual common sense, that division of the land among small owner-occupiers was incompatible with the introduction of capital on a large scale (*Parliamentary Debates*, 3rd ser., c. 595–6 [4 July 1848]). Some tenants bought their farms a short time before the 1858 Act; but this was regarded in the Commons as a gratifying surprise. In June 1851 T. McCullagh introduced an Incumbered Estates (Leases) Bill to allow a tenant on an encumbered estate, when a sale had been ordered, to secure a lease in perpetuity on payment of a lump sum (*Parliamentary Debates*, 3rd ser., cxvii. 1230–9 [25 June 1851]). This is the first suggestion I have noticed of statutory facilities for land purchase. It met with overwhelming opposition.

was made that retrospective compensation for improvements would be a gross injustice to purchasers under the Encumbered Estates Act who had been given a Parliamentary title without notice of such restrictions.[1] Gladstone clearly had some such point in mind when he wrote to Fortescue in November 1869.

> We have done nothing touching the laws affecting the agricultural class except to aggravate the mischief at its sorest point by the Landed Estates Act and by the sale of the Tenant's improvements over his head.[2]

A false and untenable policy or even a reasonable policy carried too far does not merely positive ill. An equally unfortunate consequence is that it tends to waste what little time there is for finding and pursuing the true policy.

W. L. BURN

[1] E.g. in the debates on Shee's Tenants' Improvements Compensation (Ireland) Bill, 19 June 1855 (*Parliamentary Debates*, 3rd ser., cxxxviii, 2230–40 [5 July 1855]), and cxxxix, 464–86; on Maguire's Tenants' Compensation (Ireland) Bill, 14 May 1858, in *ibid.*, cxlix. 1046–97.

[2] B.M. Add. MS. 44122 (Gladstone Papers, xxxvii), Gladstone to Fortescue, 25 November 1869.

11 Russia and Pan-Slavism in the Eighteen-seventies

When twenty years after the Crimean War the Near Eastern question again absorbed the attention of Europe, among the various changes in the setting of the crisis of 1876–8 as compared with that of 1853–6 appears conspicuously the new force styled pan-Slavism. It is the purpose of this paper to attempt some analysis of its growth and its main elements with a view to indicating its position and potentialities on the eve of the crisis of 1876. Since pan-Slavism was in general not so much an organised policy, or even a creed, but rather an attitude of mind and feeling, it was at the time correspondingly difficult to gauge its power, just as it is now to analyse its different elements. At least there is no doubt that during the late seventies pan-Slavism bulked in the eyes of Buda-Pesth and Vienna, of Constantinople and London as the most dangerous force in Russia, and as will be seen in the course of this paper there was indeed much in it to give good ground for the denunciations of foreign alarmists.[1]

One major difficulty in giving specific meaning to the vague, general term pan-Slavism was that when and in proportion as it gained wide influence it did so very largely by transforming itself into a very pronounced form of Great Russian nationalism. It was in fact during the sixties and seventies in a period of transition when the watchwords that appealed to the older generation were sounding less clearly and did not chime in harmoniously with the harsh clanging of a younger

---

[1] On the pan-Slavs and the Slavophils, besides their own writings, I have found specially useful: M. Gershenzon, *Istoricheskie Zapiski* (2nd edn., Berlin, 1923); N. L. Brodsky, *Rannie Slavyanofili* (Moscow, 1910); T. G. Masaryk, *The Spirit of Russia* (2 vols., London, 1919); A. N. Pipin, *Panslavizm v proshlem i nastoyashchem* (St. Petersburg, 1913; originally published in *Vestnik Evropy*, October–December 1878); A. Fischel, *Der Panslavismus bis zum Weltkrieg* (Berlin, 1916).

generation. In a sense it was the difference between pan-Slavism, or Slavophilism as it had been originally styled, and pan-Russianism. What had begun as the religious and intellectual strivings of small coteries of Muscovite landowners ended by being transformed into nationalist mass-emotions.

The Slavophil movement, which grew up in the two decades before the Crimean War and attracted considerable attention abroad under the description of the struggle between the Slavophils and the Westernisers, had neither any organisation nor any clear political programme. The conditions of the later years of Nicholas I's reign made the open expression of political opinions almost impossible, but a further reason for the predominantly non-political character of early Slavophilism lay in the fact that for the majority of the Slavophils it was the outcome of individual struggles to express a satisfactory philosophical and theological formulation of their religious convictions and a justification of their view of the world: hence the vein of quietism, of social and political conservatism which runs through much of the writings of the Slavophils — it is particularly noticeable in Ivan Kirievsky. Yet they were by no means conservatives of the official Uvarov brand; they tended to look upon the State and the machinery of law as acting only by force and as entirely secondary in comparison with the living reality of a community (*obshchina*) morally free and morally united in the collective realisation of faith. They were first and foremost steeped in Orthodoxy. But they were also intellectuals, belonging to the middle or upper strata of the nobility; well off and well educated; acquainted with Western thought and literature; specially influenced by Schlegel and Hegel. The opposition between them and the Westernisers was ultimately due less to divergence of historical or political views than to differences of temperament and psychological approach — the one religious, the other rationalistic. Nearly all of the Slavophils were closely bound to the Russian land, for they were not only serf owners, but were born, bred and resident much of the year on their country estates.

Like spreading oaks, these families grew in the easy soil of serfdom, their roots invisibly intertwined with the life of the people and drawing life from its waters, while their topmost branches reached up into the air of European culture.[1]

Instinctively they represented the country as against the town. Their one town was Moscow, and that was a great, sprawling clutter of gardened houses, peasant huts and countless churches. St. Petersburg was psychologically and physically, just as it was symbolically, entirely alien to them. Thus bound to Moscow, thus linked with the land, they inevitably reacted profoundly against the catastrophic failure of the St. Petersburg bureaucracy, largely non-Russian in personnel, in the Crimean War. In the 'liberal' years that ushered in Alexander II's reign, when the Press was relatively free and political activity to some extent possible, the Slavophils entered the lists prominently in the struggle for reforms, above all of course concentrated on the fundamental problem of serfdom. It was thus in the sphere of internal reforms that the Slavophils first openly appeared upon the political scene. Though bitterly critical of the breakdown of the foreign policy of Nicholas and his Baltic German diplomats, their efforts were in the first place mainly directed to saving Russia herself. Only a healthy, cleansed Russia could come forward as the saviour of Slavdom.[2] In this respect at least they had come round to the point of view of the Westernisers.

Prior to the Crimean War Slavophil circles had in general taken little sustained interest in the non-Russian Slavs. The linguistic and cultural revival which began among Czechs, Serbs and Bulgars in the first half of the century looked far more to Russia than vice versa. Russians when they travelled abroad went normally to Germany, Switzerland or the West, not to the Balkans or the Slav lands of the Austrian Empire. The official world looked askance at any incipient

[1] M. Gershenzon, *Istoricheskie Zapiski*, pp. 44-5 and 94-5 (2nd edn., Berlin, 1923); referring to such families as the Kirievskys, the Koshelovs, the Homyakovs or the Samarins.

[2] A noticeable feature in the writings of the later pan-Slavs, such as Aksakov, Danilevsky and O. Miller, is the emphasis placed on the changed position of Russia *vis-à-vis* the other Slavs as a consequence of the emancipation of the serfs and the other reforms of the early sixties: Russia they claimed could now, as she could not formerly, appeal to them in the name of liberty and a new range of cultural development.

pan-Slav stirrings, and Nicholas I, only too thoroughly supported here by Nesselrode and his closest confidants, frowned severely upon any Slav movements which might infuse a further dose of revolutionary principles, above all if they infected the Habsburg Empire. No raising of a Slav banner was possible without a break between St. Petersburg and Vienna, and such a break Nicholas was, to his cost, the last to think possible. Only on the very eve of the Crimean War did he as a last resort sanction an appeal to the Christians of Turkey to rise in common defence of Orthodoxy — but not of Slavdom. It was at this point that there came into play the first attempts of the Slavophil Movement to influence foreign policy. These were due mainly to the activities of the energetic and widely known Pogodin, one of the few among the friends of the earlier Slavophils to interest himself vigorously in the other Slav peoples.

Professor of history at Moscow University, Pogodin was the leading representative of the type of academic propagandist and philanthropist which was to be very prominent in the pan-Slav movement in the sixties and seventies. Though stoutly Orthodox himself, his Slav interests and sympathies were founded rather upon the historical achievements of the past than upon a spiritual basis of the reuniting and redemptive powers of Orthodoxy. As for the present, he conjured up a picture of brother Slavs groaning under the yoke of the foreigner and gazing expectantly at Russia, by whose undisputed and unaided might they were to be rescued. This breezy optimism of Pogodin was rudely shattered by the Crimean War, but he was possessed of a buoyant perseverance and he had the invaluable capacity of giving some life to vague sympathy by harnessing it to practical and organised work. Almost alone of the Slavophil sympathisers of his generation he lived on in activity for long after the war (he did not die until 1875), and he was one of the founders, and the second president, of the Moscow Slavonic Benevolent Committee.

This committee was set up with the approval of Alexander II in 1858 with the declared aim of assisting the Southern Slavs to develop their religious, educational and other national institutions and of bringing young Slavs to Russia to be educated. In practice it concentrated almost entirely upon the Bulgars, upon whom it had an important, though by no means always the desired, effect. From the start it was closely connected with the Church, and various ecclesiastical dignitaries both in Moscow and the provinces gave the movement influential assistance. It had the backing of the Department of Asiatic Affairs in the Foreign Office, and in particular the energetic support of Ignatyev. The St. Petersburg committee, founded ten years later, was largely directed by professors of the university and concentrated mainly on relations, by no means always amicable, with the Czechs. Similar committees were also set up in 1869 and 1870 in Kiev and Odessa, where the Bulgarian colony served as its nucleus. The membership of all four was very small: they did not issue propagandist literature on any scale in Russia until 1876 and they had no regular Press of their own.[1] Their influence within Russia was not widespread before 1876; outside Russia and especially in Bulgaria they were by then of definite importance. But their greatest effect probably lay less in their actual achievements than in the exaggerated alarm which their activities in the Balkans and Austria-Hungary had inspired in the world of diplomacy and journalism.

The most spectacular achievement of the Moscow Committee had been the holding in 1867 of a Slavonic Ethnographic Exhibition in Moscow which was much advertised in Russia, and much commented upon abroad as a thin cultural cloak for political propaganda. On the whole it was not much more than a platonic declaration of Slav sympathies, and no effect was given to the one practical proposal put forward (by the Czechs not the Russians), namely, the organisation of a permanent Slavonic institute and of biennial Slavonic cultural congresses. Its Russian organisers hailed it as for the first time arousing Russia to the Slav question and as converting what had been an abstract, literary question into a living problem of actuality. Yet these same men eight years later, when the Eastern question again festered into a crisis, had to confess that Russian ignorance of and apathy to-

[1] Aksakov founded three short-lived papers, *Den* in 1861 and *Moskva* and *Moskvich* in 1867 and 1868, but they fell foul of the censorship on account of internal policy and further funds were not forthcoming, until 1880. Aksakov and the Slavophils in general were among the most prominent in the struggle against the Press censorship.

wards their Slav brethren were still only too widespread. By 1875 not so very much had changed since 1860 when Turgenev's *On the Eve* depicted the father of the heroine as unable to distinguish her Bulgarian revolutionary lover from 'a vagrant Montenegrin'.

But at the least the Slavonic committees did form a skeleton organisation which might be rapidly expanded if circumstances were favourable, for besides the rigid Muscovite patriotism which was their core they now had, what they never had before, powerful supporters in both the Winter Palace and the Anichkov Palace and powerful allies in a new stream of anti-foreign hostility. Of their Muscovite core the most typical representative was the leader of the Moscow Committee, Ivan Aksakov, a man of vigorous personality, who rose to the height of his career in the crisis of 1876–8.

Born in 1823, sprung from the central Russian land and bred in something of the atmosphere of his father Sergei's *A Russian Gentleman*, Ivan Aksakov belonged spiritually, like Dostoyevsky two years his senior, to the older Slavophils born in the first decade of the century.[1] With him as for them the roots of Slav feeling lay in absorbed devotion to the Orthodox Church. With them likewise his main energies lay outside any professional or official service. Neither learned nor widely read, but passionately outspoken with all the conviction of a doctrinaire fanatic, he became the prophet of the small circle of the Moscow Slavonic Committee, announcing in semi-apocalyptic terms the divine mission of Russia, the freeing of her brothers in faith and blood from a foreign religious and political yoke. This historical mission of Russia, her moral right and duty, is founded in the fact — never argued nor 'proved', merely didactically stated — of Orthodoxy as the one pure form of Christianity, the essential basis of true civilisation, of which the Russian Slavs are the only true and effective repository and up-holders. Over against Slav Orthodoxy is set the old decaying Romano-German world of the West, with its poison of unbridled rationalism and individualism, its cancer of internecine competition, and its ruinous social and industrial struggles. As for almost all the earlier

[1] His pan-Slav writings are collected in the first volume of his collected works, *Slavyansky vopros*: there is a valuable, though very hostile, article, by A. N. Pipin, reviewing this in *Vestnik Evropy*, August 1886, pp. 763–807.

Slavophils Catholicism is the symbol for Western civilisation, and for Aksakov the arch-enemy. Protestantism bulks far less, appearing merely as a subsidiary form of declension from the true principles of Christianity. Thus the Catholic Slavs have been guilty of the great betrayal. The Slavs stand at the parting of the ways; either the way of the West, of Rome; or the way of the East, of Orthodox Moscow. For the Czechs and Croats there may be some hope if they return to Cyril and Methodius, to Orthodoxy; to the Poles Aksakov offers nothing but the cup of irreconcilable bitterness. The essential prerequisite for the idea of pan-Slav fraternity is the idea of the highest spiritual unity in faith: secure the purity of the Slav ideal of faith and Church, then all things will be added unto you. Hence political combinations, the political aims of Russian foreign policy are left vague and unanalysed. All the strength of the Slavs lies in Russia; all the strength of Russia in her Slavdom. Russia cannot achieve healthy national development save through realisation of her vocation as the great Slav power, through a break with the post-Petrine, Petersburg period of her history. Just as Russia is unthinkable apart from Slavdom, since she is both spiritually and materially the leading expression of it, so also is Slavdom unthinkable apart from Russia.

These views are little else than a restatement of those of Ivan Kirievsky and Homyakov, but the emphasis is now laid on Orthodox Slavdom rather than on Greco-Slavonic Orthodoxy, a significant transition towards the newer pan-Slavism. And further, while earlier writers, as too Aksakov's contemporary Dostoyevsky, hankered after some synthesis which should save Western civilisation from the consequences flowing from the over-developed rationalism of its philosophical and theological bases, Aksakov was content to summon Orthodoxy and Slavdom to do battle with the principle of evil. Russia's messianic calling was no longer to be that of the saviour of humanity at large, but was now limited to Orthodox Slavdom alone. On the other hand, he took over from his predecessors, besides their fundamental religious outlook, their antipathy to institutional forms of constraint and regulation and their criticism of or hostility to Peter the Great and his semi-German successors with their tentacular bureaucratic despotism and their desertion of true Russian ways of life for Western importations.

Thus the *mir* and later the *zemsky sobor*[1] became slogans for Slavophil or pan-Slav groups as genuine, national products of Muscovite Russia; thus the Holy Synod was repudiated as an erastian creation of Peter which had shackled the true life of the Church and bent it into subservience to the State: thus the governmental machine was attacked as an alien incubus, controlled by Baltic Germans and other non-Russians, totally unable to respond to the deep currents of national life; thus, finally, the dynasty itself was the target for accusations of being but a German brand of military autocracy without roots in the soil of Russia.

Such an attitude of mind, to some extent traditional among certain sections of the landed power, owing much now to the reaction against the régime of Nicholas I and something to the economic and social dislocation following on the emancipation of the serfs and other reforms, was by no means confined to Aksakov's followers. With different colourings and different trappings, it was common to many among the landowning class for whom St. Petersburg meant government by bureaucrats, loss of power, and economic displacement. Here were potent feelings, essentially unconnected with pan-Slavism which yet might be utilised by it in an assault upon St. Petersburg foreign policy if that policy refused to move in consonance with the true aspirations of the Russian people as the standard bearer of the Slav cause.

This anti-governmental element, together with the anti-dynastic streak, in the pan-Slavism of Moscow circles helped to make them profoundly antipathetic to Alexander II himself and to most of the high functionaries of the St. Petersburg machine. Yet they were not without allies or sympathisers in the very highest circles of the Court. The Empress and, later, the wife of the Tsarevich with all the enthusiasm of converts to Orthodoxy imbibed the traditional view of the mission of

---

[1] The historical origin and development of the *mir* or village community was the subject of acute controversy between the Slavophils and their opponents. The former took little or no account of certain aspects of the *mir* which in fact had been imposed from above by the State within the last two centuries. The *zemsky sobor*, roughly comparable to the *Etats généraux*, had not met since 1682. A revival of it in some form might serve as a curb on the Tsar and the bureaucracy on the part of the landowners.

Orthodox Russia and surrounded themselves with a circle of ardent devotees of Homyakov's and Tyutchev's brand of religious, poetising nationalism, of which the Countess Bludova's salon was the most conspicuous centre. There reigned Tyutchev's dreams of a 'great Graeco-Russian Orthodox Empire' which should gather together Slavdom with 'the pan-Slavonic Tsar' at its head, and

> as ye gaze,
> To east and west, to south and north,
> The sun's glad tidings shall ring forth,
> The summons of his conquering rays.[1]

In such an atmosphere, and with Pobedonostsev as tutor, the future Alexander III had been brought up. He was probably not deeply influenced by this mixture of pan-Orthodox and pan-Slav symbolism, but he was as Tsarevich generally supposed to be an adherent of pan-Slav ideas, a supposition which could find confirmation in the undoubted fact that a number of his entourage, as well as his wife, were warm supporters of the cause. These Court allies were not an initiating force, but if a crisis arose in Turkey, if feeling rose high, they might act as a powerful influence on Russian foreign policy and as invaluable collaborators with Aksakov's following in Moscow.

Although Aksakov and his like fiercely denounced Peter the Great and so much that followed after him, they omitted from their counts the expansion of Muscovy into the Russian Empire. It was Peter and his house of Holstein-Gottorp who had annexed the Baltic provinces, the southern steppes, the Crimea, Poland, Finland, Bessarabia, the Caucasus, great tracts of Asia. This tremendous heritage was silently accepted. So far from there being any murmur of undoing any part of this work, Moscow and the pan-Slavs were the loudest in demanding

[1] On Tyutchev's pan-Slav ideas, see G. Florovsky, 'The Historical Premonitions of Tyutchev' in *Slavonic Review*, vol. 3, pp. 337–49. Countess Bludova, a fanatical anti-Pole, was a close friend of Bashanov, the Empress's confessor, and of Tyutchev's two daughters, both ladies-in-waiting, and one of them subsequently married to Aksakov and an important link between Aksakov, Pogodin and Katkov, and Court circles. For Pobedonostsev's connection with Aksakov through the daughters of Tyuchev, cf. 'Pobedonostsev and Alexander III' in *Slavonic Review*, vol. 7, pp. 31–2.

that the borderlands be fully absorbed in the great Slav mass of central Russia, the core of the old Muscovy. The Polish revolt of 1863 had unleashed again century-old hatreds and fears. Katkov in his *Moskov-skiya Vedemosti* had led the first great Press campaign which Russia had known, with resounding effect against the Poles and against foreign intervention. In the years which followed the old 'Congress Poland' was swept away, mercilessly dragooned within the framework of the administration common to Russia proper (a framework that largely consisted of a state of siege), while 'the western lands', Lithuania, White Russia and the right-bank Ukraine, were subjected to every measure of Russianisation. Contemporaneously was initiated a campaign of the same nature in the Baltic Provinces and Bessarabia; and, to show without mistaking that Russian meant Great Russian alone, the Little Russian or Ukrainian cultural revival of the time was successfully attacked by Moscow, above all by the prohibition in 1876 of the use of the Ukrainian 'dialect' for any academic or literary purposes. Symptomatically two of the men most actively associated with this denationalising, Russianising policy were among the most prominent of the Slavophil or pan-Slav Muscovites of the day: Prince Cherkassky (1824–78) and Yuri Samarin (1819–76), both of them friends of Aksakov.

Completely different in character and attainments, they were both at one in regarding the problem of nationality within the Russian Empire as requiring urgent and drastic handling. Samarin admirably summed up an increasingly widespread feeling when he ridiculed the ideal of a denationalised empire in which Russians, Poles and Germans lived side by side but apart from each other 'comme qui dirait la reproduction très en grande de l'hôtel Ragatz (he was writing from Brussels) où Russes, Américains et Français venaient, sans se connaître, s'asseoir à la même table d'hôte'; over against this he set a Russia in which a Russian 'would feel like a Frenchman feels in France or an Englishman in England', entirely at home.[1]

For Samarin and Cherkassky the only solution possible for the great western fringes of the empire was an undeviating policy of Russian-

[1] B. E. Nolde, *Yury Samarin i ego vremya* (Paris, 1926), p. 186, quoting a private letter of Samarin written in 1864.

isation: of the success of this in the central Polish provinces with an overwhelming pure Polish population they were admittedly doubtful, but it could at least serve to stifle the nationalistic chauvinism of the upper classes until such time as the Polish peasantry had been transformed by the new legislation for which both men were largely responsible. Samarin had been one of N. A. Milyutin's right-hand men in working out the details of the abolition of serfdom in Russia and was subsequently employed in the somewhat similar task of agrarian reform in Poland. An earlier period of administration in the Baltic Provinces had likewise given him first-hand practical experience of the Letts and Esthonians and their Baltic German landowners. Prince Cherkassky, a wealthy Tula landowner, had taken a prominent part in the emancipation of the serfs and also worked with Milyutin and Samarin in Poland and distinguished himself in the campaign for reuniting the Uniats with the Orthodox Church. For three years (1868–70) he was still more in the public eye at the head of the Moscow City Council, until his protest against reaction, in concert with Aksakov and Samarin, called down the displeasure of the Tsar and he was forced into retirement. Both were noted members of the Moscow Slavonic Committee, though Cherkassky, unlike Samarin in his closing years, did not deeply concern himself with the Slavs outside Russia until he ended his life, in 1878, as civil administrator of Bulgaria.

Both men are significant in the pan-Slav movement in that unlike Aksakov or the earlier Slavophils, and unlike the professorial type represented by Lamansky, Miller or Grot, they were active in administration and politics and were well-known public figures. Cherkassky in particular represents the doer — by fits and starts — as opposed to the thinker or prophet. Samarin, endowed with an exceptional capacity for hard work, combined practical ability with deep intellectual and religious interests grounded in him by his early upbringing and his student years at Moscow university. Himself a considerable theologian as well as the author of the widely influential *The Borderlands of Russia*, the textbook of the 'Russifiers' of the seventies, he may be accounted a bridge between the older type of Slavophil steeped in the learning, the rites and the mysticism of Orthodoxy and the newer type of forceful administrator, diplomat or soldier to whom such a religious and philosophical grounding was of little or no concern. Both men are also, above all, significant as leading protagonists of the transformation of the idea of pan-Slavism into that of pan-Russianism. To the success of such views on internal policy was largely due that continuance in Western countries of the picture of Russia as the brutal oppressor of her subjects and peoples which remained one of the strongest springs of Russophobia in England and elsewhere.

At the same time this internal aspect of developing pan-Slavism was paralleled by the note of hectoring domination or overweening pride which was becoming more and more marked in relations with the Slavs outside the Empire. It is of course obvious that views such as those of Aksakov sketched above would raise in an acute form the fundamental contradiction contained in the combination of pan-Slavism and Orthodoxy. A thousand years of the history of the Western Slavs were virtually ignored. More than half of the Slavs living outside Russia dwelt within the bounds of the Austro-Hungarian Empire; and the great majority of these were Catholic and had been for centuries deeply affected by Westernising influences. Still more formidable was the problem of the Poles, the second most numerous of the Slav races and with their long and great tradition of civilisation binding them to Catholicism and the West. It was impossible in the long run to ignore them, and yet at this period that was the deliberate attitude of the Russian pan-Slavs, hot with the acrid fumes of 1863. At the Slavonic Ethnographic Exhibition held in Moscow in 1867 to display to Russia and the world at large the fraternal union of Slavdom the Poles were conspicuous by their absence. In all the round of speeches on that occasion the Poles were scarcely mentioned save by Pogodin who called upon them to rejoin the Slav brotherhood by humbling themselves before the Russian Tsar. At the close Rieger, the Czech leader, remonstrated in cautious terms. Promptly Cherkassky, true to his reputation, arose to pour forth minatory reproaches on any meddling with what was a purely Russian question.

It is evident that pan-Slavism as long as the Orthodox Church remained as its basis could only be applied in the main to the Slavs in Turkey. Only in proportion as it shed its ecclesiastical and religious elements, might it be capable of appeal to the majority of the Slavs in Austria-Hungary, or to the Poles. Even then there would remain the stumbling-block of the lack of any common language. It was symptomatic that Šafarik's correspondence with Pogodin was written in German, and that the proceedings of the Prague Slavonic congress of 1848 were likewise conducted in German. The Russians in their attempt to impose Russian as the common language for all Slavs encountered the most emphatic opposition: unedifying and fruitless wrangles with Lamansky, Hilferding and other Russian philologists in the pan-Slav camp were the only result.

Lastly, a third stumbling-block in the path of pan-Slavism lay in the fact that, although Russia was indisputably the only effective political and military Slav power, her claims to cultural predominance seemed thin and arrogant in the eyes of many Western Slavs. Thus Homyakov's *Address from Moscow to the Serbs*, in 1860, with its tone of dictatorial superiority, had aroused much ill-feeling in Serbia. Palácky and others were not behindhand in repudiating any idea of Russian hegemony; and the same antipathy to the patronising dominance of Moscow was scarcely veiled during the celebrations of the 1867 Ethnographic Exhibition. Despite the reforms of the early sixties, Russian Tsardom ran counter to the traditions and aspirations of every other Slav people. Emancipation at the hands of the Russian Tsar might mean but an exchange of domination. Gorchakov, always an opponent of pan-Slav schemes, was justified in writing, 'Je ne vous dissimule pas qu'il m'est difficile de croire, à une sympathie sincère, des races Slaves pour la *Russie Autocratique*.'[1] However much some of the Czech leaders might blind themselves to the nature of Russian Tsardom, the trees of liberty were likely to have very queer blooms if transported from the banks of the Neva or the Moskva. Certainly they were not recognisable along the Vistula.

These three major obstacles to the development of pan-Slavism were abundantly apparent throughout Alexander II's reign. Towards its close they became less apparent to foreign eyes when a different form

[1] Gorchakov to Novikov, 9 May 1872, in notes kindly lent to me by Baron A. F. Meyendorff and made from the archives of the Imperial Russian Embassy in London.

of pan-Slavism was in the ascendant which put either no or little store on the test of purity of religion, or on the overcoming of linguistic differences, or on the civilising mission of Russia, but proclaimed a nakedly political programme for the annihilation of the Habsburg and Ottoman Empires through the military might of Russia. This may be said to mark the final stage of the development of pan-Slavism into pan-Russianism, and this was the form in which during the eighteen-seventies pan-Slavism was above all represented to the rest of Europe, mainly through the work of two men, the one forgotten, the other still remembered: Rostislav Andreievich Fadyeev and Nikolai Pavlovich Ignatyev.

Fadyeev (1824–84) was a military man, belonging to a country family of the nobility serving in the army or civil service. His father rose to be governor of Saratov: his mother was a Dolgorouki. He himself served for twenty years in the Caucasus, where he became an ardent supporter of expansion in Central Asia and a lifelong henchman of Prince Baryatinski, the conqueror of Shamyl and 'the pacifier of the Caucasus'. In 1867, inspired by the field-marshal chafing in retirement, he joined in the attack then being engineered on D. A. Milyutin's army reforms which he subjected to drastic criticism in a series of articles entitled *Russia's Armed Forces*.[1] As a result he was forced by Milyutin to retire from the active army, and he soon joined forces with Chernyaev, the Central Asian lion of the day who had likewise been broken by Milyutin, and with his swashbuckling friends grouped round the violent nationalist paper *Russky Mir*. From this period dates Fadyeev's championship of the Slav cause, first pronounced in strident tones in his *Opinion on the Eastern Question* (1869), which at once made his name in the Slav lands. In January 1875 he went to Egypt to reconstruct the Egyptian army at the invitation of the Khedive — an invitation which apparently was extracted by the intrigues of Ignatyev.[2] This task was undertaken as a practical means for working towards the disruption of the Ottoman Empire, in the hope of being able in five or six years to utilise the Khedive's army against his suzerain in conjunction with a

[1] *Briefwechsel des Botschafters General v. Schweinitz* (Berlin, 1928), p. 47.

[2] Stanton (Cairo) to Derby, no. 17, very confidential, 15 January 1876, in F.O. 181/535.

rising of the Balkan Slavs. Events moved too quickly; and in any case Ismail Pasha intended his army for a very different use, against the Abyssinians. Fadyeev hurriedly set out for the real scene of action and was back in Russia at the end of May 1876. The authorities succeeded in stopping him from proceeding to Serbia as he intended, but they allowed him to re-enter the active army, and he gaily continued his career as a stormy petrel figuring prominently, after war had been declared by Russia, in Belgrade and Cettinje.

It is not surprising that the views of such a man on the Slav question should present radical differences from the ideas already analysed. Fadyeev had no interest in the past, no concern for the Slavophil tradition of emphasis on the spiritual and cultural union of the Slavs, no feeling for the unique mission of the Orthodox Church and the civilisation based upon it, no rooted belief in the virtues of the Russian peasant. He looked upon the Moscow Slavophils as having finished their role and as having, since the emancipation of the serfs, no practical programme.[1] Significantly he lived, in his later years, in St. Petersburg or Odessa, not in Moscow. He had the mentality of a militant adventurer. He could be direct and briefly to the point, but was apt to be carried away by fantastic exaggeration and atrabilious judgement. Of the Slav lands he knew little at first hand, and he had never visited any of them until his unwelcome appearance in Serbia in 1877; but he imbibed much from his friend Ignatyev and from the pan-Slav group in Odessa. Above all he had a perfectly clear idea as to two fundamentals in the Slav question — force and Austria-Hungary.

His first book *Russia's Armed Forces* (which appeared in 1867 and was soon translated into German with an alarmist, anti-Russian preface by Julius Eckardt), contained little of a political or non-technical character and pan-Slavism is only incidentally urged, and in relatively moderate terms, but it enunciated without qualification the doctrine that force is the sole final arbiter in international affairs and the inevitable prerequisite for any great nation with a mission to fulfil. That the Eastern

---

[1] *Russkoe obshchestvo v nastoyashchem i budushchem*, in his collected works, vol. 3, pt. 1, pp. 102-4. He is writing specifically of Slavophilism in relation to the internal problems of Russia, but the views here expressed are, I think, typical of his attitude to Slavophilism in general.

question could only be solved by war on a great scale was even more emphasised in his *Opinion on the Eastern Question*. This brief, easily read, violently provocative outburst from Fadyeev was the most influential of all the expressions of pan-Slav views of the time. First published in 1869, it was rapidly translated into most European, and all the Slav languages, and was generally taken abroad to sum up the quintessence and real programme of pan-Slavism.

Its resounding keynote was the watchword attributed to Pashkevich, 'the Eastern question can be solved only in Austria, not in Turkey; the way to Constantinople lies through Vienna'. The Eastern question can only be terminated by war on Russia's western frontiers, for it is not a question affecting only the Slavs in Turkey, but the Slavs in Austria-Hungary as well, and the Poles: i.e. it is 'the pan-Slavonian Question'.[1] Austria-Hungary cannot without committing suicide act otherwise than in a sense diametrically opposed to Russia: free Slav states in the Balkans would be impossible for the Austrians and the Magyars with their subject Slav races. 'Austria can hold her part of the Slavonian mass as long as Turkey holds hers, and vice versa.' Turkey is looked upon as being in complete decadence, and neither her army nor her fleet are regarded as of any consequence. Militarily Russia can always forestall her Western opponents not only in the Balkans but on the Bosphorus: with 100,000 men to mask the Bulgarian fortresses and a striking force of another 150,000 she can be in Constantinople in six weeks. But, her line of communications is fatally threatened by the strategical situation of the Austrian Empire. Hence the necessity of settling with the Habsburgs and of annexing Eastern Galicia and Bukovina, with their brother Slavs 'groaning on the Russian borders'.

Russia's 'historical individuality' is now pronounced, but it is not realised, and it can only be realised by expansion as the welder of the Slavonic world. She cannot be consolidated save as the centre of her Slav and Orthodox world of Eastern Europe.

> The whole of Europe stands up against the historical development of Russia, threatening, as it does, a still greater breaking up of present systems . . .

[1] My quotations are from the second English edition, published in 1876.

The historical move of Russia from the Dnieper to the Vistula was a declaration of war to Europe, which had broken into a part of the Continent which did not belong to her. Russia now stands in the midst of the enemy's lines — such a condition is only temporary: she must either drive back the enemy or abandon the position.

She 'must either extend her pre-eminence to the Adriatic or withdraw again beyond the Dnieper'. Save for the members of her own family the Slavs and the Orthodox, Russia has, and can have, no reliable allies. Least of all must Prussia (which Fadyeev already regarded as virtually united Germany) be accounted such, for she will stand with Austria-Hungary for the traditional German preponderance in the Danube valley, and for continued Germanisation of the Slavs. 'Russia's chief enemy is by no means Western Europe, but the German race in its enormous pretensions.' Thus foreshadowing developments of the late eighties, he went on to argue that 'all the more substantial interests of Russia and Prussia are much more antagonistic than those of *Russia and France*'.

Fadyeev was not a whit depressed by his picture of an irreconcilably hostile Europe in the struggle that was inevitably to come. Russia must stand alert and prepared to act alone — with her Slav allies. He did indeed admit as a weakness the small amount of interest that had hitherto been shown in these allies by Russia and her omission to establish herself as their undisputed leader, but he readily comforted himself with the recommendation that time and propaganda would rectify the mistakes of the past. In any case the immense sympathies of the Slavs for Russia could be securely counted upon as her greatest asset when the opportunity came and her armies struck victoriously against their common foes. Then seven hundred thousand Slavs (a typically exaggerated figure) would rise in arms to fight on Russia's side. The Rumanians were to be won over by the gift of Transylvania; the Greeks by the gift of Thessaly, Epirus and the Isles, but nothing more. Unlike Aksakov and others, Fadyeev was ready enough to supply some outline at least of the political aims of the struggle for Slav emancipation. The objects were two-fold: to secure to each branch of the Slavs its independent political and social life; and to combine with Russia in some form of confederation in which Russia was to be militarily and internationally predominant. 'Each tribe requires a Sovereign of its own for its domestic affairs, and a great Slave[1] Tzar for the affairs of all collectively.' Thus foreign policy and military affairs must be in the hands of the Tsar. He added that it was very desirable that Russian Grand Dukes should sit upon the new Slav thrones. Russia, however, was to make no annexations, except in the case of Eastern Galicia and Bukovina, and of course the southern districts of Bessarabia torn from her in 1856. Constantinople was left in the vague position of a free city for the confederation. As for the Poles, they were summarily offered the alternative between entry into a Slav confederation and ruin. 'The Polish nation will have to choose between the position of a younger brother of the Russian people and that of a German province.'

Such a programme of pan-Slavism, aiming nakedly at a Russian domination of the whole of Eastern and South-eastern Europe to be realised through the overthrow of the Austrian and Turkish Empires however reckless in what it assumed and fantastic in what it omitted, could rouse all the more alarm abroad when in the course of the eighteen-seventies the renown of the Russian ambassador at Constantinople came to be widely spread as the able, unscrupulous, tireless propagator of closely similar ideas. It was above all the influence of Ignatyev which transmuted the aspirations of the Moscow pan-Slavs into one of the main realities of the Eastern crisis when it came to a head in 1876.

Ignatyev (1832–1908) was a man of exceptional abilities and ingeniously flexible determination, whose active life was entirely spent in the army, in the foreign office and in diplomacy. He made his name, when only twenty-eight, by his resounding success in the Far East in securing for Russia the 1860 Treaty of Pekin. From 1861 to 1864 he was Director of the Asiatic Department of the Foreign Office, which dealt not only with purely Asiatic countries but with Turkey in Europe as well. In 1864 he took over the Constantinople legation (it was not raised to the rank of an embassy until three years later), and he

---

[1] Slav was frequently at this time spelt in English Slave, thus evoking a wholly different range of associations from those suggested to Slavs themselves by their common name — *Slava* meaning glory.

remained at that post continuously until just before the outbreak of the Russo-Turkish war in 1877. He came to be on increasingly bad terms with, and finally the avowed rival of, his nominal superior Gorchakov, and he never acquired the real confidence of the Tsar; but he had multiplied connections with the Court, the army, the big landed nobility (to which he himself belonged), and especially with the Slavonic Benevolent Committees. By 1875 he stood out not merely as a diplomatist but as a leader on whom was pinned much of the hopes of Russian nationalism and whose influence both in Russia and in the Balkans was of the greatest practical consequence.[1]

Ignatyev in sketching in his memoirs his general policy in the Near East laid down three aims which Russian diplomacy must follow: the revision of the 1856 treaty of Paris (including the suppression of the collective guardianship of Turkey by the powers), the command of Constantinople and Straits, and some form of common action by the Slavs under the direction of Russia. His attitude to pan-Slavism is predominantly political, the religious and cultural aspects being merely means which could be useful adjuncts for the attainment of Russian predominance in South-eastern Europe. Ignatyev was not a man for whom the Orthodox Church meant any deep religious experience or mystical communion. His attitude during the struggle between the Greeks and the Bulgars over the Exarchate is an excellent illustration of the way in which political calculations were the determinant factor. He knew that a schism would lead to internecine struggles among the Eastern Churches and a general lowering of the prestige of Orthodoxy which would be not at all to Russian interests: hence his original policy appears to have been to secure a compromise which would provide some nucleus for the nascent Bulgarian nation but which would not entirely alienate the Greeks. But as the prospect of any such agreed settlement receded he was quite prepared to tip the scales more and more decisively in favour of the Bulgarian extremists. Unable to prevent the Greeks from offering unyielding opposition, he appeared undisguisedly as the main protagonist of those in the Russian diplomatic

[1] The following paragraphs on Ignatyev are based mainly on my article 'Ignatyev at Constantinople, 1864–74', in *Slavonic Review*, vol. 11, pp. 343–4, 569–71.

service who thought in terms of Slavdom rather than in those of Orthodoxy. There could be no stronger contrast than that between Ignatyev
and his subordinate Leontyev, occasionally, though with doubtful
ustice, classed as a Slavophil. Leontyev was for some ten years in the
consular service in the Balkans and Constantinople. There his first-
hand acquaintance with both Bulgars and Greeks served to fortify his
convictions as to the primacy of 'Byzantinism' (the Greek-Orthodox
culture and view of the world) and caused him to recoil in horror from
the deliberate rending of the Orthodox world by the Bulgarian intelli-
gentsia in the name of that false nationalism, linked up with the
principles of 1789, which for Leontyev was the curse of Slavism.[1] For
Ignatyev, on the other hand, the whole question of the Exarchate was
simply one as to how could be secured for the Bulgars 'un noyau
national qu'on serait libre de développer ultérieurement'; and by 'on'
he meant primarily Russia.

The difference between the pan-Slavism of Ignatyev and his like, and
the philosophical and religious Slavophilism of the older type, is
equally well illustrated by Ignatyev's frank repudiation of any pretence
at idealism in his championship of the Slavs. Sooner or later, he held,
Russia must fight Austria-Hungary for the first place in the Balkans and
for the leadership of Slavdom: only for the attainment of this task
should Russia make sacrifices for the Slavs under Austrian and Turkish
rule and be solicitous for their freedom and growth in strength. To aim
merely at emancipating the Slavs, to be satisfied with merely humanitarian success would be foolish and reprehensible. Slowly they must be
united in the form of a defensive union subordinated to the general
military, diplomatic and economic direction of Russia. Against Gorchakov he insisted that the Slav standard should be borne exclusively by
the Russian Tsar: better to adjourn any idea of solving the Balkan
question or of liberating Bosnia and Herzegovina from the Turkish
yoke rather than yield anything to the inevitable rivalry of Austria-
Hungary.

[1] For Leontyev's views see his *Vostok, Rossiya i Slavyanstvo*, vol. 1 (Moscow,
1885), a republication with some additions of his articles on the Eastern
question, notably *Panslavizm i Greki* (1873) and *Bizantism i Slavyanstvo*
(1875).

All Ignatyev's efforts were directed towards working for the time when the development of Russia's strength and favourable conditions in Europe would allow of the attainment of a purely Russian solution of the eastern question, *viz.*, the Straits at the disposal of Russia and the creation of brother states in blood and faith linked to Russia by adamantine ties. Of first importance was the command of Constantinople and the Straits, as necessary for the security of Russia's Black Sea coastline as for her political and economic expansion. She must be master of Constantinople by one of two means, either by complete diplomatic predominance there, as was largely achieved between 1871 and 1875, or by direct conquest if the opposition of the Turks and the powers rendered the former policy impracticable. Ultimately in any case a radical solution of the Eastern question would have to be found involving the disruption of the Ottoman Empire in Europe, and defiance of the Habsburg Empire: if the other powers combined with Turkey against Russia, Constantinople and the Straits must simply be conquered, and the Greeks, Bulgars and Armenians won over to act as obedient tools of Russian policy.

Thus with Ignatyev, as with Fadyeev, predominated the ideas of an independent, anti-European policy of force, and of a Russia whose destiny was to utilise the growing nationalism of the Slav peoples so as to facilitate the disruption by her own might of the Austro-Hungarian as well as of the Ottoman Empires, leaving in their stead South-eastern Europe (and for Ignatyev above all Constantinople and the Straits) under her unquestioned control. Ignatyev himself was to play his hardest for these high stakes in 1878 when with the signature of his treaty of San Stefano for a moment he was at the zenith of his power, only to taste the bitterness of defeat three months later.

Of this newer type of pan-Slavism no theoretical or systematic exposition was supplied by Ignatyev or Fadyeev. This lack was met by Danilevsky's *Russia and Europe*, subsequently styled 'the bible of pan-Slavism'. Though first published in 1869 it was not very influential in Russia or much known abroad until a later period.[1] Ponderous, very

[1] There is no English translation of it in the British Museum. The only German translation that I know of was not published until 1920, and in a very much shortened version.

lengthy, and graceless in style, it was certainly not designed for wide consumption. It did, however, introduce a new note which helped to give it some immediate vogue. Danilevsky (1822–85) had been trained as a student mainly in botany and the natural sciences and throughout his career, which was that of a government inspector of fisheries and other departments of agricultural economics, he retained the closest interest in them; Darwin becoming his particular bugbear. From his botanical studies he derived the idea of the struggle for existence as the dominating factor in the relation between states; force was justified as an inevitable, natural concomitant of the development of any healthy species. *Russia and Europe* built up with much parade of scientific argumentation, seemed to give to pan-Slavism the *cachet* of science as then fashionable.

Danilevsky's political views, apart from their setting and presentation, are closely similar to those of Fadyeev. He, too, denies the conception of humanity or civilisation as a whole, and places in the forefront that of the struggle between different cultural–historical types, based mainly on language groupings. While in general agreement with the other Slavophils or pan-Slavs as to the opposition between the Romano-German civilisation of Europe and the civilisation of the Slav peoples, he considers this opposition to be fundamental in the sense that it is insuperable. Thus he, too, repudiates anything in the nature of Dostoyevsky's striving towards a universal brotherhood to which Russia should guide, not merely her Slav brothers, but the whole suffering world. Slav civilisation, above all as represented by Russia, is inevitably destined for a glorious future, but this future depends upon the political emancipation of the Slavs from Western Europe, and such independence can only be attained by war. Thus only can the Eastern question receive its final solution. Danilevsky has no doubts as to the outcome. His political outlook and reasoning are, as with nearly all the pan-Slavs, extremely optimistic. Russia is taken as a match even for a combined Europe, and the Slavs can have the fullest confidence in their moral superiority over a Europe diseased through centuries of violence and now through economic dissensions and the undermining threat of socialism. Victory is assured, and will bring to birth a Slav federation under the leadership of Russia, into which must enter, besides the Poles, the non-Slav Greeks, Roumanians and Magyars, and the capital of which is to be Constantinople.

Here again is apparent the unsubstantial sketchiness of pan-Slavism as a political programme. It was in fact, except in the case of Ignatyev, far less a political programme than a political manifesto. With too little backing of real knowledge of the Slav lands and with insufficient facing up to the obstacles in its path, pan-Slavism was much more of an emotional force than a planned creed of Russian imperialism. It is significant, for instance, that on the vital question of the future of Constantinople there was no agreement among the Russian nationalists. All were indeed agreed that Constantinople 'must be ours'; but there were wide differences as to what exactly that meant. When the crisis of 1878 was reached, the lack of any clearly thought-out solution was only too evident. While Dostoyevsky feverishly preached the necessity and rightness of the annexation of Constantinople by Russia as the head and guardian of Orthodoxy,[1] and while pious Orthodox circles, and particularly the Court devotees would not be satisfied 'until they sat cross-legged upon the crescent of Santa Sofia',[2] Fadyeev and others urged some kind of internationalisation in the form of a free city, and Danilevsky and Leontyev on the other hand diatribed against such an idea as converting what should become the capital of a Slav or an Orthodox confederation into a hotbed of hostile intrigues of every description.[3]

Such were the main strands going to make up the tangled web of pan-Slavism in the eighteen-seventies. Clearly it was not the organised power or carefully worked-out plan which it was represented to be abroad. Yet the foreign view of it, though exaggerated, had sensed correctly the fundamental element of danger which lay in it. The pan-Slavs, divided and few in numbers though they were, represented a sounding-board of the new, restless Russian nationalism. Through

[1] *Dnevnik Pisatelya*, in his collected works, 6th edn. e.g., vol. 11, pp. 281–3; vol. 12, pp. 71–3, 78–82, 354–60.

[2] Gorchakov on the Countess Bludova, *Russkaya Starina*, vol. 133, 1908, p. 96.

[3] Danilevsky in articles published in 1877, reprinted in P. Streltsov, *Rossiya, Tsargrad i prolivi*, pp. 66–70: Leontyev in *Grazhdanin*, 1878, reprinted in *Vostok, Rossiya i Slavyanstvo*, vol. 1, pp. 249–50, 254–5: cf. 76, 239.

them, with their connections with the Moscovite nobility, the Orthodox Church, the Court, the diplomatic service and the army, this
nationalism might, if events abroad gave the requisite shock, be capable
of effectually diverting or even directing the policy of the Tsar and his
immediate advisers. An outbreak in the Balkans, massacres of Christians, tales of heroic resistance could be made to arouse again among
the immense mass of the illiterate population of Russia the old traditional feelings that God had made the Turks to be the oppressor of the
Orthodox and the Russians to be their saviour. With the tiny minority
of the educated this same appeal of the pan-Slavs to religious and
humanitarian sympathy for the Balkan Christians could bulk large,
while they could also, of course, appeal to mere, ordinary chauvinism;
in the case of a few to a deep and solid interest in Slavdom; in the case
of many to a desire to escape from aimlessness and inaction by plunging
into a cause. This last element in the pan-Slav appeal in the late seventies
brings out one of the two deepest motive forces lying beneath the
turgid and often bombastic externals of pan-Slavism. In its call to self-
confidence, to action, to a belief in Russia as a mighty power destined
to shape the history of the world and fulfil a mission of her own, it
responded to a deep craving for national recognition, all the keener
when the humiliation of the Crimean War was set in such sharp contrast with the achievements of Italians and Germans in moulding their
national future. And as a second motive force lay the reaction, so
explicit in all forms of Slavophilism or pan-Slavism, against the claim
of West European civilisation to set up as the one, true civilisation to
which all other peoples are or should be adapting themselves, a reaction
which still remains, in different guise, one of the most potent influences
in the Russia of today.

B. N. SUMNER

12 The New Course in British Foreign Policy, 1892–1902

In one of his characteristic outbursts to the British military attaché at Berlin, the Kaiser complained, 'All my life I have worked for a good understanding with England, but you do not help me.'[1] This is only one of the oft-repeated complaints, made sometimes to the British ambassador and more often to the military attaché, but its frequent repetition, in varying forms, represented a genuine conviction of German goodwill and British lack of response. In the history of the ten years which began in 1892 this reproach has a special significance, for one at least of the important results of the developments of British policy in this period was that the era of co-operation between Britain and the members of the Triple Alliance was ended.

Sir Edward Grey, who was Under-Secretary of State for Foreign Affairs in 1892–5, put this view clearly in an important speech at a meeting of the committee of imperial defence in 1911, a meeting attended by the dominion delegates of the imperial conference then in session.

> To explain [he said] what the present situation is as between our-selves and other Powers of Europe, I think I must go back a little into history, because we cannot understand the present situation without knowing how we came to arrive at it. I must go back rather an alarming way to the time when I first became Under-Secretary at the Foreign Office in 1892. . . . In 1892 the situation then, and for some years previously, had been this: that the two restless Powers in Europe were France and Russia. . . . The solid quiet group . . . was the Triple Alliance of Germany, Austria, and Italy. It had been the policy of Lord Salisbury before 1892, and it was the policy of Mr. Gladstone's Government of 1892, not to join the Triple Alliance or

[1] Lt.-Col. A. Russell to Sir E. Goschen, no. 4, secret, Berlin, 3 March 1911. Gooch and Temperley, *British documents on the origins of the war*, vi. 594, no. 442, *encl.*

come under definite commitment to it, but generally in diplomacy to side with the Triple Alliance as being the stable Power in Europe, and the one which was securing the peace. . . . Soon after 1892 the situation began slowly to change.[1]

Sir Edward Grey, in this exposition, did not give the reasons for the change, nor did he attempt to date it. He contented himself with describing some of the difficulties of the years following 1892 with Germany and with France and Russia, and leaped forward to the time when, as he said, 'the late Government, I imagine — I was not of course a member of it — got tired of the situation', and set out on an investigation of what the troubles with France in fact were, and then to resolve them in the Anglo-French agreement of 1904. The subject of the present inquiry is the interval over which Sir Edward Grey in his speech passed so quickly, the interval before the final negotiations began which led to the great liquidation of long-standing difficulties with France. The 'new course' in British foreign policy was primarily a movement away from the triple alliance.

The secret of the movement cannot be found in any one episode. There are, indeed, several possible explanations, no one of which is satisfactory alone. The general trend of Sir Edward Grey's argument when he looked back on this period after the passage of nearly twenty years, suggested, if it did not state, one main reason — the rivalry of the fleets. Sir Edward Grey's speech, however, was only incidentally a historical narrative, and its form was determined by contemporary conditions. The emphasis on the fleet was natural enough in 1911. Britain and Germany were then in the midst of their long-drawn-out negotiations in search of a naval understanding; only two days before this speech, Sir Edward Grey had circulated to the members of the cabinet committee a memorandum summarising the history of the recent negotiations with Germany.[2] The critical conversations with the German ambassador were taking place at this very time, broken into a few weeks later by the crisis of Agadir. Moreover, the imperial conference, of which this meeting of the committee of imperial defence

---

[1] *British documents on the origins of the war*, vi. 782. Minutes of the meeting of the Committee of Imperial Defence, 26 May 1911.

[2] *Ibid.* vi. 631–6, no. 468 and *encl.*

formed part, was concerned primarily with the decision on the part of the dominions to develop a shipbuilding programme of their own. In 1911, therefore, the fleet was necessarily in the forefront of discussion. This was not so at the beginning of the century. Mr. Woodward gives the year 1906 as the opening of the period when naval rivalry with Germany was an effective force in political relations. 'The first stages of the development of the German navy,' he said, 'did not cause great anxiety in Great Britain.'[1] Much the same could be said of another subject of discussion, which had great popularity at one time, among the wiseacres who pronounced on Anglo-German relations — the Bagdad railway, though here the importance should be dated even later.[2]

There are other possible explanations. One of them — which might well be popular now, for views of the past are all too liable to be dominated by the present — gives pride of place to the problems of the far east. This theory is expounded in full in Mr. Joseph's book on *Foreign diplomacy in China*,[3] and receives some support in Professor Langer's exhaustive survey.[4] The Kaiser, in one of his outbursts, attributed the British antagonism — for that naturally was how the problem presented itself to him — to another reason. 'You don't like us,' he said — it was in a conversation with the military attaché in 1895 — 'because our commerce is beginning to rival yours in many parts of the world. It is inconvenient; but it is your own fault — it is the result of Free Trade.' And then he added, characteristically, 'Perhaps also you don't like us on account of our Politics because they also are "made in Germany".'[5] There was no doubt a measure of truth in this view.

[1] E. L. Woodward, *Great Britain and the German navy* (1935), p. 2.

[2] There is no study of this subject comparable in thoroughness with Mr. Woodward's book, though the sketch by E. M. Earle in *Turkey, the Great Powers and the Bagdad Railway* (1923) is valuable. The subject is, however, very fully documented both in *Die grosse Politik der Europdischen Kabinette, 1871–1914* (see vols. xvii, xxv (i), xxvii (ii), xxxi, and xxxvii (i and ii)), and in Gooch and Temperley, *op. cit.*, particularly vols. ii, vi, and x (ii).

[3] P. Joseph, *Foreign diplomacy in China, 1894–1900* (1928).

[4] W. L. Langer, *The diplomacy of imperialism* (2 vols., 1935), cf. pp. 167 *sqq.*

[5] F.O. 64/1351. Memorandum by Colonel Swaine, 20 December 1895. Cf. the Kaiser's account of the conversation, *Die grosse Politik*, x. 251–5.

Anglo-German rivalry in trade was making itself felt in a formidable degree, as a steady under-current, the force of which it is difficult to measure. Joseph Chamberlain, in his famous 'long-spoon' speech of 13 May 1898, attributed popular hostility to this cause, though he used less picturesque language to express his view. Then there is what is, perhaps, the most popular theory, and one which it is difficult to counter. Britain, it is often held, decided — the date given is generally 1898 — on a fundamental change of policy. Briefly, it is described as the 'end of isolation', and the circumstances of the time, particularly in the colonial sphere, determined that the new connection would be, ultimately, with France and Russia. There is much that is tempting in this traditional view; but it is at best only a half-truth, and it leaves un-explained Britain's own contribution to those circumstances of the time that drove her to choose France rather than Germany as the partner in her entente.

British policy during these ten years, dominated first by Rosebery and then by Salisbury, was confusing to foreign powers. It was, in fact, not one policy but three, and the interaction of these three constituents — for they were coincident and not successive — was responsible for the final result. The first was a matter of general principle. From time to time general principles were enunciated, which were described as governing relations with other powers. They provide the broad out-lines of policy, the authoritative statements of the direction in which statesmen were aiming, and of the principles which they were seeking to maintain. The second policy, or rather, the second constituent in policy, worked in contrast in secret. It may be defined as that element of realism in policy which is always present, but at times decisive — the knowledge that there were some things which in given circumstances might be achieved, and some which could not. It appears in this period, mainly, in three very different guises. In the first place it is seen in the repeated application of the underlying assumption that Britain's effec-tiveness in foreign affairs — like her security — depended on the use of sea-power. Secondly, it is seen in the conviction that in the last resort there were some things which would be impossible, because of the de-cisive force of public opinion. And, finally, it showed itself in the belief that for some purposes the essential condition was the maintenance of the concert of Europe. Then there was the third constituent in policy, represented by a series of specific decisions in different questions arising from time to time in widely scattered areas; and these decisions were in the final sum the most important. To some extent such differing forms and facets of policy are a matter of common form; but their differentiation was for various reasons particularly important in British policy of this period — not least because, in a world of great European powers whose interests were for the most part clearly defined, British interests were widely distributed in far corners of the world. Some, at least, of the confusion about the period has arisen from the failure on the part of both contemporaries and historians to note the working of these different influences.

Yet, it must be owned that there was another reason for the confusion: British ministers did not always say the same thing. In May 1898 Salisbury and Joseph Chamberlain both made important speeches. Salisbury, on the 4th, in a speech at the Albert Hall, known commonly as the 'dying nations' speech, referred to 'the jargon about isolation'.[1] It would be pleasant and convenient to be able to quote it as a proof that the government of the time, at least, was not thinking of itself as isolated or of a new policy that would bring isolation to an end. But Chamberlain, on the 13th at Birmingham, in a speech which also has a short title — for it was the 'long-spoon speech' — asserted that for fifty years British policy had been one of isolation and urged a policy of alliance with a great military power.[2] England was speaking with

[1] Cf. *The Times*, 5 May 1898, p. 7. The relevant passage is as follows: 'We know that we shall maintain against all comers that which we possess, and we know, in spite of the jargon about isolation, that we are amply competent to do so. But that will not secure the peace of the world.

You may roughly divide the nations of the world as the living and the dying.'

[2] *The Times*, 14 May 1898, p. 12. 'Now the first point that I want to impress upon you is this. It is the crux of the situation. Since the Crimean War, nearly 50 years ago, the policy of this country has been a policy of strict isolation. We have had no allies — I am afraid we have had no friends. . . . Now, what does history show us? It shows us that unless we are allied to some great military power, as we were in the Crimean War, when we had France and Turkey as our allies, we cannot seriously injure Russia, although it may also be true that she cannot seriously injure us. . . . If, on the other hand, we are determined to

two voices, by accident or deliberation, and the only conclusion
possible, if we base our views of policy on utterance alone, is a lack of
cohesion in the direction of policy itself. The contradiction becomes
intelligible on one condition: if we accept the view that British policy
in the period is to be found rather in the realm of action than in public
utterances or even written statements of policy. If the continental
powers, and Germany in particular, thought in the language of
alliances, Salisbury, perhaps more than all other British statesmen,
thought in terms of practical co-operation. Hence the special importance, in a period of which he was the dominant figure, of taking
into our reckoning the specific decisions on questions of detail and the
practical considerations of effective action.

If we view the period as a whole, the most important of the general
principles on which pronouncements were made, in private or in
public, was still the time-honoured refusal to enter binding alliances.
The principle was as old as the age of congresses — older indeed than
Joseph Chamberlain's fifty years — but it had taken new shape since
the transformation of the European system in 1870–1. It was a principle
common to both the great English political parties, even at the time
when their foreign policies in other respects most widely differed. It
had been proclaimed by Salisbury in 1871, and by Granville in 1872.[1]
But the significance of the principle grew as the great European alliances
developed. By the time Salisbury started his long administration of
1886–92 the alliances of Germany with Austria-Hungary and of these
two powers with Italy dominated the European scene, while already
the first tentative moves of Russia and France were taking place, which
were to lead ultimately to the alliance of 1894. The statesmen of the
great powers of Europe came to assume that good relations between
states found their natural expression in an alliance; Britain alone refused
steadfastly to use the common European language of the time, and
her refusal was of great importance. It is interesting to compare the

---

enforce the policy of the open door . . . then . . . we must not reject the idea of
an alliance with those powers whose interests more nearly approximate to our
own.'

[1] Cf. Temperley and Penson, *Foundations of British foreign policy* (1938), pp.
344, 516–20.

reactions of other European governments to the British refusal. It was a source of constant irritation in Berlin, where, at least after the fall of Bismarck,[1] it was never fully accepted. On the other hand, in Vienna, during the long tenure of the ministry of foreign affairs by Kálnoky, it was accepted with understanding.[2] At the end of 1894, when Kálnoky was trying to disperse the clouds of distrust that overhung Anglo-German relations, he gave the German ambassador, Count Eulenburg, a careful exposition of the British attitude.[3] The failure of his efforts is not surprising, if we compare Count Kálnoky's own records of the conversation with that sent home by Eulenburg,[4] but his subsequent attempt to convey the explanation through the Austro-Hungarian ambassador at Berlin seems to have had equally little effect. The British objection to binding alliances remained one of the fundamental obstacles to Anglo-German friendship.

Salisbury's objection to binding alliances was based primarily on a regard for public opinion. This characteristic of his policy — of which evidence can be found as far back as the seventies — grew more prominent in his later years. His attitude was not merely the slavish consistency in a principle, for the conditions of the time in this period, in both England and Germany, were unfavourable to friendship, and a bad augury for what might happen if the contingencies foreseen in an alliance came to pass. The atmosphere of hostility, the result of several causes, was kept constantly to the fore by the colonial question. In this period, indeed, colonial disputes were probably the most influential cause, for their force as a factor in English opinion had grown greatly

---

[1] As an example of Bismarck's attitude, cf. Malet's letter to Salisbury of 25 October 1887, Gooch and Temperley, *op. cit.*, viii. 14.

[2] Cf. for example Kálnoky to Biegeleben, no. 2, secret, Vienna, 25 October 1887, Gooch and Temperley, *op. cit.*, viii. 9–10; Kálnoky to Bruck, secret, no. 1, Vienna, 22 June 1891, W.S.A., Pol. A. Rot. 465, secret, xxiv/ii; also Kálnoky to Deym, no. 3, very confidential, Vienna, 4 December 1894, Deym to Kálnoky, no. 40F, secret, London, 13 December 1894, W.S.A., viii/172, iii.

[3] Cf. Kálnoky to Szögyény, very confidential, Vienna, 5 December 1894, and to Deym, nos. 1, 2, very confidential, 4 December 1894, W.S.A., viii/172, iii.

[4] Count Eulenburg's account is given in his despatch to Prince von Hohenlohe, no. 249, very confidential, Vienna, 4 December 1894. G.P., ix. 172–6.

as the years passed, encouraged by the growing sentiment of imperial pride and solidarity. The year 1894 was particularly rich in incident from this standpoint. First, in March, there was the question of the Niger basin, where France and Germany came to an agreement, based partly on a common opposition to the activities of the Royal Niger Company. We must, wrote the British Secretary of State, Lord Kimberley, 'be strictly on the guard against this possible combination [of Germany] with our rivals there and elsewhere in Africa'.[1] This was, indeed, only a ripple on the surface, for Kimberley's tone changed in April. Then, in the summer, the Congo question came as the irruption of an uncontrolled force in the quietened waters of the entente between England and the triple alliance. Rosebery went so far as to threaten a reversal of his European policy.[2] Again, after reflection, he gave way, though this involved a public humiliation, and a few months later Kálnoky confidently assured his German ally that the incident was forgotten as far as England was concerned. (The language used in Eulenburg's despatch of 4 December 1894 shows that it was apparently not forgotten in Germany.[3]) Already, however, when Kálnoky sent this assurance of the British recovery in December, a new question had arisen. Samoa was suggested by Germany as a suitable pledge of English goodwill, and on this the British Government could not give way, for Samoa was a question on which public feeling was strong in Australia. After Australia came South Africa as a cause of firmness. Germany at this time was beginning her long contemplation of a possible collapse of the Portuguese Empire in Africa, and England was obdurate on the question of Delagoa Bay. Feeling on the German side ran so high that once more Austria-Hungary stepped in as a mediator — for to her, if not to Germany, the maintenance of the British entente was an essential object of policy. Kimberley explained that the South African factor was decisive. The territory south of the Zambesi was so vital to England

[1] Minute by Kimberley, 31 March 1894, F.O. 64/1332. Printed Temperley and Penson, *Foundations of British foreign policy* (1938), p. 488.

[2] Cf. Deym to Kálnoky, tels. nos. 29 and 31, secret, 13 and 14 June 1894. W.S.A., viii/172, iii. Cited *Foundations*, pp. 491–2. Cf. Eulenburg's report of a conversation with Kálnoky on 15 June, G.P., viii. 455.

[3] Cf. G.P., ix. 172–6.

that she would not even be able 'to recoil from the spectre of war'. 'If England were ever,' he is reported to have said, 'to permit Delagoa Bay to pass to other hands, Cape Colony, whose interests would thereby be most seriously damaged, would immediately secede from the mother country and separate from England.' (It is worth noting here that the wording is that reported by Deym, the Austro-Hungarian ambassador.)

> The maintenance of Cape Colony [the report continued] was perhaps the most vital interest of Great Britain because by the possession of it communication with India was assured, which otherwise might be cut off any day. Cape Colony was of even greater importance to England than Malta or Gibraltar, and it was just this which the German cabinet would not understand — that the English government are compelled to support the interests of Cape Colony if they do not want to lose it.[1]

A year later it was in Africa that the final blow came. When, in January 1896, the Kaiser sent his famous telegram to Kruger he created a long-remembered popular ill-feeling, which was still in operation to stiffen Anglo-German suspicions during the South African war. The Kaiser's emphasis on his devotion to his English grandmother, or his far stranger insistence that England and Germany should hold together as 'the two great Protestant nations' — such arguments could have little effect in view of the trend of public opinion which gave substance to Salisbury's caution. Nor was the ill-feeling on one side alone. It was fed here by the belief in ill-feeling in Germany, and there by similar belief in British hostility. In 1901 when Salisbury made his classic exposition of his reasons for opposing an alliance, he asserted that 'A promise of defensive alliance with England would excite bitter murmurs in every rank of German society', and added in words that suggest, perhaps, that Salisbury himself shared in measure the popular feeling, 'if we may trust the indications of German sentiment which we have had an opportunity of witnessing during the last two years'.[2]

[1] Deym to Kálnoky, no. 35B, very confidential, London, 1 November 1894, W.S.A., viii/114.

[2] Salisbury's Memorandum of 29 May 1901, Gooch and Temperley, *op. cit.*, ii. 68–9, no. 86.

And the last two years were, of course, the years of the South African war. Five years before this Salisbury had written, 'The French and German *people* both hate us.'[1] Again, earlier still, in November 1894, Kálnoky had complained to Eulenburg of the attitude of the German foreign office to Britain. It had continued to be unfavourable, he said, despite Rosebery's surrender on the Congo question; the Press was hostile, and German representatives almost everywhere were showing themselves antagonistic. It was unnecessary, for example, he said, for the German Press to have adopted an offensive tone on the occasion of the British attempt at intervention in the Sino-Japanese war. In this conversation, too, he gave serious warning of the importance of public opinion in England. 'What I fear,' he said, 'far more than the irritated moods of statesmen would be *the impression on public opinion in England.*' There were influential people — even in the cabinet — who were utterly averse to any *rapprochement* with the triple alliance or to anything that would draw England into an active foreign policy, whose ideal would be a pure peace policy and one of good relations with all foreign powers, 'but especially with Russia, France, and America', and who would pursue this policy 'even at the cost of national self-esteem'. He said further that 'if public opinion in England were once to envisage the possibility of good relations with Russia and thence also the prospect of an understanding with France, no Prime Minister could resist such a current which would have all the radical elements behind it'.[2] The words 'no Prime Minister' are significant. There was a feeling in Germany, as the British ambassador there reported, that they had only to wait for the return of Salisbury and a satisfactory solution would be found. But this view — based mainly on the experience of the eighties — was an entire misreading of the situation when Salisbury returned to office at the close of the century. On colonial questions public opinion in England was now stronger than the personal predilections of any statesman. Salisbury stood firm at Fashoda against France, maintaining — and publishing as a state paper — the declaration of his Liberal predecessors on the Nile Valley. The whole tenor of

[1] Salisbury to E. B. Iwan-Muller, 31 August 1896, *ibid.*, vi. 780.
[2] Kálnoky to Szögyény, no. 2, very confidential, Vienna, 30 November 1894. W.S.A., viii/172, iii.

his policy makes it unlikely that he would have been less insistent on African questions where Germany was concerned.

But, if public opinion, roused on the colonial question, made an alliance impossible, there was no such objection to an entente. Co-operation between governments was, in Salisbury's view at least, a wholly different matter. Throughout the earlier period of Salisbury's influence the practice of co-operation had been a consistent feature of his policy. It was essential for the development of Egyptian administration, and it was the only possible alternative to the maintenance of the European concert in connection with Turkey. An entente relationship had many advantages. It worked, for the most part, in secret (perhaps that is the difference between an entente and that curious and sometimes meaningless form, an 'entente cordiale'?); the action that it involved was not military but diplomatic, or at the most extreme it might show itself in a naval demonstration, and it was for military action that the support of public opinion was in the last resort essential. Above all, however, it had the advantage that it was a matter of practice, and not principle. It is true that in 1887 Salisbury had hesitated before agreeing to the entente proposals of Italy and Austria-Hungary, that before he accepted the December agreement of that year he had stipulated for a written expression of Bismarck's support, that he repeatedly refused to renew these engagements — in 1895, 1896, 1897 and 1902 — as resolutely as did Rosebery in 1893. But it was the written engagements which made British ministers so dubious. When Salisbury left office in 1892 his letter to Sir Philip Currie urged in effect the maintenance of the policy of the agreements, and, in particular, the continuance of friendship with Italy.[1] Rosebery, as is well known, refused to look at the documents, but made statements which reiterated their policy, and this was in effect the line taken by Salisbury on his return. There was no sudden change of policy. The conclusion of the Franco-Russian alliance made, it is true, a vital change in the European situation, but its effect was not the reversal of British practice. The effect was rather — if we attempt to sum up these years in one generalisation — that for Austria-Hungary and Italy the entente was more essential than before,

[1] Lady Gwendolen Cecil, *Life of Salisbury*, iv (1932), 404–5. The letter is dated 18 August 1892.

and that for England the support of Germany, for which Salisbury had stipulated in 1887, was more vital than ever. The British fleet, according to Rosebery, could deal with Russia alone, but if Russia were aided by France 'we should need the help of the Triple Alliance'.[1] It was unfortunate that, in the spring of 1894, the support of Germany was lacking. The government of Caprivi reverted to a policy of reinsurance with Russia. A minute by Kálnoky shows clearly enough the difference in outlook of the two allies. He was commenting on a proposal from Berlin for negotiation with Russia by the triple alliance powers alone. 'We,' he said, 'could not consent to be drawn into discussions with Russia without bringing in England.'[2] The correspondence of this time between Germany and Austria-Hungary makes clear the diplomatic atmosphere in which British policy began its movement, not away from isolation, but away from the practice of co-operation with the Central Powers.

The movement was not complete until the end of our period. As late as 1901, when Salisbury and Lansdowne were discussing the question of a German alliance, Lansdowne suggested, as an alternative to the abandonment of the negotiations, a limited agreement on the model of the Mediterranean agreement with Italy in the spring of 1887.[3] The discussion is illuminating. Lansdowne's proposal was, in his own words, for a 'declaration of common policy and of a desire to maintain close diplomatic relations'. He himself does not seem to have had much hope of the acceptance of such proposals, and Salisbury thought there was little advantage in them. Both were probably right. The regions in which Lansdowne looked for co-operation — on the model of 1887 — were the shores of the Mediterranean, the Adriatic, Aegean and Black Seas. Here he suggested that both parties might assert their desire to maintain the *status quo*. There were even greater obstacles to such an arrangement than either of the British ministers knew. The undertaking, as we now know, would have run counter to Germany's obligations to Italy under the triple alliance, and, perhaps

---

[1] *Vide Foundations*, p. 482.

[2] Minute by Kálnoky on despatch from Szögyény to Kálnoky, no. 17A, secret, Berlin, 31 March 1894. W.S.A., viii/172, iii.

[3] *Vide* Gooch and Temperley, *op. cit.*, ii. 79, No. 93.

most fatal of all, it carried with it no countervailing advantage of colonial concessions. In 1901, in contrast to 1887, or even perhaps 1894, the colonial question was more important than the Near East. The attempts to reach an understanding on overseas issues — the Portuguese colonies in 1898, Samoa in 1899 and the Far East in 1900 — had failed to achieve their object; the promise of common action in the Near East was no compensation. Constantinople was an issue of burning urgency in the eighties; in 1901 urgency had turned elsewhere, to Africa where the Boer War was not yet ended, and to the Far East where the coming conflict between Japan and Russia was already casting its shadow.

The change, in this respect as in others, had been gradual. Rumours were rife in Europe that Rosebery, and after him Salisbury was carrying out a revolution in the British attitude to Russia and Turkey. The negotiations with Russia of the Rosebery period, which led to the treaty of the Pamirs of 11 March 1895,[1] were given a false importance by the assumption that the *pourparlers* dealt also with European questions. In fact, the treaty was one of the same local order as the Zanzibar–Heligoland treaty with Germany of 1890 which had led to similar rumours, or the Anglo-French treaty of 1898 concerning the Niger which did not. Rosebery gave repeated assurances to Austria-Hungary that the question of Constantinople and the Straits was not even mentioned in the negotiations.[2] And when, in January 1898, an overture to Russia of a more general character was in fact made, it arose from the situation, not in Turkey, but the Far East. Although both regions were mentioned in Salisbury's proposal, it was China that came first. And the occasion of the overture was the German occupation of Kiao-Chao. What had happened as far as Anglo-Russian relations were concerned was that the scene of rivalry and distrust had shifted; it had gone East, with the development of Russian expansion into the vast

[1] A.P., 1895, cix [*c.* 7643], 159–62.
[2] Cf. Kálnoky to Szögyény, no. 3, secret, Vienna, 30 November 1894. The assurances were reported by Deym in his telegram, no. 72, secret, of 21 November. W.S.A., viii/172, iii. Kimberley gave similar assurances. Deym to Kálnoky, no. 39A, very confidential, London, 30 November 1894. W.S.A., viii/172, iii; cf. also G.P., ix. 165, 167.

Siberian hinterland, and the decline in the strength of the Chinese Empire. In Salisbury's overture to Russia in January 1898 — as in his 'dying nations' speech in May — the region which gave urgency to his argument was not Turkey but China. The failure of Salisbury's overture to Russia was followed by the negotiation of the so-called 'Yang-tse' agreement with Germany. But this proved only that German co-operation in the Far East was no solution of Britain's problems in that area. And in this region there was no Austria-Hungary to mediate. The reaction from these abortive attempts at co-operation was the Anglo-Japanese alliance of 1902.

The character of the change in British policy in the Balkans is still a subject of controversy.[1] Evidence is conflicting and still incomplete. The traditional view, before the archives of the period were available for study, here or elsewhere, fastened on the evidence provided by Salisbury's speech in the House of Lords on 19 January 1897 — the speech in which, in referring to the period of the Crimean War, he used the oft-quoted words we 'put all our money upon the wrong horse'.[2] Among the many documents from various sources which have been published in recent years, there are some that support and others that confute this tradition. Six months before this speech Salisbury wrote in a private letter: 'I do not know that I can sum up the present trend of English policy better than by saying we are engaged in slowly escaping from the dangerous errors of 1846–56.'[3] Palmerston, he said, was 'guided by common sympathies' (and by this he means political sympathies) 'instead of by common interests. He made war with Russia; he insulted Austria; and he ostentatiously made friends with

---

[1] Cf. W. N. Medlicott, 'Lord Salisbury and Turkey', *History*, October 1927, and H. Preller, *Salisbury und die türkische Frage in Jahre 1895* (1930).

[2] *Vide* Hansard, *Parl. Deb.*, 4th ser., xlv. 28–9, 19 January 1897. 'But I am bound to say that if you call upon me to look back and to interpret the present by the past, to lay on this shoulder or on that the responsibility for the difficulties in which we find ourselves now, the parting of the ways was in 1853, when the Emperor Nicholas's proposals were rejected. Many Members of this House will keenly feel the nature of the mistake that was made when I say that we put all our money upon the wrong horse.'

[3] Salisbury to E. B. Iwan-Muller, 31 August 1896. *Vide* Gooch and Temperley, *op. cit.*, vi. 780.

France. In order to baulk and baffle Russia he, and his school, set up as a political faith the independence and integrity of the Ottoman Empire. The whole tone of the letter supports the view that Salisbury's views on the Near East were reasonably represented by his famous metaphor from the turf. Against this, however, and the considerable supporting evidence of the German record of conversations in 1895 with Count Hatzfeldt,[1] there is one main body of evidence to be put. Throughout this period documents can be found, some in the British archives and some in those of Austria-Hungary, in which British ministers persistently denied that any change of policy had taken place. When the Kaiser spoke to the British military attaché in terms based upon Count Hatzfeldt's reports, the implications were immediately and specifically denied.[2] On the question of the Straits, which to Salisbury as well as to other powers was the 'key to the Eastern Question', both Salisbury and his successors held insistently to what became in the course of time the new wording of the old policy: if the Straits were opened they should be open to all. The first time that the right of Russia was recognised to special privileges in the Straits was not 1895 or 1897 but 1936. British ambassadors could still throughout the period that we are considering 'deny categorically' that British policy in the Straits had changed.

Yet the change had come, even if it was not, properly speaking, one of policy. It was a change of vital importance, for it was based on something more decisive than statement of professed doctrine, on what I described earlier as the element of realism in policy. There were three main ways, I have suggested, in which this ingredient in policy showed itself: public opinion — certainly present on this occasion, for it was outraged in England by the Armenian massacres; the maintenance of the European concert, rendered uncertain now by the fluctuations in the

---

[1] Cf. *G.P.*, x. 9–13, 16–18, where Hatzfeldt reports conversations of 30 July 1895 and early in August; Hatzfeldt's reports from Cowes, *ibid.*, pp. 22–7, and his subsequent reflections, *ibid.*, pp. 28–36, *passim*.

[2] Cf. *Foundations*, pp. 494–5. Perhaps the most illuminating comment on Salisbury's views is that of Baron de Courcel in August 1895: 'C'est du reste un homme qui aime à envisager les problèmes de l'avenir et à les discuter.' *Vide G.P.*, x. 34.

relations of the powers, and especially of German policy, but still essential for effective action on behalf of Turkish Christians or effective development of Egyptian administration; and the use of sea power. It is the third point that is decisive here. Salisbury had consulted his 'nautical experts', alarmed by reports that Turkey had followed a policy of 'the elaborate fortification of the Dardanelles, and the utter neglect of the Bosphorus'. The balance of opinion, as he said in 1897, among these experts was 'strongly unfavourable to any attempt to force the Dardanelles by the action of the fleet' alone.[1] This was in 1897 — the despatch is dated the day following Salisbury's 'backed the wrong horse' speech. His doubts were, however, of earlier origin. There is a minute by him as far back as 1892 — just before he left office to give way to the Liberal administration. 'If the opinion of the Directors of naval and military Intelligence held good,' he wrote, 'the protection of Constantinople from Russian conquest must cease to be regarded as a great aim of British policy, for we cannot defend it, and our policy is a policy of false pretences.' In 1892 the idea was clearly still new to him. 'All that England and India can furnish of naval or military strategic knowledge,' he added, 'should thoroughly examine the question so that the real facts should be ascertained, and presented in the clearest light to those who are responsible for the policy of the Empire.'[2] Two months later Salisbury was succeeded by the Liberals. The results of the careful examination are not known, but there continued to be regular reports on the fortifications, and memoranda commenting on them were prepared in 1893 and 1896. They give meaning to the reference made by Salisbury in his despatch of January 1897 to this vital practical consideration. Further news of importance reached Salisbury early in 1896. Bulgaria was reconciled to Russia, a reconciliation typified, as Salisbury noted, by the 'recent conversion of Prince Boris'. The political conversion of Bulgaria was of an importance second only to the strengthening of the defences of the Dardanelles — (Salisbury had never been under any delusion as to the

[1] *Vide* Salisbury to Rumbold, no. 6, very confidential, 20 January 1897, printed in Gooch and Temperley, *op. cit.*, ix (i), 775–6.

[2] Minute of 4 June 1892, quoted in Memorandum by F. Bertie, 19 October 1893. F.O. 78/4592.

strategic importance of Bulgaria) — it affected decisively the ability of Austria-Hungary to act by land. The 'nautical experts' thus completed the convincing of Salisbury for they held that the co-operation of land forces would be essential. German help could not be expected — the period of German indecision was developing into that of the policy of increasing German influence at Constantinople. Marschall, in 1897, was sent to Turkey to make that policy his main concern. The Kaiser paid his famous visit to Constantinople in October 1898. The whole political scene in the Balkans had changed, and however strongly Salisbury might feel on the question of the Straits the impossibility of effective action was decisive. In 1902, when the Kaiser was visiting Sandringham, Lansdowne asked him whether he expected trouble in Macedonia in the spring. The Kaiser said that he did not — 'neither Germany nor Russia desired it, and Russia was not likely to permit it'.[1] 'Germany nor Russia' — the new era in the diplomatic history of the Near East was starting, and the old policy based on the conditions of an age now passed was no longer applicable.

Britain at the time was in no position to make the necessary adjustment in her policy. The crisis of 1898 over Fashoda was followed closely by the opening of the South African war, and Britain was without a friend in Europe. In 1899 the visit of M. Delcassé to St. Petersburg gave publicity to the strengthening of the Franco-Russian alliance. The diplomatic position was in reality even more dangerous than the English statesmen knew. The Delcassé visit was followed in 1900 by a meeting of the French and Russian chiefs of staff at which a draft convention — on the model of that of 1892 — provided that in certain eventualities Russia would support France in the event of a war with England. Delcassé visited St. Petersburg again in the following spring and an exchange of letters with Count Lamsdorf approved the conditional arrangement.[2] The contemporary *rapprochement* between

[1] Lansdowne to Buchanan, no. 301, very confidential, Sandringham, 14 November 1902. F.O. 78/5248.

[2] Cf. P. Renouvin, 'Les engagements de l'alliance franco-russe. Leur évolution de 1891 à 1914.' *Revue d'Histoire de la Guerre Mondiale*, 1934, pp. 297–310; *Documents diplomatiques français (1871–1914)*, 2nd ser., iii. 601–14.

France and Italy completed the cycle of diplomatic change.[1] Both series of negotiations were secret, and only the broad outlines of the developments were known, but these were enough to make the outlook dark from the British standpoint. It is small wonder that the British ministers redoubled their probing efforts to find some point at which an entry could be made through the closing lines of European relationships. The Franco-Russian negotiations deepened the danger in the far east and on the Indian frontier; the Franco-Italian *rapprochement* removed one source of the readiness of the central powers to work with England — at the very time when the changing position in the Near East destroyed the other.

When Sir Edward Grey, in 1911, looked back over this period his review contained one sentence which is significant from this point of view. He was explaining the dependence of the foreign policy of Britain on the measure of her sea power, and he referred to the one serious danger — lest Britain should be put into the position of measuring her naval strength against not one other power or group of two powers, but against *five*. This danger, if it was not actually present at the beginning of the new century, was closer then than at any other time in the era of the alliance system. It was in these circumstances that Salisbury and Lansdowne responded favourably to the overture of 1901 from Japan, and agreed in January 1902 to stabilise — as they thought — the situation in the Far East by the conclusion of the Anglo-Japanese alliance. The conclusion of this treaty gives the measure of the British alienation from the powers of Europe, and marks the recognition of the failure of the old policy of co-operation without alliances. At the very time when Britain was once more refusing — in her conversations with Germany — to use the *lingua franca* of the Continent on this subject, she entered into an alliance treaty with an Asiatic Power.

Behind the Anglo-Japanese treaty there lay a series of actions in the past which made this departure from general principle a natural development. They belong to the third category of the constituents of policy which, in this period at least, was the most important of all. The period with which we are dealing was one of constant change in the

[1] *Vide* A. F. Pribram, *The secret treaties of Austria-Hungary* (Harvard University Press, 1921), ii. 231–57.

European scene. The fall of Bismarck in 1890 was followed by years in which German policy seemed unreliable to England — and for that matter to Germany's ally Austria-Hungary. The attempt of Austria-Hungary under the guidance of Kálnoky to take the lead in the triple alliance — the prospect by which Deym had consoled himself for the dangers of Bismarck's fall — this attempt had failed even before Kálnoky left office in 1895. And Goluchovski was from this point of view a poor substitute. The formation of the Franco-Russian alliance, and the apparent fluctuations in the relationship of its partners, were again productive of uncertainty in Europe — as were also the variations in the force and direction of Italian designs in Africa. British statesmen were working in a constantly moving scene, and variations in policy in one direction dictated others elsewhere. Yet, in this medley of negotiations, in all the cross-currents of European politics certain points can be found at which the British decision in one direction or another was of momentous importance. In these decisions, perhaps above all, the force is to be found which dictated the final development of British policy in this period. Policy, as Grey later complained,[1] is often spoken of as if it were a carefully worked-out plan; as if first the broad lines were sketched, and then all the details made to conform to them. Sometimes, indeed, not often perhaps in Britain, there is a measure of truth in this picture. But in this case the details were generally settled first, decided by a bewildering variety of differing motives, and the plan or policy emerged from them.

These vital decisions belong to many different spheres of interest — it is the diversity of British interests that was the commanding feature of the situation. The decision to increase the fleet in 1894; the decision, slowly reached in 1892–6 that by the fleet alone Britain could not defend the Dardanelles; countless decisions of a minor character in the regions of Africa, in Uganda, in the basin of the Congo, the Nile Valley or on the borders of the Red Sea — decisions made often by men on the spot, with little notice taken of them at home, save perhaps by the African department of the foreign office, or by Salisbury tracing the course of events on his maps. There were two of these regional decisions, however, whose importance far outweighs that of the rest:

[1] Cf. *Twenty-five years*, i. 6.

the decision, announced by Sir Edward Grey on 28 March 1895, that Britain would view as 'an unfriendly act' the penetration of another power to the Nile Valley,[1] and that of the same year when Britain refused to join Russia, France and Germany in their joint note to Japan which led to the retrocession of the Liaotung peninsula. The first of these decisions started the series of events which led ultimately to the Anglo-French agreements of 1904. It constituted a public disavowal of the policy often proclaimed, of an early withdrawal from Egypt, and made it certain that Anglo-French rivalry could be settled only by either war or direct negotiation. It is important to note here the vital part taken in the negotiations of 1903–4 by Lord Cromer. The decision of 1895 with reference to the Liaotung Peninsula was also the beginning of a policy. It was based on a profound distrust of the professed disinterestedness of the European powers in the Far East, and constituted a new departure in Far Eastern policy from which, as events proved, there was no escape. The Anglo-Russian overture of 1898 and the Anglo-German agreement of 1900 both failed and the Anglo-Japanese alliance was the natural sequel.

It is a legitimate criticism of British policy in this period that it was haphazard and without sufficient general direction. Britain was led into an international position where the objects of her main concern could be obtained only by new combinations with Powers which could not fail to react unfavourably on relations elsewhere. Kálnoky, in 1894, spoke of a party in the English Cabinet which wanted a policy of absolute peace and of good relations with all the Powers, and such a policy had it been practicable might well have suited the interests of Britain. In a world dominated by alliances no such plan was feasible. The alternative, when once the basis was gone of the old co-operation with the triple alliance, was worked out piecemeal and with little evidence of a general design. It was, above all, not a clever policy. There is an illuminating private letter from John Hay to Henry Adams, written on 21 November 1900, shortly after the conclusion of the Anglo-German agreement relating to China. He wrote:

> My heart is heavy about John Bull. Do you twig his attitude to Germany? When the Anglo-German pact came out, I took a day or

[1] Hansard, *Parl. Deb.*, 4th ser., xxxii. 405–6.

two to find out what it meant. I soon learned from Berlin that it meant a horrible practical joke on England. From London I found what I had suspected, but what astounded me after all to be assured of — THAT THEY DID NOT KNOW![1]

Knowledge in this case came slowly, and the realisation when it came was a serious blow to the system of policy which Britain was trying to establish in the Far East. But such slowness was a contribution to the piecemeal method by which the broad lines of policy, still maintained in much the same general directions as before, were being drawn imperceptibly into new courses. The way was being made ready for the new system of policy which characterised the last ten years before the outbreak of war.

LILLIAN M. PENSON

[1] Hay to Adams, 21 November 1900. W. R. Thayer, *Life and letters of John Hay* (1915), ii. 248–9. Cited H. B. Morse, *International relations of the Chinese Empire* (1918), iii. 328.

Index

Index

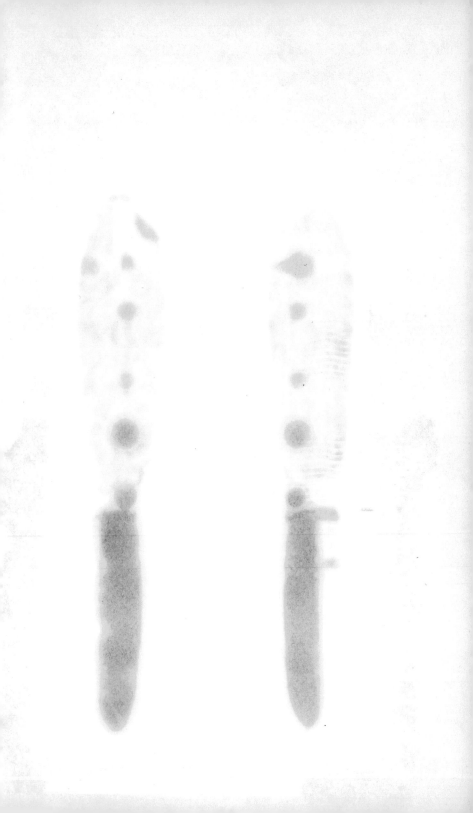

DATE DUE

OCT 0 3 2004	